D0775555

Stuck No More™

Our Love Matters
Find it, Fix it or Let it Go!

Dr. Nicki J. Monti

Copyright © 2014

Book Design: June Nagano

ISBN: 978-0-9913699-1-1

TABLE OF CONTENTS

ACKNOWLEDGEMENTS:

To my husband Konrad: his constant support, unwavering faith in my capacities, plus his humor and willingness to shuffle from room to room to allow the silence I needed at every stage of the work, were invaluable. On top of that, I give special thanks to him for teaching me again and again over these many years what love truly is, both in good times and during the inevitable challenges relationship offers. He has brought my life to an exhilarating place I never could have imagined.

To Zachary Zeiler: throughout this process, I constantly told him how this book would in no way be what it is without him. I mean it. His generous guidance, painstaking reviewing and insistence on quality has steadied me in the shaky moments and walked me through the cloudy days. My enthusiastic gratitude is thorough and unending. I thank him as well for having gathered such a wonderfully competent ID+M team, without whom it would have been impossible to create this fine result! A special shout out to June Nagano for her terrific cover and interior graphics. Such a beautiful artist is indeed a find and I am thankful.

To the Teachers: over the years I've been influenced by many, many self-investigatory travelers, including the extraordinary Beings with whom I've sat in a circle. This includes both the brilliant guides like Brugh Joy and Carolyn Conger, whose own unwavering dedication to personal evolution continuously offered a beacon for all who attended, as well as circle mates who hungered for new vista travel plus depth exploration. Out of these many circles I have managed to cull a few very special voices I am privileged to call friend. To them, I offer special thanks.

To the clients: not enough can be said about my gratitude for clients both represented here and so many others I've been honored to sit with over the years. Their stories have instructed me, elaborated my understanding, variously uplifted and/or broken my heart. Over and again they have called upon me to explore ranges I never would have braved without them. These intrepid souls have given shape to my life. I am truly blessed to serve.

DEDICATION:

For Brugh Joy, wherever you are.

For Konrad Monti, thanks for staying right here.

The breeze at dawn has secrets to tell you.
Don't go back to sleep.
You must ask for what you really want.
Don't go back to sleep.
People are going back and forth across the
doorsill
Where the two worlds touch.
The door is round and open.
Don't go back to sleep.

-Rumi [i]

To the reader:

Our love matters. It matters to you and it matters to me. I will be your guide as together we'll make sense of it all. All you have to do is open your heart and your mind. Walk with me.

In Love,
Dr. Nicki J. Monti

PREFACE

RELATIONSHIP IS AN ART—an art *easily* taught. No kidding.

I T'S PRETTY SIMPLE TO LEARN WHAT TO DO when it comes to having good, healthy relationships, and with little muss or fuss, this book will demonstrate how to have the relationship you've always craved. It doesn't matter if you're a single man or woman or already coupled, *Our Love Matters* can lead you to the changes you want and deserve.

By the end, you'll have tools of all sorts—tools you can practically apply and make your own, the means to get you into a relationship and devices to get you out. You'll acquire methods for surviving love's disappointments, for reviving stale relationships, and for thriving amidst love's promises. You'll acquire dozens of alternative ways of thinking, feeling, and acting when it comes to love of work, love of friends, love of home, love of yourself, and love of love.

Let's face it, there's really only one vital thing to be exploring for all our lives and that thing is Love. Everyone knows it. Songwriters write songs about it; novelists pen novels about it. Poets write sonnets about it. Filmmakers make films about it. Television captures it. Indeed, we are all in one way or another talking about, seeking, and worrying about love all the time—at work, at play, at home, everywhere.

There are countless definitions of what love is, what it means, how to find it, keep it, and express it. Those various definitions will be described in detail throughout this book.

All you'll need to do then is take action.

But if it's so easy, why hasn't it happened in my life yet?

THIS VERY GOOD QUESTION IS SOMETHING WE'LL EXPLORE TOGETHER. Let me offer a couple initial thoughts:

FIRST, a relationship is a great deal like chess: it's easy to learn the rules and hard to play the game well.

SECOND, for some yet-to-be-discovered reason you've been reluctant to *fully open* yourself to love.

THIRD, *reading*, listening to smart lectures, or watching YouTube are *not the same as doing it*. You can't put this or any other book under your pillow and wake up in a perfect romantic scenario.

This means that even after we discover together what's been holding you back from having the relationships you desire, plus give you spectacular tools for finding it, fixing it, or letting it go, you're going to need to apply what you've learned in the real world. Just reading what's written here can and will offer you terrific information, might even sometimes entertain, and will certainly enlarge your perspective. But to enjoy the profound change I want for you, the most important part will be practice, con

Happily, I'm here as your love mentor.

I will guide you to the right art space, teach you how to draw, and give you all the best tools: brushes, paints, proper cleaners, as well as a fresh canvas with which to work. However, it's you who needs to put it together and get to work. So, roll up your sleeves because: **Relationship is an Art that requires Action.**

What's fabulous about this call to action "mandate" is that it means *you are* the key to your own changes. That's good news, truly: Holding the key means holding the power. I'm here to tell you how to yank free from the various kinds of debilitating, underwhelming, and sorrow-driven relationships you've been having. I'm going to teach you how you can have sustained, sustainable love everywhere you go. And I'm here to let you know change *is* truly, actually, realistically possible. Change is a matter of choice.

Who do I think I am?

WHAT MAKES ME SUCH AN EXPERT WHEN IT COMES TO RELATIONSHIPS? Two things: my first qualifier is that over several decades I've successfully counseled thousands upon thousands of clients seeking help when it comes to love: how to love their current relationships; how to find loving relationships; how to love their jobs, bodies, families, themselves, and even their very lives. I've taught them how to find, keep, or leave love. Many of their stories are presented throughout. No doubt you'll see your own story traveling across the page.

The second thing qualifying me as an authority is my own personal, extensive, and often hugely fraught relationship history which I openly share intending the discoveries and learning arising out of those difficult love adventures to lead by example. Yes, years ago when it came to relationships, I, too, felt defeated and deflated.

I'd had two early and brief marriages, one benign and one horrific, and a zillion shorter and longer relationships along the way, ranging from sublime to ridiculous. Within them all, I managed to feel unlovable. Oh sure, I put on a good show, but really I was simply a lousy partner and basically attracted the same. As it turns out, the source of my problem was self-loathing. *Duh.*

In any event, after moving from New York to California, getting sober, and beginning yet another new career, I started hunting for love. And I mean hunting. I was avid and active. Even the market was an adventure in hope. Would *he* be in the frozen food section, or seeking ripe fruit in produce? Oy.

On top of this, I went to every singles event in town. This was before Internet dating, so I resorted to personal ads in local papers. I put an ad in a magazine called *Los Angeles Magazine*. Among other things, the ad said something like: *Wanted: man capable of true, intense intimacy.* I got letters from prisoners around the country—real prisoners, in prison. "Ready to be intimate," they answered. "Be out in 2 to 10." Uh, no, that's not what I meant by the word intimacy. Oops.

I began to use mantras: *My perfect, most appropriate partner is coming to me now!* I said it all day long, every free mental moment. Nothing seemed to work. The guys I did meet were…well…for the most part regrettable, with someone else, or unavailable in other ways. Whatever it was, I was mystified. I was smart, caring, and somewhat positive about my appearance, so why wasn't it happening for me?

Why? I was simply too needy, wet, and whiny—inside, always inside. To look at me, you'd never have known. On the outside, I appeared confident, funny, and abundant, but how I looked was not how I felt which was, at the deepest level, unworthy.

Finally, I got worn out and down. Everything else in my life seemed to be getting on track. I'd found my therapy career, which was like coming home to an extraordinarily beautiful mansion just waiting for me to inhabit—a gorgeous manor that had been mine the whole time, only I'd not known it. I had two great, funny cats, a decent apartment, and was nearly five years sober. I was even starting to like myself—to be the person everyone assumed I was.

The only thing missing was "him."

One day I thought: "Oh, this is ridiculous. My life is fine as is. If someone comes along terrific, if not, I really love my life. I love my career, my home, my cats, and my friends. I'm fine."

And I believed it.

I stopped looking around every corner for a relationship.

I decided to fall further in love with me.

Then I got divorced from my second husband. Though it had been ten years since I'd seen the awful fellow, I'd never filed because what I knew about myself was that I simply couldn't say no—to pretty much anything. So I figured if I wasn't divorced, I couldn't fall into another it's-just-what-came-along marriage. By then, I trusted myself more. And also, I realized the depth of my foreboding. Thus, if love was to come, I wanted to be ready. And if it wasn't, I wanted to be ready also.

I got divorced easily with no former husband contact and settled into my new contentment. Three weeks to the day I met the husband I've been with ever since. Three weeks after meeting him, he asked me to marry him. In pattern, I said yes. He's been the love of my life and my lifetime.

What is the moral of the story? Let go of expectations.

Really let go.

When I've suggested over the years to certain folks that they stop "looking" and love themselves and their lives, I've made clear there's no pretending. It needs to be real. Because one thing I know for sure: Shifting belief is essential to true, fundamental, and lasting change. And we can't pretend; it needs to be true blue.

The Universe won't be fooled.

The Universe is listening, always.

Yes, let go of expectations.

Focus on loving yourself. But you don't need to be all fixed and finished to find love.

I wasn't.

When I met my husband, one of the first things he said to me was: "I hope you love yourself enough for me to love you." I thought it was brilliant. I said yes, I did. Really, I had no idea what it actually meant. And as it turns out, I was lying. It has taken years to catch up to that yes, but I really do finally love myself enough for him to love me. Now it's the question I ask you: Do you love yourself enough to let another love you? Do you?

Vulnerability...

THROUGHOUT THIS BOOK, I WILL SPEAK OFTEN ABOUT VULNERABILITY. That's because it's through understanding, working with, and expressing vulnerability that I've been able to move myself from a love-challenged life to a love-filled life. Thus, I am vulnerable with you. Here. Now. I want you to see, know, and feel the ways in which I walk beside you in this journey. All offered stories and examples, whether mine or those of my clients, are meant to amplify, illuminate, and reveal the universality of our love experiences.

But why write this book now?

WELL, THE REASON I'M FINALLY WRITING AGAIN is because I'm simply bursting with information. It spills out of me daily, and has demanded to appear on the page. My clients have inspired me. My life has inspired me. You have inspired me.

On top of all this, a few years ago my long-time teacher and mentor Dr. Brugh Joy died. It was a difficult and life-altering experience for me. I went into what I'd call an uninspired fallow period. My work continued, but nothing new was being born. For a creative person, that's a challenging occurrence.

In spiritual circles, it's believed a student can't truly find their own voice until their teacher has passed. At the time there was much discussion about this. Now, I've long exhibited a strong, authentic voice, but honestly, something, well, special has happened to me in these last years—a more profound connection to aspects of self apparently long waiting to appear. Not that it's been magic, but it has been magical—because like a glorious sun bursting through a cloudy day, I feel infused again.

The difference between magic and magical is that I labored for this expanded understanding to emerge. In fact, I toiled as hard as I'm going to ask you to work throughout the course of this book, because I know it's worth it. This point about living the work and walking the talk is central to who and how I am. Yes, I'm well-educated. Indeed, besides formal schooling I've read and honor through my teachings many of the enthused educators before me like Carl Jung, Joseph Campbell, Donald Kalsched, James Hillman, Edward Edinger, and many, many others.[1]

I've studied with extraordinary teachers like the aforementioned Brugh Joy, Carolyn Conger, and Hal Stone, to name only a few. I've attended many hundreds of traditional workshops as well as explored more tangential areas such as Tarot, I Ching, shaman practices, rituals, psychic phenomena, astrology, Kabbalah, and more. I could go on and on. But of all the things I've ever done, the greatest teacher I've encountered is Life itself and the relationship life has brought me into, starting with my challenging family of origin.

I wouldn't give up any of it, even the so-called terrible parts. Not for anything. I love the way poet/novelist Rainier Maria Rilke puts it:

> Perhaps all the dragons in our lives are princesses who are only waiting to see us act, just once, with beauty and courage. Perhaps everything that frightens us is, in its deepest essence, something helpless that wants our love.[ii]

---

[1] If these names are foreign to you, Google can give an introduction to their philosophies and perspectives, quickly showing how they influenced each other and me.

[2] For a thorough exploration of defenses, check out my website where defenses are discussed in detail. And get my book *Stuck In The Story*. NPMong. e

[3] When I reference Self with a capital "S", I'm talking about the core of who

Yes, it's through both the struggles and the triumphs that I've become who I am proudly today: a teacher and mentor capable of imparting truly helpful, healing information.

What I will show you, then, comes from trial and experience—both from what I've personally encountered in my own life and from how I've been able to lead others in their relationship lives from lousy to laudable, from awful to amazing.

Others paved the road, now you get to walk it as I offer this life-changing information to you. Let's venture forward to discover why in the world it is that Our Love Matters!

INTRODUCTION

W ELCOME TO *OUR LOVE MATTERS* GPS. With this map, you steadily and safely navigate the sometimes fun, sometimes treacherous love terrain—routes and passageways for getting and having the relationship life you want. Here you will find methods and means to enliven, expand, and illuminate. Things you've never thought of or tried before.

Let's right off dive into the prickly often-moaned question: *Why* doesn't the kind of love that we say we crave show up?

We'll start with what I call a **Stunner**—an idea meant to splash cold wake-up water on your face. This is the first of many to be found throughout this book.

Stunner #1: You don't have what you say you want because you haven't been ready!

Really.

It's fair to assume you've never actually considered this alarming idea! That's understandable, as not many people have. After all, as far as the majority can tell, the whole love business seems mostly circumstantial.

Certainly, at first this can be a hard notion to swallow. Indeed, the idea that finding great love is all about readiness might very well make you snarl and snap. "Hey, I'm ready!" You might rabidly proclaim, "I want love. I do!"

Yes, I know *your brain believes* you're ready, but look at your life. Is that what reality reports? Hold onto your hat because here comes:

Stunner #2: Our lives consistently reveal the truth of our intentions.

Let me immediately give an example. Because I'm considered a relationship expert, both men and women often arrive in my office with a list of complaints in hand. One such example was a mid-twenties woman we shall call Melody. Already deeply saddened by the state of her relationship life, Melody had spent a number of years in partnership with a man who not only couldn't stay sober; he was quite the liar. She kept saying she wanted out.

But she never got out. Round and round we went, with me telling her there was no evidence she was truly "done" with the relationship. She argued it was over. She took out restraining orders against his violence, and then broke the orders herself by returning to him. Each time he proclaimed sobriety, she believed him and back into his arms she'd fly.

Was she finished? How could we say she was?

In her case, the staying, it became quite obvious, was father-related. In fact, the partner was practically an exact replica of her dad—charming, charismatic, alcoholic, narcissistic, controlling, sneaky, and emotionally undependable. What needed to happen for Melody is what's more or less true for us all: She needed to repair the original wound so she'd be able to move onto a relationship which was not constantly disappointing.

Turns out, this letting-go process in her case took *years*. At first she'd break up completely, declaring that it was really, absolutely over, and then make up, imagining he'd changed. But he hadn't, because underneath it all, he didn't want to. And that's key. For real change to happen, *sincere* desire must be present. There's an oft-quoted statement in the Twelve Step programs: *The only people unable to stay sober are those incapable of being truly honest with themselves.* This is brilliantly true in all areas when it comes to change.

We know that Melody's partner wasn't being truly honest with himself, but was Melody being any more truthful? On the surface maybe, but not every single part of her was ready to let go of her old unconsciously compelling story, which turned out to be, in short: If only I can get Andrew to prove his love by staying sober, it will make up for all the things Dad did.

In this example, we can clearly see that initially Melody's *true intention* was not to let go. We know that because she didn't. In fact, she stayed through betrayal of many kinds, until; finally, she'd done the deeper work of addressing the profound father hurt. Only then could she break free.

What have you been telling yourself the problem is? What if I could convince you that *you* are actually the centerpiece of everything going on in your life? And I mean everything.

Just for an instant, start by checking out the evidence. Do you find yourself in the same relationships time after time—you know, the faces change but the relationships and situations turn out to be nearly identical? Do you have the same kind of troublesome or disappointing friends—same job or colleague, struggles, same life obstacles, and same dissatisfying partnerships? Perhaps you've been thinking it's them, or the world.

It's not.

It's you.

Buck up: This is totally great news. Because that means you can **actually change your relationship to love matters!** It works like this:

- ✓ We begin by accepting that we have the life we've unconsciously designed.
- ✓ We become willing to figure out the root cause of that unconscious sculpting.
- ✓ We recognize that it's our *unconscious* intentions that require changing.
- ✓ We accept that it's up to us to shift the behaviors that report those intentions.

I realize this idea of having what we intend is an alarming, counter-intuitive, and even audacious proclamation. I'll provide plenty of supporting information as we move forward together. In the end, you'll discover that your brain, contrary to popular opinion, is simply not driving the bus, but rather that the *unconscious* is the one behind the wheel. I'm going to show you not only that this is true, but also *how* it came to be true and *why* it doesn't need to be true any longer. In other words, just because you've been *saying* you want love, doesn't mean you've been actually ready, willing, and able for spectacular love to appear. Let's change that.

First things first...

LET'S START OUR JOURNEY with this little-known fact: When it comes to having high-quality healthy, supportive, growing relationships, *there's no one-size-fits-all method.*

That's right. No matter what anyone has previously told you, it will be necessary to—or more accurately, *you get to*—find the voice of **your** relationships!

Here's a funny example: A couple decades ago, I worked with a lovely woman in her late-thirties we'll call Amy. Amy was extremely well-educated and quite fit, both of mind and body. Amy was simply unable to find the love she wanted. We spoke frequently about the underlying *why* of it; however, when all was said and done, there were just certain perspectives Amy was unwilling to shift. It quickly became pretty clear Amy's priority was to partner with someone physically beautiful to convince herself she was still a lovely viable woman, even in the face of threatening age. Absolutely no other qualities were important to her.

So, one day, Amy comes in saying, "I've met the perfect guy for me!"

"Oh," I respond, "how so? Where did you meet this magic man!?"

"At the carwash!" she answers.

I say, "Oh, was he washing your car?"

Now, please understand I have zero energy one way or other when it comes to who partners with whom, and certainly any hard day's work well met is worthwhile; however, knowing PhD, well-job-placed Amy, I was already getting suspicious.

"Yes!" She laughed.

"And…." I continued.

"And he's *really cute*!"

"Uh, huh. And…."

"And he speaks no English. And he's 21. And he's deaf."

Oh. I see. "Let me review: You've found a guy who is over 15 years younger, with a menial job, speaking a language you don't speak, and who can't hear you? Amazing."

She laughed.

Many years later, I got a message from Amy through the grapevine that she'd finally gotten everything she'd been looking for. Now, as you can imagine, I have no idea what this means, but I'll bet it's different than what I, or even you, might think would suit her. Guess what; that's her prerogative.

And it's yours, too.

The long and short of it is, you'll be figuring out *techniques that work best for you* as well as with your particular friends, family members, career colleagues, and in your primary partnership. I'll propose many, many potential avenues and you'll decide which road to take.

Over and again, I'll emphasize how essential it is that you discover **your unique voice**. That means you'll need to start listening to yourself. As spiritual author and lecturer Marianne Williamson points out: "No one will listen to us until we listen to ourselves."[iii]

Happily, all the tools offered in this book are applicable both to your relationship experiences in the world and to the discovery of individual Self. That means, *Our Love Matters* helps you with others and it helps you with you! So let's get straight to the point: Relationship is an art that requires action and that action begins with first knowing the Self.

The three steps...

The Three Steps

PREPARATION	PROCEDURE	PERSPIRATION
Do a diagnostic - What brought me to this point? Is it time for self-overhaul or just work on specific issues?	Familiarize yourself with the tools for moving-forward. See the fresh approach and the key ways to apply them.	You learn how to utilize these new tools and practical applications of how to incorporate them into your daily life.

TO ESTABLISH FIRST-RATE RELATIONSHIP SKILLS (with Self, with Other) there are three stages: *preparation*, *procedure*, and finally, *perspiration*.

1) **Preparation**: We start with learning what's been going wrong up until now. In order to fix what ails you, we need to first do a diagnostic—figure out what's led to the current dissatisfaction. It's like being in a car accident and needing to see which part of the vehicle got hit. Are we talking about a total overhaul or just banging out some of the crumples?

2) **Procedure:** We move onto discovering new, improved ways and means of traveling forward. All sorts of wonderful, fresh approaches to love await. Indeed, to fix that crumpled vehicle, we need the right equipment. Thus, fantastic fix-it tools are offered throughout.

3) **Perspiration:** Now it's necessary to put those new, improved ways and means into actual practice. This is where the all-important heavy lifting comes in. Together, we'll look at precisely how this works.

Relationship every day, everywhere, all the time…

EVERYTHING WE DO IN LIFE MORE OR LESS INVOLVES RELATIONSHIPS. Whether at work or at play, we need to know how to connect with others in viable, helpful, and healthy ways. And yes, I will over and again reinforce how this strong, workable connection with others begins with a nourishing connection to Self.

Throughout this book, I will present questions about relationships and immediately offer answers to those questions. I'll show you *why* many of your previous relationships haven't worked at home, at work, and in life; how you can *change that story right now*; plus how you can take control of your love-life and of loving your life. It's not too late, regardless of how young you are, how old you are, if you're a woman, a man, straight, gay, or undecided. It doesn't matter what nationality you are, what ethnicity, if you're from a tiny family or a large one. In other words, *everyone* can shift their relationship to love matters. And for those of you who feel that *some* areas function better than others, I'll demonstrate how *all* areas in your life can stand fresh eyes.

You'll be able to apply these carefully outlined means and methods everywhere, every day. Apply them in your job, with your families, with your friends, and in love. Use them to change how you experience the relationships already present in your life, or employ them to find and include the kinds of relationships for which you've always yearned. And, of course, utilize them to discover how to have a better relationship with your Self.

What's in the big tool chest?

BY THE END OF OUR TIME TOGETHER, you'll have a floor-to-ceiling stack of tools to assist your real and lasting transformation—an exciting array of change choices. Here are some of the titillating topics we'll deeply delve into:

- ✓ **The Four Wheels:** Basics for change.
- ✓ **The Four A's: Accolade, Appreciation, Attention, and Approval:** What we seek.
- ✓ **Connect the Dots:** Recognizing the flow of yesterday, today, and tomorrow.
- ✓ **All In:** How to give 100%.
- ✓ **Timeline:** Creating a flowchart of events.
- ✓ **Mirror, Mirror on the Wall:** Learning to see you through others.
- ✓ **The Four Gateways:** How to achieve real self-love.
- ✓ **Practicing Presence:** Tools and treats to bring you into now.
- ✓ **The Change-It-Up Plan:** Ways to achieve a new life.
- ✓ **Relationship Rules**: Important relationship canons.
- ✓ **Relationship Tenets:** Six ways to establish and maintain a healthy partnership—the ins and outs of making a relationship that really works.

- ✓ **The Trifecta** of terrific relationship: What it takes to get what you deserve.
- ✓ **Nine Heartbreak Guarantees & Nine Heartbreak Solutions:** How to stop doing what you're doing and instead do what works.
- ✓ **The Four C's: Communication, Collaboration, Contribution, and Compromise:** Details on ways to make love work both for now, and for the long haul.
- ✓ **The 10 Healthy Relationship Essentials:** The foundation stones for building a healthy relationship structure everywhere you go.
- ✓ **Imperatives for Dating & Mating:** A find-what-you-want-and-need template.

Consider this list to be the appetizer menu. Wait until you get to the real spread! By the time we're finished, your love questions will be answered and you'll be ready to either fix what you've got, find what you want, or let go of the toxic relationships you've been nursing.

The Exercises...

AS YOU MOVE THROUGH THIS BOOK, YOU'LL FIND a few initial exercises. These are the ones for you to immediately attend to for instant understanding. These selected procedures move you from one discovery to the next.

On the other hand, you will find a more complete description of ways for real and lasting change in the *Love Works* chapter. Indeed, *these offerings are vital to eventually explore.* Inevitably, a nagging worry over and again scratches through me, like a tiny mouse in the walls of my home. What if you're entering our process together imagining some big payoff, magic-wand moment will happen without doing any solid investigatory work? I truly, fervently want you to heal and because of that, I anticipate this book to be the beginning of a new relationship life for you and that by the end of it, you'll have come to understand why and how love matters, it's important to emphasize that the essential ingredient for change is your participation. That's where the suggested exercises in the *Love Works* section come in. These exercises can be done along the way if you prefer, in which case when you find the *Love Works* referenced, you immediately turn to the exercise before going back to reading.

Of course, other readers will want to move all the way through this book before engaging in any exercises. That's okay, too.

Now, you may not kindle to all of the offered means and methods, but at least pick out a few striking your fancy. In other words, do it your way, but **do it**!

Recovery begins with self-discovery...

THE ROAD TO REAL RELATIONSHIP SUCCESS starts with *us!* It's a kind of map-making process where we discover the mountain ranges, valleys, riverbeds, desert places, and even secret, previously undeveloped ranges.

What I'm talking about is determining *who and how* we've been from the start. Yes, from the start. I know—sounds cumbersome. Part of you is already shouting at me: "Ugh! I don't want to dredge up the past or dwell in it either! I just want to get on with it—just want to focus on the future." The thing is: real recovery necessarily begins with taking a long-view perspective. Checking in the rear-view mirror allows us to realize how close to our bumpers the cars behind us are driving. Besides, as everyone knows, history repeats itself. You've certainly seen it in your own life. We keep getting into the same messes, over and again. We don't mean to, we think, but it happens. We're mystified. Well, there are certain elementary, essential ideas supporting everything we are and do. Throughout this book I'll offer these ideas as **Fundamentals**. Here's the first. **Fundamental:** If you do what you've done, you'll get what you've got.

Pattern peace...

WHAT WE'LL NEED TO BEGIN WITH IS A CONVERSATION ABOUT PATTERNS. Like everything in nature, we live in pattern. Winter always follows Fall. The three stars of Orion always stay together. Winter never ever says: "I think just this once, I'm coming *after* Spring!" And none of the Orion stars ever imagine it'd be better to jump ship in order to spend a night with the Big Dipper. Nature has a plan. It may not be a plan we always understand, but it's irrefutable.

Animals further amplify this point. Perhaps you've wondered how birds know to migrate south in the winter. Or how forest animals know danger's coming. Or how perennials know they're perennials, or why the sun rises every time in the east. There's an inborn flow and go to all things in nature. No instruction required—instinct, intuition, genetic coding. We too have a flow and go. We simply each need to discover what it is.

How does the pattern work?

WHEN IT COMES TO HUMAN BEINGS, THERE ARE TWO KINDS OF PATTERNS. The first is ORGANIC PATTERNING, which operates much like nature. In this case, our association to pattern is also instinct, intuition, and genetic coding.

This organic version of pattern arrives with us at birth. It's what we can refer to as *genetic heritage material.* Our innate fabric is reported by such obvious things as hair color and height, but also includes certain behavioral tendencies like: extroversion, the potential for addiction, specific creative talent, and more. In fact, I suspect the extent of our genetic coding and the effect of that coding on our unfolding is sorely underestimated at this point, except perhaps by a few geneticists in the field.

Nurture: All too often a room without a view!

The second version of pattern is NURTURING PATTERNING (or lack thereof). This is defined as: "The sum of *environmental influences and conditions* acting on an organism."[iv]

There are several subsets of this second kind of pattern and all of them affect us. First, let's address what I term LOCAL NURTURING. This includes such matters as: a) how well we're physically fed, housed, and taught as a child; b) what peer member influences we've had; c) the physical location in which we're raised; and d) the historical times in which we're raised.

A couple decades ago, for instance, I worked with an Irish fellow named Clancy. Clancy, then in his late thirties, had been raised in Ireland by a violent, mean, alcoholic, single father left to raise four children when Clancy's mother abandoned them all. One awful story included Clancy being sent at age six across the road to buy liquor for Dad and being hit by an on-rushing car. Hearing the ruckus, the father went to where his son lay in the middle of the road. Looking down, he said, "What a stupid idiot you are!"

Clancy was in a wheelchair for months, but as you might imagine, that was the least of his injuries.

Several obvious things exemplify local nurturing here. In Ireland at that time, a young child could run such an errand; the mother's abandonment set the stage; the dad's alcoholism and self-centered cruelty severely impacted the children.

Here we begin to address the **importance of context**. CONTEXT is not only immediate, as in city-bred or country-raised (community context), but extends to world-around-us attitudes (historical context) which speaks to time-in-history elements such as specific outlooks and approaches toward ethnicity, religion, gender, and sexuality to suggest a few. Attitudes and definitions about both alcoholism and child abuse were quite different when Clancy's story happened over fifty years ago. It's likely that a certain number of Clancy's peers experienced similar circumstances, more or less.

Context also denotes technological absence, presence, or advances as well as collective interests and attitudes (global context). This then recognizes national as well as worldwide tendencies and trends. If Clancy's experience happened today, for instance, it might be possible for him to go on the Internet and find other similar stories.

In other words, you're going to be impacted if you're the richest kid in your neighborhood, ethnically distinct from everyone else, the only person in your school to have same-sex parents, head and shoulders smarter than everyone, or naturally gifted in a particular way. You'll also be hugely affected if it's the 1900s or the 21st century—if we've just landed on the moon, now everyone has Internet, or we can teleport to other lands. Clearly, your life trajectory will be explicitly affected by all these elements. That means immediate family circumstances, community attitudes, *and* national/global conditions count.

Say, for instance, you somehow discover you have innate musical talent; however, your parents either can't afford instruments, or alternatively, can get you the best teachers in the world. What if you discover that despite your parent's wishes or assistance, you can learn music on the worldwide net?

And further, say in your community being "artsy" is more scorned than applauded (or more applauded than scorned)— obviously, you're going to be influenced. And what if the last Nobel Peace Prize was given to an artist? Or what, alternatively, if there's a national decision to remove all art funding from schools?

In light of all these things, you may work even harder at your gift to prove everyone wrong, or you may fold up your tent and silently steal away into the dark night. Whichever you choose could very well depend on your nature.

Or consider if you're a naturally terrific athlete in a place that highly values athleticism? Great, right? But what if your folks are simple, hard-working types who worry about your good-job future and athletics looks to them like a pie-in-the-sky avenue? Or maybe your school has no decent facility. Or maybe you read a book or saw a movie about big city scouts discovering little recognized unknowns in unexpected corners and now you keep that book under your pillow like a bible!

How about you're gay and it's 1950 versus 2030? Or everyone in the whole world is expected to go to war versus war is a distant beat. Obviously, how we reveal who we are will be impacted by circumstance.

The plot thickens...

AN EXTREME EXAMPLE OF ORGANIC NATURE AND LOCAL NURTURE WORKING TOGETHER is offered through author Christy Brown's story, which you might remember from the film *My Left Foot*. Now, this particular film reference may be a bit dated and if you've not read about him or seen this brilliant movie, I would absolutely do so as it will open your eyes, heart, and soul to unexpected ranges. I use the story here as it's both timeless and inspirational. It's another Irish story, but quite the opposite of Clancy's!

> Brown was born to a working-class Irish family at the Rotunda Hospital in Dublin in June 1932. After his birth, doctors discovered that he had severe cerebral palsy, a serious neurological disorder that left him almost entirely paralyzed by spasticity in his limbs. Though urged to commit him to a convalescent hospital, Brown's parents were determined to raise him at home with their other children. During Brown's adolescence, social worker Katrina Delahunt became aware of his story and began to visit the Brown family regularly, while bringing Christy books and painting materials as, over the years, he had shown a keen interest in the arts and literature. He had also demonstrated extremely impressive physical dexterity since, soon after discovering several household books, Christy had learned to both write and draw with the only limb over which he had unequivocal control—his left leg. Brown quickly matured into a serious artist. [v]

Amazing, right? Christy Brown evidenced what I'd call *Soul Intention* (we'll further discuss this innate drive shortly) and also had the family to back his play.

To summarize: First comes our nature—the organic patterning with which we're born; second comes our local nurturing, which includes parents, ethnicity, neighborhood, school experience, amplification or minimization of natural abilities and tendencies, era context plus collective attitudes, interests, and pressures.

You get the drift. All of this influences our growth patterns and those growth patterns determine both how we relate to the idea of love, as well as how we actually pursue (or don't), express (or don't), and reveal (or don't). That is to say *how, when, where, and who we love has a long, multi-layered history before we even leave the starting gate.*

That means what we do in the face of all this influence—how we adapt to circumstances or defend against them—and *what we can do* to shift our relationship to some of the undermining and unhealthy habits established along the way is part of what we're here to address. Up to now, if you're like most, you've been operating on automatic. We need to change that. Because it's time to have a splendid life in all your love matters.

Context matters...

I WANT TO EMPHASIZE THIS IDEA THAT THE TIME WE LIVE IN IS CRITICAL to consider. For example, if you're a person of any age living at *this* time in history and don't know how or refuse involvement with the Internet, you're quickly seen as out of the loop, off the grid, a relic—and will be regarded as such.

What's does this have to do with finding love?

Turns out, for better or worse, how the world views certain experiences cannot help but affect the way, at every stage of life, we view ourselves; more importantly, the way we see ourselves inevitably affects *who* we love and who we let love us, because love reflects our sense of personal value—or lack of value. That self-view also challenges *how* we love others and the ways in which we permit love to enter our lives. This remains true at any age. So whether you're a young person just starting on your love-life trail or an older individual seeking either new love or to revitalize the partnership you're in, self-esteem is where real love capacity begins.

Love at any age! Is that possible?

TALKING ABOUT THE "OLDER INDIVIDUAL" SEEKING LOVE— when it comes to aging, we have long been turning our noses up, like something stinks. Meanwhile, being young has been deified (elevated into god-like status). For sure, the power of youth's lingering temptations has had widespread repercussions for one and all—like we tend to refuse to give up that "youth" period in its natural timing.

Problematic results abound.

This brings to mind a charming thirty-six year old man we'll call Simon. We worked only briefly together, but it was great fun. Simon was charming, inventive, creative, and funny. He was also very stuck in youthful ways. For example, Simon's usual transportation to session was his skateboard!

Simon was in therapy to deal with conflict in his relationship. At the time, he was living with a gorgeous woman who loved him deeply. Everything she did said that. And he loved her, too…kind of. Thing was, he simply couldn't stop wanting something fresh and new. The idea of not sleeping with or conquering every beautiful woman he met was horrifying to him. He simply *had* to pursue them, he'd say with a wry smile.

Naturally, we worked on figuring out what was behind this, but quickly Simon realized he simply wasn't ready to give up his hunting. He and the gorgeous, loving woman broke up. He proceeded to do what he did and no doubt, she moved on to give her love to another.

Simon's a terrific example of how early life now appears to last many years longer than ever before in history. Concerns over aging and an emphasis on looking young seem to be an increasing focus. Plastic surgery statistics show our increasing obsession with holding onto youth. Check out any billboard or magazine to see the many ways that young beauty is idolized.

All this affects our relationship to love—driving whether we feel deserving at any age to find the partnership for which we long. We might pretend to believe finding love means everybody at any stage and age, but even the Internet dating sites geared for over fifties have everyone looking fresh as a daisy. Most people believe when you hit a certain age, your opportunity to find beautiful love is over. This simply isn't true! And I'm going to show you it isn't true.

Different times, same ideas...

IN SOME WAYS, THE MORE THINGS CHANGE, THE MORE THEY REMAIN THE SAME. Back in the '60s, anyone over thirty was considered the enemy. "Older" people got us into war. Older people didn't understand freethinking. Older people joined the dreaded corporations.

But really, that was never the main problem. Underneath it all, we have long confused growing old with growing up. Most are worried about aging too quickly. Twenty-two year olds sit in my office, moaning about life passing them by.

It is true growing up means that there are certain requirements—obligations both annoying and fear-provoking. Unfortunately, many translate this to indicate the end of "fun." Really, we've misunderstood the whole growing-up business.

Indeed, we somehow maintain the concept that childhood is freedom. It really isn't. Oh sure, you're free to basically play all day, but is that what freedom really means to you? To me, freedom means having the ability to consider options.

How do we figure out how to be a "quality" grown-up?

Often, the problem is that we're not given good instruction. Childhood trains us, often at best, to not talk to strangers, never take candy from people we don't know, or to do all our homework. These are certainly not enough. The essentials we seem rarely to be taught, but must understand, are: self-esteem, partnership, parenting, and money.

The enormous, over-riding benefits of responsibility are poorly understood as we move into so-called adulthood. Yes, benefits, for the more personal accountability we take, the more opportunity there is to truly change our circumstances. Change of circumstance feeds outlook. Outlook affects circumstance. This means **how we see a thing is central to how we do a thing**. How we see and do things hugely determines the arc of our lives. Conscientious awareness prepares us for real-world impact. This adds up to what I call a **Newsflash**. Newsflashes are headlines for healing.

Newsflash: Perception rules and determines 90% of our life experience.

Another word for Perception is PERSPECTIVE, which means Attitude. Attitude greatly determines the route our lives take along with how it feels to be us. It also hugely influences who and how we love.

One thing's certain: When we see our existence as a series of calamitous catastrophes, we stay stuck because *what we feed grows.* If we feed discontent and the belief that we are failures in love or in any other realm, then that's what grows. If we approach life as a brilliant experiment in discovery (and especially if we nourish that belief with estimable acts), self-esteem will be what blossoms.

And as a bonus, all we are and do affects everything and everyone we touch. When we change our attitude toward responsibility or commitment or even aging, the world around us begins to shift. Needless to say, such altered perception is no easy matter. That's why this very important topic will later be covered step-by-step.

Okay, but why are we afraid of this aging business?

THAT'S PRETTY EASY. LOSS OF POWER—the fuel that runs most lives. Power is something we'll discuss in depth as we move into this book, but for now, look at the fear of power loss as quite simply the need to control outcome and even worse, the false idea that we actually *do* control outcome!

That's a wildly foolish notion.

This desire to control outcome means trying to manage not only how well we eventually do in the world, but how and what others think of us, which is a losing game to be sure. In truth, *we have absolutely, categorically, no authority over what others think about us.* In fact, we do not really have the slightest idea if anyone thinks about us at all. Of course, everyone's in basically the same boat— worried about what we're thinking too.

But back to aging: Okay, the first reason we're afraid of aging is loss of power. Naturally, the greatest example of loss of power is death itself. So, aging means dying and even if we think of this as later than sooner, we'd rather avoid the topic altogether since thinking about it only threatens to tumble us into even scarier territory, as in: What happens then? We'd rather exhibit and exert control efforts, no matter how puny those efforts are, than consider such foreboding things. Here's a very confronting relationship issue and a very common question most face at some point:

Q. What's going to happen to my relationship when I'm old? What if I get sick or suffer sexual impotence or whatever? I'm terrified I'll end up alone.

I OFFER THIS QUESTION HERE in the introduction for two reasons. First, it's not something we'll cover in detail in the body of this book; however, it's most certainly a topic of concern and worth mentioning. Second, as a way of introducing the form and context, questions will appear throughout.

Naturally, there's no absolute answer to the first two questions but rather "solutions" that will rely on the nature of your particular relationship, as well as on your own individual development. No matter what, these issues should be discussed openly rather than forcing them underground as so often happens.

On the other hand, the ending-alone issue is relevant to us all; our fear of pain and our fear of being alone are connected. We'll dive deeply into these two important topics as we further negotiate the love matters terrain, for certainly we can easily make many disastrous love decisions based (unconsciously) on these two fears.

Why so morbid? Why all the death talk?

THE RESULT OF OUR PUSHING AWAY FROM THE DYING TOPIC is more far-reaching than you might imagine. Definitely one of the more obvious downsides of our disrespectful attitude toward aging is that in too many cases, it has left us without wise role models and solid mentors. Ignoring the insight that can only arrive through tried and true experience inevitably short-changes us both as individuals and as a society.

Additionally and horribly, it also results, all too often, in the elderly being tossed aside like smelly garbage, but that's a topic for a whole other day—unless an elder is one of the relationships in your life that could use love mending.

In that case, you'll also find applicable tools offered here.

Perhaps more relevant to our topic is that refusing the death conversation often means refusing relationship closure. How many times has someone you're dating simply disappeared? Have you done that as well? Or how about in close friendships where one minute you're inseparable and the next minute you have little or no contact, with no conversation about why?

Closure involves bringing any situation to a conscious, decently-expressed conclusion. There's finality to closure and as such it tends to strike us (psychologically) as a mini-death experience. This fear/incapacity/unwillingness to say a suitable goodbye applies in numerous circumstances: where illness occurs; where a job is being left; where a friendship is ending; and where love relationships have ended...or should.

The short goodbye...

NOTICE, FOR EXAMPLE, HOW WE TEND TO GIVE GREAT ATTENTION to planning a grand wedding—approaching the event with ceremonial airs and attending to the details with excited verve. At the same time, zero attention is given to recognizing divorce as a ritual conclusion deserving our profound consideration (except legally with regards to finances, furniture pets, and children, for instance). By then, we are often too disappointed or angry to think of such a thing, but I'm telling you that refusing to acknowledge the intense psychological importance of endings undermines healing and makes it ever more difficult to authentically embrace new healthy relationships that might actually work. I'm not talking about our horror over what's happened or our fury about what's happened either, because those are the easy parts to see. I'm speaking about the kind of closure that puts the period at the end of the sentence, allowing an effective moving on. Sure, moving on is challenging and letting go isn't easy, but if we want a graceful, bright new day, it's a necessity. Know anyone who continuously talks about their ex, though supposedly the relationship has been over for years? I once met a woman who'd been divorced ten years and was still talking about the partner's leave-taking as if it happened yesterday. Do you wonder if she'd managed to find new love? Of course, the answer is no.

On the other hand, some folks do *appear* to move on by dating and such. But if we listen carefully, we can hear the last partner still shuffling amongst the sheets of the new bed.

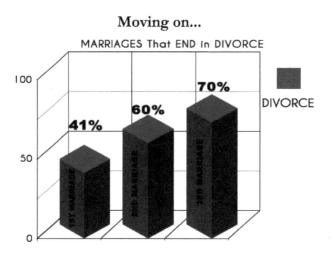

Moving on...

REVEALING WHY AND HOW getting to the next happy relationship moment is so loaded is in part what this book is all about. Let's face it, there's a reason why:

- ✓ 41% of first marriages end in divorce.
- ✓ 60% of second marriages end in divorce.
- ✓ 73% of third marriages end in divorce.

Apparently, we're not learning anything. Now, you don't have to be part of these gloomy statistics; instead, you can help create a new paradigm. I'm going to insist again and again, that you have the power. The more you know about yourself, the better chance you have of truly shifting your *long-term relationship* to love matters.

And I'm going to show you how.

Drinking from the fountain…

ALL OF MY COMPLAINING ABOUT ATTITUDES TOWARD AGING ASIDE, we must acknowledge that bringing a fresh, youthful viewpoint offers bounty for all.

Anyone of any age can keep up with the news minute by minute (requiring, of course, parents of youngsters, for better or worse, to establish new boundaries, limits, and vigilance).

We can all type in any question in our heads and Google provides us an answer. We can check out (and obsess) over every ache and pain arising in our bodies. We're able to read books and magazines on electronic screens. We're joined across the planet by images, thoughts, and curiosity.

What this means is that we live now in the deep end of a technological ocean with nearly every minute of our lives being catalogued, reported, visible, and "permanent." Or so it feels. As if we're constantly on display.

Yes, through YouTube, on-camera reality TV, Facebook, and other Internet venues, we can see moment-to-moment what everyone else we know and don't know is doing with their life. This means that attempting to refrain from comparing ourselves to…well…the world, becomes increasingly challenging. In many ways, both subtle and obvious, this adds yet another layer to what's coming to feel like standard daily stress.

Try to remember though what you're comparing is your insides to their outsides—what you *feel* measured up against how they "look" which is, I promise, not how they actually operate. Inside, believe it or not, they feel pretty much the way you do.

Thus, on top of the daily grind, try as you might to stay private, all secrets tend to surface like gutter grunge. Somebody saw you dancing with that new guy or witnessed your meltdown at work (and filmed it) or read your so-called private emails and texts; perhaps they publically pointed their bony, accusatory finger at you for a moment of "bad" behavior. Everyone's a critic. Everyone feels free to voice his or her most strident opinion.

But don't mistake me: Technology has definitely brought us more than it's taken away. Today, for example, in this age of youth-driven technological advancement, whether we're 60 or 20, we can meet our mates through the Internet—we can partner with someone who started out living hundreds or even thousands of miles away.

Let me pause to say now, though I'll repeat it later, that when seeking love through online dating, it's important to please make sure you're using a reliable site. Also, though this is hardly popular or "romantic," before getting serious with someone you've met online, I recommend that you rigorously investigate their history. Use a professional to do this, as that takes emotion out of the equation. Yes, trust is important, but so is safety. Along with great Internet reports of friendship, collaboration, and information, too many difficult stories have come our way from this mostly brilliant venue for finding love. For example, some of the more awful tales include vicious cyber-stalking or worse, young kids egged on through cyber bullying to kill themselves who've gone through with it. It's not that I'm blaming the bullies, who've been around since the beginning of time and who should, of course, under any circumstances be aggressively dealt with, but technological access can certainly amplify dire consequences. The bottom line is: Stay alert.

Burdens and benefits...

ACTUALLY, NOTING THE DISADVANTAGES ALONGSIDE THE GAINS of technology offers a golden example of how to view everything in life. Indeed, assessing the upside and downside of *anything* is inevitably helpful. Assessment assists our decision-making process as in, for instance, should I stay or should I go; is this the career path for me; is it time to give up this awful habit; is this habit really awful?

The idea is to notice that everything has both burdens and benefits. The question will inevitably be: *Do the burdens outweigh the benefits, or do the benefits outweigh the burdens?* Ask this about your job, your friendships and, of course, your love life.

Around the planet and in our homes, it's easy to see how this works. Your friend is great when it comes to a shoulder to cry on, but not so terrific when you get sick. Your boss is smart as a whip, but a horrible manager. Your dog loves you with fervor, but snarls at others. Your lover is amazing in bed, but no Mr. or Ms. Fix-It. Burdens and benefits: Both are present in every circumstance.

Summary: All of this is to say that living in the 19th century is a far cry from living in the 20th; and living in the 21st century is far different still—as increasing technological influences inundate us and throw us into a whole other startling framework.

For many, feeling beaten down or stressed out or simply robotic in the face of all these technological advancements; what arises is a fervent yearning to return to earlier times—to recover beliefs and appreciations so often appearing now elusive—a want to remember a more intimate seemingly simpler era where faith was standard and overwhelm appeared, at least looking back, less egregious. This was a time when falling in love easily was assumed to be standard operating procedure.

Thus, there's an excited re-visiting by some to the worlds of mythology and mysticism, as well as a more passionate investigation of spiritual and religious paths—paths we hope will reveal clearly how, when, and where our love matters.

Sometimes we are enlarged by these explorations. Sometimes we are disappointed. Perhaps that's because all the spiritual pursuit in the world doesn't seem to teach us how to allow *personal love* to flourish, moment-by-moment, day-by-day.

Why?

Over and over, we feel wounded by love…

OUR NATURAL, ORGANIC TENDENCY TO TURN TOWARD LOVE is complicated by how often we face disappointment. Many even imagine it's better to hold onto their fantasy of love where they feel in control of outcome than risk losing hope forever, which is their assumed response to unrequited or unsuccessful "real-world" love. That thinking keeps them from even adventuring into actual commitment. In that regard, here's the first of what throughout this book we'll call the **Universals**, by which I mean a never-changing fundamental standard fitting everyone.

Universal: That which wounds us offers to heal us.

I've spent a great deal of time working with this prickly psychological notion. How could it be that the source of our pain could be the source of our recovery from that pain?

Actually, it turns out love is the most constant and familiar example of how this maxim operates. If we let it work for us. Imagine all early-incurred family traumas and dramas—the ones that leave us feeling broken and unlovable—being healed eventually and finally through love itself. Yes, for most of us the passageway leading to vigorous, nourishing love is through challenging love experiences. It's a kind of hair-of-the-dog proposition, conceptually operating much like homeopathy, which postulates like cures like—it's best to take a stiff drink if you want to fix your hangover.

I make no case for or against homeopathy and certainly don't advise drinking to fix drinking, but do firmly stand behind the notion that toxic adult love *tries* to be the cure for damaging early-life love. As I will over and again emphasize throughout this book, we're drawn to the person we're drawn to because (unconsciously) we're insistently attempting to heal original wounds. We want to fix what got broken at home, school, church, or wherever—some inner perceived crack in our foundation. We imagine if we can just rescue or repair or even punish the new folks, the old feelings will be eliminated or overturned. Of course, this doesn't work. So, we move on to try again. And again it doesn't work.

And again.

Instead, we must address the original circumstances as well as the attitudes plus actions growing up in us as a response to those circumstances. Meanwhile, *all* the terrible relationship efforts we engage are important.

They teach. They train.

This means that great love mostly happens after not-so-great love. And eventually, with real effort, clarity, and a true understanding of fundamentals, we can actually turn things around and be able to have a loving life both at work and at play. So celebrate all those awful encounters, for they've been laying the groundwork for something wonderful.

I'm not kidding.

Let me be clear: I'm not saying even beneficial love, when finally appearing, *automatically* fixes all that ails us. There's tons of conscientious effort that must first precede such profound repair. What I am indicating is that original abandonment (smashed love) can begin its healing process through repeated encounters with such abandonment again and again. It's hard to imagine but true—if, of course, we learn from experience.

And there's the rub.

Sounds great…let's have at it!

WELL, WHEN IT COMES TO QUALITY RELATIONSHIP there's an even trickier piece, and it's a dozy. For wholesome love to appear in our lives, *we must be ready* for it. And I mean really ready. And since everything surrounding us reflects who and how we are, **the strong love we seek starts with self-nurturing**. If we don't care about ourselves at all, we'll either not recognize healthy love when it's offered or we'll not be able to absorb it even when soaked in it. Instead, we'll ferociously bat it away with our relentless distrust.

In other words: Self-love is key.

As Maya Angelou says:

> I do not trust people who don't love themselves and yet tell me, 'I love you.' There is an African saying: Be careful when a naked person offers you a shirt.[vi]

I remember my client Sabrina, a loving woman of unparalleled heartfelt caring. Everyone wanted Sabrina on his or her team. Everyone loved her unabashedly. But when it came to having lasting love, Sabrina struck out again and again.

I met Sabrina when she was 48 and though she insisted marriage was an aim, she'd never been married. Her career was well on track. She'd been a long-time homeowner. She'd many friends who revered her dearly, but no man—no one to hold her in the dark times or the sweet moments, either.

No true love.

Of course, there were father threads hanging around her neck. And mother as well. We got to work, following the path of self-love—moving her steadily toward a new self-view. She worked diligently, taking workshop courses and setting her fine heart on real change.

And change she did. She opened herself, then, to love in ways she never before had. When she did that, love came. It came in the form of Sam, a man her age who also all his life had slipped through love's real embrace. They came together with dedication. As they both turned 50, I was honored to be able to perform their marriage ceremony, a glad beginning for the life they've happily shared ever since.

So no matter how great we already are and no matter how many people already seem to know it, *we must love ourselves to love another.* Luckily though, the journey toward strong, nourishing self-love and the inviting of healthy love from others can happen simultaneously. Sabrina didn't stop her self-work the minute she met Sam. She kept at it and eventually their mutual love won out.

The moral of the story is: We don't need to be all perfectly put back together again and complete in our self-love process to allow love, but we do need to stay the course for the happy ending we seek.

Water, water, everywhere and not a drop to drink...

UNFORTUNATELY, MANY FEEL IT EVER MORE DIFFICULT to satisfy their thirst for love. It's as if we're getting further and further away from whatever natural abilities we have to commune—especially through the heart rather than through the mind. **True Intimacy**—defined here as **heart-to-heart vulnerable, authentic connection**—seems more difficult to find and embrace than ever before.

To a great degree, that's what you and I are really addressing here: how to get back to Heart-Full basics—how to offer ourselves in love to others while, at the same time, knowing how to receive the love that comes our way.

Sabrina did it.

You can too.

Let me repeat: Our greatest lifelong adventure involves learning *how to give and how to receive love.*

We must open our minds, relinquish old ideas, and find that small, sometimes quiet, hope-springing-eternal part we've over-clouded with anxiety, power grabbing, and pouting. It's not always easy but IT IS POSSIBLE. But, as it turns out, vulnerability is key.

Vulnerability? You've got to be kidding me…

MAYBE YOU THINK BEING VULNERABLE means letting folks walk all over you, or that it implies allowing everybody into your "business." Or, that you'll be perceived as "weak," that'll make you a mark or, a zillion other avoid-revealing-your-heart reasons you could come up with. Besides, you might protest, it simply sounds too hard—even unachievable.

Well, Heart-Full intimate connection is far from unachievable—and more, it's necessary to having an authentically loving life. I'll reinforce this important theme as we move along, teaching you in exact detail both what vulnerable, heartfelt love is and how to express it.

Is it difficult to learn? No.

Learning how is not the challenge, but practicing what we learn is. Because decrepit beliefs will challenge change and because fear is a powerful advocate for stasis—the noise around us insists we turn back at the gate.

Turns out, how we handle our day-to-day experiences is where we actually have that authority (power) we crave. This is true even when things with love are going all to hell. Indeed, there are ways to face collapse without completely crumbling—ways to regard loss as learning. I'm not talking about some airy-fairy philosophy that leaves you high and dry at the critical moments. I'm talking about a doable, get-the-job-done sustaining path to real love!

Let us together walk that path now.

Why bother anyway?

WHY, MANY REASONABLY ASK, DO WE TRY OVER AND AGAIN TO FIND LOVE, often in the face of extraordinarily disappointing circumstances or dreadful history?

Good question. Well, first, we're simply naturally built that way—designed to desire connection. After all, we're born in a stomach linked by a hose. Can't get more connected than that. So we could easily say the search for inter-relationship is instinctive, resting on our natural beginnings.

Those beginnings call to us, I believe.

In fact, to some degree we tend oh-so-unconsciously to spend our lives trying in a sense to get back into the womb—trying to recover warmth and safety and nurturing without angst struggle. Attempting to feel organically attached to something.

And in addition to this basic desire, there is also, I postulate, an unconsciously held *rudimentary desire to be healed and whole.* Somewhere inside, we know we've lost pieces and parts of a more complete version of ourselves. There's an organic want to reclaim those pieces. So, we attract people who have some of those missing parts and we partner with them in the hope of finding ourselves.

This premise will be further elaborated in Chapter One.

Stunner: We love who we love because we're trying to put ourselves back together again. None of it happens by accident or mistake.

Soul matters…

AS STATED, CONTEXTUAL INFLUENCES ARE NOT TO BE DENIED. If you're a young black man living today, you're most likely to have a whole different view of your possibilities and rightful place in this world than did your ancestors.

But there's yet another wrinkle to this fabric formula of genetic design plus local nurturing plus contextual effect: It's what we can call SOUL PATTERN.

Let's define soul as *life-spirit consciousness.* It's the interior landscape blueprint for that vessel we identify as "Me." This *me* design is often referred to as essence or core or psyche.

The word Soul translates from the Greek meaning *to cool or to blow, as in wind.* You can appreciate how we might take that to mean Spirit, right? Spirit, then, is something to metaphorically feel against our cheeks or hear rustling the trees outside—something we *sense* but don't exactly *see.*

With that understanding, it's easy to envision Soul as the animating principle of our lives (from the Latin *Anima,* which equals Life Force)—the vehicle of consciousness that propels us in and through our days and years. Noted psychologist James Hillman described Soul as: "That which makes meaning possible, deepening events into experiences; whether in love or religious concern…"[vii]

I'm particularly emphasizing this as psychology—yours, mine and ours—is actually the study of soul. And what we're going to be about together here, to some degree, is a discovery of the SOUL OF LOVE. That is, the soul of your personal relationship to ideas about love, as well as the soul of the love perhaps already present in your life, or the soul of love you're yet to find.

Wait, Hillman mentions religion and I'm not religious!

LET'S PAUSE to discuss the words *religion* and *religious.*

> Religion is: A set of beliefs concerning the cause, nature, and purpose of the universe, especially when considered as the creation of a superhuman agency or agencies, usually involving devotional and ritual observances, and often containing a moral code governing the conduct of human affairs.
> Religious is:
>
> 1. Imbued with or exhibiting religion; pious; devout; godly.
> 2. Scrupulously faithful; conscientious.[viii]

Now always there's a great deal of controversy about the existence of a Higher Being or even of a Universal Construct that includes any or all such concepts as: Eternity versus Temporality, After-life, Karma, Reincarnation, God versus no God, which Deity, one Deity versus many deities, and on it goes. From my perspective, *it simply doesn't matter much what precisely you believe.*

"What?" you shout.

Really though, I mean it. What I feel to be more important than going to war over the content of our beliefs is the necessity of deeply considering these questions in the first place. I become increasingly troubled, as it appears we're turning away from not only relationship with others, but from a more profound relationship with the Self. Taking the time and energy to be quiet long enough to discover deeper perspectives is required to do this. Most, I'm afraid, will never afford him or her such time or energy.

Why, we might wonder? Fear, most likely. Fear of what we might hear in the dimly lit silence. Fear of what we might come across inside ourselves that we didn't want to know.

That's because we've been taught to disdain and criticize the unknown—been instructed, though subtly for the most part, to turn away from profound discovery. Better keep your head down, says common sense, best stay on the move. How can we achieve, those naysayers put forth, if we don't travel on the fast-moving train?! Time's awastin', they proclaim. Production is the point, not process.

Hogwash. There's no rush.

Where do we think we're going anyway?

Imagine, for a minute, a world that sees lovers holding hands in the quiet dusk as an achievement; a world that reveres real, intimate communication above all other things; a world that values the investigatory process as being equal to perceived outcome.

Am I pontificating? Maybe just a little.

But to deeply pursue this offered notion that **TRUE, REAL, SUSTAINABLE, SUSTAINED LOVE**—love of work, love of friends, love of partner, love of self, love of love—**IS POSSIBLE**, it just very well might be necessary to consider some of these obscurely romantic notions. Of course, what "real" love might mean for you and how it gets revealed will be surely impacted by cultural mandates. Rubbing noses to express affection might be wonderful in Alaska, but not so great in New York City.

Thus, while discovering what love means to you, keep in mind you'll need to check in with those you meet. It's not that you can't partner with someone holding a different viewpoint. In fact, such differences can be stimulating and enlarging. As Rick Warren says: "You can like somebody without agreeing with all of their policies." And I'd add, in love matters, complementarity (different strengths, weaknesses, and positions) is often more effective than exact reflection. However, in love matters, it's important to know and appreciate specifically *what* that other person's outlook is at first with regards to your biggest, most throbbing questions; otherwise, disappointment is sure to ride in like thunder.

Our religious hero's journey…

CONSIDERING HOW MUCH WE ADORE HEROES—the fire-fighters who stride into the blaze without self-consideration, the passing stranger who fights off our purse-snatcher, the citizen who stops to help by the side of the road, the returning wounded warrior—it's odd that we ourselves, when it comes to real change, are so often willing to tremble in the shadow of our own fear. Where's all our inherent fight? Where's the survivor of forests and plains? It seems as if the more complicated daily life gets, the more cowardly we become.

Yes, it requires courage to truly know ourselves. And to love what we know. It takes a decision to stop running like hell to the nearest bright-light noise. Courage to stop hiding in whatever form whether its addiction (food, drugs, alcohol, gambling, smoking, the Internet, sex, porn, work) or in any other way.

Indeed, when it comes to profound change, we must dive beneath the surface. For change of any kind, we must brave the facing of Self and brave the facing of life itself. But you can do it; I know you can. I've seen it thousands of times, and I've done it myself. I've gone from being a steeped-in self-loathing person knowing little about love to a woman whose life bursts at the seams with esteem-enhanced clarity of loving purpose.

Does all this change business seem somehow risky?

You bet it is!

Giving up old ideas and ways, even though previous procedures cause misery, feels hazardous somehow. But remember: the greater the risk, the bigger the reward.

Summary: All great love begins with the Self. Love is an art that demands your active participation and asks your courage. As you valiantly proceed through this book I ask you to do so *religiously*—that is: scrupulously, faithfully, and conscientiously. And if you do this—if you move forward with intention and integrity as if your life depended on it—if you become the hero of your own experiences, you are guaranteed in all your *Love Matters* to thrive in ways you've never yet imagined!

This is my promise.

CHAPTER ONE
PREPARATION

- **Why love keeps disappearing down the rabbit hole –**

PART I: WHAT HAPPENED?

The beginning of love is the will to let those we love be perfectly themselves, the resolution not to twist them to fit our own image. If in loving them we do not love what they are, but only their potential likeness to ourselves, then we do not love them: we only love the reflection of ourselves we find in them. - Thomas Merton[ix]

L ET'S BEGIN AT THE BEGINNING. How do we turn out to be who we are: love-wise or love-foolish? How come we feel and act the way we do? In other words, where, when, and how did all the notions, precepts, reservations, and responses start? Because if you don't know where you've been, it'll be double-trouble-hard figuring out where you're going.

As touched on in the introduction, the first essential ingredient to understanding our relationship to love must include recognition of pattern.

Start with the appreciation that each of us is stunningly unique and at the same time splendidly similar. That is, our Being is unique, but many share our ways of expressing that Being. We most resemble, in this way, one-of-a-kind *haute coiffure* garments. The design may be entirely unusual; however, there are a limited number of fabrics to use while creating that exclusive creation.

Pattern making...

WHAT KINDS OF PATTERNS EXIST and how our individual patterns develop, as well as the source of our uniqueness will be discussed as:

1) **Soul Patterning** that includes heritage material plus genetic coding;

2) **Environmental Patterning** which notices the influences of family, community, the global historical times in which we live;

3) **Developed Behavioral Patterning** that includes defensive developments.

As we move along, we'll weave in and out of these three pattern discussions as together they form the braid trailing behind us.

All of this will reveal how, whether with friends, at work or at home—alone or with others, *you can free yourself* from the love-stuck life you've been living.

Soul matters when it comes to Love...

As mentioned in the intro, psychology is actually defined as the study of soul—the examination of our relationship to the fundamental nature of our creation.

But what does this really have to do with getting and holding onto good-quality, healthy love, which is why you're reading this book?

Let's look at the luscious tale of Cupid and Psyche, which illuminates the ways in which Love lights up awareness of that rich, fundamental "you" called True Self. True Self is the one living underneath all the chatter and fear. True Self is the part of you who really knows how to love.

Psyche's quest to win back Cupid's love when it is lost to her first appears in *The Golden Ass* of Lucius Apuleius in the 2nd century AD. Psyche is a princess so beautiful that the goddess Venus becomes jealous. In revenge, she instructs her son Cupid to make her fall in love with a hideous monster; but instead, he falls in love with her himself. He becomes her unseen husband, visiting her only at night. Psyche disobeys his orders not to attempt to look at him, and in doing so she loses him. In her search for him, she undertakes a series of cruel and difficult tasks set by Venus in the hope of winning him back. Cupid can eventually no longer bear to witness her suffering or to be apart from her and pleads their cause to the gods. Psyche becomes an immortal and the lovers are married in heaven.[x]

Cupid, as we well know, represents love and Psyche is Soul. As the tale tells, without love the psyche/soul meanders through life devoid of oomph or zest. Without the psyche/soul to enlighten, love stays—as in the story—a child tied to mother's apron strings, never reaching its full glorious maturity. Love cannot stand by to merely witness psychological pain, but must attempt to intervene. Love, then, is an intimate part of our psychological development.

Indeed, this early myth explores the ways in which love gives verve to our lives—how it sustains us when all seems lost. Without love, we're left to wander in the cold night air, unguarded. Love encourages us to fulfill ourselves. Love guides our experience with purpose. According to this perspective, taught through story and known through event, we can say that love and soul are inextricably wound together—two hands with intertwined fingers.

This denotes Soul to some degree as that which guides our very presence and thereby **Soul** that's **primarily responsible** for **describing and defining uniqueness**.

What all this means is that our avid, active search for lasting love is really, underneath it all, a longing to connect to our very soul! No small impulse, indeed. And too, it means that who and how we love can very well determine how much we are able to access and remember our own true, best, essential self. Love helps us realize the special who-am-I of it all.

Hard to swallow...

THE IDEA IS THAT SOUL plus love equal the essential us which equals uniqueness certainly flies in the face of our usual habit of pinning "specialness" on the "content" of our lives—the details we tell about ourselves. Many are so used to wearing their personal tale like a badge they can't imagine any other way. Others just don't believe in the whole soul concept in the first place, as in, "We're born, we live, and we die. 'Nough said. Done deal." Still others feel it's simply too precious or complicated or distracting a notion. That's okay. For those thinking this idea is a hard sell, instead simply use the term "psyche." Whatever word you choose, the concept stays the same.

Here's the bottom line: you are unique—inimitable. There's no one in the world exactly like you. Just like no two fingerprints are alike, no two Souls/Psyches are alike as well. It's one of the reasons why, for instance, you and your identical twin *look* alike but are not the same.

Yes, you're special. Why and how, we'll figure out as we move along. But guaranteed it's not what you currently think or imagine. It's better. Far better.

And most importantly love is at the crux of the matter.

How does it work?

YOU KNOW HOW DIFFERENT YOU ARE from your siblings and how you view life quite dissimilarly though *appearing* to be brought up in the same family?

Why might that be?

Well, in the first place, though we come from the same mother and father, how precisely we're put together—our genetic construction—shifts everything. Think of it like a cake. If you were to make two spice cakes with the same ingredients, but change the amount of spice or butter therein, or you were to cook them at different temperatures for different amounts of time, they'd not taste nor look exactly the same. Thus, how those elements called "you" are assembled is very much a part of what determines uniqueness.

Newsflash: The problem isn't how we're put together—the problem is *our attitude* toward how we're put together.

Indeed, more than the so-called facts of any situation, it is our *interpretation* of the circumstances that gets us into trouble.

By example: Let's say all our life we know ourselves to be more or less introverted. Then we interpret that to mean others easily make friends, while we have more difficulty. Maybe we take a negative attitude toward our difficulty and begin telling ourselves a story about what's "wrong" with us. Our solution, then, is to hang back when it comes to expressing feelings (using withholding/withdrawal defense). We'd like to join in, but a growing sense of self-consciousness shuts us down.

Also, we criticize ourselves about this. Each time we shut down and then criticize ourselves about that, we magnify the self-consciousness. Thus, the challenge grows.

Alternatively, maybe we get defensively pompous about our inwardness proclivity with a snarled or pouty: "That's just the way I am. If they don't like it, they can lump it!"

But there's a whole other way to look at any situation—a more self-supportive, balanced viewpoint. Let's take this introversion topic by example.

Renowned psychotherapist/psychiatrist Carl Jung had an interesting take on this particular topic along with its so-called opposite, extraversion:

> Extraversion and introversion are typically viewed as a single continuum. Thus, to be high on one it is necessary to be low on the other. Carl Jung and the authors of the Myers–Briggs provide a different perspective and suggest that everyone has both an extraverted side and an introverted side, with one being more dominant than the other. Rather than focusing on interpersonal behavior, however, Jung defined **introversion** as an "attitude-type characterized by orientation in life through subjective psychic contents" (**focus on one's inner psychic activity**); and **extraversion** as "an attitude type characterized by concentration of interest on the external object," (**focus on the outside world**).[xi]

Notice Jung's point about extraversion and introversion being on a continuum—like a street running east to west. There's no statement saying east is better or more right than west. This is important. We tend over and again to judge ourselves and others—to stare and compare. As if there's a right, better road to follow that will more easily get us to the finish line. Usually in doing that, we ignore the particular qualities we're bringing to the party.

Yes, it's actually possible to honor the gifts of our innate tendencies instead of bemoaning our rotten luck while roaming the land of self-contempt. Mainly, we need to stop thinking we're something broken that needs fixing. That's bunk.

So what then makes <u>me</u> special?

What describes and defines our **unique specialness** then **is** actually **the** *particular way* **in which we're organically, contextually, and behaviorally constructed**.

Newsflash: *You are exceptional,* but it's not because of the excruciating, stunning, or even potent details of your daily experiences or the stories you tell.

Right away I hear you cry, "Wait! Isn't it the trials and tribulations of my daily life and my history that make me special?"

Nope.

Not in the least. In fact, not even the products you create make you exceptional, for those products only report the more essential who and how of you.

Let me explain.

In life, as in film, there are only 7-10 universal stories told. Sure every "new" version tries to wow us with its distinctive approach; however, when all is said and done, we find ourselves hearing and viewing the same tales over and again. Here's the list often offered to budding screenwriters:

- ✓ Man vs. Nature
- ✓ Man vs. Himself
- ✓ Loss of Innocence
- ✓ Revenge
- ✓ Death as a Part of Life
- ✓ The Battle
- ✓ Individual vs. Society
- ✓ Triumph over Adversity
- ✓ Love Conquers All
- ✓ Good vs. Evil

There are different ways to write these archetypal stories of course. Here are a few specific film and television examples: the journey from Girl to Woman = Loss of Innocence (*Wizard of* Oz and *Silence of the Lambs* or *Orange is the New Black*); the Outcast Hero's journey = Individual versus Society (any Mel Gibson film or *Ray Donovan*); and the Search for Meaning = Man versus Himself (*American Beauty* or *Mad Men*).

All of this is to say: As human beings we have a limited number of tales to tell. Just because we get snagged on the particulars of "our" story doesn't mean it's a rare one. What makes us special and distinct is a whole different pot of stew.

So what then do those pesky events mean?

IT'S NOT THAT EVENTS ARE COMPLETELY IRRELEVANT. EVENTS PROMOTE FEELING-FULL ASSUMPTIONS. Yes, confronted by life's occasions, we accumulate ideas about how we do or don't fit into the world.

Adolescence, for instance, spectacularly advertises this challenge. Torn between discovering our individual voices and being popular, as adolescents, we often find ourselves in a fretful swirl.

Okay, maybe as a kid you did catch hold of a personal posse to hang with, but then you probably thought of your whole group as "different." And most likely, even within that crowd, you questioned your appeal. Or possibly you distinguished yourself by being one of the popular kids, but then the required maintenance felt like it was just about going to kill you.

And to this point, I think people misunderstand the real meaning of fitting in. We tend to think it's about being acceptable, which we then think equals being lovable. That's not really it.

How many people have you met in your whole life who grew up feeling like they truly "fit in?" Most of us go through development like blind men feeling different parts of the elephant, trying desperately to figure out what in the world we're touching. In actuality, *we all fit in*—because we're members of the human race. For many, naturally, that's simply not enough.

The human race, huh?

Sounds a bit trite?

Well, just because it might sound corny or simplistic doesn't mean it's not genuine truth. In fact, it turns out that our humanity, and how we express that humanity, is very much at the center of our issues and capacities around true love. More on this point will be revealed as we move along.

Well, say what you will, I'd do anything to feel like I belong…

TO ACCOMPLISH A SENSE OF BELONGING we are often willing to go to great lengths, developing such defenses as people-pleasing (*whatever you want, I'm on board for*), withdrawal (*if you can't see me, you can't hate me*), and co-dependency (*I can take care of everything*), to name a few.

But in truth, so-called fitting in is over-rated. For instance, I've known many homosexual folks who spent their childhoods in pain pretending to be straight while knowing very well they weren't, in order to fit in—an awful state of affairs.

What really needs to happen all along the way is a thorough, clear appreciation of true uniqueness. This isn't about puffed-up boasting, flagrant bragging, or unbalanced ego thumping. It's about an honest assessment of quality and capability. Easier said than done. The trick then, is learning how to offer those faculties through love.

I'm remembering June, a woman I counseled for many years. When we met, June had already been in decades of therapy, achieved over ten years of sobriety, been married and divorced, and raised two kids. Despite all that, June seemed like quite a child herself. Not only was her voice pitched high in her throat like that of a little girl, but at the age of fifty, she dressed in such things as bib overalls and childlike dresses.

On top of that, June was a major accommodator. In fact, I don't think I've ever met such an extreme case. If, for instance, she was interacting with someone and they leaned to the left, she automatically followed suit.

When they moved, she moved.

As you might imagine, June seldom expressed her opinions about anything. All of this was especially surprising considering she reported quite the wild-child history.

Point is: Since her early marriage, June was all about fitting in. Somehow in her search for acceptance, her psyche had come up with a plan: Mirror everyone all the time. Be the best little chameleon in town. Then everyone will like you and no one will get continually mad the way mom had.

Of course, in choosing this path, June had completely ignored her capacities while simultaneously throwing her true well-being aside. In fact, following a soulless marriage with a man turning out to be a pedophile, she worked for a loathsome, mean boss who constantly took advantage of her meek ways.

Right away, it was obvious that group process was the ticket for June as a place where she could practice visibility. And practice she did. Slowly but surely, June found her woman-voice. She began to explore new, undiscovered ranges of Self. She found aptitudes she didn't know she had. She left that awful job and went back to teaching, which she'd loved years before.

One day when she was about sixty, she arrived to announce that she'd finally bought her first car. We were thrilled. What is it, we asked?

"An Echo," she responded gladly.

I embraced her heartily, but had to laugh.

An Echo!

Pattern, pattern, pattern.

Everywhere we go, there we are.

In the long run, June left Los Angeles to be with her children and grandchildren. Having found her voice and an ability to celebrate her uniqueness, she was able to get in her new Echo and drive off into a joyful future. And as you can see by this story, it's never too late to heal!

Where do I begin?

YOU'VE ALREADY BEGUN TO DISCOVER THE LIFE YOU WANT AND DESERVE by accepting the idea of Soul/Psyche-pattern uniqueness. Of course, *profound acceptance* can be more confronting than it seems at first glance.

Here's a radical example. What if you're simply not meant to partner or marry or birth children? Yes, such experiences are not inevitably in Soul Pattern for *everyone*. Does that mean you need to forgo nurturing love altogether? Absolutely not! Rather, it simply indicates you're unlikely to follow the same relationship trajectory many of your friends might pursue.

And that's okay.

The idea is to embrace it. For instance, I've known many childless individuals who express bountiful nurturing proclivities toward their animals, and others who are stellar caretakers of their friends.

Or let's say you imagine yourself as a big-hero kind of person, but your psyche refuses to put you on the path to, say, discovering a cancer cure because a medical career turns out to be simply not your deal. At the same time, you discover a sincere love of flowers, which sends you into the field of homeopathy.

What if you have a passion for the creative arts, but find yourself without an inborn artistic gift—maybe you'll instead determine that the love of joyfully supporting other artists with time, energy, or money satisfies this craving.

The point here is that there are dozens of ways to attend the Soul's yearnings—finding the shoe that fits is part of the journey. The thing to remember is that **all** paths to Soul-yearning satisfaction are beautifully, wonderfully, and importantly paved with love. Love is the beginning, the middle and the end of any well-fashioned story.

Summary: All too frequently we see the *who* and *how* of us as being unacceptable. Our attitude toward our self, in other words, is that we're simply not good enough (for love, success, acceptance etc.). In fact, our fear around this idea often drives some of our more unfortunate behavior. Such fear-driven behavior turns out to confirm our worst notions. So we worry about how we're perceived in the world; we behave in self-conscious, defensive ways and then people treat us the way we suspected they would. Our interpretation of this experience is that we've now been given proof positive that our original negative notions about ourselves have merit. Oh my. It's a vicious cycle.

The truth....

BUT THE TRUTH IS, your *essential Self* is not damaged, inadequate, or unlovable. There's something amiss with the way you view that fundamental Self and, maybe, with the conduct reporting that viewpoint.

Do you hear me?

Practice saying it to yourself right now. *I am not damaged goods.*

Am I being adamant? You bet. Because we keep trying to "fix" the wrong part of the wagon and then wonder why the wagon isn't rolling along.

The idea is to come to the place of not wanting or needing to change our organic pattern—a helpful intention to set since dynamic Soul/Psyche blueprints *cannot be changed* anyway. Here's where it's handy to "accept the things you cannot change" (Serenity Prayer).

Let me be completely clear: Our Soul/Psyche pattern creates the platform on which our life most dynamically stands. As such, this pattern actually offers in great part the stability we crave. **The issue is not the blueprint itself**, but rather:

- ✓ *Our* attitude toward the blueprint.
- ✓ *The* story we tell ourselves about how and who we are.
- ✓ *The* behaviors we establish to defend those distorted, negative ideas of Self.

Identifying these three elements and then offering practical solutions is what *Our Love Matters* intends. However, to accomplish real shift, you will need to begin with the following commitment: Stop settling for easy answers and quick-fix solutions. Superficiality will only give what it's always given you: Nothing.

Q: I've always thought things are just what they are! If my love life, or any other part is awful, so be it. Things are pretty much set in stone. No?

Well, things are rarely as they "appear", especially through our dirty, history-heavy lenses. The key to change is to shift habitual ways of perceiving. If we spend life looking out one particular window in the house, we're always going to see the same view. Maybe we get an impression of viewing different things as the seasons change and new folks walk by and such, but really, we're limited by what's directly outside that window.

Try going into other rooms—maybe even other floors of the house. Broaden the picture. Someday, maybe visiting the house down the road could be possible, might be fun. Or how about traveling to another town or, oh my, another country altogether.

What I'm *not* suggesting is that you try buying an entirely new dwelling. The residence you already own is just fine. It's not your home that needs changing; it's your perspective.

Over and over I'll challenge you to consider such radically new notions. Way back when, you supposed the glass to be either half full or half empty. Well, I'm here to tell you it's both. Depends on how you look at it.

All of life is like this.

We get locked into narrow outlooks, believing ideas that in many cases don't even belong to us. Notions taught by family or church or community. The plan here is to figure out what's really yours and toss out the rest. Essentially, we're mining for the gold called the AUTHENTIC SELF.

Loving it ALL? Really?

OF COURSE, BEING NATURALLY EXTRAVERTED OR NATURALLY INTROVERTED, as in our previous example, may be slightly easier to accept than, say, being better at art than math, or being less of a basketball player than our height would imply. Part of the problem is we're told or believe we can force-march ourselves into changing these propensities and abilities. Well-meaning parents offer statements like: "You can be anything you want to be!"

Debilitating wishful thinking.

We can't be *anything*.

I, for example, was never physically built to be a ballerina, nor do I have natural technical aptitude. That means when it comes to the computer, for instance, I do the best I can and get experts to do the rest. Same goes for you.

You can improve your athletic prowess to some degree, but it's unlikely you'll end up turning "not bad" into Kobe Bryant or turn adequate technical prowess into Steve Jobs' business acumen.

The point is: So what?

Over and over I'll suggest you explore the "so what" of any situation, attitude, or encounter. We become quick experts at making mountains out of molehills, while minimizing truly important moments and experiences. At this point, try turning everything upside down, entertaining an attitude adjustment, and experiencing the wonderment of seeing things in new-fangled ways. I don't need or want to be what I'm not. Of course, that contentment took some doing. But it's a contentment you, too, can find.

The idea then is: **discover how to do what comes naturally—the things that enthuse you—and do those things with full intention.**

That's the way we develop the best version of Self. Because no matter what direction nature takes us, fighting it with complaint or shame or pouting won't change the story, whereas accepting obvious limitation positions us for an honest, authentic acknowledgment of true gifts.

Does that mean I'm stuck?

NO. YOU'RE NOT STUCK; you're simply (still) the blind person touching the wrong part of the elephant and getting confused about what manner of animal stands before you. What's wanted is a full understanding of what can and can't be changed.

So what can we change?

This brings us to **Developed Behavioral Patterns,** described by *the actions, deeds, activities, and manners of conduct exhibited in everyday life.* These expressions are more commonly known as defenses. Everybody has them. Everyone exhibits them. It's not a matter of if, but how.

Let me pause to say: The problem here is that all too often we fall under the spell of particular defenses looking as if they're offering us salvation, when in fact they're compromising our well-being. These defenses originally arise to protect us with our family, peers, community members, and the world-at-large. At some point, though, they gain way too much power and begin to take over our worldly ways. When this happens, we're no longer in charge of how we do what we do. At that point, defenses and defensiveness has come to define and bind us. [2] We'll talk about this further in the next section.

When it comes to healing, I can't even imagine where to start...

THE FOUNDATION TO EVERYTHING IS HONEST SELF-ASSESSMENT. This starts with acknowledging and exploring our everyday behavior. Naturally, this wants to be done with as little self-criticism as possible. Yes, I know, I know—that's a hard one. But really, everything you've been doing isn't awful, nor does your past conduct make you unlovable today or proclaim a tortured tomorrow. Oh sure, sometimes it feels like everyone would be appalled and disgusted if only they knew the depth of your self-loathing, or how little patience you (secretly) have for those you meet and greet daily; or even for how fed up you are with humanity in general. Thing is, we're less alone in these feelings and stances than we imagine. Nearly everyone shares our doubts, desires, and desperations. But we only come to know this if we get brave enough to reveal them.

Now I'm really feeling defensive...

"EXPOSE MYSELF!! CRITICISM, SHAME, AND EVERYTHING?! ARE YOU NUTS?" Seems crazy, I know. Before every group I run, participants tell me how shy/fearful they are of being vulnerable and visible, but it's these very exposures that alter our inner landscape like little else, especially when it comes to relationships. Just as keeping secrets or telling lies in any relationship can be a killer, regularly refusing personal revelation throughout our lives undermines true connectedness.

---

[2] For a thorough exploration of defenses, check out my website where defenses are discussed in detail. And get my book *Stuck In The Story No More.*

Indeed, sharing is (eventually) important and necessary for healing. Openness is the faster route to real change. You see most disgust, whether aimed at ourselves or pointed toward other people is actually defensive. We simply don't want to show our soft underbelly. We don't reveal our feelings or show them because we're afraid. Because we just don't think we can stand the blowback; because we've had no wise instruction when it comes to how.

Because we imagine no one's really interested.

The idea, though, is to turn your self inside out and eventually, to let the insides and outsides match. To be revealed. This begins to crack the defensive shell. As intuitive Laura Dimmino says:

> For a seed to achieve its greatest expression, it must come completely undone. The shell cracks, its insides come out, and everything changes. To someone who doesn't understand growth it would look like complete destruction.[xii]

Yes, it's in fact the fears, doubts, and assumptions that snag us (more commonly called "hang–ups"). These hang-ups, revealing themselves as defenses, encrust the True Self. [3] It's like we each have a Presidential security team following us everywhere we go, maintaining privacy. At first it makes us feel safe, then we feel cut off from everyone else, and eventually, as with everything, we adapt to and accommodate the circumstance. By then, we hardly notice that no one can easily get in to see or touch us.

Even more, protection turns into a problem as defenses promote, elaborate, and reinforce self-consciousness—that awkward embarrassment with regard to the "who" of us. At that point, we begin to believe that everyone's thinking about us the way we think about ourselves—badly. But in truth, basically no one's considering us at all. Everyone's really far too busy being worried about themselves to give us much thought. And if or

---

[3] When I reference Self with a capital "S", I'm talking about the core of who we are. This idea, really, in all self-work is to reveal our essence by removing the layers of socialization, defense and distortion covering up that essence. Mostly, however, our earliest investigations will be attending to the "self" taking us through our current days and ways.

when they do think about us, they're probably going to be a heap more generous toward us than we are.

Of course, the bar's not set that high.

Indeed, self-consciousness is a brain problem with no heart, which is why it's the prime instigator of the disconnection that bedevils relationship.

Now, picture being *free of self-consciousness*.

Really.

Free.

Consider liberty from either the loud or whispering voices telling you: "Must have, must have constant protection. Beware. Beware." Imagine instead, **love as your primary intention**.

Wow.

Well, in any event there's always great news about any posture, no matter how squirrelly it might at first glance appear, and self-consciousness is no exception. Indeed, self-consciousness lays the groundwork for Self Consciousness in the sense of being self-aware and even, eventually, Centered in Self. Terrific: When we can remove the scummy layer of sweaty doubt, unbalanced regret, and pinching fear.

Alternatives are just a glance away...

THE PROBLEM IS, WE'VE NEVER BEEN VERY GOOD at clearly knowing what we want and need, let alone going steadily toward those wants and needs.

How might that work?

In the case of introversion, for example, imagine *being able to choose* when you spend that very important alone-time you crave. Historically, we instead tend to cause rifts in order to get away; or maybe we stuff our feeling needs or the words that would report those needs. We suffer in silence, which means living in a state of constant frustration.

Indeed, I've known many who simply can't find a healthy way to ask for needed alone-time while in relationship, so they just keep breaking up with people and starting over with someone new. In fact, there are those who break up with the *same* person over and over. Is that you? Do you use "we're done" as a way of either getting space or feeling heard? There are far more effective ways to operate. I'm going to show you how.

Or sometimes, alternatively, sulking works as such a turn-off that they finally get the leave-me-alone time they're aiming for when folks stop inviting them to join the party.

There are some notable exceptions: individuals who truly don't care much for humanity, for whatever their reasons. This brings me to the unusual and stunning story of Jessie, a wildly self-conscious gal with whom I worked for many years. Jessie had an overwhelming self-contempt combined with natural introversion, plus a terrible fear of growing up that kept her constantly isolated. After being shut off and shut down for most of her life, she'd managed to successfully repress most of whatever natural empathy she'd been born with.

Jessie definitely wanted a better job life though, for which enhanced self-esteem would be essential. Initially, I assumed that like most, she'd also prefer at least some relationships in her life––even the most undemanding of friendships perhaps—so I put her in groups where she might make friends. All attempts ended the same: People would befriend her and she'd have brief, intense interactions before finding some reason to pull away. Finally one day, she declared: "Really, I just like being by myself!" The way she said it made me believe her.

Meanwhile, her career improved and she got along better and better with work colleagues. Also, she threw herself into loving her animals. So much care did she afford these creatures, it was hard to believe she would choose to eschew love forever. Still, as teacher and therapist, it's important to stand behind the client, rather than try dragging them into *our* opinion of what would be best.

Even with Jessie, however, there was one chink in her leave-me-alone armor. First of all, come hell or high water, she never missed a session—sometimes attending two or three a week. Second, for all the many years I worked with Jessie, she remained quite attached to me. In fact, the idea that I might somehow disappear struck terror in her. The deep affection she had for me (even aside from the transference, attachment and projections) [4]

---

[4] Transference is a psychological term basically meaning the therapist becomes "other" people in the client's life, such as Mother or Father. Some instances it

was palpable, so I knew that deep down lived the same desire for connection the majority of us have—the understanding that love matters. So, to this day, I continue to hold space for Jessie's love to blossom.

For many who crave such extraordinary amounts of alone time, some milder version of Jessie's story is common. Fortunately, for most there are less egregious get-what-you-want-and-need "solutions." If you're an "I-often-need-my-space" kind of person, for instance, try answering your basic, organic need for inward reflecting by *consciously choosing* a good quantity of alone, quiet time.

No *defensive* withdrawal needed.

You wouldn't have to get mad at anybody or move into resentment or become irascible or convince yourself you're unloved to do it. You could actually speak your wants and then act on them: "Hey honey, I need some alone-time. I'm gonna disappear for a while and we can connect later!"

Then off you'd go.

Sounds delicious and scary...

BEHAVING IN NEW WAYS INVARIABLY BRINGS FRESH INFORMATION. When we also tune into our inner responses, all sorts of valuable material can surface. In choosing solitude, for instance, we might discover that our avoidance is actually based in fear of confrontations: they might get mad at me (the way mom did); folks will think I'm stuck up/arrogant (the way schoolmates did); everyone will disappear (the way dad seemed to) and I'll always feel alone.

Sound familiar?

Here's a promise: good quality communication and chosen privacy do not need to be mutually exclusive.

---

is expected and in others a valuable part of the work; however, in certain more extreme cases, the transference can become quite debilitating.

Well, I try to do things differently, but it never seems to work for long. How come?

DECIDING TO CHANGE BEHAVIOR DOESN'T MEAN THAT BEHAVIOR WILL ACTUALLY CHANGE. Why have you stopped smoking or lost that pesky weight or intended to cease outraging a zillion times and every time gone back to the way it was before?

Fundamental: Extreme, defensive behavior is a symptom not a problem.

Let me repeat: **Behavior is the symptom, not the problem**. It's the news report after the thief has committed the stick-up, been caught, and gone to trial. Behavior is our response to underlying sticky bits and pieces: history unresolved; grief avoided; anger and disappointment unmet.

Sitting around forever *talking* about so-called "issues" doesn't change our life. Simply attacking the symptoms doesn't change anything either—at least not permanently and in a sustained way. Even understanding our organic patterning won't change things.

For real change to occur we must understand the true source as well as the value of all our experiences, and we must learn from those experiences. That means that everything that happens with us and to us has some gift to offer.

Newsflash: *Our experiences are not mistakes.*

Stop calling experiences mistakes.

PART II: WHAT WE FACE, WE GRACE

For me, trees have always been the most penetrating preachers. I revere them when they live in tribes and families, in forests and groves. And even more I revere them when they stand alone. They are like lonely persons. Not like hermits who have stolen away out of some weakness, but like great, solitary men, like Beethoven and Nietzsche. In their highest boughs the world rustles, their roots rest in infinity; but they do not lose themselves there, they struggle with all the force of their lives for one thing only: to fulfill themselves according to their own laws, to build up their own form, to represent themselves. Nothing is holier; nothing is more exemplary than a beautiful, strong tree. When a tree is cut down and reveals its naked death-wound to the sun, one can read its whole history in the luminous, inscribed disk of its trunk: in the rings of its years, its scars, all the struggle, all the suffering, all the sickness, all the happiness and prosperity stand truly written, the narrow years and the luxurious years, the attacks withstood, the storms endured. And every young farm boy knows that the hardest and noblest wood has the narrowest rings, that high on the mountains and in continuing danger the most indestructible, the strongest, the ideal trees grow.
- Hermann Hesse[xiii]

I N ORDER TO TRULY HEAL OUR LOVE MATTERS, we must get to the root, for we also, in the best of all possible worlds, shall fulfill ourselves according to the laws of our nature that we might build up our own form—thereby representing to the world our boldest and best selves. To do this, we check out behavioral inclinations *from the start*:

✓ Notice when and how damaging behaviors initially showed up
✓ Recognize the original childhood triggers for those behaviors

Yes, today's patterns started many yesterdays ago. For instance, that shutting-down-when-we're-hurt behavior was established as a kid at home because we felt no one was listening; or in a house too overwhelmingly chaotic; or in a school environment where we got bullied or believed we couldn't fit in. These defenses were fine way back when. Without them life would have been intolerable, truly. That's why I proudly proclaim: I never met a defense I didn't like.

I once had a client we'll call Malcolm. When I met Malcolm, he was so depressed he literally couldn't move off the couch. He'd been practically carried into session by a girlfriend who could stand it no more. For the first few months, nearly the whole time he was with me, he lay down. Even a lifted arm looked like a struggle. Malcolm's true, organic and obvious depression was exacerbated by daily pot smoking—a great way to magnify difficulty.

We began digging in to the deep causes of the depression, while simultaneously, a collaborating psychiatrist gave him anti-depressants. I must emphasize that there are cases where psychiatric drugs are an important ingredient for healing, while in other instances they merely serve as a way to avoid any real in-depth work. In Malcolm's case, they were indispensable. Of course, sobriety was also crucial for recovery.

Happily, Malcolm made a full turnaround and now lives a vital, splendid life. It didn't happen overnight, but it happened. What saved him in the first place? The pot that took him down (defense of compulsivity) and the depression (both organic and defensive). Long after the virulent strains of depression had abated—long after the drugs were a distant memory, as was the girl who brought him to therapy—Malcolm got to be grateful for all he'd experienced. He realized that his dependencies led us toward the real problems underneath those symptoms.

In the long run, Malcolm found a whole new life based on enhanced perspective and a profound understanding of what made him tick. Without the addiction and depression, Malcolm could very well have suffered an unrealized, beige life—more hopeless than hopeful. It happens all the time. Or he could even have committed suicide. But his symptoms were so radical that they forced him into an awakening.

This is a wonderful example of how our seeking of solutions can get initiated when over-the-top defensive behavior simply isn't working effectively anymore—when such behavior is taking more from us than it's giving back. That's when it's time to move from tolerant surviving to zealous thriving.

That's what happened to Malcolm.

I just want to be me...

Seems these days in our whirling, swirling, demanding world we're getting further and further away from what can be called the Authentic Self. All too quickly, we can barely remember who we started out to be. Sure life is challenging. Still, I'd assert, it's the intense pressure *we* exert through defensively perpetuating negative assumptions that creates the current feelings I call *stuckness*. This is a term I coined alongside my "stuck no more" banner.

The stuckness that alienates us from our True Selves is why sometimes we feel so lost or like we've "lost our self." But the original "me"—soul pattern matter and organic matter as well—is inside awaiting re-discovery. We haven't really lost anything, but rather have simply misplaced that connection—like misplacing our keys. And just as with those keys where all we need to do is look down to see they're right where we put them, when it comes to reconnecting with True Self, all we need to do is look deep inside and there "we" are.

Digging Deep...

EVERYBODY'S IN A HURRY TO FIND LOVE, thinking they need change *right now.*

Thing is, quick fixes just don't work.

If they did, I'd be totally on board.

It turns out this delving/digging/unearthing process is the fastest, most far-reaching, *and* most lasting procedure we can follow for real change. Plus, when actively attending and intending process work, we very quickly find that our load is actually lighter than expected. In fact, by avoiding, we make things doubly hard on ourselves because what we repress causes stress, while what we face, we grace.

Besides, what better preoccupation could we possibly have than figuring out how to best manifest the astonishing life we've been insisting we want? And really, it's not as awkward as it appears. The trick, as with so many things, is to take it one step at a time. (If you're feeling impatient about getting started, jump ahead for a hot second to the *Love Works* chapter and do the Autobiography exercise.)

Here's a great example of how these deeply-buried messages can operate. Over the years, I've often worked with adults adopted either at birth or later. Even those adopted right out of the gate inevitably evidence abandonment issues, getting often covert (unheard but still felt) messages like: you're not a keeper; you're a throw-away; we don't want you; you're too much trouble. It doesn't matter what good reason originally encouraged the adoption. It doesn't even matter if the individual ends up with a fabulous family. Naturally, a terrific adoptive family scenario means less challenging outcomes; however, invariably *something* lingers in the person's psyche with regard to love and belonging.

One such fellow, James, was adopted into a family that already had a couple of girls, but who'd lost a son. James was a kind of replacement child. James' adoptive parents had a tumultuous relationship ending in divorce. Dad remarried a nice but rather distant woman.

What James was left with after all this was an aversion to a sustained, sustainable relationship. The messages he'd taken from his life story included: relationships never last and can't be trusted; relationships are always chaotic and leave you heartbroken; relationships hurt.

James wanted relationship, for sure, just not anything that threatened to last; he was absolutely convinced they'd inevitably land him in disappointment. Actually, James was a deeply sensitive man and nearly any kind of hurt impacted him profoundly. Therefore, something inside him decided as far as loss goes he'd had enough. To avoid any more love defeat, he consistently chose far younger women not at all on his wavelength and with little capacity to meet him as a full partner. Because, then, he could always (rightfully) point to their inappropriateness for long-term partnership, he maintained a cycle of breaking up with one and hooking up with another.

Though frustrated and lonely and even well-informed, it was difficult for James to break the cycle. His fear of loss remained bigger than his desire for true love. James is now in his 40s. He's a dynamic, handsome, fun guy. We're still waiting for him to turn the love corner.

Fixing the break…

ALL RIGHT THEN, WE KEEP TRYING TO FIX WHAT FEELS BROKEN through superficial means, with people who look or sound different from before or by changing our own appearance, locale, or circumstance. And (mysteriously) we find ourselves constantly in similar situations—with partners who are unavailable, mean, unmotivated, or whatever. Suddenly, we're meeting critical pressure equal to what we experienced in our original families. We run around trying everything we know to please the never-satisfied parent. Or, to infuriate, maybe, because we're still so mad about what happened in our family of origin. It *looks* like current relationships push us hither, thither, and yon, but it's really old news displayed and replayed.

Eventually, of course, we get hurt, livid, or just plain pissed-off. Or deflated and defeated. What often follows with a *thud* is depression about the whole love business—or worse about life itself.

Bitterness is just a glance away.

Certainly, it's hard to imagine all those rotten experiences could serve up a dish both potent and tasty. But they do, when you're given the right recipe.

What is the right recipe—cause I'm really, really tired of terrible relationships and an unfulfilling life?

AT THE ROOT OF OUR TOO-OFTEN TERRIBLE RELATIONSHIPS is the defensive behavior noted just a moment ago. As established defenses are ways we organically and early on in our lives establish protection. At first they were helpmates, but at some point, they became blockades to a whole and healthy life.

Maybe at the beginning, it was a good idea to be sparklingly over-compliant, flagrantly rebellious, or vividly caretaking; however, once those originally established procedures take over present-day life, they need modification. Unbridled, they come to own us, own our decisions, and own our possibilities—capturing and imprisoning potential. That's most likely what's happened to you and why good quality, sustained, and sustaining love is eluding you. And worse still, the root problem is showing up everywhere.

Yes, everywhere we go, so do our defenses—at work, with friends, and even as we look in the mirror. But the most obvious place of all is in a relationship where defenses darkest and ugliest face threatens to stop love in its tracks.

Q: What are the most often used defenses when it comes to keeping love out?

REALLY, ANY AND ALL OF THE DEFENSES can be effective for keeping love out…because defense happens primarily in the ego-mind, which is the aspect of us that directs our day-to-day functioning.

The ego and heart are frequently at odds.

That's mostly because the ego and its representative defenses circle around power and control. To discover how that works, we need to pay attention. For instance, are outrage, irritation, snappiness, frustration, and impatience frequent responses for you (defense of anger)? Or do you tend to get embarrassed, feel shy, or self-conscious (defense of shame)? Or do you find you've got a lot to complain or whisper or "share" about when it comes to others (defense of gossip)? Or do you go silent, get sullen, shut down, or isolate in reaction to uncomfortable situations (defenses of withholding/withdrawal)?

Naturally, as there are no less than fifty defenses, this only names a few. To start with we need to recognize which anti-hurt defenses our egos have chosen to "protect" us. Luckily, noting this is easy because they show up everywhere: at work and at play; in business partnerships and in love partnerships, in how we deal with our doubts and with our certainties.

That's the *behavioral pattern.*

Once we realize what we're doing to defend against love, we can find ways to shift gears. Employing new actions to support fresh attitudes is how change happens.

Driving the better relationship road…

CHANGE IS A PROCESS. FIRST THINGS FIRST. There are four basics for change. Think of them as the wheels for your vehicle. No matter who you are, what you do, where you live, or what kind of defenses you're mainly involved with, these four wheels are essential. You can go fast or slow. You can go off-road, take the scenic route, or move straight ahead on the highway; but whatever direction you choose, these four wheels are needed to support forward movement. We'll start with two.

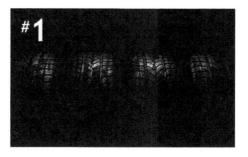

WHEEL #1: STOP TAKING THINGS PERSONALLY

This first point is a biggie. Turns out that 99% of how others behave toward us actually has zero to do with us. I know most of what happens in life *feels* personal, but it isn't. And similarly, 99% of how you behave with others has zero to do with them.

Newsflash: *Nothing* is personal. Nothing is *personal.* Nothing is personal.

I mean it.

Let's talk about that for a moment.

We looked at how easy it is to get jammed up by early notions telling us we're center of the universe. Because no one much confronts that idea, we get in the habit of taking everything personally, while in actuality pretty much *nothing is really about you*!

That's right.

When your boss is mean as usual, it's not about you. And when your partner screams because you've forgotten to take out the trash, it's not about you. And when your friend is always late, that's not about you, either.

> Self-importance is our greatest enemy. Think about it. What weakens us is feeling offended by the deeds and misdeeds of our fellow men. Our self-importance requires that we spend most of our lives offended by someone.
>
> Carlos Castañeda[xiv]

The point is that everyone, including you, operates out of private fears, defenses, concerns, hopes, wishes, dreams, and longings. You're simply a momentary player in their private show. And vice-versa.

This is not to say we remain unaffected by how other people act and what they do. Our inner data damage can certainly be amplified by challenging exterior events and people. It happens constantly. But *the volume of our reaction* has nothing to do with the person standing in front of us.

So if deep down we feel undeserving of respect, then our partner forgetting the trash for the billionth time can easily plug us into deep inside injury. At that point we might move to fury or grief or even guilt. Then every time we're disrespected, we revisit dark pain. Like when we bite the inside of our cheek and all day long, keep biting it.

What if your mother was inevitably late to everything? Well, lateness might incite you. Or if you're constantly mean to yourself, something you learned at the feet of your dad, your boss' meanness could feel like the proverbial straw breaking the camel's back.

It takes some digging to appreciate how deeply held that don't-deserve-respect conviction might be. To understand the wound inspiring such belief...stay tuned. Meanwhile, I rush to say: It doesn't mean ignoring a reasonable request is acceptable in a partnership. How to negotiate these dropped stitches and come to collaboration as well as compromise will also be soon discussed.

The key to understanding the truth of what's being offered here is to recognize how the same things don't bother everyone. Like Pat's lateness drives you crazy but when you grouse to mutual friend Jewel about it, she seems unfazed. Or being exceptionally neat is vital to you, but no big deal to your roommate.

Universal: The bigger the reaction, the older the significant stories supporting the reaction.

Let me reinforce this vital point.

When you're tempted to slam viciously into the slow driver in front of you, it's *not* because he's a slow driver. Rather, it's because the slow driving is poking some tender, old unmet hurt regarding how important or unimportant you feel; or how respect-worthy or not respect-worthy you feel; or how vital it is that you be thought well of by the person waiting for you on the other end of your drive; or some other not-of-this-moment feeling.

This is why I'm so fervently pushing you to meet your history through writing. Ignored early pattern beginnings and denied wounds will continue to haunt and control your life.

The question becomes: Do you want to be the driver or the passenger of your life?

Try this favorite "mantra" of mine:

This is not personal—it's not about me—it's not about me—it's not about me—it's not about me.

Repeat about a billion times. Say it throughout the day whenever you have a free mental moment. Do this consistently for thirty days and see what happens.

Projection...

EVERYONE—AND I MEAN EVERYONE—ACTS IN RESPONSE TO HIS OR HER OWN INNER LANDSCAPE MANDATES. That means the rude bank-teller, demeaning boss, thoughtless date, and churlish in-laws are all throwing their own personal, unresolved, often-unconscious fears, thoughts, wishes, fantasies, hopes, dreams, and disappointments on you. They're the projectors and you're the screen. This holds true everywhere in life. Even in your partnership. Even with your parents.

You, too, are in nearly constant projection. Let's talk a moment about this common, it's-everywhere-we-go defense called **projection**. We all project. It's our primary way of seeing the world.

I have a young dog named Bruno. He's a very passionate rescued pup, and always wanting attention—desperately trying to get all the love all the time. He'll growl for it, shove the other animals out of the way for it, all while using his sweet eyes and wagging tail to plead for it—makes no difference that for years now he's been safe and sound. He's obviously still referencing his where's-my-mama roots.

Once in a while Bruno will catch a glimpse of himself in a mirror, at which point he'll rush the mirror, attacking and growling. You see, Bruno has no idea that the image he's barking at is *him*—he only knows he must defend his turf.

We're all just like Bruno. We don't realize that there's no one "out there"—that the images we see called Other People are really just mirror images of us. And we're all referencing our where's-my-mamma-papa roots.

So the first way to drive that new terrific relationship road is to deeply, clearly understand this projection business. Intense realization about projection wants to reveal how **clearly other people's actions and reactions have nothing whatsoever to do with you**, and vice versa.

We're simply reflecting each other.

Fundamental: We live in a house of mirrors.

This means if you don't like something in me, it's really something in you either you don't like about yourself (often unacknowledged or even unrealized) or something you wish for. Notice that projection isn't just about the so-called negative aspects and attributes, but also about the positive ones. That means, whether I'm demeaning or *exalting* something in you, it's merely a quality I need to find and look at in myself.

Bottom line: Just as our parents were our first reflectors, everyone we meet after our parents reflects us also. Everyone: the grumpy boss, the flaky friend, the brilliant co-worker, the creative collaborator and even the all-too-often MIA lover.

In other words, beauty and ugliness, kindness and meanness, creativity and calculation, vivacity and sluggishness, abundance and scarcity all live *in you.* Our friends, colleagues, and partners might very well carry these qualities in more obvious or clearly different ways from us, but that doesn't in any way leave us out of the equation.

This inevitable looking through a particular lens based on expectations, training, preoccupations, hopes, and dissatisfactions means we're simply not clear-eyed. Part of the intention of this book is to offer new focus and vision. We'll do this by providing bi-focal lenses so that you can see clearly what's up close and then, simply by shifting the intention of your glance, also see equally well what's in the distance.

How do I stop projecting?

WELL, WE CAN'T REALLY STOP PROJECTION, but we can stop being ruled, enamored, or distracted by our projections. Once we do that, we easily see what a teacher and ally projection can also be.

As a first glimpse at how projection works, it's fun to check out who in our life most aggravates us—who makes us squirm. And isn't it amazing how the thing that bothers you so much about the colleague working on your left doesn't at all trouble your other co-worker! What do you make of that? What if upon deeper investigation you realize the most annoying trait of that colleague reminds you somehow of your mother? Now assume for a moment the person's holding up a gigantic sign: *The characteristic or attitude or manner you're wrinkling your nose at lives inside you, too. Look. See. Know.*

This idea can be quite disturbing when first considered. We never want to think we're carrying those qualities we despise or disdain. Yet, we are. I say this without doubt because, in fact, we each contain *all* characteristics. And the funny thing is once we understand and appreciate this we become far less reactive. Eventually previously irksome people and challenging situations barely bother us at all.

To get a feel for how this works, you can do a little or a lot. For now you may simply want to glance at this and approach it more aggressively upon first completion of this book. I merely want at this point to awaken the understanding of how much in charge we actually are of how things land on us emotionally. You'll find an exercise exploring the projection phenomena in *Love Works*. It's called: **Mirror, Mirror on the Wall.**

As always, none of this is meant to give you more grist for your self-loathing mill, so please, please refuse to use what you discover against yourself.

Summary: Projection is extraordinarily helpful once we get past the annoying part, as we realize projection puts us in contact with something we need to know about ourselves. The more we know about us, the more authority we have to determine the course of our lives. Indeed, the greater our understanding of Self, the less those "aggravating others" aggravate. It's win-win.

So eventually, I just get rid of those old hurts and the behaviors, right?

NOT REALLY. IT'S NEVER ABOUT GETTING RID OF ANYTHING; it's about discovering the benefits and teachings of all experience. It's like we have a piece of shrapnel embedded deep within—a war souvenir. We can't make the war not have happened. It was what it was. Wisdom says trying to remove the shrapnel would be more dangerous than leaving it in, and anyway it's a kind of badge "celebrating" experience. If you'd never gone to war, you'd not know what you know and be who you are. In the end this is a terrifically handy perspective since those original wounds simply aren't going anywhere.

A better focus, instead of trying to toss history aside, is discovering the stories you've been telling about your original experiences. For example, I once had a client whose brother died when she was only 10, and all her life the client believed it was up to her to make up for her parents' loss. In adulthood, she became a diligent worker and in relationships, she was the person working harder than anyone to make sure the partner was satisfied. She worked so hard, in fact, that each partner ended up feeling incompetent, unable to keep up or smothered by attention, or simply turned-off by the woman's busy-bee approach to love. Which brings up the all-important question: *How do the stories we continue to play out perpetuate original wounds?*

The salient questions allowing truth to emerge will be: 1) what's our attachment to our told and re-told story-of-history; 2) how have we wrapped our identities around the details of that dusty, musty tale?

For healing, it's time to clear the air.

But I really, really, really want love!

DO YOU? LET'S CHECK OUT THE FACTS, because as it turns out the evidence of our intention is inevitably visible in our lives. This is to say: If dominant inner aspects truly want love, *and if* simultaneously your psyche believes you to be ready for that love, you have love. To repeat: *you have what you intend to have.* But if you don't have it, or can't fully give yourself to what you do have, that means on some level there's more fear than desire.

I know how hard it is to grasp the concept that what you have is what you intend to have. Take a deep breath. Read the line again. Stop shaking your head and think about it.

Let's go at it another way.

Do you, for instance, know someone who's always saying they want to lose weight but never does? Or they lose it temporarily and inevitably put it back on? Why do you think that happens? It can't be about the how-to because there are a billion programs pointing the way. Something else must be going on. Would you say that individual truly *wants* to be thin?

Or how about the friend insisting she's going to leave her awful partner, but instead stays, putting up with unspeakable behavior? Are there really any *terrific* reasons for staying? The kids? Honestly, do you think those children are better served by living in a house of pain?

For all of us this is true. Some part—not the brain—is deciding (intending) to proceed just as we are. I don't care if you're on a dozen dating sites, going to every meet-up in town, and telling all your friends you're ready.

Fundamental: What we intend to have, we have.

It doesn't mean you're an idiot or incapable—or irredeemable. It means you don't really yet understand the driving force behind your actions. That's in part why you're here with me.

By the by, this is a good time to remember whatever connection you have to faith, which I think of as assumed trust. I don't mean some pie-in-the-sky desperate hope or even belief in divine force. Rather, I'm suggesting a profound link to the part that fully realizes there's mystery in the world beyond our understanding and, most importantly, beyond our need or ability to control it. And further, faith that the part able to entertain confidence in the psyche's intention for long-term well-being is alive and well. To me, faith feels like a hand at my back. Naturally, no matter how much temporary confidence such well-being generates, sustained faith happens only with our active participation.

Not long ago, I was preparing for a video shoot. To the makeup woman, I laughingly said: "I'd like you to make me look 20 pounds thinner and 20 years younger." To which she replied with what she later explained as an old makeup business quip: "This is a brush, not a wand!"

And so I say about this book. This is a brush, not a wand. Change depends on you—what you start with, what stage of life you're in, and how much work you opt to do. Faithfully.

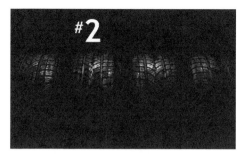

WHEEL #2: REALIZE THAT YOU'RE THE CENTERPIECE OF YOUR OWN STORY

You have the power to change.
You.
What happened way back when influences but does not determine.
You decide what your future will look like.
Smile.
This is astonishingly good news.

All right, I'm IN! So I do the history writing...what comes next?

OPTIMALLY, RECOGNIZING WHAT HAPPENED WAY BACK WHEN is followed by a process called **redemption**. Redemption means to find value. As hinted, believe it or not, *all* instances and incidences of our histories offer something worthwhile. "What?" you shout. "Now, Dr. Nicki, you're really going off the rails! To say that, you couldn't possibly understand what it was like living in *my* house!"

I can and I do.

And still, I shall maintain—there's gold in them thar hills.

So, just for a minute, imagine taking a coupon into a venue called The Learning from History Store. Picture such a place: bedraggled souls coming in carrying their burdens in baskets and bags; faces fallen and ashen; most everyone disbelieving that anything too great could come from the coupon they've brought.

Sound familiar?

But then, notice their eyes light up as everyone begins to appreciate how in this store a person can truly realize the full value of experiences. All of what you bring. You can cash in on what's happened and walk out holding tangible riches firmly in hand. You can understand the precise opportunities past significant encounters offer.

It's amazing to realize that when those experiences are transformed, our entire perspective alters. And even better: **Transformed experiences are transformative**. Once we redeem the events and experiences of our history, we are forever changed.

The adventure called history...

I'M TELLING THE ABSOLUTE TRUTH HERE. No matter what you at this moment believe, you *can* discover, uncover, and reveal the stunning resources gleaned from *every* heartbreaking adventure. And that's the way I look at history—as an adventure. People often talk about "failed marriages," for instance. To me there's no such thing. There are lousy marriages that collapse. There are marriages that have disaster written all over them from the start. There are marriages in which the individuals simply outgrow each other. However, it's my perspective that from the very start, our psyche is up to something particular when it chooses a specific other, no matter how "random" that choice may seem to the casual eye.

So let me be more specific about the idea that *we love who and what we love because we're trying to put ourselves back together again.* As we grow up, out of perceived necessity, we begin to toss parts of ourselves away—aspects that simply don't work in our families, with our peers, or in the world. We stop maybe, for instance, showing our feelings; instead, we don a shiny protective suit of Teflon armor. Or maybe we become the clown, masking our underlying sadness and self-consciousness. Or perhaps we start outraging—noisily spilling our disappointment over the landscape of our lives like hard beans rattling along a tiled floor.

Later, as we begin searching for partnership, we most often find ourselves attracted to individuals carrying the parts we've discarded. How alluring or impressive or potent we find that person who cries easily and expresses all the time. Or, how amazing the one is who says what's on their mind without pause.

After all, that behavior is simply no longer in our wheelhouse. This finding of partners who appear unlike us is commonly called opposites attract. Really, that phrasing is a bit incorrect. It's actually opposite *characteristics* attract. Thus, we discover ourselves drawn to people carrying the features we've tossed away—because we have a vague, distant memory of being more complete (whole); whereas, now we feel as if something's missing. We want to put ourselves back together again like Humpty Dumpty.

For a while!

Then something happens—all unconsciously. We begin to find those previously abandoned traits just as distasteful in the person we've attracted as we initially did in ourselves. After all, we did toss them out in the first place. That's when some of the trouble starts as we set out to make the other person more like us.

Oops.

Greeting life on life's terms...

THERE'S AN OLD JOKE: WE MAKE PLANS AND GOD LAUGHS.

The point is: Life happens.

The trick is to learn how to greet the life before you.

Let me quickly insist: This has nothing whatsoever to do with the idea of settling. Settling is something people do when they believe they've no options. Guaranteed when it comes to love matters, you have countless undiscovered alternatives. Stick to your do-the-work guns and those opportunities shall appear.

Meanwhile, greeting the life before you means: *Envision what you wish for, take action to fulfill your dreams, and at the same time be open and able to welcome life's surprises.*

Actually, not getting what we want when we want it is most often for the best. Think back. Remember when the desired job didn't happen, or the lover chose another, or the house deal fell through? Most of the time something far better came along, right?

Oh, and by the way, making choices about how to proceed is not and shouldn't be as simple as: *But it's fun* or *I wanna*. It's appalling how often these two notions are the current standard for decision making. Actually, both concepts are usually code for *I've been stab-grabbed by my inner adolescent.* Feel into the truth of this. Listen for it when others talk. Do we really want our inner 16-year-old deciding the best direction for our lives? Eek.

Why now? What's getting our psyche's dander up?

THE LIST OF HOW AND WHY WE GET IN A PSYCHOLOGICAL BOIL IS LONG. It includes things like death in the family, realization of career unhappiness, financial stress, and/or reaching certain ages. Plus, any personal crisis or extreme change can turn up our inner emotional flame like moving residences, a brutal physical experience, or job change.

And as if that weren't enough, collective discontent such as a worldwide economic crisis or global trauma—or even violent outbursts like the random killing of a number of children or the collapse of apparently steady landmarks as in 9/11—throws fuel on the dissatisfaction fire.

Indeed, *context* is important and impactful.

As stated, the time in which we live is as relevant to our unfolding personal story as anything else. Far back and long ago, we were affected most often by local gossip—"news" spread by word-of-mouth. We learned about the way the world worked through stories (mythologies).

Then newspapers came into being and the way we obtained information shifted to some degree. Then radio came along, followed by television. With the advent of the Internet, everything was altered again. "The Inter-Net": Think about the name itself—a brilliant tangle of organizational structures that entice and ensnare. Now news across the globe is visible as it happens. We're more greatly informed, but seem at the same time increasingly inured to the importance and vitality of each event. Meanwhile, gossip remains one of our favorite avenues of so-called communication.

The overall effect?

These days, it seems to take more and more stimulation to wake us up. We require our television, movie, and video game violence and/or special effects to be ever bolder and more vivid. Screens are growing in size. Sounds roar louder than ever before and now, movies are even revisiting the 3-D experience.

As a society, we've come to believe more is better—faster rules. It's no wonder so many of us feel overwhelmed, out-paced, and behind before we begin.

But the thing that inevitably turns up the interior flame most vividly is a relationship. Indeed, no matter what happens around us or how the world shifts, nothing seems to inspire, ignite, alarm, and incite the psyche like partnering—especially when it includes sex. When love and sex appear on the scene, it's with full lights and sirens.

That's because the psyche is like a big pot of stew, with vegetable, meats, broth, and spices. Now, if this stew sits on the stove for quite a long time with no heat under it, all the ingredients will fall to the bottom of the pot until you turn on the fire, then things begin to bubble to the surface. The carrots rise up and the onion pieces appear, floating like casual summer swimmers. Eventually, the meat begins to swirl around, too. Sure, after the broth has been sitting for such a long time you may need to skim off and discard the top greasy layer, but finally, the real tasty juices will begin to show themselves.

Several things can act as fire under the pot including life crisis of all kinds; however, relationship is the one surefire fire! And once that fire's lit, you can end up with a delicious meal, a burnt offering, or something, though tolerable, not-so-satisfying to the appetite.

Faces change, the relationship stays the same…

BUT HOW IS IT, WE WONDER, that we keep attracting the same relationships over and again? Bad luck? Naw. Stupidity? Nope. Actually we attract terrible relationships mostly because we don't deeply comprehend what triggers attraction in the first place.

But we can grow to understand, just as we need understand to grow.

The trick is *complete focus on the Self*. Change happens when we look at us rather than pointing at the other guy. How awful or unfulfilling or abandoning the other was is not ever the point, even if they were actually all those things. Let's dive into a hugely difficult conversation to further illuminate how important this point is: The topic is violent abuse.

There's inevitably a surge and wave of furious reactivity when we hear or speak of, say, men who beat their women. Everyone takes up the shout. Poor woman, they say. How horrifying, they proclaim. She's seen as victim and he as perpetrator.

I implore you to reject this posture.

I'm certainly not saying violence is laudable or should be overlooked—not at all. Nor is this a conversation about blaming the victim. What I'm encouraging is the idea of viewing this as yet another example of relationship as a mirror. So, for example, even if someone believes the beaten woman doesn't unconsciously know the upcoming situation she's getting into—which I'd argue—what about after the first hit? Why does she stay?

Certainly, we give many "reasons."

None of them really hold upon careful inspection.

None.

What's more valuable in these cases—and what offers true eventual freedom for the receiver of the violence, whether the relationship is short-lived or long—is for the woman to investigate the violent nature of *her own* self-loathing.

Before you rush to judgment about what I'm saying, please understand that I *personally* know what I'm talking about. I entered such a violent relationship and stayed nearly a year before being able to walk away. And as long as I "blamed" him, I was stuck long after my leave-taking. What really released me from the shame of having participated in such an awful bonding was the profound acknowledgment of my own breathtaking self-contempt. And that's the point. *Our* release. It's not as much about getting free of *them*—though that's a result—but more important to understand our own behavior. Otherwise we're doomed to repeat our terrible choices in some form or other.

No matter what we think.

No matter how we protest.

Maybe next time he doesn't hit but only screams. Still, the self-hatred has sustained.

Oh sure, we want to feel sad, perhaps, for the undeveloped stuck-in-history aspect of Self that makes these lousy choices in the first place; however, real freedom and the actual change that allows us to have a future different from the past is never found in glaring at the other person, but rather in gazing directly at the Self.

So what might that sound like in a more benign case?

Perhaps: "My last boyfriend never let me know what was going on—no phone calls about lateness or planning about what's to come. I allowed this because..." (I was desperate to keep him; I thought I could change him; my father was just like that and my parents stayed together forever; I never knew I deserved something different, etc.)

Can you see how this works?

Once you figure out this first little piece, you've opened the front door to actual change. Then you can further explore the house, including the attic and the basement.

Summary: Mostly we keep having terrible, disappointing relationships because we imagine it's other people needing to change.

It isn't. It's us.

And also because somewhere along the way we decided we're insufficient to the task of love.

This is an idea, not a truth.

Let's smash that illusion.

PART III: HEARTBREAK

The heart was made to be broken.
- Oscar Wilde[xv]

Talking about heartbreak…what exactly is it and why does it continue?

O Well, we don't *want* to stop it. Not really. We simply don't know how to behave differently. We're stuck in deeply rooted VERWHELMING SORROW, GRIEF, DISAPPOINTMENT these are the benchmarks of heartbreak. It's my opinion that most adult heartbreak—at least the kind that feels irredeemable, unfathomable, and non-negotiable—stands squarely on the shoulders of childhood; indeed, most first heart damage happens at home.

Now certainly, some early pain and loss is necessary, doing the job of propelling us into an identity. These are the little shocks— like realizing mom isn't there *every* second of the day. Or that we must learn to feed ourselves. These sorts of wounds have natural compensations. Like while alone we get to discover ourselves, and picking up that spoon means having the freedom to fling it across the room.

But not all heartbreaks are organically and naturally repaired. Some are simply cruel beginnings. You see, Dad and Mom are our first loves and if they leave us longing, our hearts break. Then, primarily, we spend our lives chasing repair. We might chase it through "others," through attempted success, by constantly attempting to garner approval, by trying to look perfect, or a zillion other ways. None of these secondary efforts scratch the original love-loss itch.

Happily, the solution lives inside. That's where mother and father, as we perceive them to be, exist. Changing our relationship to those original wounds means changing how we regard those interior figures.

As a side note: This idea that ineffectual or negative or even cruel parenting was unintentional is completely irrelevant. Of course, they did the best they could, considering their own inner struggles, historical dynamics, and projected material. It's not that mom and dad *thoughtfully* did what they did or acted the way they acted—exactly the opposite. In fact, our parents' behavior wasn't at all personal—wasn't about **us** *per se*. None of that matters. What we need to keep looking at is impact. So we don't pass it on to our children or to the world-at-large.

It's vital to realize this. Because, no doubt, all these years you've been thinking it's about you and responding to life based on the assumption that what happened hinged on something you were or weren't doing or on some essential flaw.

It didn't.

It does now though.

Many times when individuals realize they have lingering anger, resentment, grief, or heartbreak, from childhood they rush to "inform" their parents about their discoveries. Don't do that! It won't, for the most part, help in the least. Again, it's not the outside parents that are the point, which means talking to them about old wounds is unlikely to have any salutary effect. Besides, the heartbreak happens when we're little. It's the little people in us who need to be addressed.

On this point: Perhaps you imagine original parental slights have mended because today your relationship to the folks feels just dandy, or at least, the best it's been. That's lovely, but not completely relevant because to add layers to this already many-tiered cake, we don't only have one inner relationship to one inner set of parents. In fact, we have different perspectives of our parents at different ages. That means the child of four relating to the parents from that time is not the same as the one at 12, 20, or 35.

Thus, the work of today needs to be with the *various interior images* of the parents of yesterday. How great is that? After all, perhaps the in-the-world parents live thousands of miles away or are people we rarely or never speak with—or are dead. Or maybe our current relationship with them is dandy and we'd rather not poke old wounds. So the fact that we must make our alterations without them means no big confrontation or strained Thanksgiving dinners, or family meetings to tell everyone what's what. Just you—doing the inside job needing to be done. Wonderful. And in the end, even if you have a decent relationship with them to start with, it will be all the better.

The thing to discover is how to find an inside part that can be the nurturing, attentive, invested father/mother we originally lacked. Because how we react and respond in our life as adults and the choices we make are most often based on outdated ideas of who and how we are. So every time we choose heartbreak— yes, I said choose—we reinforce the erroneous notion that heartbreak is what we deserve.

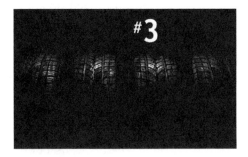

WHEEL # 3: FIGURE OUT WHY YOU'VE *CHOSEN* RELATIONSHIP SABOTAGE

THE TRUTH WILL SET YOU FREE, so it's vital to get down to brass tacks. I know in many ways you're entirely sick and tired of life's heartbreaks. You're over it. When oh when, you ask, will it be my turn to have a great career, be surrounded by amazing friends, and/or find the love of my life?

The answer remains the same: Whenever you're *truly* ready. Harrumph, you say. I've been ready. To which I again answer without hesitation: I don't believe it. Sorry.

I shall keep impressing upon you the **fundamental** notion that we actually have the life we intend. This is always a truth. To change our lives we need to change our intentions.

Just for fun, imagine I'm right—that you're getting something out of your apparent loneliness, disrespectful friends, or flaccid bank account. What could it be?

Sit with the question.

Write down whatever comes forward. Now, dive beneath the first few answers, which I guarantee are superficial no matter how plausible they sound. To further and more deeply explore this process, check out the **True Intentions** exercise to be found in the *Love Works* chapter.

Stopping the heartbreak madness…

WHEN IT COMES TO *REPEATED* HEARTBREAK, I INEVITABLY FEEL SUSPICIOUS. I'm talking about the kind where someone seems to pick the same sort of lousy, no-account, MIA, mean, unsupportive, unavailable, or inappropriate partner over and over. Faces change, but the relationship remains the same. We keep saying we want something different but never find something different. Like the person who gets a couple DUIs and says they'll never again drink and drive, but then does.

Doesn't that make you wonder?

Indeed, we repeat our self-sabotaging behavior at every turn, each time blindly expecting different results. That's the common sense definition of insanity. And all too often this relationship dance feels exactly that way—insane.

That means, we find ourselves time after time lolling about in the love dumps precisely because we've actually got some psychologically sound (if not happy and healthy) reasons. It's also because it's mega-difficult for us to realize our lessons. To believe what hasn't worked before won't work again. Rather, we learn the way children learn—by repetition, lots and lots of repetition. Weren't you at some point thinking about your child: "Does she really need to watch that video for the millionth time?" Well, yes, she does. It's how she learns. And besides, it's comforting for her to go over known territory.

Still, it's as if each time we begin again, we get amnesia. We overlook, ignore, deny, and repress instinct and intuition in order to "get" what we so desperately imagine will lead us to happiness. More often than not, we instead trot ourselves down a weed-infested garden path, acting in ways guaranteed to stop real, nourishing, healthful love in its tracks.

Q: Why would we want to stop healthy love in its tracks…after all, isn't that what all of us desire?

Well, we don't *want* to stop it. Not really. We simply don't know how to behave differently. We stuck in deeply rooted myths based in personal history. And there's little real, valuable instruction that can uproot old ideas or turn aside toxic beliefs about lack of worth or deservedness or lovability. If dad was unavailable, we find unavailable others. If mom was critical, we find critical others. Or we ourselves become unavailable and/or critical. Until we break the cycle.

The question always to ask is: *How does this serve?* [5]

That means, like it or not, believe it or not, we always get something out of repetitive, even clearly undermining, behavior. The "serving" point might not be what you'd normally think of as a so-called good thing, but it is something! This is the central point of my thesis:

Fundamental: Everything we do—*every behavior in which we engage*—has a purpose.

It may not be an obvious purpose or a healthy purpose, but still, it serves. If it didn't we'd stop. Like we used to have tails and now we just have tailbones.

Q: So why do we do it? Why do we keep going after the pain?

---

[5] In psycho-spiritual circles, this oft-asked query is called "the forbidden question".

Here are the basics—what we'll call The Four A's. Having to satisfy the call of these dynamic needs is in many cases central to our pain problem. Decide which of the four shoes fit. The trick is to look for exaggerated thinking, feeling, and behavioral examples in your life. This takes huge amounts of self-honesty. It's worth it though, for honesty is truly the gift that keeps on giving. Of course, following the realization with wondering about origins of such would be dandy. The more you know, the faster you can heal.

The Four A's:
Accolade, Appreciation, Attention, Approval

The Four A's

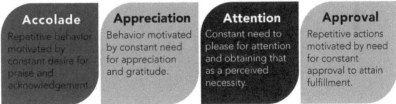

Accolade	Appreciation	Attention	Approval
Repetitive behavior motivated by constant desire for praise and acknowledgement.	Behavior motivated by constant need for appreciation and gratitude.	Constant need to please for attention and obtaining that as a perceived necessity.	Repetitive actions motivated by need for constant approval to attain fulfillment.

Accolade: For some of us, the need for praise and acknowledgment has no limits. We continue dancing as fast as we can in every scenario, just for the sake of the applause. *Everybody loves me when I'm funny, so I'll just be funny all the time, even though I'm swimming in inside tears!*

Appreciation: Gratitude for a job well done is one thing, but when we're driven to get *quid pro quo*—when we're keeping score and making internal lists and when we never feel we get as good as we give—we've veered into murky territory. *I don't believe anybody ever really notices or sufficiently acknowledges how hard I work!*

Attention: When this need is given superpowers, we can easily become cartoons of ourselves. The drive to vividly please (or with equal vivacity, displease) becomes central to our lives. *Look at me, look at me, look at me!*

Approval: A pesky little hunger, though it can appear in more subtle ways than the want for attention, it has enormous authority when it comes to ruling and ruining our lives. *Is this good enough? Am I doing it right? Look how much I've achieved.*

The problem, as usual, is not the above delineated wants themselves, but rather the degree to which our need for their fulfillment propels us. Desperate to get what we believe we must have (to survive) we keep doing the same things over and over again, even though the outcome is dismal.

Discover how the "*As*" weave through your life. And when you're feeling super brave, track back to where it all started. We call that **Connect the Dots**. Here's how it works:

NOW: I need to be sure I'm the center of attention.

THEN: In my first marriage, I would go to any lengths for attention, including getting hysterical.

WAY BACK:

> *I do that with constant jokes*
> *I was always life of the party*
> *I put on little shows for daddy*
> *I can never let anyone know I'm not okay*
> *I pretended it was all right even when it wasn't*
> *When I made him laugh I felt happy*
> *He always seemed to love me most at those times*

Again, you can glance at this now just to give yourself a running start toward healing or you can revisit the *Four A's Connect the Dots* exercise more extensively through the *Love Works* chapter. It doesn't matter when you do it, it only matters that you do it.

The deadly duo: loneliness and fear...

Indeed, very often, underneath it all no matter which "A" we favor or how our behavior reports our need, lives a nagging fear that we simply don't belong anywhere or to anyone. That leads us to the often-excruciating, hugely common experience called loneliness.

The answer to how to deal is likely to displease.

It's the same for loneliness and fear as it is for any other uncomfortable feeling: The solution is to *go toward it*. That means, sitting still long enough to truly feel fear's throaty scratch and to discover the deep gasping ideas fueling that fear. Running away won't help. Ignoring won't help. Numbing out with bustling business or calamitous compulsivity of any kind won't help. We need to dive right into the center of the stinking pool, go all the way to the bottom, and see what we find. Maybe there's buried treasure. You'll never know 'til you try it.

Universal: The only way through it is into it.

Is something being better than nothing? Nope: bad fish is not better than temporary hunger. Bad fish will give you food poisoning. So stop running away from yourself and into the first arms that come along or back to something awful or whatever. Yes, instead of going out to that maybe dangerous bar, or joining a rigid organization promising salvation, or feeding your envy of people appearing not lonely, sit still. What are you running from anyway? There's interesting, valuable, and exciting information inside you; but if you never stop long enough to listen, you'll never get the gold. Face the loneliness. It's an important teacher. Beyond and right behind that loneliness live inner wisdom voices. Listen. There's plenty to learn just sitting perfectly still in the quiet of your own breath.

Q: I've tried everything and am still alone. What do I do now?

I know that sounds lousy, but assuming relationship is truly in the cards for you, maybe you're not yet fully following the guidelines offered here.

This is not to say it's easy.

Most likely you're battling deeply-held shame, which is a sense of basic defectiveness. Such torturous feelings are often at the center of what we experience as excruciating loneliness. Exploring the family messages received right from the start about what being alone supposedly means about us can reveal much.

Suggesting you find peace with your aloneness is likely going to be *very* unpopular.

Preposterous, you might insist.

Cruel, you might spit. However, hopefully by now you've accepted how—on some level—you've designed things to be the way they are. How and why might that be true? Keep in mind, this doesn't mean you're broken or unlovable. Your life can still be full and luscious, whether you're partnered now or ever. And as it turns out—though true for the few, not the many—partnership isn't everyone's cup of tea. And it doesn't mean something's wrong with you. Besides, with or without a partner, love can be very much a part of your days and ways without a primary "other" partner in it.

The best way to explore these points is through meditative silence followed by writing. Here the idea again will be to, in as non-judgmental a way as possible, face the truth about how your life has so far reflected your inner thoughts or beliefs. Realizing the honest how and why of this affords the possibility of changing direction.

Well, invariably we all need to improve the way we talk to ourselves about our love matters. That means loving self-talk is *critical* to practice. It sounds old-school simplistic, but it works.

Starting sooner than later is best.

When ready, go to the **Loving Self-Talk** exercise in the *Love Works* chapter and begin taping over those old negative inner messages.

Do it now.

Summary:

- ✓ See if you can discover what you're doing to contribute to your lack-of-relationship.
- ✓ Consider whether or not you feel truly, really ready to be partnered. Try being profoundly honest about this. Wonder if the lonely circumstances are something some part of you has set up. If so, explore how you've set them up and why.
- ✓ Become sincerely at peace with aloneness. Remember that not everyone is supposed to be partnered.
- ✓ Start practicing loving self-talk as soon as you can.

Give Up or Step Up? That is the Question.

Q: Seems like the loneliness is even more excruciating after relationship heartbreak. So what do you do when you just want to give up on love altogether?

Sure, when our heart-breaking loneliness is exacerbated, the first place many go is to the idea of never allowing love again or imagining that even if it is allowed, it will never be as beautiful as it once was.

The reason we feel so pummeled by loneliness at these times is because our feeling center is wide open, like a heavy door finally escaping its rusty hinges. When this happens, naturally, all sorts of critters and harsh stinging, wind-swept possibilities can get in. But it's worth it to be able to feel and know the sweet breezes and soft summer scents also wafting through. For next time. When you find the one in whose arms you can truly, finally rest.

We take the bitter with the sweet.

So, ask yourself these questions. What happens if I 100% give up on love? What's the gain and what's the pain? How would it actually look to give up? What would change?

Alternatively, how would it look to go all in—make a 100% commitment to love? This commitment need not be person-specific, so no excuses, please. Commitment can be practiced every day, all the time. It's a way we feel walking through the world.

> Sometimes it's a form of love just to talk to somebody who you have nothing in common with and still be fascinated by their presence. - David Byrne [xvi]

When we're 100% in, we know it. But just in case you're wondering about your readiness, interest, or ability to fully commit either to a particular person or to a circumstance, there's a brief recommended exercise delineated in *Love Works*, which I call **The 100%**. This is meant to help you discover what's *really* true for you. It's also a terrific exercise if you're one of those should-I-stay-or-should-I-go relationship folks. Check it out.

Make your own rules…

Actually, there are **Nine Heartbreak Guarantees**—ways of thinking and behaving that will absolutely, undeniably land you smack-dab in the center of heartache pain.

Let's start by addressing the last one first and work on the others later:

Heartbreak Guarantee #9:   READING FROM AN OLD RULEBOOK!

This one will definitely drive you to heartbreak hotel. Your room's all ready. No reservations needed.

In our desperation for ways to make love "work", we all-too-often cling onto the strongest perspectives we can find, never much pausing to determine whether they truly fit our personal style and needs. In fact, we're so hungry for "right" answers; we'll listen to pretty much anyone with a strong voice. I guess that's good for strong-voiced me, but there's a ton of bad information out there, so it brings me to worry—especially when it comes to exact rules and regulations about love. We simply don't live in that kind of "rules" world anymore. There's no longer a straight trajectory for pretty much anything, let alone love.

Of course, I understand the desire to have a plan. Don't have sex until…don't call them until…don't tell them too much…don't tell them too little. And on it goes.

Bunk.

The idea, instead, is to figure out what *you* need and want. Some people need to take less risk. Some need to learn spontaneous risk-taking. It's the great news and the tough news. Instead of trying to establish some carved-in-stone regulations for dating and mating, you get to shape your own path. What works for you may not be what works for your sister or friend. I once briefly knew a couple who'd been together 23 years when we met, and had had no sex for 17 of those 23 years. Mostly that worked for them, which is why when the couple and I parted company, everything remained as it was. And that's okay. Such a plan is not for everyone, of course.

I bring this important point forward only to emphasize yet again how vital it is to discover the *soul of your* relationships and to the best of your ability, honor what you determine.

Mother, Father, Child…

THOSE OF YOU WHO'VE READ MY PREVIOUS BOOK, *Stuck in the Story No More*, know this formula. In the course of our lives, we only have three relationships: the one we have with our father, the one we have with our mother, and the one we have with the child we used to be. That's it! That's all we've got. Throughout the remainder of our days, every relationship we have is either some copy of one of those three or a combo-pack version.

That means when we find ourselves over and again, for example, rescuing everyone we come across at work, at play, and in partnership, it's likely because: we're rescuing little us who lived in wretched childhood circumstances; we're rescuing mom who got beaten by dad; or we're rescuing dad from his depression and so on.

Get it?

Perhaps as a kid you were constantly disappointed by dad in some way or other: he was unavailable, absent, violent, etc. Now, as a woman, you're furious at men; alternatively, as a man, you hate, don't trust, or demean yourself.

The important point is that based on history and according to our natural predispositions, expectation runs today's show. We get what we expect. If because daddy was an abandoner, we keep anticipating abandonment, for instance, we magically, inevitably fulfill those catastrophic expectations. In this example, there would be four primary ways in which to satisfy negative belief:

- ✓ Find people who abandon you
- ✓ Push people to abandon you
- ✓ Abandon others as a preemptive strike
- ✓ Abandon yourself

All this, naturally, is mainly done unconsciously.

It's not as if we determine these things with our brains.

No. In fact, when it comes to relationships, our brain has very little influence on our decision-making. Hard to believe, I know, but true. Mostly, we're driven by deeply held psychological forces—accumulated fears, doubts, fantasies, and needs—sitting in the psyche waiting to be projected onto the world.

It works this way: As previously stated, we start out believing ourselves to be the center of the Universe, with all events and experiences being, far as we can tell, *about us.* This gives us a gigantic amount of power—or at least, imagined power.

So, as infants, when mom isn't with us, she simply, for all intents and purposes, ceases to exist. Then when we (mostly through crying) make it known she's expected to show up, usually (hopefully) she does. We make our needs known and things change.

It feels like strong magic.

That goes on for a while until eventually we come to realize there's a world outside our crib. Still, we believe that world is for and about us. Why would we think otherwise? In fact, it's *supposed* to be that way. If it isn't like that, or if our importance is ignored too young, there's trouble. Our psyches are severely impacted by such turn-away and that effect can follow us throughout our life––especially if we lack instruction about how to reverse that influence.

In any event, at some juncture something else happens—something disturbing. We notice mom and dad aren't always cooing in our direction or paying the kind of attention they used to. And then there's those additional faces coming toward us: big brothers and sisters, cousins, aunts, and others.

We hear our parents arguing. We don't understand why or even what arguing is about, but it doesn't feel good. No one seems to respond as quickly to our needs during these times. We begin unconsciously to form a picture of a world that's no longer paradise. Paradise, in fact, feels lost. And since we remain center of the universe, we assume this "problem" of loss has to do with us.

Maybe it does and we intuit that. Maybe mom is exhausted and dad has no sympathy, or maybe dad thinks our upbringing should be one way and mom disagrees. Or perhaps, it really has zero to do with us. But we don't know that. We never know that.

And we begin to hold onto the atmospheric negativity. We grab hold of it just like we grab a hold of everything at that young point, putting it in our mouths and trying to swallow it down.

Now, it's not that most *know* this want to reclaim paradise lost, and really that knowing or not doesn't much matter. But this desire, I'd postulate, is a motivating force for us all. And since conscious realization of primary intent is unlikely, that means someone we don't even know is driving the car. In other words, the person driving the car is the chauffeur we hired. That driver is garbed in defenses, reactivity, projection and assumption. They're wearing glasses with thick lenses and often driving through foggy terrain.

Sounds bleak....

NOT REALLY. BECAUSE IN ACTUALITY, the *unconscious is our ally*—the unconscious is a collaborator and is, in fact, contrary to how it may sometimes appear, always working on our behalf, attempting to re-unite us with the One; whether that means to you the one that is all of humanity or the one that is unified Self or the one that is Divine force as you perceive it to be.

Let's look at this another way.

Right from the start, and as a function of being organically separated from the source (showing up originally as mother), we begin a life-long search for wholeness.

Universal: The Search for Wholeness is the rule, not the exception.

Certainly, this natural, hungry exploration looks different on different people. For some, it's a clear shot to the wholeness endgame and appears as a lifetime of spiritual quest or philosophical delving and study. For others, it shows up primarily as relational—be it through primary partnering or through relationship to the greater world, especially in terms of finding and exhibiting purpose. And for still others, it comes forward in the search for contented satisfaction, whatever form that might take. We don't need to be talking about it or even understand we're invested in it to be participating.

Also, buried within is a True Self, yearning to break free and to be known. Another way of saying this is that the psyche wants us to be the best, most complete Self we can be. We crave re-uniting with our original inner state. The voice we had before life interrupted.

We say it all the time: "I just want to be me."

Accordingly, our encounters happen because some (unrecognized) aspects want/need the lessons that come with experience so we can reclaim that "me." Our healing intent wants to involve, therefore, to the best of our ability at any given time in our development, an invitation to the "true" vehicle owner to get behind the wheel. If and when that happens, *every* experience becomes a learning experience.

And, too, we crave uniting that True Self with all. This combination, we sense, will give us the Wholeness we naturally seek.

This might sound annoyingly woo-woo or granola thinking or like spiritual pabulum, but play along for a second.

Imagine this to be true.

Picture what it might have meant to *learn about yourself*—deeply learn—in that last tumultuous, go-nowhere partnering you had, or even in the difficult relationship you're currently having. Consider how doing that could allow you in the future to avoid the same bad choices or behaviors. And even further, what if the happy contentment you seek is actually an expression of a more deeply-held unfulfilled want—a desire vaguely remembered somewhere in the back of mind, like a snippet of a dream that annoyingly dissolves upon awakening.

So consider that maybe, just maybe, all this grunting toward love has been not so much about finding "the one," but more about …well…getting back to our roots, so to speak. About re-connecting with the little kid in us that somehow got lost along the way.

All this means is that *understanding the root* of your feeling, you're thinking, and your behavior is the start of authentic change, which adds up to the wonderful news that your future can positively be different from your past. It'll just take a little digging!

No wonder I'm heartbroken...

OKAY, OKAY—IT'S EASY TO SEE WHY LIFE'S SO CONFUSING. And amidst our puzzlement, we somehow get convinced we're unlovable because we blame ourselves for our bewildered condition of separation from the source.

I want to emphasize here that this occurs to *all*, be it more or be it less. This condition doesn't depend on great parenting or lousy parenting. The state's not reliant on social status, ethnicity, or local context. It's an organic experience common to us all. Of course, the context elements we've been enumerating then intensify everything. Still, the fact that this is natural to us all goes far to explain why even the well-healed or fabulously parented among us suffer esteem problems and are most often hard-put to establish patterns indicating True Self-Love.

Let's skip to an example of how great parenting can still leave us unable to partner well. This is the short story of Samantha, a dear 20-something career gal whose early life had been stellar. Her folks loved each other and their three kids. They set appropriate boundaries, encouraged self-esteem, and offered a stable growing-up atmosphere.

What's the problem, you might well ask?

Well, so great was the parental relationship role model, and so very close was Sam to her family, that she found great difficulty "getting out." This is a far more common issue than you might imagine. I call it: The problem of coming from an intact family unit.

Thus, for Sam, all relationships paled in comparison to her family dynamic. No one was as great as dad. And no partnership matched that of her parents.

Of course, what Sam hadn't realized before our work together is nothing's perfect. Naturally, her parents had their challenges— Sam had simply refused to see them. Actually, bringing those trials to light allowed two things: first, she admired and loved them even more for the work done to move through the difficulties; second, she was able to realize that a quality relationship takes effort and attention. It doesn't instantly show up as *all* it's meant to be. There are no perfect pictures.

Happily, Samantha was able to partner with a terrific man, whose own attempts to grow alongside her continue to prove invaluable as they now move forward together.

All right, so left feeling adrift with no clear path back to the Self, we begin wandering the land, like returning war vets; homeless, dazed and confused. We're in a state, really, called Post-Traumatic Stress Disorder. According to the A.D.A.M. Medical Encyclopedia:

> The cause of PTSD is unknown. **Psychological, genetic, physical, and social factors are involved**. PTSD changes the body's response to stress. It affects the stress hormones and chemicals that carry information between the nerves (neurotransmitters). **Having a history of trauma** may increase your risk for getting PTSD after a recent traumatic event.

Symptoms

Symptoms of PTSD fall into these main categories:
1. "Reliving" the event, which disturbs day-to-day activity.
   - ✓ Flashback episodes, where the event seems to be happening again and again
   - ✓ Repeated upsetting memories of the event
   - ✓ Repeated nightmares of the event
   - ✓ Strong, uncomfortable reactions to situations that remind you of the event (*I'd add that much of this "reminding" is at an unconscious level*)
2. Avoidance
   - ✓ Emotional "numbing," or feeling as though you don't care about anything
   - ✓ Feeling detached

Now, though I've been clear about PTSD being pretty much a lock for us all just by the condition called birth, no matter how challenging or apparently easy our lives following childhood, early trauma exacerbates everything.

In fact, many well-documented conditions (and defenses, I'd say) report symptoms of PTSD. One of our currently most commonly thrown-about terms, for instance, is depression. Apathy and numbed feelings are generally part of depression and in the case of PTSD, we can often layer on the defense known as dissociation, which feels like leaving your body. It's easy to glimpse this dissociative experience in sex—as when we're sometimes outside watching ourselves perform.

Or, as another example, are you the kind of person who holds cards close to their chest, keeps things buttoned up, or thinks of themselves as "private?" Maybe this process has become so natural; you hardly realize it as defensive. But it is. It can also be another symptom of PTSD.

Having a lack of interest in normal activities, showing less of your moods

These things can easily read as indifference. But you're not indifferent really, are you? No—maybe you're just scared; or maybe you've merely gone to sleep.

> The opposite of love is not hate, its indifference. The opposite of art is not ugliness, its indifference. The opposite of faith is not heresy, its indifference. And the opposite of life is not death, its indifference. - Elie Wiesel [xvii]

You're exhibiting an odd kind of self-control by attempting to mask your underlying moods. Of course, as with much of PTSD, we're often not even conscious that underneath the sluggish or lethargic feelings lives trauma.

In actuality, the above-delineated PTSD symptoms can be helpful, sounding the alarm that alerts you to the need for finding the source of pain. Once we know what underbelly issues we're actually dealing with, we can address them head on.

Finding out what we were like as a young child can be very instructive. What's the family lore say? For example, for the so-called private folks—were you always that way? Or alternatively, as a young one, were you bubbly, talkative, or constantly interrupting? If so, when did the holding back start? What was happening in your life when this holding back began?

I'm remembering now the story of the terribly depressed 25-year old woman named Amanda. She was verging on suicide when her mother accompanied her to the office. Amanda was a wildly talented, artistic person having terrible trouble finding lucrative and exciting ways to express her aptitude. Her mother was an artist herself, of a very different type. While Amanda tended to be creative in what we might call a "messy" way—always drawing outside the lines, so-to-speak—the mother's art took the form of painting tiny pictures on small enamel objects.

Very detailed. Very organized.

Neither of these artistic choices is wrong.

That's not the point.

By the time Amanda was around four, the mother told me, she was already "out of control." What did that mean? I wondered. "Well, she'd constantly interrupt me while I was working—wanting to show me what *she* was drawing. I simply couldn't get her to simmer down!"

Out loud, I questioned what this woman imagined mothering a four-year old would entail. More importantly, in the short span of that simple story, it was easy to see Amanda's life pattern emerge. All her adulthood, she held herself back, afraid of being "a visible interruption" in the world.

Hopefully, the picture is getting clear and you're seeing how the broad effects of early life must not be underestimated. Maybe the following PTSD symptoms even sound familiar:

- ✓ Avoiding places, people, or thoughts that remind you of the event
- ✓ Feeling like you have no future
- ✓ Difficulty concentrating
- ✓ Startling easily
- ✓ Having an exaggerated response to things that startle you
- ✓ Feeling more aware (hyper-vigilance)
- ✓ Feeling irritable or having outbursts of anger
- ✓ Having trouble falling or staying asleep

Thus, PTSD can be situational or more constant, depending on how traumatic our history was and how that history impacts our nature. As such, it is accounted for through both psychological impairment and through commonly exhibited defenses. Indeed, one way or other, looking around in the world, it's easy to see how widespread it is for folks to seem extremely detached, wildly uncomfortable in their own skin, or strongly reactive to others and to circumstance.

I'd call this PTSD in action.

Understand and remember that none of this is about blaming our origins, but rather about appreciating their impact. Certainly, it's not helpful to loll around in family-of-origin, or awful early peer-life regret. Mostly, that just leads to acting like a victim, to fury, or to depression. Identification of when, how, and where is the key to authentic change.

Thing is, when it comes to my childhood, I don't remember much...

MANY REPORT AN INABILITY TO REMEMBER BIG CHUNKS of their history. Most likely the psyche wisely dumps out what it considers too much to bear; or maybe we dissociated so entirely we simply weren't present enough for the original experience to remember it. That's okay, because healing can occur without our needing to shine a light on every nook and cranny. Still, most of us do maintain some specific story memories, whether they are tales passed down through the family or our own recalled experiences one way or the other. Our *pattern material* can also be revealed by noticing the way today's thinking, feeling, and behaving correlates to personal historical "facts"—family stories repetitiously told or details about how old we were when our parents divorced or when our sibling was born or when dad died.

Let's explore an example.

On a television show called *Millionaire Matchmaker* where I appeared a number of times as expert, one client talked about how all his relationships lasted no more than a year and a half. I asked what happened in his life when he was between one and two. Instantly, he looked stricken. "Oh," he offered, "my father died." Shortly after that, we arrived at the even more devastating truth: "My father was murdered." Thus, that's when his faith in lasting love also got killed off.

It's a simple formula, really, but one seldom considered.

Look back at what was going on in your life at particular junctures. Simply explore the facts through what we'll call **Timeline**, noticing how the timing of notable occurrences corresponds with current circumstances. (For further exploration, use the chart provided in the *Love Works* chapter.) Create a kind of flowchart describing how things unfolded, timing-wise. This will be a huge help as over and again you practice **Connect the Dots**.

Ah ha, I hear you say!

"I was 2 when mom started having her affair…"

"…got pregnant with my brother…"

"…dad left…"

"…we moved and kept moving every couple years…"

Start to notice the timing parallels between now and then. You might not even remember much about how you felt back then, but you can begin to see how a pattern formed by examining the "facts". *Dad left when I was two. All my relationships last approximately two years.*

Maybe as you're constructing the timeline, feeling details arise. Great: Explore them. In addition, once we start a thorough discovery of the Self, very often long-buried, previously forgotten memories surface that might make you nervous to consider. Fear not, for forgotten memories only return when we're ready to greet them.

The task in any event is to figure out what initiated core beliefs and the primary defenses guarding those beliefs—to discover where and how we became ensnared by the ideas and procedures holding us back from love. We determine what happened, who we are, and then *learn to love both our stories and what happened in the wake of those stories.* This is called loving yourself first. As Martin Luther King said:

Darkness cannot drive out darkness: only light can do that. Hate cannot drive out hate: only love can do that.[xviii]

Symptoms, symptoms everywhere and not a drop to drink…

AT FIRST, ALL WE CAN SEE IS **SYMPTOMS**. A few symptom examples are:

I can't find love;
I get really, really attracted and excited by someone then somehow quickly lose interest;
Everything starts out well it seems, then before you know it they disappear;
I keep attracting losers;
I inevitably end up being the caretaker.

Well, you get the drift. Whatever the repetitive love pattern in your life (or career pattern, friendship pattern, health pattern, or money pattern), it's a symptom with deep roots. But, of course, not all symptoms are created equal and some are far more egregious than others.

Indeed, when it comes to symptoms for what ails us, there's a broad range, both obvious and obscured. These indicators include anything from self-consciousness to compulsivity to self-contempt. They'll show up in three prime ways:

✓ Thinking
✓ Feeling
✓ Behaving

Each of these avenues wants exploration.

Still, no matter how entirely we recognize and even course-correct symptoms (contain compulsivity, reduce self-contempt) sustained, sustainable change can only happen by dealing with what lay beneath.

Fundamental: We can never fix a problem at the level of the problem.

That means getting our partner to finally take out the trash will not "fix" relationship woes—smelly trash isn't the problem. The "problem" is feeling ignored, unimportant, over-burdened, or disrespected.

In a relationship, this often leads to what we might call the not-enough syndrome. He says: "You wanted the trash taken out and I did that and you're still not happy. I can never satisfy you!" He's mystified. She remains bereft. He hasn't gotten the real point and neither has she.

Aiming at superficial solutions is mostly why so many programs, plans, and treatments fail to scratch the actual itch. For true shift, digging deep is required. It's like finding the liquid gold called oil.

> ...[geologists] use a variety of methods to find oil... finally, and most commonly, they use seismology, **creating shock waves that pass through hidden rock layers** and interpreting the waves that are reflected back to the surface.[xix]

Yes, in the long run to access our own deeply buried liquid gold, we often need to be shocked into an awakening. Still, we must *start* with what is presented to the naked eye. We'll want to apply sensitive measurement techniques and begin with an exploration of symptoms. Then we'll utilize *psychological seismology* to pass through hidden rock layers and interpret those symptoms (waves) reflected back to the surface. That means we'll explore daily defensive habits and methods of interaction. Eventually, through that effort, we'll slowly but surely sniff out the important effects of history. That's when we will have struck oil.

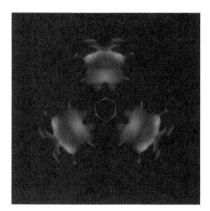

PART IV: PSYCHOLOGICAL SEISMOLOGY

T HROUGHOUT THE REMAINDER OF THIS CHAPTER, WE SHALL EXPLORE WHAT I CALL *THE ELEVEN ELEMENTALS*. These are paving stones on the road to True Healthy Love. Once we fully grasp these vital basics, everything promises to change forever.

Yes, *promises.*

Don't approach the Elementals, though, like you're in a race to some mythical gotta-get-love/fix-love finish line. In other words, like great food, these need to be savored slowly and fully digested.

Overall, the suggested method is to hang out with each, as if it's a new friend you're just getting to know. Ask questions. Wonder about rhythms. Make play dates. Get intimate. However, as you're moving along if one or several elude immediate understanding or are particularly irksome, travel to the next. You can always return to the more challenging ones at another juncture.

In all self-work the idea is to set ourselves up for success. Viscously pounding away at something doesn't allow that. It only discourages. Make every attempt, but when truly overwhelmed stop for the time being and come back to it later.

I'm not suggesting you take the easy road, nor turn away without much genuine effort. And I'm not at all recommending permanently ignoring what irritates or mystifies. I'm just saying take your time. Be kind to yourself along the way. And remember to be impressed by your own efforts.

Radical, huh!

All right then—the intention here through an understanding and appreciation of the Elementals is to—as in our oil-digging example—dig into the deeper effects of history so we can determine the best direction to walk toward a new kind of future loving life.

Get ready.

Responsibility: the gift that keep on giving...

OFTEN IN LIFE, OUR FIRST LINE OF DEFENSE IS BLAME.
It's other people, we protest.
It's circumstances, we proclaim.
It's not my fault, we insist.

ELEMENTAL NUMBER ONE: **AVOIDING RESPONSIBILITY FORFEITS THE POWER TO ACCOMPLISH REAL CHANGE.**
I'll bet you're imagining taking responsibility might only exaggerate your tendency to be cruel to yourself, to find every little thing wrong with you, and to do what you do best which is to beat yourself within an inch of your life.

Oddly enough, exactly the opposite happens.

The thing to know is that nearly everything begins with clarity. In this case, there needs to be excruciating clarity about the specifics of how we've thus far undermined happiness.

First question: What have you been doing to guarantee your love problems? We need to begin with what's *not* working before we can move onto a new plan.

To elaborate understanding you will find nine dreadful heartbreak guarantees woven in amidst the Elementals. These heart breaking procedures insist that your usual ways of behaving, thinking and feeling toward love mean your future will most definitely mimic your past.

Guaranteed.

Keep in mind that all nine heartbreak habits can show up also at work, with friends, and elsewhere. What's great is that there are equivalent solutions, which we'll explore together a little further along.

Yes, hold on, help is on the way!

Heartbreak Guarantee #1: REFUSING TO RECOGNIZE YOUR CONTRIBUTION TO THE DISREPAIR

All change arrives through self-responsibility while abjuring responsibility by imagining it's all about terrible luck lousy partners, or world circumstances, promises the same dismal outcome each time. The faces encountered change, but our relationship-to-relationship stays the same.

However, repetition of events is also a call to action. It indicates lessons not learned, in the same way that repetitive dreams try to give us a message we're not completely gleaning. Once we get the message, we can move on to the next moment. Looking at past history and current behaviors directly in the eye will allow genuine life shift.

Fundamental: When we tell the truth about our profound complicity in the disrepair of our relationships, we find new freedom.

The buns might be burnt, but the rest of the meal tastes delicious, including the amazing desert soufflé. Take responsibility for what doesn't work and credit for what does.

Alternatively, when we blame others for everything that goes wrong in our lives—or blame our weight, our puny bank account, society-at-large, the times in which we live, or the city or state in which we reside—we're lost. We've labeled ourselves as a victim, which is a rotten, slumped-down, overwhelmed position.

Ugh.

The thing is though, that taking *responsibility earns us real power* while pointing the finger everywhere but toward ourselves gives all the power away. After all, what do we really think we can do to *make other people* different?

Nothing.

Attempting control through complaining, cajoling, seducing, or insisting are all guaranteed to leave us feeling underwhelmed and disgruntled. Not only that, sitting around waiting for other people or the world to change throws us into a serious holding pattern, circling the airport waiting for permission to land. Eventually, we run out of fuel. Maybe you have. Perhaps that's why you're here with me now.

Stunner: The only real authority we have in life involves the choices *we* make.

Once we know what's truly driving our choices, we can shift our relationship to the dynamics of such. That can be followed by new actions reflecting deeper understandings.

The long and short of what to remember about all this is that continued and current problems don't happen because of past "bad" decisions, or even prior bad acts, but because we don't learn from those past decisions and acts. But please understand that when it comes to love, the learning needs to be many-layered. Cataloguing superficial traits will not scratch the itch. We must realize *why* we made the choices we made. It doesn't matter that he's bald or she's short. It makes no difference, even, if he's always late or she's constantly critical. *The question is, what inner dynamic supports our attraction to such an individual?* And I promise it's not just because they were cute or good in bed!

I'm sick of all the heartbreak...

It takes courage to love, but pain through love is the purifying fire which those who love generously know. We all know people who are so much afraid of pain that they shut themselves up like clams in a shell and, giving out nothing, receive nothing and therefore shrink until life is a mere living death. - Eleanor Roosevelt [xx]

ONE VERSION OF DEFEATED AND DEFLATED is the individual who says they're never ever going to again open their heart to another because they got hurt.

Really?

If that's your position, you've truly learned nothing. Because the broken heart is the heart that lets the light in; which means, when the heart gets cracked wide open, the light pours through the way a sharp morning sun penetrates a bleak day—if we choose to let it. But if we use lost relationship love as an excuse to shut down, we're guaranteed a small, unfulfilled life.

Q: But I only seem to be attracted to people who don't want or aren't available for a committed relationship. Why?

THE FIRST IDEA IS THAT WE CHOOSE UNAVAILABLE PEOPLE BECAUSE IT'S SAFE. Well, that's the easy answer. The more thoughtful response is: **we choose unavailable people because we aren't ready to commit.** In other words, because *we ourselves are unavailable.*

Now, this doesn't mean we're not right about our partner. Maybe s/he is cruel, childish, or unreliable; but once more, that's not the point. In other words, just because our lover is truly critical in a way that makes us cringe, doesn't mean we're not just as critical (at least to and about ourselves) so that their criticism mirrors ours. Just because every boss we've ever had actually over-burdens us with responsibility, doesn't mean we've not somehow (unconsciously) set it up that way. And that string of unavailable people you've been dating reflects an unavailable you also! No matter what, the buck always stops with us.

This is a hard one.

You're probably going to want to shake your head or push such a notion away. "No, no...*I am* available! I WANT a relationship. I do, I do." Or, "Really, I'm completely beat at work. I gotta have less on my plate. It's not something I want or ask for."

Universal: Our true intentions are revealed by the reality that stands before us.

If we want to know our real aims, we need to check out the evidence as revealed by the occurrences of our life. The long and short of it is: Whether you realize it or not you're choosing unavailable people for a reason.

You are choosing.

Ouch.

Yep. There it is again—that shift back to the Self as our source of sorrow. I remind you though: This is good news. You have the power to change your relationship to the story you've been telling and living.

You have the power.

You.

Here's a great, awful—and very familiar—story:

Long ago, I worked with a man we'll call Jake—a fun, terrific good-looking early 40s fellow married to a smart, attractive same-age woman who held a high-powered CEO job. They had two children. By the time I knew of them, they'd comfortably grown into the life they led—becoming a well-oiled corporation to some degree, as such couples can tend to do over time.

When Jake first got together with his wife, she had no career track and had hardly discovered the woman she was to become. In a sense, he mentored and helped her while she developed—a process he dearly loved. That development also grew in her a somewhat latent relationship with control. She was a big planner and liked things super-organized. Over time, she got better and better at keepin' Jake constantly busy with honey-do lists.

Now, in the course of Jake's job he—as the story goes—spent many hours at the office, and therefore, with certain co-workers. One such co-worker was an attractive 20-something gal. She seemed like an up-and-comer—a yet-to-be-formed person like his wife originally was.

I'll bet you can see where the story's going. That's because it's so common.

Yes, inevitably Jake and the young woman became close, and as you might guess, began an affair.

When Jake arrived in my office, he was in terrible turmoil. He loved his family, but was overwhelmingly drawn to the woman who'd become his mistress. And their sex, he explained, was incredible!

No kidding!

In these cases, the sex is *always* incredible. Because no kids bounce in interrupting and there's no mortgage conversation to have and no trash to take out. Assignations are inevitably sexy, planned for, highly anticipated, and thrilling.

Jake could not figure out what to do. Should he stay in his wonderful, beautiful home, where his kids were happy and where he and his wife still *appeared* fine and, in fact, were still sexual as well? Or should he leave what had become a more mundane relationship experience to be with the exciting young mistress?

Then on top of all the other confusion, the wife got pregnant.

Oh my.

Jake and I went round and round. One day, he announced that his wife had discovered the mistress and was still wanting to work things out with him—was willing to come to therapy to see if they could put the family back together again. Then he informed me that the mistress, obviously separately, also wanted to join therapy to see how they could happily become the couple she was hoping they'd be.

It was a sticky situation at best.

As we worked, Jake and I looked at his history and the story he was playing out. I warned him that seldom in these circumstances does the I'm-leaving-to-be-with-the-mistress scenario have a happy ending. Of course, there are always anecdotal stories, but they are the exception, not the rule. But Jake was by then being run by desire, as well as by the inner saboteur that had taken over.

So, leave the lovely wife and family, he did.

The subsequent collapse of his relationship with the young mistress-suddenly-full-fledged-partner didn't take long. In fact, in a somewhat startling twist, she somehow magically discovered "religion" and decided pre-marital sex was no longer appropriate. She then became more and more distant. Eventually, she said she no longer loved him. They broke up. The new baby had been born, but by then there was no going back—too much betrayal and hurt.

What were Jake's true intentions?

He already had love in his life, and beauty—and success. But something in him wasn't finished with his original family story—

a story he'd reacted to by believing he didn't deserve a stellar, smooth life and by allowing an idea to take over making him unconsciously feel the only way he could "prove" his value was to be the mentor. Eventually, Jake married again, this time to another controlling woman needing rescue and development.

This is only one brief story of infidelity.

Further examples are presented later in this book. We best remember that such behavior is inevitably symptomatic, which means there are underlying psychological and emotional prompts. Even with this often-met and delicate infidelity topic, sincere healing can occur, but that means that in order for it to happen, we must, as always, dive below.

Meanwhile, the mistress story....

ON THE OTHER SIDE OF THIS STORY, we find, of course, the mistress, who, quickly changing her mind about the evils of pre-marital sex, in short order went on to some other unavailable fellow. Her tale is no less commonly met and the reasons for her choices are no less potent.

Why do we choose unavailable folks?

In this woman's case, as happens often, her need to "conquer" unavailable men was connected to her history with an unavailable father. Obviously, this can have several sub-sets: seduce and discard (still mad at you, Daddy); conquer and claim (choose me, Daddy); seduce and cling (you have to see I'm good enough, Daddy), to name a few. Sometimes, such behavior stands on the shoulders of what we might call the over-close father/daughter relationship resulting in *I'll never betray Daddy by having a relationship that actually works.*

Obviously, these are super <u>unconscious procedures.</u> They're also gender neutral (meaning everyone does it no matter what their gender or sexual orientation). Naturally, we've just barely tickled the edges of this involved topic.

However, even approaching the *why* at a more surface level garners some fairly universal answers. For instance, I mentioned earlier choosing unavailable partners happens because it's safe and because we're not ready to commit. This is important to reinforce, so I'll say it in an uncharacteristically categorical way:

Individuals choosing to partner with someone already in relationship are in the business of avoidance.

They are simply not ready for real commitment. They choose someone who can't entirely follow through, allowing them to imagine they're giving themselves over completely to love, which they've actually not learned how to do. The partner's unavailability permits them, as it were, to have the illusion of controlling outcome.

They're never really at risk for a full union.

Naturally, few mistresses believe this to be true. They blame their circumstances on bad luck (I can't help it if she met someone before me, I still love her); fantasize about a fairy-tale outcome (he'll leave her and we'll finally be together, which is all I want); somehow imagine things will be different for them in the end (I know people say once a cheater always a cheater, but they don't understand—this is my soul mate. With me it will be different).

By the by, let me pause to say firmly: Women also cheat and I never mean to imply otherwise. In fact, even though statistics still confirm men as cheating more, it shows women catching up:

> Men are more likely to cheat than women. But, as women become more financially independent, women are starting to act more like men with respect to infidelity."[xxi]

And most certainly, not all men can be expected to cheat. Outdated ideas might keep us stuck thinking women never and men always. Gay women cheat and straight women cheat. Gay men cheat and straight men cheat.

Cheating is an equal opportunity employer.

In fact, our lives are now filled with electronic assists for long-term cheating, for sleuthing potential deception, as well as for quick-fix hook-ups. In this regard, according to *Bloomberg Business Week*, there's a new app in town called Tinder: "a pathologically addictive flirting-dating-hookup app. One year after launching, Tinder's hordes have swipe-rated each other 13 billion times— 3 billion in August alone—and 2 million matches happen each day. It's the fastest-growing free dating app in the U.S." Funnily and awfully enough, actually, folks using Tinder frequently find themselves being pursued by the same potential "dates" pursuing their close friends.

As we can see, everyone seems to be on the fast track. Quick liaisons are frequent.

What does this mean?

It means *millions* are veering away from well-considered love and going for instant-soup liaisons. It means that our desperation is taking a strange turn. Or maybe it merely means this is a new age with new rules. Still, it reminds me a little of the popularity of gay bath houses back in the day and we all know how well that turned out. Guess we'll have to wait and see.

Meanwhile, here are current infidelity statistics from Statistic Brain. Appreciate though, when perusing these numbers, that since infidelity is generally secretive the numbers are likely to be under-reported:

Marriage Infidelity Statistics	Data
Percent of marriages where one or both spouses admit to infidelity, either physical or emotional	41%
Percent of men who admit to committing infidelity in any relationship they've had	57%
Percentage of women who admit to committing infidelity in any relationship they've had	54%
Percent of married men who have strayed at least once during their married lives	22%
Percent of married women who have strayed at least once during their married lives	14%
Percentage of men and women who admit to having an affair with a co-worker	36%
Percentage of men and women who admit to infidelity on business trips	35%
Percentage of men and women who admit to infidelity with a brother-in-law or sister-in-law	17%
Average length of an affair	2 years
Percentage of marriages that last after an affair has been admitted to or discovered	31%
Percentage of men who say they would have an affair if they knew they would never get caught	74%
Percentage of women who say they would have an	68%

affair if they knew they would never get caught	
Percent of children who are the product of infidelity	3%

Q: If my partner cheats, should I forgive?

CAN WE FORGIVE DECEPTION OF THIS OR ANY OTHER KIND?

Not only can we, but perhaps…well, let me put it strongly…perhaps we *should.* Of course I'm not saying this is true all the time for everyone. Some circumstances call for severe response. However, I can't tell you the number of couples I've counseled who've returned to a far stronger, more resilient relationship following infidelity—if both parties involved do the hard work of self-discovery.

What might that self-discovery include? First, each member of the couple needs to recognize their contribution. Remember: This isn't about "fault" so much as it is an acknowledgment and understanding of complicit inner psychological factors and how those factors impact choices made. "Cheating" here becomes a symptom rather than in and of itself a problem. Second, it's helpful for each party to see how personal history is at play; in other words, we're dealing with something often called "the crowded bed," which talks about how the parents of both members of the couple climb into the relationship bed, so to speak. That means parental attitudes and behaviors about sex and about partnership will want to be investigated.

Summary: Taking real responsibility and ownership of both emotional and behavioral contributions to *any* circumstance is an essential love solution, otherwise we're needing to wait for everyone else to change which means we're stuck.

In engaging this take-responsibility process you can right away start making new decisions and adopting fresh perspectives. No waiting needed. Step to the front of the line. It's important to look your actions in the eye and even more essential to figure out what motivated those actions so you can alter both attitude and behavior.

And remember: no matter what your history, you're not "damaged goods." Stop thinking of yourself that way. Everyone makes mistakes or, as they say, "to err is human." Indeed, we're human. No more. No less. Really, that's an extraordinary thing to be. Falling down is how we human beings learn to walk.

But the question inevitably continues to be: what are you learning from your mistakes? If the answer is "nothing", you're caught in a vicious cycle promising no happy ending.

ELEMENTAL NUMBER TWO: **OUR EXPERIENCES ARE NOT PROBLEMS—THEY'RE OPPORTUNITIES.**

We spend far too much time looking outside ourselves for the source of our so-called problems. Sure it's true that services are declining and times are tough. Certainly, slicing our way through the thick technological jungle is fun but trying. And indeed, we're offered a million choices, but hugely challenged as to decide what's best. Thus, we're left frequently feeling overwhelmed and under-prepared.

It's easy to appreciate why we turn to complaint. Besides everybody's doing it. In society it shows up as passing the buck, suing, and asking for bail-outs. It's the attitude of "I can't fix it so you should fix it for me."

Time to realize *they* and *it*, however, are not the problem.

Actually our own psychological structure is the crux of the "issue." You see, we attract what reflects our interior landscape. It's what I call the magnet-to-the-refrigerator effect. If I put a magnet on a wall it will fall down, but if I put the same magnet on a refrigerator it will stick because it's the right material finding the right material. That's how people and circumstances come into our lives. Something inside us "pulls" them in.

For our own good.

"Are you nuts?!" you spurt. "I don't want bad relationships and terrible bosses in my life. Nor do I want friends who disappoint or ignorant co-workers!"

Well, as I keep insisting, some part of you actually does "want" those things. Why? Because:

✓ We're getting what we expect which only confirms our long-held assumptions. Psychologist Abraham Maslow smartly put it as: "when the only tool you have is a hammer everything starts to look like a nail."

✓ Our psyche wants us to heal, so it repeatedly encourages familiar situations and people to let us to try, try again.

✓ There's often a part of us "insisting" that others become what we assume they are.

What's the proof?

Notice how same circumstances and equivalent sorts of people repeatedly show up in your life. Now maybe you're thinking that's coincidence or happenstance or bad luck.

It's not.

I remember one fellow who firmly described his three ex-wives as terrible, complaining bitches. "Wow, three in a row," I said with inside amusement. "How did that happen?"

"Dumb luck!!" was his certain answer.

In this fellow's case, he was a bitter, negative man who had something terrible to say about pretty much everyone. Were the women actually awful or did he perceive them that way? Or was it the combo pack? Of course, we have to wonder why his partners chose to be with someone so dismissive. What that indicated about *their* self-esteem is obvious.

Summary: As long as we assume others and circumstances are the problem, we give up all power to make change happen. Focus on changing yourself rather than concentrating on what's wrong with everybody else.

ELEMENTAL NUMBER THREE: **STOP IGNORING THE SIGNS.**

Ignoring the nose on your face doesn't mean the nose isn't there. Every relationship you've ever known *has told you what it's made of*—you simply refused to notice. Proclaiming yourself to be a victim of circumstance won't help. Turning a blind eye only guarantees we'll get lost along the way. Signs are there for a reason. Pay attention.

We like to imagine we're an exception to the rule. We hear millions of stories about how individuals rarely form a long-term partnership with the next person they meet right after a big breakup, but that maxim doesn't include us. Or, we decide "playing hard to get" means she's interesting when it plainly means…she's not really ready for love. Or, we imagine he never makes plans because he's spontaneous when actually…he's just not a planner!

This elemental comes with two heartbreak guarantees:

Heartbreak Guarantee #2: REPEATING OLD PATTERNS OF UNDERMINING BEHAVIOR.

UNIVERSAL: If you do what you've done, you'll get what you've got.

Once you realize and recognize the signs, really, really hear what's been told to you by your potential or current partner or boss or friend or family member, the idea will be to change course rather than doing what you've always done. Of course this is no small feat. It means discovering new methods of operation and new ways of looking at things.

Heartbreak Guarantee #3: REFUSING TO HEAR

This is another way of ignoring signs. People tell us all the time about themselves—who and how they are; what they want; what they're willing to be or do. They tell us with words and they tell us with actions. Unfortunately, we often don't listen.

Enter projection.

Remember how it works? Instead of really seeing and hearing what others present, we interpret them according to our assumptions, preoccupations, fears, and wishes.

Oh my.

Someone says: *"I'm not ready to settle down."*

And we think (usually unconsciously): *"Oh with me, it'll be different."* Another individual gets hugely jealous about every minute not spent with them and we decide that means caring rather than the huge unprocessed insecurity it really indicates! In the case of extreme jealousy, there's a crushing sledge hammer about to land on you. Prepare.

Oops.

Still another says: *"I don't ever want to get married,"* or *"I simply don't want children,"* and something inside believes that will change because, we imagine, *everyone* wants marriage and children. We assume and imagine these things based on our own desires.

I recently heard a startling version of this from a Filipino client. I mention the culture to again emphasize that context is important for certainly Filipino family structure differs greatly from many others. Still, this particular report is so startlingly obvious it stands anywhere as a beacon.

The client explained she has one brother and numerous half-siblings. Those additional siblings came from dad's other wife and from his mistress. The tricky part was he'd had most of the children with all the women simultaneously. So dad managed two wives and a mistress all at once. Everyone knew about everyone else, kind of.

But here's the kicker. On the father's *first date* with mother, he showed up with two other women in tow! Get it? First date. Pick you up at 8. And here are the two others who'll be coming with.

Talk about writing on the wall.

Realizing a pattern is one issue, while truly hearing what's said in the first place is another. But listening is a form of true closeness, which unfortunately in today's world is last on many lists. Sometimes, as in the case of Filipino who thought, according to her culture, at her so-called advanced age of *thirty*, she was out of options, we sometimes take what we imagine to be the best we can get.

Ugh.

Anyway, for genuine *intimacy* to occur (which I define as vulnerable visibility), we first need the ability for *presence* (a full exploration of presence will ensue on page 190). It's easy, though, to imagine intimacy to be dangerous and thereby avoid it with everything we've got. We have many helpful evasion aids these days.

Getting foggy

A GOOD, SIMPLE EXAMPLE OF INTIMACY AVOIDANCE, for instance, involves the social lubricant called drinking. Let me be clear: I'm not railing against alcohol, though in many cases I might, and just because I'm sober doesn't mean I think everyone should be. Moderate drinking for those who can is fun and relieving. I'm simply offering a case in point in the following brief conversation about dating.

All right—as we all know, beginnings are already loaded with full-throttle projection, while we imagine who, how, and what the other person is or can be. Add alcohol—get further distortion. After all, alcohol is the "take the edge off" drug, which translates as blurring focus.

I remember having a date in early sobriety with a drinker—how much of a drinker, I didn't realize until the end of the date. In any event, he offered me a drink. I said, "No thanks, I don't drink."

He looked shocked. "*What do you mean you don't drink?*"

I repeated. "I don't drink."

"*Wait,*" he persisted, "*you never, ever drink?*"

"No," I answered, by now amused. (Side note: When someone goes on and on like this about the importance of drinking, they have a drinking problem. Clue.)

Anyway, he then said: "*Well, how about drugs? Do you do drugs?*"

"No," I answered, keeping it simple.

By now, he was spinning like a top.

"*So let me get this straight,*" he said, huffing his astonishment and looking like someone having outgrown himself and about to burst through skin seams, "*You never, ever drink and you never ever do drugs. What do you do for fun?*"

At that point out of my mouth came something I didn't even understand at the time. An idea and way of believing that took years, actually, to catch up to. I said: "For fun, I'm present in all my experiences." Date over.

Being present in all your experiences is what I want for you too. Not all the time —I just doubt that's possible for any of us humans —but more often than not.

Therefore, I have a radical suggestion: Try having your initial liaisons be alcohol-free. This doesn't guarantee clarity, but it sure gives you a fighting chance. Especially since everything you need to know about the other person, you can glean on the first date.

By the way, with many of my single clients, I love playing the game "What do you know about this person after the first date?" I promise what you notice at the start is what you'll still be talking and complaining about five years later.

The Filipino woman told her daughter that after the monumental first date, she knew very well what her next twenty years would be like. And so it was.

One way to play the what-do-I-know game is to write down your complete experience of the date right after. Leave nothing out. Did s/he show up early or late? Did they ignore or attend requests? Did they ask questions or just talk about themselves? Did they take charge or make no decisions?

This is not a judging process, simply an assessment tool. And it's entertaining. Right away we absolutely realize far more than we tend to admit until we see it written in black and white.

ELEMENTAL NUMBER FOUR: **WE'RE STEEPED IN OLD ROUTINES.** You've been attached to customary practices the way barnacles attach to the side of a ship. You keep following these same maneuvers; each time supposing things will turn out differently. Perhaps now, you've begun to recognize how you've been behaving and thinking.

Recognizing the nature of our habitual ways and means is a great beginning. Guess what though—insight is not enough to create real, lasting change. In fact, insight is the gateway. The garden is still a couple steps away.

Indeed, you've read all the (previous) self-help books, gone to coaches and counselors, talked to smart friends, taken seminars, and to tell the truth you feel basically no better off than you ever did. How come?

Because *deep* digging is essential.

Have I rung this bell enough to convince you yet?

Q: Well, this is all hard to fathom. I always figured whether love comes into our life or not is basically a matter of luck or circumstance. Isn't it?

NOT AT ALL. LUCK HAS NOTHING TO DO WITH IT. Would you say its "luck" that the sun rises in the east every day and sets in the west? Like the sun, we too are living out patterns that bring us into particular kinds of relationships. These designs travel us down specific work situation roads, put us in distinct friendship groupings, and too they choose who/how we love.

Do we *know* these patterns—are we conscious of how they operate in our lives? Mostly not. That's the point of this book.

Well, when I say *we* don't know these patterns, I'm referring to Ego Mind. The ego mind imagines that just because it directs day-to-day operations, it's running the show. The ego-mind decides that making an exact plan will determine precise outcome.

But it doesn't work that way.

Actually, it's the unconscious that's mostly orchestrating our lives. We think we decide who to love based on their looks or smarts or money or whatever our yard stick may be; however, what's truly motivating us is our relationship to personal history and our inner association to mother, to father, and to the child we used to be with regards to mother, father, and family. As stated, those three bonds form the foundation of every connection we have.

Thus, until we at least understand and shift our perception as well as attitude toward those early dynamics, we're hard put to find the community or career or partner for which we wish.

Q: Yeah, but why are relationships SO difficult—what does this unconscious stuff have to do with that?

BECAUSE *RELATIONSHIPS ARE HARD-WIRED INTO PERSONAL HISTORY*. It's that simple...and that complicated. Imagine old files you thought you'd deleted suddenly popping up again on your screen. Boom! Pictures appearing in vivid color. Old barely remembered saved files demanding attention. And before we know it, we're revisiting our shoved-aside, repressed, ignored, still-fuming, heartbroken, hungry parts. Feeling fragments we've been running from like hell.

This brings us to...

ELEMENTAL NUMBER FIVE: **MOVING FORWARD REQUIRES LOOKING BACK.** I know this sorting-through-history business sounds arduous; however, **recognizing what happened and how it happened is essential to creating sustained, sustainable change.**

Any other approach is most likely to yield only a temporary effect. For change to last we must drill down with insistent, respectful intention. Superficial "decisions" about what needs to be done simply never last.

Thus, our lives are filled with broken off pieces of emotionally impacting historical material, much of which has sunk to the bottom of our psyches (often thought of symbolically in certain psychological circles as a deep ocean). Refusing to accept, acknowledge, and understand the effect of personal historical experiences attempts to force-march the past into the yawning shadows; but not only doesn't such relegating delete the on-going influence of initial experience and the stories growing up around those occurrences, it amplifies them. That means the result of our refusal to face the past does exactly the opposite of what we intend.

Indeed, brilliant psychologist Carl Jung emphasized: *What we resist persists.* This means that the things we avoid or deny gain momentum inside us and in our lives. In other words, if we ignore things, be they past experiences or present issues, they only get bigger, bolder, and more dreadful. Like that appendix pain we pretend isn't there, eventually history erupts in our lives showing up as terrible relationships, awful often-unfathomable circumstances and even ill health. According to this thinking, what happens around us, then, is not at all distinct from what happens within us.

Now you may not be completely on board for this notion, but I encourage you to at least consider it. Again, if the unconscious is the source of what occurs in our lives—and thereby the life we're having is a direct reflection of confusions and considerations going on *within* us—we actually have more power to change the way things go.

Thus, the idea is: instead of pulling away or turning our back altogether on inner thoughts, struggles, remembrances, and even regrets, look them in the eye. Overriding or denying issues, concerns, or emotions only fuels them.

Yes, moving forward requires looking back...

LET'S RETURN TO THE CONVERSATION about the lag time between the wounding and the visible scars of the wounding. Take a quick look at the life of trees.

Ever wondered how a tree that is hollow on the inside can be alive, or have not fallen when the wood is hollow in the middle? Internal decay is a common phenomenon in trees. I wouldn't call it good, but it is normal (very common). These cavities are caused by Mother Nature's decay fungi.

The *decay process usually gets started from some large wound*. It could have been from a lightning strike, broken limb, or even a damaged root underground. Any large wound usually leads to decay. Wounds larger than about 3-4" in diameter (can vary depending on tree species and health) take the tree so long to callous over and close up the wound that rotting fungi get established and start breaking down the inner column of wood in the tree.[xxii]

Have you calloused over the rotting fungi of your history? If you have, it's likely to be hugely influential when it comes to your love matters today. The reason to identify the genesis of our behavioral patterns—which means spotting original wounds—is to awaken.

Stunner: Current insistent ways of thinking, behaving, and feeling actually have little or nothing to do with NOW!

This doesn't mean we have more excuses for self-doubt or lack of motivation. Stop BLAMING your historical experiences for your dissatisfying life. Rather, to get the ball rolling on real change we must accept how, when, and where patterns started. Name the wound to claim the cure. This is where Connect the Dots comes in handy.

Okay, let's bring it home: It's **not** because there are no good men in the world that you're without a satisfying relationship; and it's **not** because all women judge you for your lack of largess that you can't find love. It's **not** because you're a loser that you don't have the career of your dreams. It's **not** because you're socially inept that you have no close friends. It's because your life is shrouded in old ideas, anciently rooted reactivity, and cumbersome behaviors.

Change how you view your story and you will change how you live your life.

But I'm so, so tired of it all!

Carrying the unmet scars of your past is a heavy burden. It gets tiresome.

Q: Why do past hurts linger on so long?

The answer to that is easy. Past hurts hold on because we never truly face them in the first place. Think of these hurts as termites lining our house. Oh sure, when we found little winged something-or-others dead on a sill a while back, there were only a few; we didn't know quite what they were, so we dismissed them. Then there was the neighbor who got her house tented and we thought, hmm…termites. I should probably have my house checked, too. But we never did. Things came up. We got busy.

One day, though, we woke up to part of the house actually falling down! No ignoring the problem anymore. Signs of visible collapse are everywhere.

> …termites…are capable of compromising the strength and safety of an infested structure. Termite damage can render structures unlivable until expensive repairs are conducted. [xxxiii]

Same with unmet wounding: It nibbles at the edges of our lives until, if ignored long enough, it takes us down.

Time to survey the infested interior: In doing so, we'll reveal the damage while in an equally important way realizing with a shout of genuine glee that **we are completely lovable just as we are**.

I don't want to dwell…

Of course, I fully understand how the idea of tracing back to the beginning seems daunting and naturally many are afraid, thinking it's a betrayal of family or a waste of time or simply too emotionally thorny a proposition—unless, of course, you're a history flaunter who lets traumatic event define your entire identity. That's as unbalanced and undermining a way to go as never looking back. But even history flaunters are well served through this process because it means looking at the past with fresh, unadulterated eyes.

All right, so right now you're grumpy—wondering with a sneer how looking at the past is going to get you *right now love* and happiness, or fix the love pickle you're currently in.

Stunner: We love who and what we love because we're trying to remember ourselves—put ourselves back together again. We're actually *born to love*, but have merely forgotten how because fear has taken the place of faith.

Yes, as I've implied, we're trying to recall the Original Self. To call back into aliveness who we're actually meant to be. Beginning in childhood and continuing, this organic, True Self got distorted, over-layered, and distracted by life's events. Thus, if we want to understand what's blocking our happiness today, we need to appreciate what actually launched our hesitations, fears, and awkward self-consciousness yesterday.

What's being said here is that none of the specifics of a partnership, friendship, career, or anything else happen by accident. Everything is part of an interior (albeit mostly unconscious) program.

This is how it works: As we're (apparently) ambling along through life, we take ourselves over and again into circumstances equivalent to history in some direct, or circuitous, way. We *must do this* because we're unconsciously driven to heal original wounds. But internal bleeding doesn't stop when you put your leg in a cast. Wrong focus: That's precisely what we're doing when we try to repair our earliest hurts through current relationship.

Healing doesn't happen that way.

Can't happen that way.

Here's a personal example. My husband of many years is enormously attentive. He lets me know every day how beautiful, smart, and talented he finds me to be. He lavishes me with sincere love. Even strangers can see the appreciation he has for me in his eyes. Meanwhile, I adore and admire him. He's the brightest, most interesting man I've known—my best teacher. All this doesn't mean he finds me easy to deal with or that we don't fight or that I haven't entertained leaving, as has he. My own parents fought viciously, so I concluded that love and fighting are connected—a belief that has insistently clawed its cutting way through my life. It's made for a lively, if challenging, marriage. Now as I said, my husband sincerely admires me, so that means the marriage has probably "fixed" me, right? Not on your life.

In fact, throughout, I've needed to examine and reexamine my relationship to self-esteem when doubt rears its dark head. How come? Shouldn't his unflagging devotion make up for my childhood of constant abandonment?

Not at all.

Why?

A true healing of my daunting personal history is an inside job. That's the way it is for us all. My husband's unflagging love is the sweet icing on my cake, but I must put the cake ingredients together and do the baking; otherwise, there's no cake to ice.

And frankly, I wouldn't have it any other way—because without walking this stony, uneven, pothole-ridden road to healing, I'd have little to teach. It's all made me a better teacher. It's all made me a better person. It's part of what's made me an expert on love matters. So here we are.

Ugh…makes me wanna give up…

No, no. Don't misunderstand me. My husband's offered me invaluable contributions. Without it, my development would have likely taken a far different course. His love lets me know safe places and safe people exist in the world, and teaches me that *unconditional* love is possible.

By the way, unconditional love is hugely misunderstood. Many throw the idea around with little real understanding of its aim or possible impact, which is like throwing a piercing javelin with your eyes closed.

Unconditional love can be defined as love that dives beneath all the nasty defenses. It's a love of the Being, rather than the Doing. We can unconditionally love people we don't like even a little. We can unconditionally love murderers and thieves. We can even (eventually) unconditionally love the cruel mother and cruel father.

But unconditional love doesn't override or ignore bad behavior. We can hold unconditional love and still exhibit strong healthy boundaries. As you might suspect, such an elegant position is a learning process. The *how* of this we will discuss more fully as we move along. But the bottom line is this:

Newsflash: The only way through it is into it!

Summary: It's important to keep our eye on the what-it's-all-about ball. Most likely so far in your life you've been working on the wrong part of the accident-impacted car. If what got hit in your collision was the passenger side door and you decide to fix the front left, your vehicle remains a damaged mess. Damage assessment is essential. Such assessment needs to be thorough and ongoing.

ELEMENTAL NUMBER SIX: **INSIGHT IS JUST THE BEGINNING.** Okay, you've realized a *little* something, but not enough to facilitate a truly changed life. Your eyes are open, but the brilliant sun is yet to fully shine and the glad birds still refuse to sing. You now know how to avoid the exact same pitfalls. All of that's great.

Far as it goes.

What's next?

Unfortunately, many stop at this point in their self-discovery process. That's a problem because all too quickly things get static. Sure, something's different—there's less chaos and drama perhaps. But we still don't have what we've been saying we want.

Again we feel stuck. At this point, having an intuition that...well...*some* movement is wanted, we all too often choose to travel backwards, returning to the terrible undermining habits we thought we'd left behind.

This is where remaining stalwart is key because even having moved to a realization of personal complicity, taking responsibility for what's happened so far, and getting to the fabulous point of avoiding the potholes in the road will not, as it turns out, be enough to reveal a splendid life.

Don't stop.

Don't stop.

ELEMENTAL NUMBER SEVEN: **THE KEY TO LONG-LASTING CHANGE IS** *ACTION* **THAT STANDS ON A PLATFORM OF PROFOUND SELF-AWARENESS.**

As we've begun to establish it takes a combination of: #1) alert self-understanding; and #2) the action that will change a hapless series of love and living experiences into something that supports and expands your life. It's so easy to stand in our own way when it comes to implementing this two-pronged attack. To begin with attitude plays a huge part. Several heartbreak guarantees are included in this Elemental category with most of them being generated when we trot after either negative or controlling thinking the way a baby duck trails its mama.

Heartbreak Guarantee #4: EXPECTING THE WORST.

As earlier indicated, we tend to get what we expect and just as a bad day builds on itself so does negative expectation get reflected by our lives.

Q: When I look around I see that relationships don't seem to work very well in this world—so many folks seem unhappy in their love lives...so why bother?

SURE IT'S EASY TO FIND DREADFUL RELATIONSHIP TALES. It's much like newspaper stories. The ones showing up are dramatic and deadly. Good news too seldom makes it into print, or catches our attention. But just because terrific relationships are not what you've so far noticed doesn't mean they're not out there.

Really.

Are these great ones flawless? Naw. You know our fairytale "happily ever after" notion's been quite misunderstood. It doesn't mean and-ever-after-we'll-never-again-fight-or-have-a-bump-in-the-road. How could that be because that would say never again will we grow or change or form our own opinions? Dumb.

My version of happily ever after means: *we're committed and willing to work through the tough times as a team with continuing discovery, unfolding respect, mutual encouragement, and a lifetime of curiosity.* It signifies feeling safe with a particular other in a way that invites discovering the profound meanings of our love matters.

But if all we notice around us is relationship gloom and doom, then best check our early history at the door. Yes, maybe you're afraid to open your heart because you haven't been taught how to have healthy relationship, but that certainly doesn't mean you can't learn.

Fear keeps us down and holds us back when it comes to love. We're afraid to get hurt and/or to be abandoned. Because that's our interpretation of what happened in our family of origin. And often we've come to the erroneous conclusion—in fact, we become deeply "convinced"—that we ourselves are unlovable.

Sometimes our response to this dark belief is to refuse real love. We can commit to this refusal in numerous ways, including: never staying in a relationship past the first disappointment; being attracted to wildly and obviously unhealthy relationships; staying in those lousy relationships too long; sabotaging potentially good relationships; constantly doubting ourselves, and more.

Naturally, behaving in these ways merely confirms our worst notions and convinces us we're right. Worse still—without risking real and thorough love—we never truly come to know the depth, breath, and scope of our capacity. It's called living in your parents' house. You can take the person out of the home, but taking the family of origin messages out of the person is far more complicated.

Love anything and your heart will be wrung and possibly broken. If you want to make sure to keep it intact, you must give it to no one, not even an animal. Wrap it carefully around with hobbies and little luxuries; avoid all entanglements. Lock it up safe in the casket or coffin of your selfishness. But in that casket—safe, dark, motionless, airless—it will change. It will not be broken; it will become unbreakable, impenetrable, and irredeemable. To love is to be vulnerable. - C.S. Lewis[xxiv]

And actually, it's this vulnerability that prepares us for an extraordinary life. The idea is to see through new eyes, at which point you'll quickly notice terrific relationships all around. Maybe by that time you'll actually be in a great one yourself.

Heartbreak Guarantee #5: LIVING IN EXPECTATION OF REJECTION

This continues and deepens our expect-the-worst guarantee. Of course, after many "bad" relationship experiences, it makes some sense that you expect rejection followed by dejection. But negative expectation based on the past only deters future positive outcome. What you're really doing is rejecting yourself—as in, I expect you to reject me because that's all I deserve.

Heartbreak Guarantee #6: MAGICAL THINKING AS A SUBSTITUTE FOR INSPIRED UNDERSTANDING

Putting pictures of perfect partners on your wall, wearing a lucky sweater, or avoiding people who look like your last lover will not magically invite the relationship of your dreams and desires.

Actually, imagining that certain actions cause particular results is mostly based on early distorted ideas of "power" formed through circumstances. Thus, for instance, if as a child we started correlating our mom's drunkenness with our "goodness or badness"—or early on became the family member who tried to "save" someone/everyone or imagined if only we'd been better, dad would never have left—we've established long-standing patterns based in ideas of false power. It's called magical thinking. I'm taking the liberty here of expanding the usual parameters of MT based on how frequently I find it weaves into daily life.

Magical thinking often sneaks by stealth in the back door through film, books, and television stories. Romance novels used to be the go-to for MT. Now, constant technological avenues for love-seeking add new permission. These forms of fantasy usually fly in on the wings of growing, growling desperation.

Current online video fantasy games, for instance, let us play everything from heroes and villains to alien creatures. Through these games we can triumph in ways often eluding us in daily life. We can join whole online communities, giving us an increased sense of belonging.

The anonymity is freeing.

Needless to say, none of this better prepares us for real worldly, committed love. What it does is offer temporary relief from daily plight and fight. Unfortunately, it sometimes also allows an already on-the-edge kid permission for violence in ways he'd never previously considered as in the dreadful *2008: How to Kill a Prostitute* game.

Indeed, the more uncertain we feel about the future and the less structured our path, the more we can tend to depend on magical notions and other errant efforts to try controlling the outcome.

Magical thinking springs up everywhere.

"Some irrational beliefs (Santa Claus) are passed on to us. But others we find on our own. Survival requires recognizing patterns—night follows day, berries that color will make you ill. And because missing the obvious often hurts more than seeing the imaginary, our skills at inferring connections are over-tuned. No one told Wade Boggs that eating chicken before every single game would help his batting average; he decided that on his own, and no one can argue with his success. **We look for patterns because we hate surprises and because we love being in control.**"[xxv]

As you already know, I'm a big fan of pattern discovery. However, superstition about certain consistent behavior creating a pattern of particular outcome is not the same as recognizing an existent true pattern. So, imagining that skipping sidewalk cracks will save your mother's back from breaking isn't finding and honoring a pattern. It is not such a big deal when engaging in these little superstitions; but it becomes quite a problem when we start battling powerlessness with garbled ideas of cause and effect. [6]

We all do this to some degree.

And *degree* is the optimal word here.

When we blow out birthday candles making a wish: that's magical thinking. When a baseball pitcher ritually brushes off the mound in a particular way or a football player kisses an object pre-game: that's magical thinking.

Obviously, these procedures neither inhibit individuals nor undermine anyone else; so again, no biggie. In fact, many things some might consider to fall into this category, such as astrology and Fen Sui, are actually supportive of a more-expanded vision of life. [7]

My husband and I sometimes watch a television program called *Antiques Roadshow*. Here we can clearly witness how certain objects as in, say, a particular actor's costume or signed baseball cards, carry "value". Yes, this is in part because those objects are attached to history; however, I'd postulate that there's also some magical thinking connected to their worth. After all, does it matter that a player used a particular bat to hit a home run? Why does that instill it with so much significance? It was the man, not

---

[6] A deeper dive into magical thinking can be described more clinically in the extreme as superstitious ideation. It can even include certain pathologies like believing ourselves responsible for turning off streetlights as well as particular paranoia, etc.

[7] Now as a side-note, I'm a big fan of astrology deeply met. That is, when an excellent astrological expert explores and reports the patterns reflected through our charts, it's both exciting and enlightening. However, taking a quick-fix look at sun-signs only and comparing them to the sun-sign only of someone you met to decide if they're love material is silly and short-sighted. Like all elegant deciphering tools, astrology is best approached with reverent depth. In that case, astrology can increase your understanding of certain attractions and the results of those attractions.

However much we may want the easy are-they-right-for-me-answers, it's important to first discover what's landed us in love confusion, doubt, or disappointment in the first place. Don't jump to astrological conclusions. Don't jump to love matters conclusions, either.

the bat, who hit it. Obviously, the bat becomes the permanent representative of the man.

It turns out that anything—personal or public—with a "unique history" gains value. Our wedding rings get passed down. For example: Recently, a client of mine experienced the death of both parents within a year. Their lush home was filled with tons of valuable silver, antique furniture, and other precious objects. One item becoming a small bone of contention amongst the siblings was the cutting board dad made for mom by hand which was considered to have sentimental value.

Sentimental value means an object has been touched with magical thought—that cutting board "holds the energy" of both mom and dad. Again, this personal investment in an inanimate object causes no harm. Quite the opposite, such investment often brings sweetness to our lives.

Now of course, as with all things, there's potential good news and potential bad news when it comes to magical thinking. The obsessive-compulsive, for instance, who need to check the door lock three times, the stove five times, and be sure all objects are *exactly* where they "should" be is forbidding full engagement with real life.

Now we're entering MT problem territory.

Wishing is another benign version of magical thinking. But wishing without substantial backup work seldom scratches the itch. I can wish for my perfect lover to appear; however, if I never leave my house, constantly keep my eyes lowered, or say no to everyone who asks me out that "perfect" person could simply pass me by.

Now certainly being absolutely disconnected from the idea of magic often leaves us sitting firmly in doom and gloom. Extremely depressed folks are often desperately "realistic." There's even a disorder known as anhedonia, which is the complete inability to experience pleasure at all. [xxvi] Individuals besieged by this dreadful perspective can't manage to locate any value whatsoever in everyday life. Believe me: Those folks would be better off giving a glance toward magical thinking.

Here's the thing—there's a great deal of wondrous, helpful, inspiring magical thinking in the world. Like everything else, the idea is not to throw the baby out with the bath, but rather to recognize when, how, and where such considerations engage or absorb us, entertain or expand us. Culturally, for instance, we can give a happy nod to MT:

> Arthur C. Clarke's assertion, "Any sufficiently advanced technology is indistinguishable from magic comes to full fruition in cyberspace—a realm of avatars and instant messaging. And magical thinking may help us pluck the fruits of digital technology".[xxvii]

Ritually speaking…

THERE'S MORE GOOD MT NEWS.

Along the magical thinking way we discover a great deal about something called *ritual*. We all engage in rituals every day, whether or not we know it. Ritual offers our lives scaffolding. Our morning activities, for instance, are usually ritually performed. Go to the bathroom, brush your teeth, make your coffee, and take your vitamins. Whatever *your* sequence it mostly stays the same. Of course, we can also talk about more formal versions of ritual:

A **ritual** is a stereotyped sequence of activities involving gestures, words, and objects, performed in a sequestered place…Rituals of various kinds are a feature of almost all known human societies, past or present. They include not only the various worship rites and sacraments of organized religions and cults, but also the rites of passage of certain societies, atonement and purification rites, oaths of allegiance, dedication ceremonies, coronations and presidential inaugurations, marriages and funerals, school "rush" traditions and graduations, club meetings, sports events, Halloween parties, veterans parades, Christmas shopping, and more. Many activities that are ostensibly performed for concrete purposes, such as jury trials, execution of criminals, and scientific symposia, are loaded with purely symbolic actions prescribed by regulations or tradition, and thus partly ritualistic in nature. Even common actions like hand-shaking and saying hello may be termed rituals.[xxviii]

I'm taking the time to emphasize ritual here as it shines light on important and often hugely supportive procedures. I shall encourage an exploration of: a) how to understand the unconscious rituals with which you're already involved as some of them are helpful and some are not. Once realizing the difference we'll look at: b) how to make supportive choices of which rituals to maintain. (For more on this, check out *Love Works*.)

Indeed, ritual can offer us structural solidity and safety in a chaotic world. It's possible to find expanded perspective and life-enhancing experience through particular ceremonial practices.

Perhaps you're balking at this conversation.

Maybe the idea of ritual sounds too extreme. The thing is, *all* relationship includes ritual. It's best that you understand the rituals your relationships involve so that you can keep what you like and leave the rest. Like that "ritual" of routine sexual engagement you've fallen into with your partner that's squeezed the very life out of your encounters!

In any event, as with all ideas and procedures presented here, I encourage you to toss aside your old standard notions and try things on for size. Hopefully, even at this juncture, I've begun to poke holes in your old ways of perceiving. Not accepting a changing perspective can be like losing a bunch of weight and still shopping for the same-size clothes. That's not really going to work when it comes to outfitting you in the best shape and style for your future. Go on—try that bright plaid shirt you never imagined wearing.

This momentarily brings up the familiar conversation about what we do and don't value, otherwise known as meaning.

Often I'm asked: "How do I find meaning?" Needless to say, we're hungry for it. We anticipate meaning to elaborate a personal sense of significance.

And it's true.

It does. To quote Anais Nin:

There is not one big cosmic meaning for all; there is only the meaning we each give to our life, an individual meaning, an individual plot, like an individual novel, a book for each person. [xxix]

Certainly it's easy to get stuck in rigid, even outdated ideas of meaning-fullness and meaninglessness. Notions we've accumulated and hang onto by rote. Still, most would agree that life without acknowledged meaning feels empty. In those cases, purpose becomes elusive and happiness seems impossible. Lethargy easily sets in. Giving up altogether travels not far behind.

My answer about how to find meaning is simple and always the same: Things, processes, people, and all of life has meaning because *we decide they have meaning.* That is to say, meaning is not absolute.

What has meaning for me need not have meaning for you. And that's okay. I, for instance, find meaning in emotional discovery. My husband finds it through the study, exploration, and compilation of historical data. Neither of us is right or wrong.

What's the point of this dialogue?

Very often, it's our judgment about what has meaning and what doesn't that gets us into relationship hot water. In order to protect what really feels like fragile belief territory, we impugn, reject, ridicule, and suspect other perspectives when it comes to what's important and what's not. We often say different strokes for different folks, but do we really believe it? Imagine having no reactivity toward others opinions, disagreements, manners, and methods—picture being clearly and firmly connected to personal perspective without needing others to concur.

Summary: Magical thinking believes that with certain routines we can influence the world to go "our" way. Some of those procedures support us and others do not. As with all things, it's not about simply discarding a process, but maintaining benefits while releasing burdens. It helps to know where we've placed our sense of meaning and meaninglessness.

Locked & Loaded: getting triggered...

TALKING ABOUT MEANING: WHEN IT COMES TO RELATIONSHIPS, FOLKS OFTEN MENTION WHAT'S CALLED *TRIGGERS*: things spinning us off into reactivity from which we are hard-put to recover. Triggers are earth-shaking provocateurs that over and again threaten to undermine love everywhere, all the time. We tend to feel at the mercy of such experiences—like we're uncontrollably rolling down a steep, sharp-rocked hill.

Part of the work of relationship recovery is to learn how to refrain from reactivity, to discover the wonderment of clear response. This in no way implies stuffing or denying feelings. At best, in fact, our feelings want to inform our words. However, there's a big difference between being informed and being ruled or ruined.

If we look at triggers like gun mechanisms, we get a more precise appreciation for what's happening. Why in the world would I choose such a viscous reference? Because oh-too-often challenging relationship struggles make us feel like we've got a gun to our heads!

In those cases, when pinched by some perceived infraction or actual blow, it's easy to accelerate our velocity from a resting state to one of energetic motion—which is just what happens when a trigger's pulled and a bullet leaves the chamber. This is called kinetic energy. Unfortunately, it takes the same amount of work to decelerate once we're firing as it did to accelerate.

Oops.

Part of our aim here is to figure out how this deceleration happens. Otherwise, obviously, we're in a constant state of war.

How does it work?

THERE ARE SEVERAL "ACTIONS" SUPPORTING FEELING TRIGGERS. What's important is to determine what our own personal triggers are. We'll spot them through thoughts and/or feelings, depending on our nature. Triggers are not themes, but will lead us to our themes. For example, I have an "I have to do everything myself" theme. Here the trigger might be disappointment when someone says they're going to do something they don't do.

It's valuable to also recognize something called a Shame Spiral. This is best described as a downward spinning whirl of self-loathing. In this example, my own version would sound like: I have to do everything myself □ I can't depend on anyone □ I don't deserve to depend on anyone □ I'm on my own because I'm unlovable.

As you can see, the trigger is merely the poke.

How we react and respond to that poke is the important piece. Now, a healthy person can get let down and simply realize the disappointing individual has a problem keeping their word, or that stuff happens or that the guy's not someone to count on, but not take it to mean anything about their own value. Someone swimming in damage takes it all personally.

Really?

Not take things personally?

How can that possibly happen?

Well, it can, and does.

When we keep focus on what *we* feel, think, and do.

Self-focus is true freedom. This I promise.

Heartbreak Guarantee #7: MAINTAINING THE ILLUSION THAT SOMETHING'S BETTER THAN NOTHING.

All too often, in the midst of emotional panic or awful self-contempt, like the thirty-year-old Filipino, we take what comes along, relationship-wise, job-wise, friendship-wise, or whatever. This starts early. Not long ago, for example, I was working with a delightful fifteen-year-old boy just venturing into relationship territory. He said, "Well, this girl kinda likes me, so maybe I should date her?"

I suggested perhaps finding more extensive criteria.

To you, I recommend the same.

Certainly, there's more to this take-what-you-can posture than meets the eye, as dread of being alone or broke or some other deeply held fear inevitably platforms these unhealthy choices. Whatever the impetus, the result is most often some way, somehow unhappy.

I guess that means out with the old, in with the new?

NOT AT ALL. IT'S NOT ABOUT GIVING UP *all* old habits. Some are benign, while others are even helpful. For instance, when I was a kid I was quite sure monsters lived in the closet and came out to attack when the night's thick darkness descended. I had two solutions: first, keep all closet doors firmly closed; second, make sure there's a light on somewhere nearby. Naturally, I'd not thought it through—I mean, monsters powerful enough to commit nighttime attacks can certainly penetrate doors and slip through closet cracks.

In any event, it didn't take much sleuthing to realize I lived in fear of the shadowy unknown. Turns out, I was intuitively onto something. Monsters did live—just not in the closet. They lived inside me, in the form of fury and of profound loneliness. This double focus became the basis for much of my self-discovery work.

Having subsequently spent a great deal of time, then, appreciating both these inner dynamics and more, I no longer imagine wardrobe monsters out to get me. But you know what— I still prefer the closet door be shut at night. Really. I don't get anxious to the point of not being able to sleep if it's cracked open, but mostly I honor my habitual preference.

And to that I say: So what?

No harm, no foul.

Here's another example: For a very long time, I perceived being sent to sleep-away boarding school from age 7-18 as meaning that I was unlovable. I deeply integrated that idea and subsequently spent many yearning years both habitually and ridiculously attempting to prove this to be true by engaging in self-denigrating, self-defeating behaviors. I got in the "habit" of throwing myself under the bus. Through diligence and by walking the path I'm laying out here for you, I recovered myself. Today, I stand on a platform of self-love.

The point is that some habits will stay and that's okay. It's the ones that impede and undermine that we want to toss out or modify.

Summary: When we've sourced behavior, come to understand the beginning points, and recognized patterns—then been given new tools to confront those patterns—we can maintain newly chosen directions. We might still be wearing a few of the old clothes, but, after all, some garments remain classics anyway.

PART V: LIFE ON LIFE'S TERMS

Welcome Surprise...

ELEMENTAL NUMBER SEVEN: **WHAT HAPPENS IN OUR LIFE IS LESS IMPORTANT THAN HOW WE GREET WHAT HAPPENS.** It's easy to notice how different people handle similar events in different ways. One individual takes the demise of their relationship as a crushing blow that forever embitters them against love, while another expresses the pain and learns what to do better next time. One faces disease with bright courage while others collapse under pressure. One finds losing everything in a fire to be forever insurmountable, others move into gratitude for lives spared.

Newsflash: We can only face our lives; we cannot force our lives.

This brings us to our final heartbreak (remember we started with #9, which involved reading from an old rule book–a book you've hopefully by now in our work together, already thrown away!)

Heartbreak Guarantee #8: TRYING TO CONTROL OUTCOME.

There are plenty of matters we actually have control of, including the integrity, intention, stamina, and enthusiasm we offer to this circumstance called Life. But when, in all our affairs, we're driven by fantasies of perfection, critical expectation, self-contempt, or several other brain-occupying defenses, we're sure to be disappointed by what ensues.

Indeed, it's foolhardy and arrogant to imagine we have control over how things turn out. We've plenty of evidence showing how silly this is, but try, try again we do anyway.

In fact, fervent, powerful need for control and the angst companioning that need block growth.

Let me repeat: *We are not in control of outcome.* Until we fully get that, we're promised to be continuously flooded with feelings of insufficiency or frustrated anger or both. Our only real authority involves our daily, moment-to-moment choices. A Vietnamese Zen Buddhist monk, teacher, author, poet, and peace activist Thich Nhat Hanh says:

> The miracle is not to walk on water. The miracle is to walk on the green earth in the present moment, to appreciate the peace and beauty that are available now…It is a matter of faith; it is a matter of practice.[xxx]

Stunner: Living in your head instead of in your life is undermining your happiness.

Stop it.

Be full-hearted in all your endeavors, including love. You'll be astonished by the glad results.

But everything feels harder these days…

I'VE SAID IT BEFORE: IN MANY WAYS THIS IS ABSOLUTELY TRUE—things are *psychologically* harder. With so many more options than ever before, and hardly any 'organized' ways to move through life, plus few everyone-does-it methods, many feel dazed and confused.

For example, used to be in vast numbers of society most everyone expected to go to college after high school, graduate said-college basically knowing the future: get married, buy a house, and have 2.4 kids. No more. That's still the flight path for some, but certainly not for the many.

Our choices have multiplied.

And with increased choice comes increased anxiety.

Ever go to a restaurant with a ten-page menu? Egads.

We've long known about *mid-life crisis*—that gotta-change-everything feeling popping up around mid-point where folks tend to buy a motorcycle though they've never before ridden, leave a long-time job though nothing in particular is on the horizon, or trade their partner in for a younger model. While such times often appear to lack volition—like that first out-spurting of semen or menopause arriving seemingly out of the blue—in actuality this mid-life psychological jolt can be viewed as a kind of wake-up call and an exciting invitation to get moving in new directions and to discover fresh inspiration. Fantastic. It can even encourage ready individuals to begin figuring out how to give back to the world.

Thus, a mid-life crisis offers all kinds of possible positive and novel tracks to take, though, of course, the better part of valor might advise awakening without blowing up your life.

Well, now just for laughs and giggles, there's a new wrinkle in the fabric of society. More recently, we've snagged ourselves on something referred to in psychological and sociological circles as *first-quarter crisis*. It occurs when you're thirty or under.

Oh my.

This time the experience has nothing to do with revitalization. It doesn't rouse us to further freedom. Rather, since it's stimulated by fear when it comes to choosing or committing to a particular future trajectory, it's usually spiced with burning self-doubt.

Minimally, there's frantic flailing.

Maximally, there's paralysis.

Oy! It all seems to go on forever...

AS YOU CAN SEE, THESE CHANGING TIMES give cause for both celebration and for anxiety. Turns out, both the "fantastic" and the "oh my" are hooked onto our unprecedented longevity.

Naturally, the things-are-harder point rests squarely on this important detail. The way it works is that though we live longer and are mostly healthier, elder-hood is still approximately 10-15 years long (starting around 80 years old, edging now even toward 85). This means so-called mid-life is wildly extended, seeming to go on and on.

Let's take a second to delineate these life sections in more clinical language. According to Carl Jung, for instance, females move through the following life stages: maiden/puella (girl); mother (procreative woman); crone (wise woman). Because of our extended mid-life, it seems there needs to be a stage between mother and crone. I've named this phase: *Feminine Matura* (mature woman). This inserted fourth stage attends that part of life that though no longer precisely about fertility, most certainly might be the most abundant stage we yet encounter. Using Jungian terms, the equivalent in males would be boy/puer; father; *Masculine Matura*; senex.

Certainly, none of these phases necessarily appear in linear fashion. Wisdom can develop early in some and youth linger on and on in others. And we might move back and forth depending upon the area. Some are quite advanced in worldly matters, but wildly immature when it comes to relationships. And so it goes. At best, the stages eventually thread together like a well-crafted tapestry.

I emphasize this stages-of-development point as a further appreciation and acceptance of the collective sociological shifts before us. Rather than standing in the shadow of an old paradigm (between 18 & 21, we decide who to marry and what to be), we best embrace the new adventuresome truth that most likely we'll linger and shift and scurry and change our minds in pretty much every area of our lives. We simply have more time, more choices, and more leeway to become who and what we wish.

It also means seldom anymore does an individual stick with one occupation for the entire course of life. Nor do they attach themselves to one lifelong partnership. Thus, change is becoming the norm rather than the anomaly.

Of course, as with all things, benefits come with burdens.

This extended mid-life also stretches out our relationship to youth. There's even a new description called Kidult: "adults interested in forms of entertainment such as computer games, television programs, etc. intended for children". (Wikipedia) "Forever 21" is in our lexicon and consciousness. It reflects, at best, a certain societal permission to linger in early developmental stages (remember skateboarding Simon?) and, at worst, actual infantilization—meaning we're reduced to children.

All this is to say, individuals are discovering direction far later, finding their often first partner later, and having children later. (Note: I'm well aware there are many, many exceptions to this "new" formula; however, if you're reading this book it's likely you've bumped up against this changing construct.) The new paradigm isn't a problem *per se*; it's simply a truth.

Marching to the beat of our own drum...

MANY THINK THIS MEANS THAT WE can do whatever we want, whenever we want to do it. Sure, now that certain rulebooks have been burned, it's tempting to imagine everyone will be on board for unique and individual perspectives on how to live life. Sadly, this simply isn't so—mostly because individuals want collusion for their own viewpoints. Complicity allows us to feel good about our choices. After all, if you've decided you don't want children while your friend or colleague is still all about it, your position might feel threatened or threatening. Maybe in conversations they even play the religion card. Or talk about having kids as an important contribution to change. Again, how your decision is perceived or greeted by others is going to very much depend on your attitude, the depth with which you've explored that decision, and your manner of presentation. And more importantly, this depth of exploration is sure to impact how successful your love experiences will be.

Q: Well, a lot of people aren't having kids these days, but what if I simply don't want a partner or marriage? No one seems to believe me!

CERTAINLY, EVEN IN OUR PERSPECTIVE-EXPANDING WORLD TODAY, not wanting children is challenging enough to express, but try telling others you really, clearly, absolutely *want* to be alone—or at least you don't ever want to get married. It's definitely hard to hold ground when everyone else appears headed in another direction. We worry about approval. We worry about fitting in. We worry that our apparent desires are wrong. We worry about what our parents will think and say.

Here's a wild and important realization to wrap your mind around:

Newsflash: "Other people" are not the point.

Turns out, for the *most* part, when we're *truly* at peace with being alone, (or childless, a stay-at-home parent, working for a corporation, working for ourselves, very social, not so social, etc.) others will recognize and respect that. Folks are far more likely to admire a position that arrives with a deep understanding of how and why. Authentic assuredness is hard to deny. They may never really get it, but at least they'll leave you alone about it. Well, maybe not your parents, but other people.

Let me give you an example that may seem somewhat afield, but that I believe carries the meaning. Long ago, I worked with a lovely man who let me know early on he was what's called an ethical atheist. Now though I myself stand on a spiritual platform, this fellow had such an amazingly clear, well-explored outlook along with no need for me to concur, that we found much correspondent connectedness, and our work together served him well.

Contrarily, there was another atheist client I'd worked with years earlier, who, unlike the aforementioned man, had done little real investigation. As it turns out, he'd landed on his atheistic position more out of rebellion against family than anything else. In fact, mostly he'd toss the word around like a randomly thrown Frisbee in the park, just to see who'd catch it. His rebellion was a defense for how hugely powerless he felt in his life. This adolescent "punch" was a way to prove uniqueness through revolt.

As I tend to do with *all* viewpoints no matter what the topic, we explored foundation. I've noticed the more we need to cogently explain our positions, the more we ourselves come to understand those positions. It's similar to what happens when we use a new word in a sentence three times.

Clarity ensues.

Anyway, Tom and I often discussed atheism, as it was one of his favorite talking-point fallbacks. A good way he'd discovered to avoid real delving. Eventually, Tom admitted he simply liked to be the "troublemaker."

Just for fun and as a true recommendation, I finally suggested he join the Atheist's Society Organization so he could carry on a deeper dialogue about it. He turned up his nose, quickly saying he'd no interest in knowing "those people."

I had to laugh.

Point of these two stories is that if your position is well thought out and strongly held, others will accept it. But it's always helpful to know why you believe what you believe.

So does that mean if I say I don't want a relationship, it's okay?

LET'S BE CLEAR: I APPRECIATE AND ADVOCATE BEING WITHOUT PARTNERSHIP, **IF** THAT'S TRULY YOUR PATH. Now many settle on being single out of fear or self-loathing or some other defense. You'll need to dig deep to see which hat suits your face. For those who discover after vigorous investigation that they've stayed alone simply as avoidance or in self-contempt, please realize it doesn't have to remain that way.

You can have love.

It starts with you loving yourself.

Loving myself is such a cliché!

CLICHÉS ARE, IN FACT, FREQUENTLY SPOKEN TRUTHS. Just because everyone knows to say it, doesn't mean it isn't so— quite the opposite. The problem isn't the veracity of the oft-touted self-love concept...the problem is: *How do we manage to do that?*

Q: How do I love myself when no one else seems to love me?

THIS QUESTION LOOKS AT THE WRONG SIDE OF THE MULE.

Yes, everything *starts* with self-love, but then it waves out from there. To some degree this is counter-intuitive. After all, we might wonder, didn't my mommy love me first? Isn't that how I know love—'cause I looked into her eyes and saw myself reflected there? That means, it would follow, you can love yourself only as a reflection seen in others.

I disagree.

I disagree because I believe love to be **an innate ability**. I feel we *do* love ourselves completely and wholly at birth. Having nothing to doubt, why would we not? But then as before stated, through the experiences of family trauma, peer drama, collective disgruntlement, heritage impact, and contextual affect, we *develop* an estrangement from natural self-love and begin moving into the complications of being alive in a world layered with questions and concerns. And then, of course, there's the conversation about blaming ourselves for being kicked out of paradise.

Whatever the source, somewhere along the line—whether immediately or later—we decide we need to be convinced of our lovability—of our love ability.

Sure, if we didn't perceive mom's love because she didn't "radiate" it or maybe because she was stoic by nature, we might have hurried into self-doubt. It's that take-everything-personally business. But as you can see, that's not all there is to it. Luckily, love is bigger than our parents—bigger than any one person really. Actually, love is more profoundly about Life itself—about celebrating the extraordinary miracle called being alive. The imperative is: Love yourself, love others, and love life. In the words of poet E.E. Cummings:

Love is the voice under all silences, the hope which has no opposite in fear; the strength so strong mere force is feebleness: the truth more first than sun, more last than star...[xxxi]

Realize here and now that the word LOVE is not being bandied about cavalierly. A sincere massaging of what-is-it, where-in-me-does-real-love-ability-live, and how-do-I-learn-to-share-it is wanted. We discover this for the personal *us*. We discover it for the public *us*. And we discover it, in fact, for the world, which grows or diminishes, as do we.

But what is it…this "love" thing? How do I know if I'm feeling it or have it or am even capable?

ACTUALLY, EVERYONE'S CAPABLE TO SOME DEGREE (perhaps excluding sociopaths). It just appears very different in different people. What love is or feels like or looks like, you'll need to determine for yourself. Is it that warm sensation moving through the chest or that experience of gladness or the can't-get-them-off-my-mind or that I'd-trust-them-with-my-life or…?

You get to decide.

You decide.

You.

Remember: Things have meaning because we *decide* they have meaning. People have meaning because we decide. Circumstances have meaning because we decide. Meaning and love are inextricably linked.

Annoying, you say.

True though—there are no absolute rules.

How we each experience love is far from standard. We talk about it, sing about it, write poetry about it, draw or paint about it, craft novels, films, and television portraits of it; however, in the final analysis, there's no oh-THIS-is-it description that fits everyone in every circumstance.

Why?

First: Because it's a matter of *feeling*. And feelings are not so easily captured in simplistic ways. Second: Because we see "others" through the lens of our own projections, which means we inevitably desire those we love (and love itself) to fulfill what can't actually be filled. Arthur C. Clarke put it perhaps devastatingly best: "The person we love doesn't exist but is a projection through the lens of our mind on the closest thing that approximates our desire." Or to put it more simply: 'Beauty is in the eye of the beholder."

So where does all that leave us?

Back at self-love: Really, not a bad place to land.

And once we really love ourselves we realize there's already other-person love in our lives. It hangs there, in fact, like wonderful, delicious fruit just waiting to be picked from the tree.

Enough is enough!

ELEMENTAL NUMBER EIGHT: **THE IDEA THAT NO ONE LOVES US IS** *A NOTION*, **NOT A TRUTH!** Just because we think it, doesn't make it so. Change your thinking perspective, change your life.

Case in point:

Long, long ago everyone believed the world was flat. They were certain of it. Although ancient astronomers such as Eratosthenes clearly proved that the Earth was round (and actually estimated its diameter with amazing accuracy), human civilization went through a period called the Dark Ages, where knowledge was condemned by the Catholic Church if it in any way conflicted with the doctrine of the Church. People were deliberately kept ignorant for a thousand years. If you are ignorant and can't read, then **your perspective** of Earth **is what you can see by looking out around you. And you will see a flat world around you—flat for as far as the eye can see in all directions**. Of course, today we understand that's not true, but if questioning that concept might get you put through the Inquisition, or get you burned at the stake, you would be very wise to not question that the Earth was whatever the Church said it was. And the Church taught that the Earth was the center of the Universe and that everything revolved around it; and that if it were round, the Bible would have told them so. Finally, when Columbus proved the Earth had to be round, the Church had to relent (eventually) and modern science was allowed to prevail once again, after a thousand years of possible scientific advancement was wasted. There are still a tiny handful of people to this day who belong to The Flat Earth Society who teach that the world is flat, but I think they do it more as a ceremonial, social thing than as actually believing it. [xxxii]

Our viewpoint is ordinarily dependent on immediate experience. If we get all our flowers from the corner store, as I did being a city gal, it's hard to imagine extensive grounds where flowers grow unrestrainedly. If "as far as we can see in all directions" is a lack of love coming toward us—a flat, flat world everywhere—it's easy to assume love is not to be ours. Once we're standing on that there's-no-love-for-me platform, it's a small leap to the nearest interpretation that is likely to be: "I don't have love because I don't deserve love." What follows is an accumulation of (made-up) reasons why we don't merit love.

All hogwash: We could call this our "Love Dark Ages."

Can't give what we don't have...

"MY PROBLEM IS, I GIVE TOO MUCH! I do everything for everyone else and there's nothing left for me!"

Is this familiar? I hear it all the time. If this is your hue and cry, let me be the first to tell you if no one else has: You're deluding yourself.

First, giving is only half the equation called loving. When we give without allowing ourselves to receive, whether with any awareness or not, the giving is most likely coming from pure ego as in "what's in it for me?" And further, if we're only giving to others and not generous to the Self, we're probably engaging a prove-prove-prove-myself-to-be-acceptable process.

It hints of masochism.

In any event most excessive giving (sometimes called co-dependency) is about control—an effort to manage how other people perceive us: "Oh she's so good"; "My, my—he's so unselfish"; "Oh, you can always count on them to get the job done!"; "I simply can't imagine where she gets all her energy—she does so much for so many people."

In the extreme, giving 'til it hurts indicates some gigantic, deeply-disturbing fear. We may not know what it is or even be mostly aware of it, but it's likely to be there. Perhaps as a brace against abandonment, we (unconsciously) hope giving enough will make us indispensable. Or maybe it's that control business. Or possibly we imagine acting like a good person means we are a good person. We hope that it equals getting rewarded in the end.

Or perhaps we're trying to give what was never received as a child in an unconscious effort to heal original wounds. Whatever the reason, no matter what you think, your giving's unlikely to be "pure."

I once had a rather wonderful client who clearly didn't believe she deserved the great financial bounty she'd achieved in her life——even though nothing had been just handed to her, but rather resulted from years of diligent hard work effort. Therefore, in the face of these lack-of-entitlement feelings, when divorcing after a brief unpleasant marriage where she'd been the sole provider, she readily gave away the farm—contrary to the advice of all who loved her dearly.

But when it comes to giving, in the long run it really doesn't make much difference why. No kidding. Except it helps *you* understand your own motivation, which is always valuable. Clarity, after all, pulls open the blinds of confusion, allowing all the little dust mites and dropped ashes littering the room to be better revealed for potential cleaning.

Still, good deeds don't have to be done from absolute purity to be effective. Plus, just because you're aiming for approval or salvation or redemption or whatever doesn't mean you're not basically a truly generous individual; for underneath the "have to" for self-esteem bolstering purposes is likely to be someone who's naturally gifted when it comes to caretaking. That talent can be a wonderful quality when better understood and not operating on automatic. Happily, then, you can at some point be generous as a style not a necessity.

We can give so much we leave no room for anyone else...

ELEMENTAL NUMBER NINE: **WHEN WE BELIEVE OURSELVES TO BE UNLOVABLE AND UNDESERVING, WE FOLLOW A PATH THAT PROVES IT**. Giving so much that there's no room for others to give back is a problem. Or, alternatively, rejecting love before it can enter the house at all is an equal snag. Only loving people who can't or won't love back, or sabotaging our own well-being over and again, is additionally quite problematic. All of these secure our unworthiness beliefs. Bottom line, as Stephen Chbosky says: "We accept the love we think we deserve."

Holding onto familiar styles and systems guarantees continued disappointment. For real change, we need to do things differently.

No one else has to adjust—only you.

And when we do, something magical happens. When we shift—really, truly exhibit the modified behavior that reflects a major interior perspective change—the world around us begins to *feel* entirely altered. You see, how we experience life is based mostly on how we perceive life to be. Money, property, and prestige don't fix things. Beauty doesn't fix things. Accolade and approval don't fix things. All day long, year after year, I sit with people who have all these and are dismally distraught.

Newsflash: Joy-fullness is an inside job.

Thus, once we change perspectives we begin to note reflections of that change showing up in unexpected ways. New people arrive in our life. Former friends and associates treat us differently. We begin getting what we've been asking for.

Obviously, it's time to alter those rotten perceptions; time to revolutionize the behaviors that undermine our possibility for glee, for success, and for true accomplishment—time to change our relationship to self-love. And then—only then—can we have the relationships and life we crave.

ELEMENTAL NUMBER TEN: **SELF-LOVE *CAN* BE LEARNED.**

For genuine self-love here are **The Four Gateways**. These gateways summarize and then expand some of what we've so far discussed. To heal your love matters enter the gateways with full intention and be amazed.

1. Awareness

We need to understand what we're doing today before we'll be able to change what we do tomorrow. Begin by seeing how deeply true it is that self-love is missing in your life. Look the spitting dragon in the eye.

Themes, showing up in repeated phrases spoken or thought, are easy to catch when written down. Once we know what they are, we can develop a solutions-to-the-theme list. For example:

As mentioned, one of my long-standing themes was "I have to do everything myself." This notion made me feel, for a start, over-burdened, and at the same time smart. It led me to refuse collaboration, reject teammates, avoid dependence, and much more. Realization and recognition of this theme—as well as developing an ability to spot the feelings plus actions that reported them—led me to solutions like learned collaboration, explored interdependence, and practiced delegating. These and other specific solutions will be well covered as we move along; however, we started this understanding with Connect the Dots. Continue to expand your picture-making process.

Awareness begins with noticing what we think, as well as how we behave in response to that thinking. For now, just start watching all the ways, great and small, that each day you reject the various forms of love coming your way. Do you, either out loud or in your own mind, toss off compliments as if they don't count? Do you refuse invitations for aid when offered? Do you hesitate to ask for help when needed?

What else?

Go as far as you can to discover your inability to appreciate the loving gestures already present in your life on a daily basis. By example, with regard to my own above-stated theme: I would never tell others I needed help; I criticized all help I did get, constantly finding people inadequate to the task; I complained about needing to do everything myself.

So, keep that list—that way you'll easily see your themes jumping out at you. This is the beginning of noticing the thinking, feeling and behaving ways you reject love.

2. Historical Triggers

Understanding clearly how, when, and with whom the past leaps forward to manage our lives provides yet another gateway to change.

What is the origin of your self-doubt?

To discover this you'll need to be brave—to overwhelm your fears with sincere intention. In my case, that 11-year boarding school experience signaled to me the importance of figuring "it" all out myself, without specific parental guidance. Also, when I was with my traveling salesman folks in the summers, they were constantly busy, so I was pretty much on my own. *Get it together,* I somewhere inside determined, *and never let them see you sweat!* My mother even tells the (unlikely) story that when learning to walk I never got up and fell down, but simply one day stood up and walked across the room. Of course, this is nonsense; however, it does carry the important message of my home life.

I want to quickly say at this point I have absolutely no negative energy on these memories. No resentment or "blame." I merely mention them here by way of offering example. And that's exactly the attitude I'm encouraging in you. You see each element of our histories, as I over and again stress, builds the house called "me." The idea is to realize that it's indeed a dandy house. Maybe not perfect, but swell just the same.

In any event, it helps to look at the past not as the enemy you've been afraid to welcome in, but rather as the hungry, disenfranchised but well-meaning relative who arrives at your door, hungry for aid and attention.

ELEMENTAL NUMBER ELEVEN: **HERITAGE MATTERS.** In our desperate effort to be politically correct, we've tended to discard the value of heritage. It's annoying.

Heritage invariably factors in, whether we're close to our roots or not. Somehow it trickles down through family messages; or slips in through societal implications and even direct statements; or filters in through local attitudes and prescriptions. It's carried through bigotry and leaping-to-judgment statements.

I once had this delicious client who truly appreciated as well as loved both me and our work together. One day as she arrived, I admired her shoes. She said unselfconsciously, "Oh *you'll* dig this—not only are they cool, but they were super cheap—a real bargain!" She meant it as a connecting statement. And she knew me quite well to be a generous, not count-your-pennies person. Really the statement came from her knowing me to be Jewish and all the common undercurrent of assumptions rippling through the world about Jews and money. She said it without thinking, meaning absolutely nothing nasty in a personal way. Rather, it was a deeply held bigotry she didn't even realize she had.

Like it or not—admit it or not—we all carry bigotry to some degree. It's important to understand, then, both our own roots (because really if we don't know where we've come from, it'll be very difficult to figure out where we're going) and our attitudes toward the origins of others.

If we ignore or impugn our specific histories, both personal and ethnic, we will at some point see damaging results. The damage might sneak up on us to merely tickle our ribs, or it might sock us square on the jaw. But one way or another, it will come to interrupt how, who, and what we deeply accept and love.

So don't ignore your own long-standing family stories and traditions. The suggested autobiographical writing can help. Look closely at those passed-down ideas and ways, whether benign or troubled. For instance, my mother left two raw eggs in the fridge for the length of my teething, supposedly to make my teething easier. At the end of that time, the eggshells were empty. When asked why she really did this, she said she didn't know except that her mother had done it.

Obviously, a gentle tradition.

On the other hand, all the women in my lineage back as far as memory were the ones who "ran the show"—the diligent workhorses who made the majority of the money, managing both business and home. Stay-at-home mother was not in my "heritage" story. I have followed that sometimes daunting, sometimes exhilarating, family mandate.

Of course, when it came to learning love, the directive often made for an uphill climb. Like all the women before me, I tended to become the man I never believed I'd find lying beside me. It's been a long road back.

One of the many wrong-headed notions we tend to carry is that our family challenges and conflicts are the "source" of our problems. This is not exactly true. There's nothing, for instance, wrong with my offered story. It's given me huge gifts. And, too, you might be able to discern how my first theme point ("I have to do everything myself") plugs into the storyline of "all the women in my family run the show."

But again I say: So what?

The question becomes not "Did I do things a particular way?" but "Did I *have* to do things that way?" What's not being said here is that heritage in and of itself is "fault" for what ails us. It contributes but does not determine. What I wanted for myself and what I want for you is choice—to take what you like and leave the rest.

Roots and trees and it's all their fault, oh my...

THIS DESCRIPTION OF TREE LIFE aptly describes the importance of knowing but not blaming our roots:

> Roots are often blamed for damage to foundations. In reality, roots are rarely the cause of the problem. Though small roots may penetrate existing cracks in foundations, they are incapable of causing mechanical damage through their growth.[xxxiii]

Thus, as everywhere in nature, roots—defined as "the part of a plant that attaches it to the ground or to a support, conveying water and nourishment to the rest of the plant"—give us form and body.

Stunner: Where we come from is not the problem. It's the promise.

As I've said before and shall repeat: even the most awful circumstances offer great gifts. What we're investigating here is actually *the cracks in our foundation*. That means: what happened; how it happened; and how we responded to what happened.

The intention is not to leave us "hating" our families. The aim is to merely establish the effects of circumstances as we perceive them to be, and to realize the messages we took from early experiences. Here's a tiptoe into understanding.

Pattern pieces

SEE IF YOU CAN *NOTICE A PATTERN.*

Repeated reactions might give a clue, especially if linked to current life. For example: Whenever your parents were fighting in the house you went to your room, closed the door, and started doing something to block out the noise. Today, in relationships with friends or partners and even at work, when something upsets you do you withdraw and preoccupy yourself, preferring to avoid confronting either the situation or your own feelings? Note the similarities between the child you were and the adult you are today.

3. Confronting stuckness

This is the third gateway to sincere shift. We've all got plenty of old stories, long-standing ideas, as well as defenses that report those old stories and ideas. Reprogramming attitude is a hard one, but it definitely can be done.

The easiest method, though it might not sound like it, involves a tool called: TAKE CONTRARY ACTION. That means, instead of shutting down, we speak up. Rather than raging, we practice engaging.

Of course, especially in work situations, we can't always hit circumstances head on, so taking contrary action under certain conditions will simply mean exploring *inner responses* to whatever's happening rather than outwardly doing anything about it. But identifying feelings is no small matter and contributes hugely to potential change.

Actually (hopefully) completing all other exercises in the *Love Works* chapter will land you in the final assignment, which involves writing a new story for yourself. It's really fun, important, and astonishingly effective.

4. Practicing the art of self-love

This book is chock-full of tools for discovery in this regard. Practice, practice, practice.

But my life seems basically kinda okay except for...

"ALL THIS TALK ABOUT HISTORY. WHAT'S THE BIG DEAL anyhow? Well, maybe I don't love my job, but it's not so bad," we say. Or, "Other people are fat and have love; my friends aren't over the moon about their lives, but seem fine. Yeah, they complain sometimes, but seem pretty okay. But what's really confusing me most is that things were going all right for quite a while, and now suddenly there's this dark cloud over me. I don't know what happened!"

A reasonable mystification, huh?

Okay, everything was fine for a long time, or so we say, and suddenly we're feeling emotionally, spiritually, or with regards to daily life, topsy-turvy. Oh yes, the party line's been: Things were fine and now they're not.

This *feels* like truth.

But is it? Really?

Many get exceptionally skilled at elbowing out any intrusive notions threatening to derail their chartered course. Just because we shove things under the rug doesn't mean they're gone. Internal decay is a common phenomenon.

Indeed, *appearing* to be okay doesn't mean we are okay, 'cause most deadly illnesses hide out of view until quite far along—until the mass shows on the lung or we're spitting up blood or the stomach pain is unbearable. Even a terrible cold can first show itself as a tiny scratch in the throat.

Everything *seemed* okay, and now it doesn't.

Seemed is the operative word here.

Of course there's the quiet (or not so quiet) rumble inside that says we're supposed to be somewhere else in our life by now—should have accomplished more, should be amidst fulfilling our dreams—even if we were never quite sure what those dreams were to include. I hear this complaint from 20-year olds, 60-year olds, and everyone in between. Few ever feel like they're as far along as they're meant to be.

Making matters worse, the world has likely encouraged us to be cavalier. Certainly, many go through life primarily skimming the surface. I call it stone skipping. It's a procedure that passes for acceptable—until it doesn't and that's when the proverbial hits the fan.

Compartmentalizing decay initially helps avoid *obvious* disrepair and despair. So if you're the kind of person who says "my life was pretty okay and then suddenly…boom," it's likely you've been simply *shoving things under the rug*; the belief being if I don't see the dirt, the dirt doesn't exist. Problem is: whether or not its front and center dis-ease continues, chewing at the edges of your life. Actually, the dirt is piling up under the rug, causing lumps in a carpet just waiting to be tripped over.

Somehow, we find our back against an emotional wall, whether it's an obstacle we hit a certain age, because all our friends get married and are having babies, our company goes bankrupt, the relationship we thought would last forever collapses, or whatever. Then the rotting, discomfort, and fear eat their way to the surface.

But we're mystified. We're mystified because somehow we didn't see it coming—mostly because we chose to ignore the signs. But those indicators were there all along, this I guarantee.

I feel so empty…

LET'S GO BACK TO OUR TREE ANALOGY [the italicized words mine]:

Decay is a tricky subject.
Tree species (*heritage material*), tree health (*family dynamics*), weather conditions (*global context*), and the location of the tree (*local context*) all play a role in quantifying the risk factor of a tree with rot. Most importantly, you should consider potential targets. If the tree is in a field, you can live with a high-

percentage chance of it falling over. If it is growing over your kids' play area, you can't tolerate much risk at all.[xxxiv]

All right, if you're most like a field tree your hollow center—that is, your lack of connection to inner self—*might* perhaps affect only you—if, of course, you spend all your time by yourself. On the other hand, if you're dry as hell amidst a thick forest—meaning if you've got other people around—everything you are and do has influence. Did you know that when we leave a room, bacterium that's been clinging to us stay behind? We're not without impact, much as we might think ourselves an island.

In a way, I often emphasize, when it comes to how we influence the world around us, we're involved in a kind of pyramid scheme.

Say we touch ten people either with our grin or with our grim. Then those ten people touch ten, and those ten more. Picture the number affected at the end of just one day. Thus, if we walk through our day grumpy, others pick up our grump.

It's easy to imagine them passing that on.

Thus, if we're forlorn, our cloud will follow but if we're conscious and conscientious, the people we interact with will be also influenced. This happens whether they realize it or not. This happens whether we realize it or not. We are the stones thrown in the middle of the pond and everything we are and do ripples out around us.

That means working on self-love affects more than just you. It affects the world directly around you, which in turn affects the global world.

Sound big? It is.

All this connection business is giving me the creeps!

THE BULK OF OUR CONSTERNATION ABOUT CONNECTION IS ACTUALLY *UNCONSCIOUS*. Ask a hundred people if they *want* connection and most will say yes.

But remember our **Universal:** Consider the evidence.

How? It's pretty simple to do really.

To appreciate how much you do, don't or won't, let's begin with a few simple questions: Do I have in my life what I say I want? I say I want to be thin. Am I? I say I want friends. Have I gone to any lengths to make that happen? (No excuses, please. Of course you're too jammed up or just moved "here" or feel shy or whatever). I say I want partnership. Do I have that?

Complaints flow from us like smooth, finely aged wine from a musky bottle. Our age, jobs, busy lives, looks, childhoods, society, and locale—you name it—there's always something we can point to as the "problem." It sounds like this: "No, I don't have (that) but I really, really do want (to be thin; have a relationship; get a better job) **but** (all the good ones are gone; it's hard to meet people here; time's not my friend; I'm so busy in my new job; there are no jobs out there; I don't have time to exercise; my body just doesn't respond when I diet; I'm always on the go)."

We're getting nowhere fast.

Going back to the termite analogy, here's what to do:

- ✓ Notice the tiny flying indicators littering the sill of your life
- ✓ Accept that the unnerving debris you see points to some hidden problem
- ✓ Realize something drastic must be done
- ✓ Prepare to get to the source of trouble
- ✓ Bring in the expert terminators for change

I know this modification of attitude and outcome to be possible because I have shifted many things, including my previously unhealthy relationship to relationship. I've gone from being a woman terrified of true intimacy to having a successful long-term amazing, imperfect, challenging, alive, inspiring, and sometimes infuriating, but always growing brilliantly, intimate life-long love. Not only have I done it, but I've witnessed thousands also accomplishing the same love-life shift—or shifting their relationship to money, to their body image, to basic self-esteem, and to success.

I'm thinking now of Anne, who comes from a long line of destructive drunks. Her grandfather and grandmother had a violent relationship, where they'd get drunk and he'd beat her.

Her mother and father were also drunks together, of the falling-off-the-bar-stool variety, but never engaged violence.

Anne herself was not an alcoholic—her "addiction" was a bit different. It circled around "healing" the partner-alcoholics she managed to find over and again. In common language, it's called co-dependency.

So, as might be expected, Anne married a drunk.

Now, he never hit her the way granddad hit grandma, nor did he drink in that sloppy way mom and dad did. It seemed as if down through the generations, things were getting better.

Anne spent many years trying to "cure" her husband Spencer of his problem. Naturally, fixing him was really all about Anne fixing her own history. As well established by this point in *Our Love Matters,* this never works.

In any event, even three kids later, divorce was inevitable.

After her divorce, Anne began dating a charming, seemingly "regular" man without apparent addiction issues. One day, she called to announce: "You won't believe it—Dave just let me know he's alcoholic! How did I manage to attract that again, and why didn't I know?"

Did Anne *want* a sober man? Part of her did. But her psyche was more intent on healing original wounds than anything else. Finally, Anne did the challenging and gorgeous inside work called for, healed her *inner father/mother relationship*, and eventually married a lovely non-alcoholic partner.

If we can do it, so can you.

How?

Start with the above-offered premise: Assume you have in your life what you intend to have. I know, I know. Ouch. Stick with me here though. Because not *all* parts of you are bent on maintaining your loneliness or stuckness in whatever area. Yes, there is an aspect choosing awful partners or refusing choice at all (or refusing health, success, visibility, financial security, etc.). But other parts *do* want it to be different. I can say this unequivocally because you're reading this book about change! Now, of course, if you actually do the recommended work that will be proof positive.

Begin with the idea that the rejecting voice inside is only **one aspect**—like a single character in a film or in a television series. Sure, they may be the lead at this point, but not forever.

All right, here's a four-part change process.

Follow the yellow-brick road to great understanding of self:

Part 1: TRUTH-TELLING: Everything will begin with this. Here's an example:

Start with the current "facts."

Current Position/the Idea: I say I want love but I don't have love.

New Truth: Part of me *does not* want love (as indicated by the dead termites littering the sill).

Again, this part not really wanting love (or money, success, good friends, etc.) is only one facet holding you back from fulfilling desire. It doesn't mean you've been lying, only that you've been blind to the whole picture.

Part 2: THE PAYOFF: The next step requires that you consider the consequence of NOT having what you've been saying you want. Again—the payoff will be found in actuality. If you want to know why you're doing what you're doing, simply *look at the results of your actions.* Let's take something a little easier than love. Body weight's a good one. Here's an exploration:

Current Position: I'm fat. I want to be thin. But I keep screwing up my "diet," so I never get to the weight I want. And try as I might, I never seem to find time to exercise.

New Truth: Part of me *doesn't want to be thin* (or doesn't think I deserve to be thin; or is angry because it feels like I have to work harder at it than everyone else).

In this case, an unmet, inner committee member is choosing to undermine weight loss and fitness intentions. The idea is to figure out how this aspect got started thinking the way it thinks and operating the way it operates.

Or here's the Anne example:

Current Position: My parents were alcoholic. So were my grandparents. The last thing I want in my life is an alcoholic partner.

New Truth: Part of me thinks my only option is an alcoholic partner.

Notice that it's important to begin speaking of this so-called "want/intention" as coming from just *a part* of you rather than a report of what the whole of you prefers.

How did this all happen?

WE ALL HOLD IDEAS, ACCUMULATED THROUGH A LIFETIME OF EXPERIENCE. Myths, really, about how and why things work or don't work. It's good to start with understanding what these notions are and how they live inside. Thin/fat is a terrific topic in this regard. Certainly, it's discussed enough. Here to make the point are just a few stats from 2012 on weight loss in America:

- ✓ $20 Billion: The annual revenue of the United States weight-loss industry, including diet books, diet drugs, and weight-loss surgeries.
- ✓ 108 Million: The number of people on diets in the United States. Dieters typically make four to five attempts per year.
- ✓ 85 Percent: The percentage of customers consuming weight-loss products and services who are female.
- ✓ 1 Hour: The amount of time spent on daily exercise by people who lost and kept off at least 30 pounds of excess weight for five years.
- ✓ 220,000: The number of people with morbid obesity in the United States who had bariatric surgery in 2009.
- ✓ $11,500 to $26,000: The average cost of bariatric surgery, which reduces the size of the stomach.
- ✓ $500,000 to $3 million: The average salaries paid to celebrity endorsers of major weight-loss programs.
- ✓ $33,000: The amount of money celebrity endorsers, on average, earn per pound lost.

Thus, the reports about the amount of surgeries targeted for weight loss are staggering, to say nothing of the lasers, ultrasounds, far-out diet plans, pills, and endless products supporting the greatest growth industry we have. I present these statistics merely to emphasize what an often-met topic this is. Again, I'm only using weight as a concrete, easy-to-picture example. Naturally, the topic of love is even more dominant. Yet another reason supporting how consumed we are and how to find it, fix it, or let it go!

Anyway, when it comes to physical appeal we've plenty of images on our various screens to propel and impel us toward what's acceptable and unacceptable. Then, of course, there are dynamic family conversations and attitudes about it.

I'll assume you've accepted the theory that indeed part of you doesn't want what you've been proclaiming. Now, let's get down to the nitty-gritty. As we switch to a conversation about body acceptance and body shame, please note these questions are equally applicable to both men and women. Although, obviously, how women are viewed and view themselves has long been a focus, men's attention to such things is certainly on the rise and has been for quite a while now.

Question #1: What myths might I hold about "thin" people or people without buffed bodies?

A GOOD WAY TO EXPLORE THIS is a fill-in-the–blank procedure as in: Thin people are _____; thin people do _____; thin people feel _____; thin people get _____.

Alternatively, a way to go is: Fat people are _____; fat people do _____; fat people feel _____; fat people get_____.

Or, if you prefer to get right to the love story, substitute appropriate questions as in: Relationships always turn out _____; People in relationships feel _____; about relationships, my parents taught me_____.

The process is to write the *same* lines over and over, filling in the end of the sentences *without thinking* like: "Thin people are all about looks; thin people hate fat people; thin people have all the luck; thin people are dumb." And on it goes. The important answers will come after many, many fill-ins. The temptation is to write a few lines and stop. Instead, try to keep going.

Notice I don't use simple or euphemistic words, such as: overweight, full-figured, plump, zaftig, etc. Not that those don't sometimes apply; however, I find when attempting to embrace new truths the "rude," direct terms are more jarringly effective.

Try it. Come up with your own beginning phrases also and proceed to fill-in-the-blank. Be creative in your approach. The more you do and the further you go the better you'll come to understand the moldy ideas driving your dismal love life.

I'm already squirming…

NONE OF THIS IS LIKELY TO BE COMFORTABLE. We don't grow from a position of comfort. Dig in, do the work, and see the change.

Now, discovering the real **personal payoff** (the hidden problem, dilemma, or fear) requires a series of further in-depth questions. These investigations can be, as indicated, awkward. Keep in mind that the greatest adventures most often require the greatest risks.

Obviously, though, you're going to need to play along with me here—assume I'm onto something and that there's an aspect *purposely* keeping you from what you want. You might as well try it because you know very well nothing else has yet worked.

Okay, here we go.

It often helps to characterize this part, giving the "aspect" a physical picture. In my case, for instance, I see this inner voice as a villainous, tall, skinny guy—the kind who might viciously tie me to train tracks.

Question #2: What's the payoff of not being thin, toned, or buffed? Or put another way: What part of me is being serviced by my hesitation to shift in this area? Or: What's the payoff of not having love (or of suffering with the love life I have)?

FOR EXAMPLE, WHAT IF THERE'S A VOICE IN YOU that believes skinny people are less liked, and not being liked feels like an awful proposition? Or maybe you believe people appearing to have love are just pretending?

This payoff question #2 is called: *How does it serve?*

As mentioned previously, questioning in this way is a well-established tradition in certain psycho-spiritual circles. When engaging such inquiry, we need to throw out the many answers. Keep asking until you have a noteworthy response, such as a chill up the spine, quickening of breath, tear, or something physical of that nature. Your body will tell you when you're "on it."

I'm starting to sweat...

MANY TIMES UNDERMINING IDEAS REMAIN INVISIBLE TO US when we don't know the right questions to ask. Here's a fun, personal, slightly humiliating example of such. For many years, unbeknownst to me, I assiduously held myself back from success. My sabotage was obvious in some ways and covert in others. After I began scraping the crud off my psyche, I discovered my declining to step into full potentiality was connected with an unconscious refusing to let my parents have any credit for doing a good job raising me.

Seriously. Ugh.

So the unconscious thinking was: "I'll be damned if anyone's gonna think I had caring, good parents. If I do really well, everyone's gonna believe it was *them!*" And so, damned I was.

Ridiculous, right?

Embarrassing to realize and admit, too.

Also, though, this recognition was key to change. I mean, even the dullest mind must eventually notice no one gets harmed in that scenario but me.

Oh my.

Years later, when I'd begun emerging from my life of dramatic disaster, my mother actually said to me: "Well, I guess we did a pretty good job!" I had to laugh. By then it didn't so much matter. And even more wonderful is that eventually I came to the profound understanding that my parent's contributions to my success were truly immeasurable—that without each and every childhood action or inaction taken, I'd never have become who I've turned out to be.

So here's the next challenging inquiry as we continue to explore both the body-image question and the love-conflict question:

Question #3: What would/could happen if I manage to have the body I crave? Or: What could happen if I have the love I crave?

EVERY QUESTION LEADS TO ANOTHER EXCELLENT QUESTION. This is a good thing. Like, if I had the body I crave, I'd attract more potential partners. Then what? What if I fall in love and end up abandoned?! I couldn't survive.

In all instances look past "logical" and accept that your psyche might at this point be a tangled delivery system, so the 'irrational' assumptions driving your behaviors are likely to make little intellectual sense. Be bold. Try to entertain the answers without the self-judgment or quick nay-saying that will turn you away at the important eleventh hour.

Question #4: What thinking activates this process and what actions or inactions support that thinking?

NOW THAT WE'VE LAID THE FOUNDATION by gathering plenty of info, it's time to start checking out the *doing* part of our procedures. In this case, we'll consider thinking as a "doing" process, considering how thinking propels action or encourages inaction.

It's important here to be specific. It might be challenging at first to catch those thoughts, like catching fireflies in a bottle. They fly in quickly, nearly escaping. But with diligence, catch them we can.

Those awful thoughts inspire equally awful deeds and before we know it, we're taking a self-sabotaging action or surrendering to a self-defeating inaction. Notice here that what we do is important; however, what we don't do is equally noteworthy.

To figure it all out, the trick is to stay awake and aware. Look at the initiating ideas: those giving you permission to drive the dark road to self-damage. Remember, we're talking here about weight and body image only by example. We could equally use drugs, alcohol, rage, continuing awful job circumstances, terrible relationship choices, and numerous other avenues of discussion. Question #4 asks us to recognize the specific behaviors we take that support our dismal thoughts. These actions inevitably perpetuate awful self-image and terrible self-esteem. Here it's important to acknowledge the ways in which we're not doing the things that *could* be done to change the picture.

A list is helpful.

For example:

- ✓ I think: *What difference does it make? No one cares anyway.*
- ✓ I act on the thinking by: *Eating terrible food; binging; eating late at night.*
- ✓ My inactions include: *Not exercising; watching TV while I eat, which indicates a lack of self-respect and unconsciousness; not cooking for myself.*

Or:

- ✓ I think: *When it comes to love, everyone has it easier than me.*
- ✓ I act on the thinking by: *Comparing myself to others; constantly finding things wrong with whomever approaches me.*
- ✓ My inactions include: *Isolating; not reaching out; refusing to meet new people.*

Wait…what's the point of all this self-sabotage?

REMEMBER WHAT WE'VE BEEN SAYING. The point is to reinforce old ideas about our unlovablity. Why? Because stuckness is familiar. Because we're afraid. Because we know nothing about self-love.

Newsflash: All sabotaging preoccupations are about lack of self-love.

Part 3: Diving Deeper: Real change usually requires drastic measures. That means yet another series of even more confronting questions to be asked. I know: frightening. It's true that genuine transformation isn't quick or easy. And anyone who tells you it is, lies.

It isn't easy, but it's worth it.

Stunner: *What you're doing now is actually harder than change!*

Yes, resistance to fully actualizing our best life is super draining. This circles the long-supported psycho-spiritual precept that *all* suffering is resistance. To realize this truth in a small way, trace back to all the times anticipating the difficult moment or activity was far tougher than the actual event itself. Remember that reunion; the friend confront; asking the boss for a raise? Certainly the advance anxiety, prelude preoccupation, worried anticipation, and halting hesitation were all worse than the experience.

Not infrequently clients call me in the middle of a panic attack so I can talk them back into presence and into their bodies. Inevitably the panic is about something they anticipate is going to happen. When the time comes for the dreaded event it is *never* as awful as the advanced panic advertised.

Breaking free from a lifetime of struggle means letting go of resistance. How? Simple: Do what you've been avoiding—no matter what.

Okay, back to our getting fit example.

Say we blame a bad body, for instance, for missing out on what we imagine to be "the relationship of our dreams." Deepening might take us to: *What if I looked just right and still no perfect prince or princess came along—how would I feel?* Perhaps the awful, bitter-tasting answer would be: "Now I'm really a loser. Now I have proof positive that no one will ever love me."

What a tragic, unbearable notion, and quite untrue.

Newsflash: If you're not in a relationship it's not because you're overweight, unfit, too short, not rich enough, not smart enough, not educated enough, not lucky enough, too old, or anything else; it's because *you're making yourself unavailable.*

As with everything else we could name and blame our lack of partnership on, there are plenty of individuals of every shape, size and age happily finding and having relationships. Indeed, there are even people who *prefer* heavier body-types. So if you're using weight, or anything else, as an excuse to stay alone, get over it. You're lying to yourself as to the *why* of it all. If you don't want a partner, or aren't ready for one at this moment, just admit it.

It's really fine.

Yes. Really.

Or let's try same topic, another direction: I once worked with a 50-something woman, April, who'd gotten quite heavy in the wake of her difficult divorce. She reported to me that she couldn't leave the house to be with friends, as she was too embarrassed to let them see her this way.

The result? Horrible loneliness.

The worse she felt, the more she hid away.

The more she hid away, the more she ate and the worse she felt. Walking this how-does-it-serve discovery path, we'd say April was getting something out of both her self-sabotage and the ensuing lonely feelings.

What might it be?

In April's case, she got to feed her belief that the divorce was all her fault—that she was unlovable and would remain so. In truth, there were profound and undiscovered, early life stumbling blocks to overcome.

How about you? Were you lonely far back as you can remember? Did you feel rejected, unloved, or unlovable in your childhood? Does your current life confirm an early story about lack of deservedness?

Or maybe you're terrified, actually, about having a relationship at all. Perhaps your parents' marriage was so awful you don't (unconsciously) trust yourself to make a go of it. So some part of you figures if you're too physically unappealing, you won't ever have to risk ending up in your parents' relationship. Maybe the opposite is true; your parents' relationship seemed so ideal you can't imagine ever measuring up.

These are called the **Underlying Dynamics**. Thus, fat and other ideas—a flaccid love-life, constant job disasters, and terrible friends—are symptoms only, indicators of deeply held ideas, hesitations, or fears.

4. Exploring Origins (get to the source).

Question #5: Where did all this start? Hmmm...where did I get the idea that thin folks are untrustworthy? Did the idea start with Mother? Father? Society? Or: What were my initial teachings about love?

CLEARLY, THIS QUESTION WILL REQUIRE DEEP DELVING. Let's return to the fitness example: When exploring, recall how mother treated her own body and shape. How did she talk about herself or about others? How did she discuss weight or appearance or beauty to and with you? Same with dad: Did he discuss looks? What did he say? Did they seem to be important? Further, what was going on in school when it came to physicality attitudes? What magazines did you read or look through? What TV shows did you watch? Who were your favorite stars?

You get the drift.

This is a look at environmental impact. While exploring this, check out your own reactions and responses to it all. Go into as much detail as you can manage. If you have old diaries or journals, read them. It's all there—advertising your present-day life.

As stated, our behavioral patterns, and the thinking that goes with those patterns, start when we're kids—so glancing back is essential. What was modeled to you as a child by your parents? A child-development friend used to say: children learn three ways— by example, by example, by example.

Also important, as previously indicated, is recognizing what was going on both locally and globally in the world while you were growing up. For instance, what was the attitude toward body image when you were growing up versus now? Or, in a whole different way, perhaps you've bought into the notion that there's not enough love, money, applause, friends, career opportunities, success, or whatever to go around. It's called holding a notion of *limited supply*. And since you're never going to feel truly satisfied in any of these areas, you figure you might as well satisfy yourself with food, or hide out, or stay in a menial job, or assume poverty etcetera.

I realize these questions are challenging to ask, difficult to answer, and a bear to confront. However, over and again I will tell you: Real change can't happen without discomfort.

Stunner: Whether you're facing your past or not, your past is always facing you.

Easy does it...

OKAY, HERE'S THE TEMPLATE—A STEP-BY-STEP DISCOVERY PATH. Let's shift gears back to the main point, which is our love matters. Drill down to get full, expansive answers. You'll be amazed at what you'll learn about yourself. Now, please don't use the info you come up with like a sledgehammer on yourself. Try being a compassionate witness to your own findings.

We'll start with Anne's story as an example:

- ✓ **The Idea:** It's inevitable that my partners will be alcoholic.
- ✓ **Payoff:** I don't have to really look at myself.
- ✓ **Truth:** I don't believe I deserve dependable love.
- ✓ **Origin:** For generations, family relationships have been undependable.
- ✓ **Underlying Dynamic:** Being with irredeemable alcoholics confirms my belief that I don't deserve more.
- ✓ **Current Behavior:** I assume all partners will disappoint and my only value is to be found in how much or how well I can help them, so I partner with men who "need" me.

Or:

- ✓ **The Idea:** Great love is impossible to find.
- ✓ **Payoff:** Since all love will disappoint, I don't need to really open up and be vulnerable to profound love.
- ✓ **Truth:** I'm afraid I'm unlovable.
- ✓ **Origin:** Mom and Dad fought constantly.
- ✓ **Underlying Dynamic:** I should have been able to fix my parents.
- ✓ **Current Behavior:** I assume I'll never find happy, satisfying love and attract lovers who confirm this.

I'm not trying to put words in your mouth here, only offering a couple question-and-answer examples from which to work.

Yeah, okay, but so what?

HOW DOES KNOWING ALL THIS CHANGE ANYTHING, YOU MIGHT ASK? Well, it does. Understanding true intention, the origins of that intention, and personal ways and means, begins to allow new choices to be considered and eventually affected.

For example: When investigating ideas about physical appeal, you might discover the underlying issues circle around a fear of being unloved and unlovable. You then could realize you're feeding (or starving) a fear that started when Daddy left you at nine years old. And because you conclude that staying unhealthy does not, nor will it ever, offer the love you crave, you realize how self-sabotage is only keeping you tied to your parents. It's called staying (metaphorically) little in our parents' awful house. Now you can begin devising new ways of "filling" yourself.

Newsflash: What keeps us in our sad, bad, troubled relationship to the Self, to others, and to life is primarily our refusal to give up the habitual behaviors that report old beliefs.

Traveling new relationship landscapes requires shifting defensive procedures. It's absolutely time for a change: so do something about it.

Change starts and ends with you.

Getting love specific

I KEEP SAYING THERE IS NO ONE-SIZE-FITS-ALL for a good relationship. There isn't. But what does exist is a find-what-you-need-want-and-deserve template. I call this template **The Six Imperatives** because it's imperative you discover the "how-to" of getting what you want and need when it comes to the 'find it' portion of our love matters program.

6 Imperatives for dating & mating

AN IMPERATIVE IS SOMETHING UNAVOIDABLE AND ESSENTIAL.

It's imperative we have air and water to survive. Without them we quickly die. Most plants need sun, and all need moisture to thrive. All animals require food and water as well.

What's offered here are the air and water for successful dating and mating survival. You might have a couple of your own. Terrific. Build on what's offered.

Get set, ready, go...

First Imperative: BECOME THE PERSON YOU WANT TO DATE. THIS IS CALLED **MIRROR IMAGE.**

A good way to start understanding what this means is to list the essential qualities we picture in an ideal mate. Do you imagine them kind? Proactive? Romantic? Fit? Really, you can put anything on your list you desire. After all, it's your 'wish list.' Make the list as extensive as you can.

Now, note which of the listed desirable qualities you embody. No excuses. Just because you're not in relationship right this minute, doesn't mean you can't evidence these things. The idea with this wish list is to name it, then claim it.

Wow.

Really? Yes.

That means growing and expanding happens *before _and_ during* a partnership because great partnership, like terrific friendship and wonderful work, encourages us to discover our greatest potential and to actualize that potential.

Second Imperative: KNOW YOUR SHORT LIST OF NON-NEGOTIABLES AND STICK TO IT. THESE ARE CALLED: **DEAL BREAKERS.**

You've made your long, extremely complete wish list.

Now, the idea is to take four or maybe five things from that inventory and realize them as non-negotiable. No, the non-negotiable does not encompass the entire catalog. If our record of must-haves is impossibly long, it simply means we don't really want a relationship because, as you may by now realize, no one's perfect.

That's happy news because you're not perfect either.

So keep that Deal Breakers list short and put the rest on a secondary what-I'd-prefer-but-don't-*have*-to-have list. You can choose to have any deal breakers you want. I remember the fabulously gorgeous couple I worked with that both had "Must Hike" on their non-negotiable list. Okay.

Another might say: can't smoke or must believe in God or must have money. Don't let anyone tell you what's right or wrong about your choices. You decide. And try like hell to not shame yourself about what's important to you.

Third Imperative: FORGET GAME-PLAYING. THIS IS CALLED **STRAIGHT SHOOTING.**

Advice that suggests specific don't-and-do rules drives me crazy. Don't call for three days; or never call before they do; or do kiss on the first date; or never kiss on the first date; or…whatever. It's so very important that you find your own way. I know you'd maybe rather have a great this-is-what-always-works answer but…well…there's nothing that *always* works. Except maybe one thing, and you might not like it much: Be authentic.

Be vulnerable.

Don't ration your passion.

I mean it.

Authenticity is the key.

This truth can't be said often enough. Now, imagine trying to be who and what your date needs, as if you know! What happens somewhere down the line when the "true you" shows up? And show up it will. Because wearing a mask or holding ourselves in a fake way cannot be sustained.

It can't.

This reminds me of a terrific client I had while still in early training. She was just barely over 30—beautiful, smart, funny, sexy, and even employed. But she simply couldn't have a relationship that lasted past four or five months.

I was mystified.

I organized my first little group of four participants—two men/two women, including her. The group happened to be homogeneous, everyone being of same age-range, availability, and socially similar.

Our first night was quite a shock. As we got rocking and rolling, I noticed my usually lively client suddenly become shy, reticent, and demure.

Gone was the humor.

Absent was the spark.

Next individual session, I said to her: "What in the world happened?! Who was that?"

She laughed. "Oh that's the way I always am when I first meet guys. Best foot forward, ya know!"

"Uh huh," I replied, "and how long does that continue?"

"Oh, a few months. Until I'm sure they like me."

"Well, there's the source of your problem," I offered. "You're presenting this completely false self, which by the way is far less interesting and engaging than you really are. And when, after a few months, the true *you* bursts through they're astonished and put off. After all, that's not what they signed up for!"

She was stunned, and she got it right away.

After investigating the history supporting this ridiculous (though all-too-common) procedure, the shift this delicious woman made was phenomenal. She vowed and proceeded to "be herself" from the first moment of meeting, no matter how much she liked them (you know, the more attracted we are, the more powerful the mask we tend to adopt). *Very quickly*, she found herself in a wonderful long-term relationship leading to marriage and children.

Naturally, the moral of the story is be as much of yourself as you can be, everywhere with everyone. I know it's scary but after practicing a while, you'll discover how much easier it is to maintain than all those heavy masks.

Fourth Imperative: BELIEVE WHAT THEY SAY. THIS IS CALLED **HEARING AID**.

"I'm not ready for a commitment"; "I have very little time in my life for relationship"; "I'm really focused on my career"; "I'm not a one person, person"; "I'm involved with someone else I'll never leave": These kinds of statements are common communication. They come at us either by word or deed early in a relationship. We too often tend to ignore what these messages inevitably mean.

We can change them, we imagine. Ha.

And then what: What do we suppose that'll mean about us? We're special. We're important. We've proved a value we never really believed we had. We made up for what we didn't get from dad or from mom.

Never happens.

I mean, we may get the guy or gal. They might leave their partner or make time for us or become the ardent admirer we crave, but that still won't prove what we think it will. Because knowing our true worth is an inside job. There's not enough outside accolade, appreciation, attention, approval, or love to fulfill the deep, fundamental longing we've been chasing.

The trick is to turn your hearing aid on loud.

Don't reinterpret what they say and do.

Believe them. If someone's super jealous, try not to assume that means caring. It doesn't. If they call and text a zillion times a day, try realizing they're compulsive. If they ignore your calls for extended periods, hear the unavailability this reports. If they refuse to discuss contraception or sexual safety, recognize their selfishness.

The list of hearing aids is long. Make one for yourself.

Fifth Imperative: Practice Public Presence *(the how-to begins on page____).* THIS IS CALLED **Center Stage.**

Fundamental: Live in your life instead of your head.

The point is to enjoy the journey rather than living in expectation of either the worst or ideal scenario outcome. This imperative asks you not to start picking out a wedding registry dinnerware pattern on the first date. I always get a little concerned with the folks who proclaim, "s/he's the one" right off. After all, as we've well established, the beginning of *all* relationships are mostly projection, meaning we can barely really "see" who we're initially dating. So how can we tell? Besides, if we're all about what will happen down the line, we're not present to what's going on right in front of us.

Oh sure, there are often complicating factors here.

These are the things that help us toward vigilance about good/bad, right/wrong, hurry/wait. For instance, a woman's age pushing her to want to breed soon; stimulating or defeating status or financial parameters; fear of loneliness; desperation; sexual need as well as personal want or doubt. But no matter what the agendas, over-layering concerns, and internal debates, we always need to start by standing front and center in the experience of now.

Sixth Imperative: Walk the talk. THIS IS CALLED **Walkie Talkie.**

If you want to have or find the relationship you've been scouting, realize that *you're* the one holding the compass. Yep. Give what you're asking for. Be the person you want to love. Love who *you* are. I keep shall repeating myself in this because it's the essential ingredient for a fit love life in every area.

So figure out what authenticity, vulnerability, and integrity mean to you. Do for others what you're asking to have done for you.

I thought you'd give me more...

Are you disappointed? Think these six imperatives are too self-centered and not enough about *them*? Well, that's the drill. I shall ring this big bold bell again and again; the source of real power is **You**.

You and your decision to change.

Start doing the heavy lifting...

AS WE HEAD INTO **CHAPTER TWO: PROCEDURES**, CONSIDER THE FOLLOWING VERY CONFRONTING, demanding question: *Where were you standing when you lost the keys to the Self?*

This is a profound inquiry.

It addresses the beginning of loss. It tackles first glimpses at the forming of defenses. It speaks to the great, yawning desperation for love glimpsed or visited or lived in. It requires that we sit still in solitude and silence—wherein the most vital and life-changing questions are posed and answered.

It asks for presence.

I'm not suggesting that you "work" this question or even try to figure out what the question means. Just feel it rolling around on your tongue or traveling down your throat and into your body. Simply allow it to sit in your psyche the way a stained shirt might soak in solution.

I realize you've been struggling—brawling with and against your backdrop story. Trying with all your might to fashion the life you desire. Kicking and stomping, or huffing and puffing, as you hack away at the weeds growing across your path. But really, is that so? Have you been holding the most life-enhancing perspective all this time? I'd say no.

Perception is the key...

Amazing poet Rainier Maria Rilke tells us:

> Only those sorrows are dangerous and bad which we carry about among our fellows in order to drown them; like diseases which are superficially and foolishly treated, they only recede and break out after a short interval all the more frightfully; and gather themselves in our inwards, and are life, are unlived, disdained, lost life, of which one can die. If it were possible for us to see further

than our knowledge extends and out a little over the outworks of our surmising, perhaps we should then bear our sorrows with greater confidence than our joys. For they are the moments when something new, something unknown, has entered into us; our feelings grow dumb with shy confusion, everything in us retires, a stillness supervenes, and the new thing that no one knows stands silent there in the midst. I believe that almost all our sorrows are moments of tension which we experience as paralysis, because we not longer hear our own estranged feelings living.[xxxv]

THE SOLUTION TO OUR ATTITUDE TOWARD "SUFFERING" IS TO REALIZE WHAT CAN BE AND HAS BEEN <u>GAINED</u> THROUGH DIFFICULTY.

This truly, then, is the seminal question to address: *What have we learned and what are we learning?* Ask yourself this question every day. Begin by entertaining the idea I keep pushing that even the most seemingly devastating experiences have something to offer. We're exactly who we are today because of each and every one of our terrible trials. Trying to eliminate any of them would be attempting to remove a few lower bricks from a building structure.

The whole construction collapses.

Recently, a dear filmmaker associate of mine offered a wonderful metaphor about all this. He said with regard to our histories and the life we pursue in light of those stories:

> If two different directors make the same movie, following the same script, you would get two totally different movies. Same script, different stories. Your life is your movie and the question becomes: How do you want to direct it? How do you want to interpret your movie? Do you want to tell a positive story, a hopeful movie, or do you want to live in a dark movie? How do you choose to experience your life—stuck in the trauma or dancing with passion? It's entirely up to you what movie you decide to live and direct. Be creative, delve into the story, be a director—the important thing is to realize there are choices. [xxxvi]

CHAPTER TWO
PROCEDURES

For one human being to love another human being: That is perhaps the most difficult task that has been given to us, the ultimate, the final problem and proof, the work for which all other work is merely preparation.
- Rainier Maria Rilke [xxxvii]

- FIND IT –

Finding and having "the" love you crave means understanding previously hidden motivations followed by taking new actions.
Learn how here and now.

PART I: DEFENDING YOUR DREADFUL LIFE

H ERE COMES THE HEAVY LIFTING as we plummet more aggressively into the **how-to's**: how to find new love, how to revive the struggling love you've already found, or even how to stop your involvement with a go-nowhere love now present in your hapless life. Let's begin with a reminder that real change takes real action. I mean it. Talking or thinking about what needs to shift is one thing. *Doing* something about it all is quite another. If you sincerely want to have a quality relationship, in you will dive. And during that plunge, remember to come up for celebratory air.

As we move along, we'll be realizing the value of three areas:

✓ Presence
✓ Perspective
✓ Vulnerability

Oh good...change NOW! Let's get to it...

RIGHT OFF THE BAT, IT'S IMPORTANT TO UNDERSTAND change does not, cannot, and will not happen all at once. That means there's not some one astonishing revelation or ah-ha moment companioned by profound understanding and even accompanied by obvious solution that then changes everything forever. This is a common misunderstanding. Mostly, we don't even know we're thinking that way—until some awful disappointment kicks in and we suddenly find ourselves back at what feels like square one.

First, all realizations and insights, as well as revelations and ah-ha moments, are only doorways to change. And just like any doorway, even once opened, it's simply an invitation to enter.

Ugh. Really?

Yes, but that doesn't mean those entryways are unimportant; it merely means they're not the end of the road. Actually, these recognitions are basically announcements of what's (psychologically) afoot.

Let me give an extreme couple example of how realizations can be doorways not only challenging us as individuals, but huge confrontations in relationships. This great story is a terrific, albeit extreme, example of how "finding it" is never the end of the road...

Many, many years ago I worked with a charming woman named Lily, who was once married and at that point a single mother, seeking new love.

Lily felt reasonably satisfied in her career; however, for her love was life's main aim and purpose. Clearly, career interest was always going to take a backseat. As I keep saying to you, not all paths are the same for all people. You get to decide what takes precedence.

One day, Lily arrived to announce she'd met a delightful man––handsome, kind, and smart. She was thrilled. Over time, the relationship progressed nicely and they fell deeply in love. And then something truly unimaginable happened. One day Lily walked into their shared home to find her beloved, Frank, dressed in women's underwear.

Lily was stunned, and then appalled.

What did this mean?

As the story unfolded, it turned out Frank was a cross-dresser and had, in fact, been so all his life. Now, as quickly came forward, 80% of cross-dressers are heterosexual, so Frank's attraction to Lily wasn't at all the issue. What was front and center, though, was that poor Frank had for much of his life kept his proclivities a secret and right up until and including that moment of being discovered, he had great shame about it all.

Needless to say, Lily immediately bumped up against many of her own conflicting feelings.

They began therapy together, plus I started working with Frank individually. It really didn't take Lily long to decide she could live with Frank's need because in the face of all he brought to the relationship party, this "issue" seemed minor. Obviously, not everyone would be able to feel this way.

There's no right or wrong here.

You get to decide what can work for you. This is a vitally important point I shall continue to emphasize. We keep thinking there's a right and wrong way to proceed toward and with love. There isn't.

Over time, Frank got more and more comfortable with accommodating his desires. He'd often worn women's underwear under his "man" clothes when going to work, but now it became an everyday event.

Eventually, Frank wanted to go out "dressed up." He did so at first by himself.

Cut to: Frank began asking Lily to accompany him in public as he dressed completely like a woman. As you might imagine, this initially was quite confronting for her. Being heterosexual herself, Lily was confused about both feelings and appearances. But again, because of her deep, abiding, and ever-growing love for him, she accommodated.

Let's skip along in our story: Over time, Frank and Lily got used to being together with him cross-dressing all of the time. Then, another unpredicted thing occurred. Frank began discovering this process was not enough. Slowly, but surely, he realized he actually wanted to *be* a woman. He began hormone therapy.

I'll jump in the tale to tell you that two major events then occurred: first, Lily and Frank married; second, eventually Frank became Frankie by having a full sexual realignment. As you might imagine, all along the way there were tremendous adjustments needed for Lily, who now, much to her surprise, found herself married to a woman.

Perhaps it will amaze you to know that this couple continues thriving in love. With great effort and a ferocious ability for unconditional acceptance, as well as a fulfilled intention to profoundly address what they each considered a priority, they found the soul of their relationship. Frankie fulfilled her version of self-love, which allowed her, actually, to become hugely successful in her career and in her marriage—while Lily decided, after immense application, that love wanted to trump all other preoccupations and previously accepted notions of right and/or wrong love.

Makes me think I have no real love quandaries!

OBVIOUSLY, EVERYONE'S LOVE STORY IS NOT THIS RADICALLY CHALLENGING. But the truth is, when it's *our* story, it feels just as extreme. Really though, it's best to think of learning real love like preparing to throw a party. First, we establish the party occasion and decide upon a date. Then we send out a save-the-date to potential party participants. I'd call this part of the procedure having a realization or insight; an example might be noticing how we keep getting into unhealthy relationships over and over. This realization/insight might even include a smart recognition such as: "*Oh my, everyone I date is emotionally unavailable just like my father! How did I not notice that before?*" At that point, we've marked our calendar so we can more consciously continue party planning as the event approaches.

Now it's time to send out the actual party invites and because we've been paying attention, and perhaps doing some internal investigation, an ah-ha moment might happen: "*Wow—the point is I keep partnering with daddy because if I can get him to notice and deeply appreciate me as special, I'll feel a worthiness I've never felt*"; "*I'm still heartbroken because I never really felt dad's love, so now all I think I deserve is repeated heartbreak*"; "*I'm out to prove to myself that all men are as lousy, unreliable, and incompetent as my father was!*"

Naturally, there are numerous other possible iterations.

In any event, most tend to feel coming to a profound conclusion is the end of processing. Not in the least. Now, in fact, it's time for the actual party to occur. The plans are made, the decorations bought, the food ordered, and the stage set. In this case, it means *feeling* the sometimes heart-wrenching or infuriating or fear-provoking effects of the original hurt.

Some party, huh?

Oh yeah, and then there's what everything looks like after the party. At that point it's necessary to realize there's still cleanup to do. Some of the mess will want to be thrown out. Other precious items will need putting away. Oh and there's the gifts brought to the party. You'll want to open those gifts and enjoy the surprise they offer. As always, some gifts will be less to your taste, while other gifts will wow you, bringing broad smiles. The greatest gifts you'll want to start using right away, as storing them in a secret drawer or closet for eventual 'special occasion' use will serve you less.

Finally, there'll be thank-you cards to write or gratitude calls to make. And then the realization—deeply, profoundly, and hopefully with some appreciation—that this is far from the last such party you're likely ever to throw. In fact, it occurs to you that the next "big birthday," you'll want to do it all over again—because by then you'll be somewhere else along the road, have fresh outlook realizations, and maybe even fabulous additional new friends to invite.

We can call such experiences **stage change** events. These proceedings happen, fingers crossed, at different phases in our lives.

Stage change...sounds dicey?

INDEED, AS IT TURNS OUT WE CONTINUE EVOLVING (more or less depending upon our intent) at different levels in various periods of our lives. A 15-year-old isn't going to explore the Self the way a 50-year-old can. And even defined pattern themes are approached differently at different ages and growth stages.

Another way to understand how it works is by looking at child development. When a child first starts talking it's basically indecipherable, with perhaps a few cogent words dropped amongst the sound weeds. We don't require them to assign meaning or to articulately put things together when they first start speaking. Their brains need to get better at recognizing connections and we know that. Eventually, through practice, there's an increased ability to form full sentences.

All of life is like this. What we can do at one stage we simply can't do at an earlier time—because we're not organically ready. It does us no good berating ourselves over this. You wouldn't scream at the child to speak before he can, right? And though there may exist some anticipation of timing based on overall statistics, we certainly don't mark our calendars precisely as to when we expect it all to occur.

On the other hand, we also don't want to glue the child's lips together so they can't talk at all. And when we don't explore fresh possibility, we're doing just that.

Stunner: There's no "I'm done" point when it comes to change.

This is good news—because it means that discovery can happen right up until the last minute. Again, what we can discover at 20 is not the same as at 30 or 40 or 80. So the next time you feel like you're simply re-visiting old themes you supposedly unearthed and "conquered" previously, realize those topic matters can now be explored from yet another angle and with even more elegant results. Besides, we only have those three or four themes we're circling around forever, so naturally we're going to re-visit them. In that way we live all our lives, as it were, in a psychological cul-de-sac.

That doesn't mean you're at the beginning when reviewing the same dynamic. You haven't failed and that doesn't indicate you've learned nothing.

It simply says: Welcome to a new stage.

Thus, change occurs in more of an upward moving spiral than a linear fashion. When we're on the back end of the spiral, we inevitably feel as if we know nothing and have accomplished little. Thing is: The spiral *is* moving upward. We're truly not at all where we began.

Presence: be here now

WHEN IT COMES TO CHANGE, everywhere we look we find the widely touted idea of **Be Here Now**. It's everyone's Fundamental.

Every stage change is best companioned by three kinds of presence: a) Mind Presence; b) Body Presence; c) Heart Presence. Probably, at this point, you won't be able or even be interested in managing all three at once. I speak of them only to raise awareness. The plus-one is True Self/Divine Presence. We will touch on this briefly.

But what the heck does presence mean anyway?

Let's start with a definition.

The excellent 1979 Jerzy Kozinsky film, *Being There*, gave us a wonderful example of what presence means (a great film to rent is you haven't seen it). In this book and film, lead character, Chauncy Gardener, spends his life attending completely to the moment in front of him. He doesn't do this to be smart, Zen, or manipulative. He does this because the simplicity of his life (and of his interior psychological system) has given him no pre-formed interactive tools. He simply reflects like a mirror those with whom he speaks. And since most people are hugely attached to their own thoughts and perspectives, this reflecting makes others think him brilliant. Over and again throughout the film, Chauncey drags the thread of his just-learned ideas into subsequent interactions. He never travels too far back, nor does he get ahead of himself. He stays exactly where he is.

Because Chauncey is "being there," he's entirely freed of anxiety. Indeed, fretfulness, as perhaps you're beginning to realize through our earlier conversation about control, is all about how things are *going* to turn out rather than how they're going right this minute. And because we can't really *know* what turns and twists await us at the end of the road, our worry is heightened. The more we focus on tomorrow, the more angst we have today.

Thus, we might say: Presence means being exactly where you are while you're there. *This* moment, then, becomes the *only* moment of importance.

Of course, this suggests when we're walking through the market we're not texting or talking on the phone. And when we're driving we're not answering emails. Or while we're eating we're not watching television. It means when our lover is talking to us we're not making tomorrow's to-do list in our head.

A great deal to ask, I know.

I'll be repeatedly addressing the concept of presence throughout the rest of this book. Why? Down through the ages, every spiritual procedure that ever was emphasizes this *practice presence* mandate. In modern times, well-respected teachers, coaches, gurus, psychologists, and psychotherapists have stressed this as well. All with good reason, I assure you—because it's the first inescapable rule for creating a truly stellar life.

Wait, I thought you were going to tell me how to find a terrific relationship?

I AM! THIS IS IT. Because the first rule of having a fabulous relationship is: **Become the person you want to be in relationship with.**

At best, that shall include presence.

Mind presence...

THERE'S NO DENYING IT: The mind is a wondrous and delicious vehicle for investigation, insight, discovery, determination, and inspiration. A good mind is an honor to possess and a pleasure to witness. However, when it comes to presence, deciding the mind to be of ultimate importance—and thus leading always with brain power—has caused us to lose our collective way. Living in our brains doesn't mean we're truly connected to anything outside ourselves—or, in fact, connected to any profound inside conversation either—for certainly the brain can help us be both superficial and self-centered. It's called being small-minded. We can be hugely smart and small-minded. We can be deliciously insightful and also heart-selfish.

So how, then, does the brain stand in the way of presence? Multi-tasking, work pressures, control issues, worry about the future, and clouds of depression are only a few of the barriers to being-here-now. Actually, it's easier to avoid, deny, ignore, or overwhelm presence than it is to attend to it. We've lots of practice. And even more societal support.

Great examples of our long travel away from the essential presence healing practice come to us through daily news stories all the time: tales about young children left home alone to fend for themselves; or stranded with a parent so depressed they get no attention; ignoring our friend whom we've met for dinner because it's so very important that we text; obsessing so much over the outcome of an upcoming talk or experience that we forget to attend situations directly in front of us; even a recent story of a baby forgotten in the back seat of a car because Daddy was so preoccupied with work, he neglected to drop him off at school *and didn't notice* 'til the school called the mom and furious Mom called him.

Think of yourself as a hoarder living in a house filled to the brim with stuff. Your life is the house and your busy mind the hoarder. Up 'til now you've been too embarrassed to invite anyone over or even if you did, no one could easily make their way across the floor. Now you could blame the house for not being big enough to hold your possessions, or blame people for being unable to negotiate the territory, or even blame your mother who passed down to you many of the items. But really, the only effective thing to do is to clean up your own mess. Make room for others to come in, all the while remembering it's *your house*. And when you do that, in they will come.

No matter what, the least effective thing to do would be waiting around for the mysterious stranger who will know just what the house needs and fix it all.

So, get cracking—time to clean up.

Indeed, we can easily spot lack of presence anywhere and everywhere—including in our own heads and beds.

But what about planning for the future? What about dreams?

OKAY, SETTLE DOWN. You're moving into what's called ego mind again. Just because we're not in charge of the outcome, the way our ego mind might wish, in no way indicates we must give up future intentions. Make those plans. Pen those lists. Imagine a path to success in all areas. However, once charted, settle into the task, conversation, or experience at hand. In other words, *enjoy the journey* instead of being the kid who says are we there yet? Are we there yet? Are we there yet?

Ever arrive at a destination with absolutely no memory of how you got there? We get so brain-busy we run entirely on automatic. That, too, is an example of a lack of presence.

Another way to look at it is that having hopes, wishes, and plans, but at the same time remaining present is a bit like setting the GPS guide. We put in the information, with the right address, and off we go. When it's time to turn, we do so. What we don't do is spend our whole drive wondering: *"When's* the turn? *Where's* the turn? *What* will the turn be like?"

Instead, watch the road directly in front of you.

How Does It Work?

PRACTICING PRESENCE WILL *ABSOLUTELY CHANGE EVERY ASPECT OF YOUR LIFE*—if, of course, you actually do the practices. There's two primary ways to practice presence: a) with others b) by yourself. Both exercises are detailed in the *Love Works* chapter. Try them. You'll be surprised, and perhaps even amazed, by the happy results. Still, because this topic is essential to proceeding well along our healing path, we will begin a brief exploration now.

When it comes to practicing presence while with others, fabulous listening is the key.

Great listening can be described as *Responsive Listening.* Turns out the first rule of hearing other people is to stop all our own inner jabber. That's right. To hear them we need to refuse, at least momentarily, to be enamored, overwhelmed, or distracted by our own brain noise.

Not so easy for most of us.

To make this happen, it's important to first address what's going on in your mind while the other person is talking. Do you wander off into your own life? Are you busy considering your brilliant comeback? Are you imagining what you'd rather be doing? Are you scheming about what the two of you can do later?

Anything that takes you out of, as we've established, "being there" undermines the collaborative moment. And that's what good listening is—collaboration. Needless to say, lack of listening presence is a quick way to slice and dice intimate relationships—

let alone great interaction between you and the boss, or terrific sharing between you and your friend. Indeed, being a great listener serves every aspect of life.

The idea is to keep our thoughts focused on the matters at hand. (Again, check out how-to in the *Love Works* chapter at end of book.)

While truly attending, it's helpful to communicate our good listening through look and sound, which are called *reflection* and *echo*. When we're really paying attention, these very natural reactions don't need to be forced. The speaker's sadness is reflected in our face. Their astonishment is heard in our brief gasp. We do it all the time with babies.

It's organic.

Thus, *Responsive Listening* includes both reflection and echoing. Now, because we're truly present and not wandering off into self-centered-thought-land, it's simple to interact with the speaker. And when we're doing that we can easily incorporate the best tool of all time when it comes to fabulous listening, which is called: *Repetition*. Often, we say things like: *I hear you; I understand; I get it*. These are all fine, but they're not at all the same. The trick here is to use the speaker's exact words—their *exact* words. You don't need to be creative or instructive. No helping or inventing, just repeating.

The speaker gets it: he or she knows you're listening because you've reported their words back to them.

At first this might seem to be a clunky process but really it's not quite as cumbersome as it sounds because the words can be weaved in, like a ribbon into a braid.

It works like this: they say "I was so hurt," and you respond "Yeah, I understand you got hurt." It's that simple; however, you might be surprised at how hard it is at first to maintain.

And then, with practice, it gets easy. That's when we can feel the rightness of it.

Once you've mastered the art of repetition, you can shift to *Active Listening*—where the idea is to move the speaker's story forward with your on-point questions. At this point we use the speaker's *precise words* and include a responsive inquiry.

For example, they say: "*I was at this party, which you know I don't love to begin with, and I was dancing with this total stranger...*" And you say: "*So, you were dancing with a stranger! Wow, I know that's tough for you. Were you scared?*" Or they offer: "*What a lousy day I had!*" And you reply: "*Really—a lousy day...in what way?*"

Active Listening involves:

- ✓ Repetition, including exact words
- ✓ Echoing and reflecting
- ✓ Curious story advancing

Most likely, both responsive and active listening procedures sound simplistic, but you'll be surprised how amazingly effective they are—and how much harder it is to remember to do them than you might imagine when reading these easy instructions.

By the by to jump ahead for a minute to the "fix it" portion of the program, this repetition and active taking-heed practice is astonishingly effective in primary relationships. There we are with our beloved in an argument...again.

We are feeling unheard and unmet...again.

What do we do?

Start by listening: That means you must stop making your point long enough to actually *hear* what's being said to you. Now, echo, reflect, and repeat. Put aside your assumptions and your I-know-exactly-where-this-is-going and instead ask questions. This procedure will surprisingly curtail the length, breath, and scope of the fight.

Quite often, all we want is to be heard.

Whether it's with a friend, lover, boss, employee, or banker, you'll find the individual with whom you're speaking truly feels heard when you repeat and reflect because *you actually must hear* them in order to effectively and correctly recap.

But—as they say on those shopping shows—there's more.

While the repetition exercise slows down our rapid-fire mind and anxiety-laden planning of a comeback, it means usual reactivity's become more measured. We tend to less often spiral out of control—less fighting, less reactivity, and more connection.

Terrific, right?

Well, yes. Unless, of course, avoiding deeper connection turns out to be (unconsciously) what we've been aiming for all along. Remember that other **Fundamental:** We have what we intend (whether we know it or not). For real change, we need to recognize our true intentions and shift those intentions.

And when I'm alone?

PRACTICING **PUBLIC** PRESENCE is all fine and good as far as it goes—but how do we actually improve our ability to be present to and for ourselves? In a way, that's even more daunting. After all, when by ourselves it's so very easy to roam our fantasy future or obsess regretfully about yesterday. We can even idealize the past, imagining it as the best of days—whether that at all resembles truth.

Certainly, it's too tempting to want to be wherever we're not.

Luckily though, practicing presence can also happen when we're alone. Such a process will most often involve the senses, meaning presence is a **living** process—a practicing of aliveness. And as such, presence is what we call *body-full* or *bodiful,* which means at best presence brings us into contact with our body-selves.

Body presence will be further discussed below.

Once beginning to brave contact with the body-self, and that physical self-connection with the environment, we're perhaps ready for an even deeper dive. Now, you might very well want to wait until the end of this book using the *Love Works* chapter to try this private presence practice; however, I'm going to offer just the beginning of instruction now. I do this primarily because I consider this particular endeavor fundamental to all other efforts. After all, if we can't be with ourselves sincerely, how can we expect to be entirely, enthusiastically, and authentically with others?

The first "rule" of practicing private presence will involve silence. Silence is something in today's busy, bustling world most of us know little about, and have even less interest in discovering. It took me a long time to appreciate and allow silence, so I entirely understand the hesitation. Once there though, you'll never turn back.

I'm not suggesting you immediately entertain such an adventure daily, but rather try it perhaps a half-dozen times. What's the worst that could happen? I promise noise will still be just a glance away and you can easily re-enter racket should silence be too challenging or unsatisfying.

Turn everything off.

No phones.

No computer.

No radio.

No television.

Oh, and by the way, if total silence feels like a completely awful idea, you can start this process with a background of patient, easy, wordless music. There are countless "meditation" albums from which to choose.

Now find a private, quiet spot—either in-home or somewhere that delights. Get completely comfortable. Lean back. Settle in. As an entirely new process, this might at first seem impossible, but give it a shot.

Close your eyes.

Try imagining yourself approaching a beautiful, deep, calm body of water—perhaps an ocean into which you are choosing to dive.

Start breathing in your nose and out your mouth.

Let all concern or anxiety or fear leave you.

Breathe.

Nothing terrible can happen in this experience.

Breathe.

Know that you are entirely safe in this moment.

Breathe.

Imagine a slippery waterslide inside. Choose a simple word to let gently roll down the slide—like peace, or how about love.

Just breathe this way for a long time.

No hurry.

No plan.

Simple.

If words or thoughts come in, let them move on through like clouds. You're not attaching to the word-thoughts or developing them. If you think, "I'm hungry," that's fine—but don't develop a lunch menu in your mind. Just notice the idea and go back to focusing on your breath.

Guess what?

You're tiptoeing into meditation!

Yep. Focus and presence are two meditation aims. Meditation brings you into the experience of presence we've been addressing. And from my perspective, it doesn't need to be fancy. Washing dishes in a focused way can be meditative. Petting your cat can be hugely meditative. You don't *have* to sit in a perfect position or in an ideal place. Your eyes don't need to be closed. Maybe you simply can't "empty" your mind the way everyone says you're supposed to.

Forget about it.

Do the doable.

This idea of **doing what can be done**, rather than constantly berating yourself for what's not accomplished, is pivotal to all my teachings. I want us to celebrate our wins, not constantly diminish steps taken by moving to "not-enoughness."

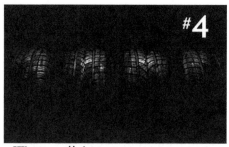

WHEEL # 4: PRACTICE PRESENCE

THE FINAL WHEEL ON YOUR BASICS-FOR-CHANGE VEHICLE suggests that you try all the presence tools enumerated here and in the *Love Works* chapter exercises. Don't dismiss any of them immediately. Nibble everything first, discarding what's not to your taste later.

Yeah, but I feel like I don't have a minute to spare…

I REALIZE THAT PRACTICING PRESENCE MIGHT VERY WELL FEEL IMPOSSIBLE. It seems like the odds are against us. How can that possibly happen in our busy, crammed-to-the-ceiling world? It can, but it takes a firm decision. The truth is we always find time for those things we deem as priorities: time to date that new potential love; time to go to that friend's party.

So there's little excuse for refusing to practice presence. In fact, of all the things we do with our time—the have-to and must-goes—this is where we have most true authority. *We* get to decide how clearly, consistently, and insistently we stand for…whatever. To discover that stance, we best go inside where all the most valuable answers live.

Yes, it's true.

Stunner: The most effective solutions for how to live a quality life live *inside you*.

So ask yourself this question: *Where do I stand and what do I stand for?* Ask it again and again. Over time, the answer is likely to change. How exciting: It's called having an examined life.

Yeah, but the world seems like an unholy mess!

I KNOW THERE'S A GREAT DEAL OF COMPLAINT ABOUT THE STATE OF THE WORLD.

Newsflash: Society only reflects the trends and tendencies rising up from within *us*.

Indeed, it turns out *we* are the society about which we complain. We're the instigators, as well as the inspiration for all that goes on around us. It's like we're Magic 8-balls and media in all its forms reports the Shake 'n Bake answers that bubble to the surface. If you don't like what you see outside, best check out what's going on inside.

In fact, even visible national and international "explosions" are far from irrelevant to each of us. They're expressions *of* us. For example, terrorists are not some vague far-away little-known group we shall never actually meet, but rather manifestations of who and how we are. Ever met a bully? Ever been a bully? *Bully* is actually a less "political" word for terrorist.

Look around.

Look in the mirror.

In fact, try asking yourself: *How does the terrorist live in me? How do I bully myself? How and when do I terrorize those in my life?*

Though these are unpleasant and even threatening suggestions, I bring them forward now to invite a more thorough appreciation of how vital it is we attend to personal change. I know you're reading *Our Love Matters* primarily because you want an improved love life, which naturally I want for you as well; however, there's more to this love business than first meets the eye. These profound how-does-who-I-am-affect-the-world-around-me questions are essential investigations.

They change us.

They change who and how we love.

They change the world.

All this means that just as we project onto partners, friends, and bosses, we also project our inside wants, needs, and perspectives onto the world stage. What happens in the world being a true reflection of what goes on inside us casts yet another vote for taking full responsibility for ourselves, rather than passing the buck blame to society for what ails us as individuals.

Fundamental: Everything *appearing* outside us is actually inside us.

Tying to ignore or throw away any particular element of the encountered Self, no matter how ugly it first appears, never serves in the long run. Besides, the more we deny or reject what leaves a bitter taste on our lips, the more likely it is we'll find some version of that nasty in our office, our friend circle, or, oh lord, sleeping in our beds.

This brings forward something we can call the **Inclusivity Concept,** which is the idea that we ourselves—each one of us—actually have *every quality in the world, known or unknown.*

I promise.

Inside each of us, whether we acknowledge it or not, lives a saint, a sinner, a murderer, a creator, kindness, cruelty, flakiness, consistency, faith, doubt, fidelity, and infidelity—and on it goes.[8]

---

[8] In Jungian terms, this is called the Shadow, which is aspects of the Self disowned, rejected, ignored, or denied. I mention this only briefly here, but later it becomes more vividly important to understand as a huge element in the "fix it" portion of our relationship work.

This might sound bad to you, but it isn't.

It means we're even more connected to each other than imagined. It allows us to be far less judgmental, irritable, and discontented with some digging. The brash finger-pointing could abate. Further understanding might arrive.

Mahatma Gandhi said it beautifully:

> It is unwise to be too sure of one's own wisdom. It is healthy to be reminded that the strongest might weaken and the wisest might err.

Thus, though we may not play out or reveal certain aspects, attitudes, or actions even to ourselves, they do exist. Before you run like hell, let me reinforce that it is these similarities with all living creatures that allow us to move toward: compassion, comprehension, and correspondence—wonderful enhancements to our humanity.

Let's look at one of my favorite examples: Compulsivity.

It's everywhere, right? It shows up clearly with alcohol and drugs, cigarette smoking, sex, gambling, body image preoccupation, food, Internet usage, and the like. Also, it appears more subtly sometimes as over-working, gaming, and now texting—which has become such a do-it-now obsession, that folks are dying over it! Literally. In fact, texting is a terrific example of how compulsivity always trains its focus on immediate gratification, while refusing to take a nanosecond to consider the long-view. Guess we need to ask ourselves if satisfying the right-now urge by driving while texting is worth crashing or even dying, as recently a client of mine did. Of course, the teenager in us thinks we're the exception not the rule.

Others will crash, but we won't. Is that *I'm-special* or the omnipotent perspective we earlier discussed? Perhaps. In any event, it's an attitude that all too often now proves deadly.

When compulsivity is used in the relentless pursuit of drugs and alcohol, it can also have disastrous results. Nor is compulsivity dandy when it takes us into a work-style that robs us completely of balance. On the other hand, when compulsivity is employed to encourage serious effort, frequent exercise, or creative pursuits, it can be a wonderful ally. Similarly, being an awful, terrorizing self-bully can be modified into a gentle voice encouraging improvement. Point is: *Every problem includes a promise.* The trick is to learn to separate the promise from the problem, so we can get the goods.

Oh sure, you'll need to know how to access the aforementioned compassion, comprehension, and correspondence, but happily this invaluable information is coming up soon, so stay tuned.

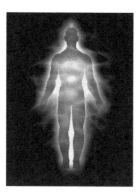

Body presence

I WANT TO TALK ABOUT BODY PRESENCE TWO WAYS: The Physical Body and The Emotional Body. In fact, most people are completely disconnected from their Physical bodies. Really, they're more like severed heads floating through life. Ever have that experience where you're watching yourself have sex?

Not so great, huh?

And by the way, lest you protest this detached-from-the-body idea based on the fact that you're fit: Just because you've shaped your body—or carved it like a pumpkin, managed it with diet, exercise, even surgery—doesn't mean you're connected to it.

Nope.

Actually, many who spend great amounts of time forming or attempting 'perfect' physical shapes are the most cut-off, for they see the body more as moldable clay rather than as a luscious vehicle to house the soul. Naturally, not all fit folks match this disconnected description.

In any event, the general consensus these days is it's all about brainpower—and as previously covered, technology gives a helping hand to this idea. Indeed, we have Internet love, email love, and, oh my, texting "love."

Let me pause to again discuss this incredible, often wonderfully convenient, world of sexting in yet another way. Sure, tremendous excitement can be generated when, while in our fertile brains, we surround what we're writing with juicy images and imagine how the words will be received. But sexting in any form sets everyone involved up for potentially disastrous consequences. Get caught and you can lose your job, status, or relationship. Plus, once it's out there, it's out there—those pictures, those words.

And worse still, this is simply not about love.

It may be about getting a surge of stimulation or feeling (apparently) connected without all the fuss and muss or "real" interaction—or diving into your own rich fantasy life or trying to make sure you're remembered. Whatever it's about, it's guaranteed to fall short in the true-satisfaction department.

So pay attention to what you text or email. What's your sincere intention?

Remember first, at all times, we read texts and emails in *our* own voice and interpret accordingly. This, then, invites huge projection. But more importantly, whatever dialogue you might want to offer can be better, more effectively, and more authentically said *to* them in person.

Let me add, however, if you're in a committed relationship sexting can be a revitalizing expression—occasionally. Not while driving, and not instead of true in-person expressions of love and excitement.

Anyway, we also have Facebook revelations, Tweets, and Instagrams that cover every second of our days. We even have something called Talking Heads:

> The image of a person, as on a television documentary or news show, who talks at length directly to the camera and usually appears on the screen with only the head and upper part of the body visible. [xxxviii]

Indeed, everywhere we turn brain power is elevated and amplified. But did you know the body has a mind of its own? The body has wisdom.

Here's a story: I was on a retreat trip with my teacher Brugh Joy in Colorado. We were camping outdoors and rafting the Colorado River—quite the challenge for a not-so-much-about-nature person like me. Now, I love to open up and expand my resources by putting myself through unexpected experiences, but that doesn't mean I find it easy.

Anyway, one day I was climbing up a tiny set of rocks with several other group members. I was trying to "figure out" where to put my feet to get to the next little ledge, when the person behind me tried to helpfully push me up. I got mentally reactive, which only further confused the situation. I asked him to stop helping, which reluctantly he did. I paused inside myself, allowing the momentary inner silence that brought me to complete presence. Suddenly, my legs bent in a particular fashion, agilely leading my feet to the ledge, like a lithely climbing goat.

Simple, elegant: No thought. My body led the way.

My mind had only complicated matters.

Indeed, it's important to realize that we're more than giant craniums. We're born in a body and are "supposed," thereby to…uh…embody. When we do so, all kinds of miracles—great and small—can ensue.

What is embodiment?

WHAT DOES THAT MEAN —TO EMBODY?

Giving concrete form to an abstract concept; soul—the human embodiment of something. [xxxix]

Looked at from this perspective, without a body, this thing called being "human" is merely an abstract concept. It's an easy jump from body-full disconnection to inhuman behavior. Look at how all the crime shows emphasize the importance of convincing the criminal, be it vicious killer or hostage-taker, of our humanity by speaking our name, etc.

Why, you might ask? In order to stay in touch with brutality, the criminal needs to de-humanize us—think of us as an "it." Remember how Buffalo Bill treated the girl he'd captured in *Silence of the Lambs* or how so many of the killers on the long-running television show *Criminal Minds* behave? Chilling.

Best we not also think of ourselves as "it."

And further, when we reject full human embodiment, we risk refusing our most profound gift: our link to both personal humanity and to all humanity. Perhaps some of what's gone off the rails in our ferocious, self-serving, grab-what-you-can world can be linked to ignoring the value and importance of this full-body embrace.

Additionally, to bring it back to lousy relationships (plus lousy jobs, lousy friendships, lousy bank accounts, lousy body image, and more), I'd theorize that much of our discontent stands squarely on the shoulders of this loss of "human" connection.

Thing is, this disconnect *will* happen—definitely.

We will forget ourselves, lose track of our association with our own humanity—maybe because we're too tired, hungry, angry, or overwhelmed or for a dozen other reasons.

That's okay. Best, assume you're a work in progress anyway instead of aiming for perfect.

There's no such animal.

Indeed, even when gaining full clarity about where things are coming from and how they express in our lives it doesn't mean "we're done" with change. Personally, I hope never to be done with change.

Is this a defeating notion? Not at all. It is, in fact, yet another example of how beautifully, imperfectly human we are.

Fundamental: Accept and appreciate that you'll always be flawed, without interpreting that to mean you're "defective and insufficient."

This is key for a happy life. And, too, it's key for finding love.

Eventually, defensive moments and reactivity, then, become clear red flags down on the play. They indicate areas we need to revisit and rework. When, for instance, we get particularly peeved about something, we're alerted to the fact that one of our underlying themes needs more attention. Such continued investigation allows a clearer and less inhibited experience of life in an on-going way. In the long run, we're able to better ease on down the road.

But I think I AM in my body!

HOW WILL YOU KNOW IF YOU ACTUALLY **ARE** "IN YOUR BODY?" Well, when we're truly "in" often, we can feel energy coursing through us—that "buzz" when the adrenaline's pumping. But even without an excess of adrenaline, you should be able to feel the blood flowing into all of your parts. It won't stop at your stomach (usually indicating you've connected with some kind of childhood material) or get stuck in your genitals (showing a specific focused interest). It won't afford you upper-body strength, but then get clogged the minute you stop your barbell lift (meaning your moment of focused body attention is over). You won't be jiggling your leg in your seat, or bouncing your foot up and down as it's crossed over your knee (an indication you want to flee the scene). You won't need to cross your arms over your solar plexus when hearing disturbing things (signifying how you're trying to shut down up surging emotions). When we're sincerely embodied we feel alive.

All over.

The body is smart. It knows what it needs—of course, most of the time we simply pay little attention. (To discover more about how to pursue connection to your body mind, check out the Love Works exercises.)

The Emotional Body...

WELL, WHEN IT COMES TO BEING EMBODIED, we like the idea, especially if it means better sex, except when through such a procedure we often find ourselves thrown into *feelings* that won't any longer be ignored, denied, or distracted from. Unfortunately, that's a dark closet many don't wish to open. Because...feelings can lead to connection and connection can lead to hurt and hurt threaten to overwhelm, which sends us into painful trauma memories.

Of course, most of us spend excessive amounts of time trying to avoid pain. As if we can. As if that's a good idea anyway. We can't and it isn't.

Pain is our teacher.

After all:

> Pain motivates the individual to withdraw from damaging situations, to protect a damaged body part while it heals, and to avoid similar experiences in the future. Most pain resolves promptly once the painful stimulus is removed and the body has healed, but sometimes pain persists despite removal of the stimulus and apparent healing of the body; and sometimes pain arises in the absence of any detectable stimulus, damage, or disease. [xl]

Certainly, we're trained to do everything we can to escape pain, including prescription drugs, obsession, and constant work, among other things. It's called self-soothing. Avoidance seems to be standard. We'll dodge, duck, weave, bob and ignore important conversations about such unpleasant subjects as aging and death.

This leads us nowhere good.

We must recognize that pain is an important, valuable feeling. No less vital than joy or lust or gratitude. Going *toward* the pain is actually our solution.

For true transformation we need to face ourselves, whatever pain that might include or incur. Yes, courage is required. Reach deep inside. You've got nothing to lose but your stuckness.

A rose by any other name....

WHEN WE TALK ABOUT EMOTIONAL BODY, WE'RE REALLY INVITING OURSELVES into the wondrous, important, and exciting adventure called **vulnerability**.

Fundamental: Vulnerability is critical for true transformation.

But what is vulnerability and how does it work?

I DEFINE VULNERABILITY AS the open-hearted, open-minded, and open-voiced expression of moment-to-moment heartfelt truth. Now, that's a mouth full.

And it sounds dangerous.

But it's not dangerous. You mostly think that because of what you've decided being vulnerable means or doesn't mean. Let's course correct your ideas right here and now.

Here's *what vulnerability doesn't mean*:

- ✓ It in no way allows us to willy-nilly say everything that occurs to us
- ✓ It doesn't let us tell everyone else what's going on with *them* or what they should do to improve their lives
- ✓ Vulnerability doesn't mean a disastrous collapse into a sickening emotional puddle or that we're waiting to get run over
- ✓ **Vulnerability does not mean that we are weak**

Here's *what vulnerability does mean:* Vulnerability is the clear, non-accusatory, and non-reactivity-laden communication of feelings and experiences.

That's it.

That's the long and the short of it.

Now, to articulate those feelings in a cogent manner, we're going to have to know what they are. In other words, we have to actually recognize our needs, motives, drives, and intentions in order to express them. This self-awareness is the crux of our excellent love matters.

Fundamental: *Vulnerability is critical for finding True Love.*

But...

NATURALLY, WHEN WE EXPRESS OURSELVES VULNERABLY all sorts of new concerns arise. Here's one:

Q: "When I'm open, people tend to rely on that openness and kinda expect it to continue non-stop. In my openness, I attract people who long for love and acceptance the same way I do, but then I find them needy which is exhausting."

PERHAPS YOU'RE CONFUSING CARING WITH *care taking*. *Care taking* often involves an attempt to control how and what another is doing or feeling and can be oh-so-tiring to maintain.

I often, for instance, work with people between the ages of 19 and 25 who are just getting out of drug, alcohol, or eating disorders rehabilitation centers—who then begin their reintegration into the world by going to what's called a sober living house. These transitional residences mean to teach life skills, often including such fundamentals as: get up, make your bed, brush your teeth, keep your room clean, talk nicely with others, attend daily to your sobriety through meetings and collaborative conversation, etc.

Now, like rehab, these situations tend to be quite pricey. The individuals living there, then, are most often funded by well-healed parents.

Here's where the trouble can start.

Over and again, I'll bump up against a lack of understanding as to how much is help and how much is enabling.

Recently, as a specific example, a young woman named Brittany came to work with me for a few months. In that time she appeared to make moderate progress. Not much though, really. You see, alcoholics often have great chatter—they can sound like they have it altogether when actually, they absolutely don't.

In any event, after a few months the girl convinced her very caring parents she was ready to return to school. So, they got her a gorgeous apartment in Los Angeles with fabulous furniture plus a car—and off she went. Her job was to go to school and stay sober.

Oh, the fact that she was still dating an alcoholic boyfriend got complained about, but mostly ignored; and when she immediately stopped therapy, that, too, got overlooked. By the by, this was, at age nineteen, her second go-round in rehab and with her own paid-for apartment. The first apartment, she'd absolutely trashed. She was with that same boyfriend at that time.

Her folks were convinced that their sincere love and support could get their daughter sober. Unfortunately though, knowing our parents worry and care about us doesn't "fix" what ails us.

When I asked the parents before Brittany left the sober living facility what they intended to do if she threw away her sobriety again, they answered: "Put her back in rehab I guess!"

I shook my head. "How about letting her make her way in the world without your largess keeping her incubated? You're only making sure she stays a child with no resources. That's not love."

Here's another similar example with a slight twist: I was working with a terrific 50-something man we'll call Brent from another country, who'd now and again comes to Los Angeles. During one period, he'd come to visit his then-25-year old son who, like Brittany, had gone from rehab to transitional housing.

After a while, it was time to go home.

Now, the son had a four-year old daughter of his own whom Brent had been long supporting, along with his son's estranged baby mama with whom the granddaughter lived. As his son prepared to go home, Brent said the following: "I've decided to continue supporting you and your ex for one more year only. By then, I expect you to have found a job that enables you to support yourself."

The son, quite miffed, asked how much he was to receive for that year. When Brent told him the very generous amount, he scoffed and replied: "I should get six times that amount!"

Brent asked him why.

His son responded: "Because you have it, so I should have it."

Brent and I laughed together about this, but it was clearly not so funny. Luckily, Brent had by then come to realize two things: first, that his generosity was really based in his guilt over divorcing his son's mother; and second, that when it came to his son, he was crippling him more than helping him.

As a side note, let me say how tremendously difficult it is for those 25 and under to stay sober. There's a typical self-centered notion that they're not "done" with drinking and drugs—that they can handle it even if people around them the same age are dying.

Really, though, each must find their own path in this.

All right—so how does true caring work then? First, it has little or no self-centered control in it. Second, it's offered without a need for recognition or particular response or even adherence. It's simple generosity. When we're in real service, we don't worry about giving too much. Rather, we openly assist, console, or simply affirm, without ego attachment. That means we tender our Open Heart having absolutely no agenda when it comes to results.

If our advice or solace is received, that's wonderful. If not, we're at least able to maintain freedom from reactivity (which is an ego response). Wonderfully, the heart is not reactive; rather, it is responsive.

In any event, when it comes to vulnerability here's an idea that might strike you as surprising: Just because our Heart is open doesn't mean we must actually *choose to respond* to every single person we meet. Let me repeat: *An open heart means we've made contact with our capacity to respond* but it doesn't demand response.

As to the "longing for love and acceptance" aspect of the equation, we're entering entirely different territory. What wants to be discovered is what that "longing" and "need for acceptance" is based in. Is it that organic want-to-connect part of our natural design, or are we talking about repairing damage?

Now, if damage is the point, we can look at the source three ways:

- ✓ Urgency about personal love based in previously unmet and/or unresolved childhood material
- ✓ A lack of sincere self-esteem also based in early material. This lack signals the gap between True Self and personality defenses and behavior. Bridging that gap is part of the work of healing
- ✓ A missing contact with Divine Love. This reference moves us further toward what's called the "trans-personal"[9]

---

[9] The term transpersonal means going beyond personal/personality matters, and reactivity—beyond preferences, private preoccupations, and individual focus in order to work with what's known as the Collective or more particularly according to the term coined by analytical psychologist Carl Jung, the Collective Unconscious.

"Collective unconscious is proposed to be a part of the unconscious mind, expressed in humanity and all life forms with nervous systems, and describes how the structure of the psyche autonomously organizes experience. Jung distinguished the collective unconscious from the

But again...

ANOTHER VERSION of disquiet sometimes spoken of when an open heart is considered sounds like this:

Q: "I'm afraid opening up the way you're suggesting will just make me a doormat. People see it as weakness and take advantage!"

THIS IS AN INTERESTING AND COMMON PERSPECTIVE when it comes to vulnerability. Many think of being open as a namby-pamby way of flagrantly spilling feelings over everything like splashed milk. It's not that at all. Vulnerability can be contained and quiet. Or it can be determined and outspoken. It has as many shades and colors as can be imagined.

Like a Columbus of the heart, mind, and soul, I have hurled myself off the shores of my own fears and limiting beliefs to venture far out into the uncharted territories of my inner truth—in search of what it means to be genuine and at peace with who I really am. I have abandoned the masquerade of living up to the expectations of others and explored the new horizons of what it means to be truly and completely me, in all my amazing imperfection and most splendid insecurity. - Anthon St. Maarten[xli]

Vulnerability turns out to be the most resilient and strongest position we can take. It takes off the defensive armor and lets us proclaim ourselves. Think about those long-ago days when men

---

personal unconscious, in that the personal unconscious is a personal reservoir of experience unique to each individual, while the collective unconscious collects and organizes those personal experiences in a similar way with each member of a particular species. "

When traveling such a road, participants tend to explore meditation, dream-work, sociological phenomena, mythological references, spirit, the unseen, guides, synchronicity, wisdom spaces, and symbol study among other things. Trans-personal exploration essentially means, more or less, leaving personality matters out of the equation. Of course, in its right timing, I'm a fan of all this.

fought on horseback wearing suits of armor. Turns out those "protections" were so very heavy that if a warrior fell off his horse, he was weighed down to the point of being unable to get upright in time to defend. Basically, he was a turtle on his back. Often, then, the challenger still on horseback could easily smite the dislodged fellow dead. So-called invulnerability—defense against authentic open-heartedness—is much like that.

Finally, vulnerability means: *I trust myself to withstand any reaction you might have to my expression of truth.* I can be my organic, authentic self. I need spend no time making sure you see me a certain way. I trust *myself* to stand upright in the face of any reaction to genuine me.

Imagine feeling as if no matter how the world responds, you're able to hold on to the belief that you're fine. Would you prefer others hear, understand, and value what you're offering?

Sure.

But even when they don't, you feel secure. Pretty powerful, huh? And that's what the practice of true vulnerability offers.

Now, remember: When practicing vulnerability, the truths you tell are about YOU.

They don't include the so-called 'realities' and observations you choose to level at others. In other words, talking about someone else's behavior instead of your feelings doesn't indicate vulnerability—even if you start the sentence with "I feel…"

This is a common, convenient misconception.

Transparency

WE'RE NIBBLING AROUND THE EDGE NOW OF SOMETHING CALLED **Transparency**. This is a conversation I often have with celebrity clients as they're entering public life in sometimes overwhelming ways: besieged by paparazzi, quoted and misquoted in the press, while facing constant public scrutiny and commentary.

Really, to some degree, we're all encountering and enduring similar circumstances. Recall our chat about projection. Well, everywhere we are and go, projection demands people make assumptions about who and how we are. These assumptive projections guide their attitudes, reactions, and behaviors. It's not really about us, but, of course, most of the time we take it personally.

Hopefully, you've been working on this as suggested.

Now, though, let's move to the next level.

Being transparent means letting comments, attitudes, and reactions move through you, much like light moves through a window. You're glass. Outside, there's a storm or slight wind or gathering dusk; inside, you maintain calm and an even temperature. You know what's going on out there has little to do with you. Sure, when leaving your inner space you're likely to encounter some weather to perhaps ruffle the hem of your jacket or blow through your hair, but it's a small enough matter and you're certain you can safely get where you're going.

This works the same whether we're famous or "regular."

For instance, we stay open to the sweet or even rude autograph-seeker wanting to make contact—which equals for non-celebrities staying responsive to the kindly, or even grumpy, corner store purveyor. With self-assuredness, we answer probing interview questions—which reminds us of dealing with family, friends, and customer interruptions. And all the time we're doing these things we remain aware of the protective yet see-through glass surrounding us. We don't need to hide or shy away for the projections coming toward us bounce off like bullets off a Kevlar vest.

Transparency everywhere all the time?

DON'T SUPPOSE YOU CAN DO THIS 100% OF THE TIME. Certainly, there will be days and times that life throws us off balance; when we're exhausted, having little reserve gas in our tank, or we're feeling overwhelmed by daily events. At these times, it's easy for transparency to bite the dust, while into a reactivity slump we fall.

Every once in a while, also, we'll run across someone so hugely inductive we get swept into their orbit before we know it. Induction works like this: we feel perfectly stable one minute and get so triggered by someone the next minute, we're suddenly on fire. Nothing they've said is exactly personal, but somehow just being with them provokes us. Maybe you've experienced this as someone's depression landing on you with a *thud*, when just before they arrive you felt perfectly fine.

Another perhaps more obvious example, for instance, can be seen in the case of a group of women working together in an office suddenly finding themselves sharing the same menstrual cycle schedule. This is to say: induction is a stealth process that happens just below the surface of things.

Often, in the aforementioned more challenging instances, the only healthy thing we can do for ourselves is get away. But we can't always leave, for instance, when a job we really need includes a toxic co-worker. That's when transparency is a development well-worth pursuing.

You can practice by finding an image for yourself. If the window idea works for you, use that—or choose another. Imagine *embodying* that transparency image as you walk through the world. Write about what happens.

Summary: Practice vulnerability and visibility everywhere as much as possible. Combine it with a practice of transparency. You'll be astonished at the glad results. People will begin treating you differently. You'll start feeling connecting in brand new uplifting ways.

Heart presence

THE WEAVING TOGETHER OF SPIRITUAL PRACTICES WITH PSYCHOLOGICAL DISCOVERIES takes us into the previously described transpersonal realms. Heart Centering and Heart Presence are practices encouraging this adventure. (See *Love Works* chapter.)

Though I dearly love transpersonal investigations, I believe it's best to do the fundamental, foundational psychological work *prior* to entertaining heightened states and lofty intentions—because such investigations can also function as escape from experiencing our wonderful humanity.

Again.

In any event, the collective ramifications of living intentionally from and through the heart have been scientifically traced by various investigators. A wonderful example of this comes through Dr. Masaru Emoto's work:

Dr. Emoto, a doctor of Alternative Medicine, introduced the novel idea that water not only reflects the physical word around it (as when we use a placid lake or pond as a mirror), but it also reflects the consciousness of the being surrounding it.

The experiment he used to discover this included bottles filled with water, that were set under either a positive or a negative influence. For example, some bottles of water were wrapped with written notes, with the writing facing inside the bottle that said, "thank you." This was done in various languages. No matter what language was used, the water in these bottles, when frozen, created complete crystals that were lovely to behold.

Water over which a priest prayed, with love and gratitude, created the same type of crystals. Conversely, unpleasant, incomplete, and malformed crystals were created in water exposed to people saying or writing, "You fool," or other negative expressions.

By exposing water to a particular word or piece of music, freezing it, and photographing the ice crystals formed, Dr. Emoto has shown that from beautiful words and music, come beautiful crystals, and from mean-spirited, negative words, come malformed and misshapen crystals. What is the significance? It becomes clear when we remember that the adult human body is approximately 70% water and infant bodies are about 90% water. We can be hurt emotionally and, as the water can be changed, for the worse physically by negativity. However, we are always closer to beauty when surrounded by positive thoughts, words, intentions and ultimately those vibrations.

It's clear our personal body has a connection to the earth's body.
   ✓ The earth's magnetic resonances vibrate at the same frequency as human heart rhythms and brainwaves

✓ The earth's constantly changing electromagnetic fields may be affecting your day-to-day health, feelings, and behavior

✓ When the sun's emission of a 2.8-gigahertz radio-wave frequency is increased, we tend to feel better

✓ Geomagnetic field disturbance is associated with lowered heart-rate variability, indicating our nervous system is not functioning as well [xlii]

Naturally, this dialogue is spectacularly important.

But what I want to emphasize here is something more practical. Listen up: Just because you're pursuing a trans-personal non-reactivity based life in no way means you're to remain disconnected—not from your feelings, not from the feelings of others, and not from the expression of those feelings. This is to say, many disciplines would have you attempting to "rise above" your emotional body.

That's not my position or suggestion. I have experienced and witnessed that being Heart Centered and still hugely emotional is possible.

✓ Feelings instruct
✓ Feelings allow
✓ Let's not leave them behind

Really, when it comes down to it, I don't want to leave any of the presence forms out. They all have value. Instead, why not hold the posture of: One for all and all for our connection with the One.

Q: Does all this vulnerable connection lead to the self-esteem that leads to love?

HEALTHY SELF-ESTEEM MEANS HEALTHY SELF-REGARD. A tall order to some degree because as previously enumerated, multitudinous elements contribute to such a possibility. There are many layers of affect to sift through. Actually, all things considered, it's amazing we can find our "Self" at all, let alone a healthy version.

All too often our sense of esteem rests on our imagining, with or without any true proof, how others feel about us. But really, like my childhood-envisioned closet monsters, there's simply no *there*, there.

Those feel-good-or-not-about-myself impressions mostly lean precariously on a wildly distorted self-view surrounded and promoted by defenses.

Yes, truth be told, we're generally making up much of they-like-me or don't of it all. Assigning our esteem to money, property, prestige, compliments, atta-girls/boys, comparisons, numbers of folks showing up at our parties or awards is a losing game. The only thing that secures positive self-esteem is a thorough recognition plus accurate, and even amused, acceptance of the whole picture of what's called "me." After that, whatever others think is icing on our cake, be that topping bitter or sweet.

Love-longing and all that jazz...

BY NOW, IT'S CLEAR THAT ADDICTION AND "LOVE" HAVE MUCH IN COMMON. Often, both ardently try to fill missing inner pieces—that hole-in-the-bucket feeling so many of us struggle with. You know, the I-can't-be-comfortable-in-my-own-skin sensibility. The idea that life just isn't what we hoped or anticipated. It is the notion that if only we can do enough, or have enough, we'll feel like enough.

In fact, when it comes to addiction there's what's called a three-point impaired belief system:

1. I'm worthless
2. I'll never really be able to depend on anyone
3. *It* will fix me!

This impaired belief system can often be applied to our love woe perspective as well.

1. I'm worthless
2. I'm going to pretend I'm depending on someone though I doubt I really can
3. That person/relationship will fix me!

In the case of addiction, the healing work begins with sacrificing immediate gratification. Usually in the case of love longing the work is the same. That is: *Stop doing whatever it is you would usually do to satisfy your need to feel temporarily good about yourself* even if it *appears* to offer a promising love outcome. Stop people-pleasing, aggressively challenging, shutting down, constantly partying, frantically dating, constantly complaining, or whatever you're doing to soothe the restlessness, discontent and desperation driving your actions.

Yuck. Sounds impossible?

NO, IT'S NOT IMPOSSIBLE.

Hard but not impossible.

And if as you say you really want to find, have and hold fabulous love, you'll try it.

The process being recommended here is called **Containment**, which means to put boundaries around our actions and/or thoughts. Put fences around the yard. Barriers to protect the dog from running down the street. Though from the dog's point of view, your confinement is annoying, think of how much safer that dog is.

Indeed, containment can offer us safety as well as privacy. As with the yard, staying on our side of the fence—without constantly spilling out onto the road (keeping some private thoughts private, for instance)—supports a sense of well-being. It helps us discover what wants to be shared when. This, in turn, lets us know that we can trust *ourselves*. It's not about withholding; it's about sharing from a place of considered clarity.

Keep in mind; however, none of this is an excuse for refusing to tell the truth. Everything we say would best be said as an honest expression.

"How are you, Dr. Nicki?"

"Grumpy! I'm in a lousy mood."

But there's no need to tell *everyone why* my mood has turned dark. The more intimate the person I'm talking to, the more detailed the answer.

An easier way, perhaps, of thinking of this containment process is what I'm calling **Shut It!** As it sounds, *Shut It!* asks us to close the garden gates entirely, whether ever so briefly or for longer. This can reference behaviors, thoughts, words, or, even in certain cases, extreme feelings like vicious outrage.

Of course, sometimes we need to *Shut It!* permanently, as with rabid addiction. In such instances, restraint is mandatory and acquiring big strong absolutely-no-matter-what-I-won't borders is essential. This is considered boundaries and containment as self-care.

Mostly, though, boundaries are temporary solutions meant to pause things long enough to allow deeper understanding. That means if I say "no" to a conversation with someone used to talking my ear off, I might be doing it:

✓ For temporary relief
✓ To reassess the overall value of the relationship
✓ To allow time to figure out why I have folks in my life who take more than they give
✓ To prepare for intimate conversation about the way things are going between us so I can deepen our connection
✓ To stop long enough to look at how and why I set up friendships this way

In other words, *Shut It!* can be either the beginning of understanding or the result of clarity.

When and how...

IN DAY-TO-DAY LIFE, HOW AND WHEN BOUNDARIES ARE EXHIBITED DEPENDS ON CIRCUMSTANCES. Sometimes, for instance, in the areas of work, family, close friends, acquaintances, or partnerships, we believe our only boundary solution is an electric fence. In other instances with the same folks a simple redwood structure with a gate that swings open, or even perhaps a nice green hedge, will do just fine. Mostly, though, some kind of enclosure is a good idea to keep certain critters or unwanted people off our property. It lets the flowers grow without getting trampled.

Of course, there are delicious occasions when no barrier at all is necessary. And in *all* instances—hold onto your hats—just because you have terrific boundaries, doesn't mean you can't be fully open and available to connection!

Now, it's easy for those having trouble getting out of the early development to confuse shut-down selfishness with self-care. But digging in quickly teaches that selfishness and self-care are not at all the same.

How do we tell the difference?

Here's the formula: Self-care leaves us feeling cared-for; selfishness leaves us needing more. You do the math.

PART II: THE CHANGE-IT-UP PLAN

"Be the change that you wish to see in the world."
- Mahatma Gandhi

Newsflash: If you want a different life, you need to do things differently.

Here's a first glance at four dandy change procedures. When it comes to love, this is an all occasion plan that works equally well for find it or fix it or let it go. For further understanding and appreciation, refer to the *Love Works* chapter. This step-by-step plan can be enormously helpful in all your transformation work:

- ✓ **Contain.** Stop following habitual, distracting, self-sabotaging thoughts and actions down the weed-thick garden path. Exhibit new boundaries.
- ✓ **Invite discovery.** Containing some routine behaviors and ways of thinking opens new doors, inviting fresh exploration. In fact, underneath the old ways lives all the terrific un-actualized potential waiting to explode out of you, like backyard Fourth of July fireworks. Let it.
- ✓ **Allow recovery.** It's like digging in the dense, dark dirt, washing off the mud, and finding out there's been rich gold nuggets buried all along. Let's unearth the hidden wealth.
- ✓ **Alter actions.** All the new info—plus the tools acquired along with innovative ways of perceiving life and love—has prepared you to pursue true happiness.

Contain	Invite Discovery	Allow Recovery	Alter Actions
STOP self-sabotaging thoughts & actions. Exhibit new boundaries.	As you begin to contain negative routines - allow for new self-exploration.	When you discover your hidden motivators be good with it. Let it come out.	You are now equipped to shed past self-defeating actions and will fulfill your true potential for happiness.

I once knew a couple, Maria and Blake, going through a terrible divorce 20 years and two kids in the making. Blake had truly gone off the rails—becoming embittered about everything in his early 50s including his career, marriage, the social system, and even life itself. He was at that time a two-decade-sober heroin addict, who'd long ceased his personal investigatory work.

It's what's called a dry drunk.

Meanwhile, Blake had always been a terrific dad, but somehow during the decomposition, even that capacity deteriorated. His kids were often chasing after him for even the most modest amounts of time, attention, or expression of real interest.

Maria was infuriated. She'd always been the family engine, including primary breadwinner, but now her hurt and vehement resentment of the situation knew no bounds. A recovered heroin addict herself, she'd diligently worked on constant self-assessment and self-improvement; she knew she'd need to dig even deeper though to topple the rabid feelings overrunning her in this divorce experience.

First, Maria began practicing *Shut It!*

Some days it went well and others not so much. Blake left awful messages and texts, indicating how everything was all her fault and describing her in loathsome ways. She felt bruised and bullied. And she worried that he was right.

Then Blake upped the ante by asking Maria to return to him anything of value accumulated during their life together. She interpreted this to mean she herself would retain little value after the divorce. That *she* was being perceived as having no worth. That the long marriage also was being diminished and devalued. She imagined never finding love again.

The rational part of Maria knew this was nonsense but staying non-reactive proved difficult. Sometimes she lashed out. Each time, she worked hard to sit herself upright again.

After some initial weeks of reeling, Maria began to track back––going over their marriage. She recalled vividly and frankly how much control she'd exhibited all along the line, trying desperately to force-march her husband into actualization. To some, it might look like she was merely supporting him to become his best self. And to a degree that's true also, but underneath it Maria had to finally accept that she'd been trying to do for Blake what she could never do for her father, who was (no surprise) a carbon copy: a constantly disgruntled alcoholic who abandoned the family.

When Maria realized the profound nature of the truth that she'd stepped right into her mother's shoes, she began to recover herself.

Now, this is not to say that the road was smooth. She'd dive deeply in and then suddenly leap out of the waters again, as if startlingly regurgitated by some ocean monster.

Plus, as always, realization was only the start.

Maria wrote and sobbed and wrote and sobbed. We worked together over and again. Finally, she devised a releasing ritual—not so much about Blake, though letting go of the idea that he was ever going to change was essential, or even about long dead dad, but more about her *inner relationship* to the disappointing, incompetent man.

What Maria discovered was that holding this image of men had kept her from allowing true parity and partnership into her life. Because of her need to stay in control as a brace against the vulnerable surrender to love she was deeply sure would kill her, she'd actually robbed herself of what she most sincerely deserved: brilliant love.

Find your own way…

AS YOU CAN HOPEFULLY TELL, each element of the Change-It-Up Plan needs personal exploration and instigation. The suggestions offered are general. Just as Maria needed to find her own path, you need to find yours. And remember: nothing happens overnight.

I'll assume to some degree by now you've invented or discovered certain directions that work for you. Whether you're actually following your own good intuition and understanding is another matter. Now, if profound solutions elude you, there's no shame in reaching out to an expert to walk with you to recovery.

No matter what you decide, one thing's certain: it's no good simply glancing over the list and imagining change. Work each aspect to the best of your ability at this point in time. Be as diligent as Maria was.

1) Contain your reactivity, whatever form it's taking.
2) Figure out *your* part in the story you're telling.
3) Allow the relief of realization to wash over you. In working with these realizations you're mining for gold.

4) Now choose new actions to take, for in raw form gold isn't as valuable as once turned into something else. In fact, it often takes a keen eye to even recognize worth amidst the dirt.

I love the story of the Optimist Boy: The optimist boy finds himself in a room covered to the brim with smelly dung. In walks his friend to find the boy leaping and frolicking—diving down into the steamy piles over and over. "What in the world are you doing?" the friend asks, holding his nose. The boy laughs, "I figured with all this crap, there must be a pony somewhere!"

Like the optimist boy, we want to dive in again and again, accepting whatever we do or don't find each step along the way, including the stink. Naturally, this process is challenging, but incredibly valuable. By eventually turning our discoveries into useful forms, recognizing what new actions to take, or innovative thinking to embrace, we can indeed find the hidden pony.

After a while in this contain-discover-recover-alter process, the oddest thing happens. We actually find ourselves longing for more of this experience. We let it touch areas not yet delved. It becomes our new go-to for respite, relief, and information.

Amidst the changes, finding True Self...

WOW. THE WHOLE THING SOUNDS AWFULLY DIFFICULT.

Well, it is, until it isn't.

And then—something astonishing occurs when we're brought into contact with a deep inner voice. Some call this the "True Self." Others would name it Divinity. At this juncture, and for our purposes, I don't see much difference.

Let's digress for a second to talk about what's usually called *mindfulness*. Actually, I'm not much of a fan of this turn-of-phrase. I realize it's taken from long Buddhist tradition, for which I have much respect; however, as Westerners I believe it tends to take us into murky territory.

Mindfulness means to direct us to "an attentive awareness of reality..."—a focus on things in the immediate. Now, I entirely get the intention and obviously I'm all for it as our long dialogue on presence indicates, but when words like "reality" start popping up I find my nose wrinkling. Indeed, I have no idea whatsoever about so-called reality.

In fact, I find the notion confusing.

Whose reality?

Invariably, conversations about reality land me firmly back in the lap of perception. And similarly, mindfulness brings me to roam the territory of the mind. Most certainly I can personally, like many, do with less of that, thank you very much.

Of course, I realize what's really being intended by mindful folks is the *mind emptiness* meant to come from exquisite focus on the now. Certainly, this can occur. But in our current sociological climate, where shiny objects so easily distract, calling something mindful feels like it walks us down a too-familiar and not-so-helpful path. All right, enough digression; let's go back to True Self Presence (Divine Presence).

Do nothing? What an order! I can't go through with it!

THIS IDEA OF "BEING" RATHER THAN DOING IS ANATHEMA TO MOST OF US. I remember well the first time it was suggested to me. A therapist asked me to "do nothing." I blinked a few times, rolling the words around in my mouth, trying to make sense of them.

What could that possibly mean?

Can I read? No, she answered, that's doing something.

Can I write? No.

Can I listen to music? No.

Finally, I sighed heavily. I just couldn't fathom what she was saying. "I have a teenage daughter," she offered. "Often, she just sits and stares out the window. That's doing nothing."

I didn't really get the point, but I did it.

Agonizingly at first and eventually, slowly, finally, I settled in. And then this completely odd thing happened. I came to love the nothingness of it all.

You will, too, if you give it a shot.

A real shot.

And sometimes during this process a kind of meditative creative mental wandering will occur out of which organically surfaces great and wondrous realizations or artful outflow.

How does it work?

THE MECHANICS OF THIS ENGAGEMENT WITH THE SELF is simple but challenging. When it comes to doing nothing, it works this way: If ordinarily you'd go to every function you're asked to, be on every committee, host each event, answer every phone call, inevitably be the listening ear for your friends and colleagues, work your fingers to the bone, say yes when no is what you really want, have sex because you think you should, or a zillion other versions of make-them-like-me, you instead forgo.

But since I do dearly love the idea of saying "Yes!" as a way to go through life, think of this shift as *saying yes to you* instead of everyone and everything else.

Oddly enough, that's the easy part.

The harder part, now that you've given yourself some space, is: "Do nothing." We sit. And sit. And sit. We be. Feelings arise. We let those feelings stir and toss and jump to the surface. We greet them as they appear without making any effort to suppress, distract, deny, or ignore.

We do this until we simply can't do it anymore.

That doesn't mean once uncomfortable we jump up and get moving. No. Actually, when we're entirely fed up with doing nothing we do…more nothing. We do nothing until we're actually *past* the point of discomfort.

After the discomfort has dissolved long enough for either ease or deeply held information to occur, there's doing. In this case the doing is: write about the feelings, understandings, insights, worries, fears, and excitements arising from the nothingness experience. This is doing in service not of avoidance, but of engagement.

What can I expect?

QUICKLY, MOST OF US FIND "SUFFERING" comes with stillness—what some call the itches, twitches, and bitches. Actually, this so-called suffering is considered a quality of engagement—a diving deep experience that enlarges understanding. This version, arising from containing desires, is generally underestimated in importance and value.

The evolutionary role of physical and mental suffering, through natural selection, is primordial: it warns of threats, motivates coping (fight or flight, escapism)…despite its initial disrupting nature, **suffering contributes to the organization of meaning** in an individual's world and psyche. In turn, meaning determines how individuals or societies experience and deal with suffering. [xliii]

Yeah, that's all very fine and good, perhaps you're thinking, but I wanna have fun. Life is hard and tiring as is, so why complicate matters with all this endless investigation?

Well, it's a reasonable question.

And there's no rule.

Intense exploration isn't for everyone.

Most likely, though, if you're reading this book something in your life isn't working. You don't have the job/career, bank account, and friendships, or the love relationship you crave. At least some part of you wants that to be different.

No one ever changes or grows by lying around on the couch with a remote in their hands. It's a nice way to spend a lazy afternoon, but not a lifetime. That means, to accomplish the life you say you want and deserve, discomfort (suffering) will be necessary. Best to face and embrace, because remember what we established: The more you resist, the worse it will be, because what we resist persists.

Let me give another personal example.

I hate needles. To some degree, you might even say I'm needle-phobic. I have terrible tiny veins and they roll. So I've had dozens of awful needle experiences leaving me bruised and needle-bullied. For years I anticipated pain, and pain there would be. Finally, in desperation, I developed this "embrace" process. Whenever I go to get my blood drawn or whatever, I spend the entire time saying to myself: "Go toward the pain, go toward the pain" and presto, the "pain" vanishes! But when I resist, it persists—and increases. It's the "I don't wanna" and "I hate it" that actually upgrades mild discomfort into stunning ache.

Indeed, suffering embraced is revolutionary and revelatory.

And as a bonus, when we make contact with profound discomfort our humanity is actually amplified. I'd postulate that this humanity—the part distinguishing us from all other living things—is our most extraordinary gift. And further, I'd say: *Humanity most generously expressed brings us into embrace with our Divinity and with the True Self.*

Q: "I *want* to give my entire self, but I feel great resistance at certain times and toward certain people. Is this ego?"

It's a combination of fear and ego. The fear is likely based on that story you've been telling yourself about who and how you are—the story begun in childhood, bouncing off your nature and exaggerated by local-plus-global time in which you're raised.

Also, often we concoct this notion that if we give everything we'll have nothing left and imagining, as earlier referenced, there's a limited supply. As if the worlds a big pie and every slice someone else gets means less for you. This perspective can give rise to vivid jealousy, vicious competitiveness, frantic fury, and more.

Actually, tendered love works the opposite way.

The more we offer the more it grows in us—which means the more we give, the more we have to give. It's a little like eating so much we stretch our stomach and then are able/want to eat more and more. Happily, in the case of true ego-free love, there's no such thing as getting too love fat. Plumped up by our loving capacity is a good thing. The only limitation we have, really, in this regard involves temporality—our dance with time limitation.

So many people to love, so little time!

Okay, so if there's a small inside voice whispering, "why should they get from me what I'm not getting for myself?" most likely *that's* ego. Well, letting and getting your own needs met is primarily up to you. Remember: Start by telling the truth about what you're actually asking for versus just expecting others to intuit, and then allow requests to be fulfilled.

What I'm saying here is that we're the cause of our own love-hunger. We sometimes expect other people to read our minds and know how to act to make us feel loved, we act in ways that indicate we're entirely self-sufficient and don't need anything from them, we reject what comes toward us when they try to offer us care, or constantly make others feel what they're giving is simply not enough. Naturally, none of these ways get us what we desire.

So the problem isn't my mind?

REALLY, IT'S NOT AT ALL THAT "MIND" IS A PROBLEM—IT'S WHEN THE EGO RULES THE MIND THAT TROUBLE KICKS IN. As far as having a "good" life goes, mind is a contributor, not an inhibitor—unless we get stuck living there, or think the mind is the only important part of us. That is, unless we give mind all the power.

Thus, if I'm using my good mind to discover, uncover, and reveal—terrific. As long as I'm not caught up in the results of my investigation—as long as I don't use what happens out of my discoveries against self or against others.

In fact, each aspect of us has, we might say, a mind of its own. Science has even discovered a mind *in* the heart—a heart mind. And as we've established, the body has a mind as well.

So remember: Ego isn't in and of itself a "bad" thing.

It helps us through our days and is the steering wheel of our daily life. We need it. But plenty of times, some ego modifying is definitely required.

Here's a thought: If you feel as if you're drowning in ego-mind, try accessing one of the other kinds of mind—either the body mind or the heart mind. This can be accomplished readily through: dance/movement, meditation, or some form of art/creativity. Just put on music in your living room and let yourself move, or join a dance class. Sit quietly with your eyes open in front of a flickering candle; or with your eyes closed meditate in your backyard or anywhere feeling comfortable. Get some paper and finger-paint or put shapes on canvas. Throw clay, or break a bunch of old ceramic dishes and create a mosaic. Or make a collage.

The possibilities are endless. Use your imagination.

Listen carefully: These constantly offered suggestions are not meant to simply fill up pages. Don't overlook them or just read them. **Take Action**. That's what will make a difference in your life. Don't let the resistant part of you, the naysayer, or the skeptic ruin your hope of recovery. Becoming comfortable in your own skin, finding and having a satisfying career, as well as supportive fun friends, and experiencing wonderful love are all waiting for you.

Relationship…the crux of our matters!

Q: "Why do the people I'm closest to make me the most nuts? Why so much reaction to those we love?"

WHEN IT COMES TO GIVING OF OURSELVES it's often most difficult with partners. This is completely connected to unresolved family material. Remember the earlier offered **Fundamental:** The bigger the reaction the older the material supporting the reaction. Let's add: The closer the relationship, the more triggered into that old material we become.

It helps us to remember that the three to four personal themes arising from this early material *are the only themes we ever have to work with for our entire lives*. How great is that. We don't keep encountering new "problems"; we only come across iterations of the same problems. Therefore, once we realize what those few pivotal themes are and have our tidy list of tried-and-true solutions we can apply the fixes that lead to fresh perspectives, no matter how odd the latest conditions may at first appear. Additionally, knowing there are only seven to ten stories for those three to four themes means we're all in the same boat. The problems you're having are the problems I'm having. You understand me because, more or less, you've been there.

When our themes arise, as they inevitably do *even after* we've come to clarity about what stimulates them and how they operate in us, we can each time be re-inspired to new levels of self-understanding.

Remember how Maria did it.

Such new experiences inevitably offer dandy specific back-to-the-drawing-board announcements. So, by example, even though I'm very well aware by now that my bleating "I have to do everything myself" is nonsense, when it arises, as it most certainly still occasionally does, I get to reexamine whatever lingering commitment there is to my original story. In doing that, I usually come to several further conclusions:

- ✓ My "doing everything" has taught me breathtaking capacity
- ✓ I actually have plenty of teammates these days
- ✓ I'm still wedded to control
- ✓ Some small inner voice still resists full surrender to love
- ✓ I enjoy being the boss of my accomplishments

As perhaps you see from this list, refined realizations can take a look at what's generally considered the good, the bad, and the ugly. My favorite (eventual) position is what I've mentioned as the "So what!" of it all, meaning, yes, I realize what my life has all boiled down to—both what's been given to me through my experiences as well as what's been lost—and I've arrived at a place of compassionate equilibrium about it all. I truly understand that *I am far more than the mere details of my story.* I've been to the redemption store. Eureka.

Summary: What I'm encouraging here, then, is an embrace of the perspective that everything that happens serves us in some way. To accept that viewpoint, we need to let go of old resentments and instead realize history through a new lens. We're not to do this letting-go superficially or cavalierly; instead, we arrive at a well-considered appreciation of cause and effect. Real freedom comes when we embrace fully the previously touted mantra that nothing that's happened is personal. That nothing-personal business actually includes our parents and their behavior. Indeed, turns out the folks were operating out of their own drama, trauma, and opinions also. Just as were the kids in school. And that terrible neighbor, officious coach, tiresome teacher, and cold grandparent. All were involved in inner struggles having zero to do with us. Perhaps right now accepting that notion seems impossible.

Hang in there.

We're not done yet.

CHAPTER THREE
PERSPIRATION

Believe in a love that is being stored up for you like an inheritance, and have faith that in this love there is a strength and a blessing so large that you can travel as far as you wish without having to step outside it.

Rainer Maria Rilke [xliv]

– FIX IT –

It's time to fix the relationships in your life. At work and at play. In the living room and in the bedroom. Fix what you've got or fix what you get. But no matter what, everything starts with you.

PART I: WHAT DO WE DO NOW?

L ET'S GET DOWN TO IT! Understanding and transforming your love matters means changing your lousy relationship patterns. There are many pathways. Some roads will seem steep and rocky, while others mean crossing once-fertile, now-dry riverbeds—and still others will have you traipsing through thick forest. Sound arduous? Well, not all efforts require quite so much, but real, lasting change inevitably includes some degree of chop wood, carry water.

Try believing you have more grit than you've supposed.

Imagine fabulous inner resources yet to be discovered.

Moving forward, the plan is to bring in the big relationship revolution cannons. This is where the fun really starts.

First, I'll continue to point out the how, where, and why of relationship undermining. Then I'll clearly enumerate what new alteration ways and means can be activated.

The rest will be up to you.

Great! I want change NOW...

IT'S ALWAYS TEMPTING TO WANT AND IMAGINE IMMEDIATE CHANGE. For you gotta-have-it-now enthusiasts, keep in mind that doing something differently on Tuesday doesn't mean everything shifts by Friday. Because the *when* of change is not our business. Annoying, I know. Our job is to persistently and consistently attend the *process* of change with intention and dedication. Quick fixes don't work. Never have. They're bandages on wounds that need real surgery. We're going to do that surgery here together.

Also important to remember is that each psyche operates at its own pace and you'll need to discover yours. It's a bit like weight loss. Some folks lose more slowly, some more quickly, even on the same exercise and eating regimen. Genetics matter. Age matters. Old habits matter, as does attitude. Thus, when it comes to change, we've got to realize and accept the odd notion that the psyche—the inner soul of us—has our best interest at heart.

Talking about pace, lets pause to discuss relationship pace. Let's say you're reading this book because you're already in a committed connection, but it's not going as well as you wish so you're looking for helpful ways to "fix it."

Now, you're definitely finding those helpers here, but there's something vital to understand: Because as just stated we inevitably grow at different rates even when everyone's really trying it's unlikely you and your partner will be or stay on the same growing page, especially for the entire length of a long-term relationship. If you're reading and working this book and your partner is not, or even if you work it together, chances are you're not going to move at the same rate, nor in an identical way. It's easy to mistake this pacing variety for impossible difference, or to get resentful, furious, or disappointed along the journey.

Instead, try respecting your partner's tempo. This might be hugely difficult and can feel frustrating, paralyzing, aggravating, and more. Maybe you wonder: Does it mean we've grown so far apart there's no coming back? A better way of viewing it is to imagine you're living in a garden with fruits and blossoms promised to bloom at various times, wanting you to just patiently wait 'til the right part of the season. Of course, you might worry: Will the garden be dead before you can reclaim it? Or wonder if there's special food and attention you can give to help a grand flourishing; however, for now, best to simply hang tight.

Unless there's been more bad than good, a relationship is well worth a sincere additional effort. Why? Because if we don't shift our relationship to the relationship we're already in, we're likely to revisit the pattern in the next one.

Stop shaking your head.

Everyone thinks they'll choose differently next time. But since it's *our* patterns that need changing, not the people with whom we exhibit those patterns, we're guaranteed to repeat experience unless we alter the fundamentals.

Remember those marriage/divorce stats!

That's depressing…what can I do to keep my relationship alive meanwhile?

ALL RIGHT, NOW THAT I'VE CONVINCED YOU THERE'S NO RULES, LET ME OFFER A FEW. To avoid confusion, we'll call them **tenets**. These relationship tenets are important if we're to resist throwing a grenade into the center of our relationship. Not that I'm completely opposed to such radical measures. After all, bombs thrown can either incinerate or illuminate.

In any event, when couples first arrive in therapy we facilitators assess for two things in our interior deliberation about how to proceed. The first is level of commitment and the second is willingness.

What is commitment? Initial ideas about commitment land us in statements about personal vows made and honored. The nature and form these vows take vary widely. And the contracts that go with those declarations are even more various. On top of all that, such contracts are invariably both overt and covert— which means there are things agreed upon out loud and things each member of the couple knows, but have never openly acknowledged.

What, then, is willingness? An agreement, if not eager at least active, to do what's required to change what's happening and to shift what's not working into something that can be sustained.

When folks come to therapy, it's lovely if they enter with a shared commitment as well as equal willingness to do the work. This seldom occurs. Usually, one person is driving the let's-work-on-this bus. Besides which, all too often a therapist is the final stop on the way to the divorce attorney, when in fact the best work is preventative rather than last-ditch efforts.

Happily, it often doesn't matter who gets you into the room. Great work can still be accomplished once you're there, even if at first reluctantly. It's a bit like the fellow getting a DUI being "sentenced" to Alcoholics Anonymous meetings. Sometimes it's just *pro-forma*, wherein the body comes but the willingness to change stays home. Sometimes, however, the fellow actually gets sober.

Meanwhile, what the couple presents as the problem isn't ordinarily really "it." Maybe some upsetting event happens to bring them in. We might start there for a short time, but sooner rather than later, what inevitably comes forward are underlying, unacknowledged issues.

Covert contracts

THIS DIALOGUE ABOUT OVERT AND COVERT CONTRACTS brings me to think about a couple who came in because the wife found out her husband was cheating. Actually, he'd been doing this for a long time, but as a travelling salesman had managed to keep his activities nicely out of view. Lately, he'd let himself be more flamboyant, bringing them onto home turf.

Now, this couple enjoyed a lovely lifestyle. He did very well financially and was able to afford a beautiful house, where his wife and child could delightfully reside. Clearly, she loved him and their life, but didn't want his proclivities thrown in her face.

Still, neither wanted divorce.

What quickly came forward were their very different sexual appetites. In actuality, they never spoke of their unwritten, mostly unconscious contract, that as long as he kept his gallivanting outside of view, she'd turn a blind eye.

The couple never did admit this directly; however, when therapy was over, I was pretty clear things would remain as they'd once been, with him enjoying the company of other women on the road with a remembered commitment to maintaining in-town decorum. The trade-off for her was keeping hearth and home as it was.

What was their willingness to do the work? Actually, they shared the same fairly tepid level of willingness. You see? It's not about answering outside attitudes or opinions about what's best. Not mine or anyone's.

What would have happened if she, for instance, were more fervent about her fidelity requirements or him about his sexual needs? Don't know. But, in fact, they were basically on the same page and she merely wanted her hurt registered. He heard and that was enough.

Could we theorize that this man and woman weren't sharing the same idea of commitment? I guess. But who cares, because in an odd but clear way, what they were doing worked for them.

Now, you and your partner also don't even need to be on the same commitment and willingness page in the usual sense for progress to be made. You can have one idea about what describes committed love while your partner has another. The idea is to clearly determine your priorities.

The trick is to be honest with your Self about that.

And to be generous with your partner also.

Astonishing, huh?

If you find you're full of requirements about the way change must occur either for you or with your mate, you might want to double-check those motives. It's likely to have far less to do with them and with current circumstances than with rising inner fears.

The Tenets

OKAY, HERE WE GO with the tenets. The language shows them geared for primary partnership however they can easily also be applied to friendship, family and even work. For example, in

Tenet #1 substitute the idea of not expecting co-workers pace to be identical to yours; or friends; or your mother's.

As you read, and hopefully more extensively explore how several apply specifically to you and your relationships, remember that these are meant to be touchstone ideas leading you to understand how you're currently thinking and acting. In other words, the tenets are both reminders and instructions.

I've included some question prompts—self-investigatory inquiries. As usual it's best to spend quality time *with each question.* Ruminate on them. Write about them. *Add questions and answers of your own.* The suggestion is to look them all over and then choose the ones that sting the most. For instance, if Tenet #3 announces yet again your tendency to be controlling, insistent, or even self-righteous in your relationships, whether it seems to be about the bigger dilemmas or the little things, be brave enough to tell yourself the truth about this and then dig in to find out why you might be proceeding in a way that cannot possibly give you the quality of loving relationship you want.

Okay, begin:

✓ **Relationship Tenet #1:** Don't expect your partner's pace to be identical to yours. Q: *In what ways does your learning, interactive and/or production rhythm differ from your partners? How do you feel about those differences? What kinds of visible reactions do you have to those differences?*

✓ **Relationship Tenet #2:** Realize that just because your partner isn't changing at your pace, doesn't mean they're not changing at all. Q: *What thoughts come up when you consider how your partner behaves with regards to change and effort? Do you, for instance, imagine the worst or ignore it or get furious or...?*

✓ **Relationship Tenet #3:** Understand that your way is not the only way. Q: *What is your relationship to being "right"? How do you handle disagreements about procedure both at home and at work?*

✓ **Relationship Tenet #4:** During the "dry" times, try focusing on the cheese and not the holes. Remember what you like and love about your partner. Stop looking at what's missing and see what's present. Q: *What good* *reasons do you have for staying in the relationship or the friendship or the job? What are the best things about your situation?*

✓ **Relationship Tenet #5:** Keep your eye on the *self-change* ball. Changing your part of the equation will change the entire equation. It may still not turn out as you prefer, but you'll have learned something that will most likely announce what's next. Q: *What's your current focus in terms of self-change? What do you imagine happening if things don't go the way you prefer?*

✓ **Relationship Tenet #6:** Stop endlessly discussing the relationship with your partner. There's an old saying: "If you're talking about the relationship all the time, you're not actually engaging the relationship." Remember, the work to be done is primarily *inside you.* Do your own work first. Q: *How often do you talk about relationship issues with your partner? How often do you complain about relationship issues with your friends or family? How much time are you actually spending doing the work of change?*

✓ **Relationship Tenet #7:** Check out your relationship patterns to see what's being repeated (i.e., do you always find something wrong; do your disgruntlements tend to surface with a particular timing; do your relationships tend to last the same length of time?). Q: *What do you know so far about your relationship patterns?*

Moving into change…

The idea will be to do *something*, but don't attempt to do it all at once. Why? Because such an attempt is a sure set up for failure.

After all, there's some reason we don't feel good about ourselves or relationships or even life. Perhaps the reason's already been discovered through the first couple chapters, or maybe it's yet to be determined; but in any case, if there weren't some deeply held hesitation driving the lousy relationship bus, you'd have already implemented all the great advice you've heard or read over your lifetime. But I bet either you haven't followed the suggestions or you've tried some of it and it simply didn't "work."

Let me hammer home this point.

You know how every New Year's Eve we make one or several resolutions? By the end of January—if it takes that long—we've "failed" to hold onto our resolve? Or remember how you decided you'd never ever eat sugar again? How long did that last? And recall your declaration about going to the gym *every day* for the foreseeable future? Or even more, how about I'm never, ever again going to say mean things to my partner, drag out my laundry list of complaints, or look at my phone while we're talking?

Yes, even though we've been working on looking at the underlying causes of undermining relationship habits, and even though perhaps there have already been some startling revelations about root causes, you still need to continue one step at a time. Because when we set unobtainable tasks and overwhelm our psyche with too much change too fast, we can't sustain it. What happens most often, then, is the system either goes into viscous rebellion or shuts down altogether. We need adjustment time for each new effort. We must listen for the psyche's readiness. We must take the baby steps that strengthen our legs for the big run across the room.

The problem is we're very often walking a razor's edge when it comes to discerning between moving at an appropriate tolerable pace and answering the less change-enhancing call of our well-developed defense system. Because sorting out this discernment is a dicey proposition, the suggestion is: try something—really, really try—and if you feel truly overwhelmed, choose something less aggressive to do.

That means, when you hear that whiney, resistant "I don't wanna" voice, ignore and proceed; but when you start feeling truly beaten-up by your own efforts, stop. Like when you decide to exercise every day for the foreseeable future, but on day four, there's an unmanageable body hurt that can't be ignored. At that point you need to let your body rest and not berate yourself for doing so. So if you're plowing through the exercises here and feelings are starting to truly overwhelm, take a break. This doesn't mean the minute you have an inkling of an emotion you flee. Be honest.

On the other hand here's a keep at it example: Often with couples, one person is hugely critical of the other. Every little thing that person does seems to create irritation. Now, the very first thing that needs to happen is that the critic must *Shut It!*

Stop all criticism.

Right away you get worried. What if letting go of vigilance results in things falling completely through the cracks! Understand two things: first, it's important that you check out your overall long-standing relationship to both contentment and to control. This is not a relationship problem; this is a "you" problem. Also not to worry—your quick criticisms will simply be lurking in the shadows waiting to announce themselves again.

Ah, the whining has begun.

But, but, but…

Here's a good example of DO IT ANYWAY!

So, you first stop all criticisms. Then you notice what happens. What feelings are coming up for you? How's this cessation of pointing-finger vitriol affecting the relationship?

Now that there's space, you can start to determine what "bigger" issue needs attention. *That's* the one to address.

PART II: FIX IT OR FORGET IT?

"Never love anyone who treats you like you're ordinary."

- Oscar Wilde

WHETHER YOU'RE TRYING TO FIX THE RELATIONSHIP YOU'RE ALREADY IN, trying to find a mate, or trying to move on, it's important to pay attention to what I'm calling **THE GRAND CONNECTION TRIFECTA–** –which is the win-place-show triple play that describes terrific relationship. These three basics want to be present in *all* intimate friendships and best be visible at work as well—but absolutely they are utterly essential in a thriving primary relationship. If after reading these you realize none are present in your current relationship, I'd suggest seriously considering what that means.

-Win-

Your partner should ALWAYS be your biggest fan.

If your partner is not your biggest fan, you certainly know it. Perhaps you experience the lack of "fan" as constant criticism or judgment on their part. Maybe you see how they don't defend you when others nay-say. Perhaps they scoff at your ideas or seem to underestimate your contributions. Maybe you can't tell them your concerns and secrets, afraid to be rejected. Certainly, some of this could be your own self-consciousness or insecurity and you'll need to diligently investigate what's yours and what's theirs.

But let me be clear: Being your biggest fan doesn't mean you have *carte blanche* to behave without boundaries. It also doesn't mean you get unmitigated approval for all your choices. What it does mean is that no matter what, the *essential you* is fundamentally appreciated, respected, and applauded.

As an extension of this I'm an enthusiastic supporter of the idea of fanning the flames of your partner's wishes, dreams, and desires, even when you don't quite agree with the aim or understand the choice—assuming, of course, that those directions are in line with your relationship agreements. Obviously, for instance, if you have a monogamy agreement and your partners "dreams" include multiple sex partners, there's a problem.

-Place-

Your partner should cherish you.

Feeling and being cherished offers you a safe "place" in the world.

Cherishing is an art that best includes action.

Word plus deed.

However, some are better at the art of cherishing, while others excel at actions. Whatever's being offered should be recognized and appreciated. We don't want to be ungenerous about the matter, or insist what we're getting isn't enough because it fails to meet our fantasies. It's always important in any kind of relationship (including primary, family, friendship, work, or even with acquaintances) to be charitable when assessing the value of what's tendered. Just because someone doesn't do things our way, doesn't mean either their actions or their words should be dismissed.

This brings forward an important point. In any relationship, openhandedness is essential. All too often we need others to find important precisely the things we find important. That's a grave error.

There's an old metaphoric story in couples' therapy circles that goes something like this: A couple is having their first excited Christmas. Partner A comes from a family where everyone gives tons of little gifts. Partner B comes from a family where everyone gives one big gift. Partner A, not considering this difference, buys partner B many little gifts. Partner B not considering this difference, buys Partner A one big gift. Even though they spend the same amount of money, both are disappointed.

Here's another tenet then:

✓ **Relationship Tenet #8:** Don't assume sameness. Check with the folks in your life to see what *they* want and need. Q; *What do you know about your partner (or friends or coworkers or family's) needs? How do those needs differ from yours?*

-*Show*-

Your partner should have your back.

Having your back "shows" through action. Your partner's there to listen, cajole, and at times when appropriate, advise. She or he invests in you, evidences true interest, and expresses caring concern for both troubles as well as triumphs.

But, again, having your back doesn't mean agreeing with everything you say, think, or do. In fact, a truly great partner will tell you the truth—which means being what's called your *black needle*. A black needle is something that punctures our inflation balloon. You know how it is: the ego swells or, alternately, gets completely flattened. We either get so puffed-up we imagine being above error, disavowing responsibility for some dropped stitch; or otherwise, we start lolling around in some exaggerated idea of wrong-doing. Turns out whether we believe we're the best thing ever or the worst piece of crap on the planet, we're inflated.

Best or worst are both wildly unlikely.

Once we're onto ourselves, we can feel our own positive/negative inflations. Still, recognizing them doesn't always mean being able to negotiate them. That's when the black needle comes in handy. The balloon deflates, and back we are, resting on solid ground.

The Trifecta sounds great...how do I get that?

THIS IS A GIGANTIC **UNIVERSAL** SO LISTEN UP: *Be* the person you want to date, work for, live with, or befriend!

"That's it??!!" you say with a snarl.

Yes, as usual everything begins with you. Again, this should be music to your ears, since it means finding relationship peace and happiness doesn't depend on a lightning strike, luck, or an apocalyptic world shift.

Because change is in YOUR hands.

Right here.

Right now.

So in terms of the Trifecta: *be a fan for the people in your life.* What thinking, feeling, behaving would *you* need to change for this to happen? *Have other people's backs.* What do *you* need to do differently? *Show or tell others how you cherish them.* Do you?

Do it today.

Do it at work and at play.

Well, of course, becoming the fabulous person you want to date needs to include also treating the Self in those fine ways.

Are you your biggest fan? In what ways?

Do you have your own back? How?

Do you cherish yourself? When?

The buck starts and stops with you.

How does it work?

WITH EACH OFFERED AVENUE FOR CHANGE, participation will be requested. Of course, whether or not you engage is your call. The more you do, the more you'll change. So when you feel ready, take a moment to write about the Trifecta. Make a two-column list. Side one: what you do now (for self and toward others). Side two: what you could do differently.

Heartbreak: slaying the monster

Life will break you. Nobody can protect you from that, and living alone won't either—for solitude will also break you with its yearning. You have to love. You have to feel. It is the reason you are here on earth. You are here to risk your heart. You are here to be swallowed up. And when it happens that you are broken, or betrayed, or left, or hurt, or death brushes near, let yourself sit by an apple tree and listen to the apples falling all around you in heaps, wasting their sweetness. Tell yourself you tasted as many as you could.- Louise Erdrich [xlv]

AS PREVIOUSLY STATED, HEARTBREAK IS that awful, punch-in-the-gut, self-esteem pummeling experience of lost love. In the moment it seems we'll never recover.

Of course we do.

It feels we'll never try again.

Of course we do.

It looks like devastation.

Of course it is.

And it's also the most enlivening, resource-expanding, humanity-engaging experience we can encounter. Remember Maria during her divorce? Ask her. Her moments of greatest despair were also the times when she felt most alive. She may not exactly have known it while the pain was raining its terrors down upon her, but looking back it's clear. This may be true for you as well. That's why heartbreak requires patience and such sweet self-care. Eventually, of course, we want access to the aliveness without the pain.

Point is, heartbreak can and does happen *within* an on-going relationship also. Happily, not every partnership challenge need end in collapse.

As so often, the "fix it" solution is simple, but difficult.

It's *constant reinvention.*

What this requires is a persistent willingness to re-view the relationship. Not review meaning go over old territory, but rather see anew: re-view. Yes, this is likely to involve some remembering, which means putting things back together again (versus dismembering, which is what we do when tearing a relationship and ourselves apart). What we never want to start from is the perspective that we've been doing something "wrong." What's more helpful and truer is that our behavior stems from unconscious conclusions, requirements, and yearnings.

I profoundly believe we come to a relationship to heal early damage, to confront basic patterns, to find new resources, and to claim lost parts of the Self. That means every so-called relationship error we make is actually a smart effort to mend—to some degree; unless, of course, you've simply been operating on masochistic overdrive.

In any event, you're here now—to make things different. To make it happen, simply reading this book won't do it. You're going to have to participate and get really active.

Try these three relationship questions on for size. Remember you can find ways to also apply the questions to other areas of your life, like job or friendship.

#1. What originally brought you into love with your significant other?

#2. What were you admiring, imagining, and thinking about them then, that you've since lost track of?

#3. How can you begin to see your partner as a "new" person?

You see, our excitement and enthusiasm about other's lives primarily in our heads.

Yes, our heads.

That doesn't mean there wasn't grist for our mill—elements making us sit up and take notice. Oh certainly, perhaps there was a soul connection or an instant sense of "knowing," or maybe over time we discovered more and more layers that brought us into a sense of this being a truly wonderful person. But mostly, when we first meet, we simply make it up and make them up. Imagine them to be who we need them to be.

We become enamored. Fall under a spell. Then somehow, along the way, original inducements fade.

Or get over-clouded with resentments. It may take only a short while or many years. Still, the process is the same. Expectation and appreciation are replaced with uneasiness, disappointment and desire perceived as unfulfilled.

The work at that point is to penetrate those resentment clouds with the light of our...uh...let's call it Love Vision. Hokey? Maybe, but right too. We need to re-vision the love we used to so easily touch.

Q: What do you do when the passion dies?

HOW MANY FRIENDS DO YOU HAVE THAT TALK ABOUT THIS? It's everywhere.

We all know most use the word "passion" as code for sex. Certainly passion includes more, for it might include lust, but usually involves much beyond lust—such as, for example, fervent emotional connection. We can be passionate about work or friends or sports or anything else.

It's vivacity.

Life force.

Carl Jung calls it Libido.

In a relationship when passion begins to die it often shows up sexually, because as mentioned, sex is the repository and reflection of all sorts of inner psychological precepts, thoughts, feelings, desires, disappointments, etc. It might look like daily stress or money problems or health issues or intrusive kids or whatever is interrupting primary relationship passion but for sure a more probing inquiry will be wanted. Proof is, when suddenly dating someone new you without doubt manage to find the energy, time, and interest to express passion in whatever form.

Right? Right.

In any event, long before lack of sexual passion rears its head, passion has begun to die on the vine in other areas. Guaranteed.

Still since it's such a popular go-to topic, let's hover over sexual chat for a hot second to make this basic point: when it comes to reigniting great or even good sex with a partner, you need to remember: If you had it, you can get it back. If you never had it, that's another conversation.

Good sex

Newsflash: GOOD SEX IS MOSTLY IN OUR BRAINS.

That means the zest with which we perceive and approach our sexual experiences depends more on our own readiness than on the partners we pick. Needless to say, there are exceptions. Some folks will be lousy lovers no matter how much pizzazz and positive intention we bring to the party.

Okay, so how does this work?

When we first meet, all we can think about is the person we're attracted to. We imagine, hope, and invent. In our minds, we work it and work it. By the time we actually meet up with our new lover for a liaison, we're primed, pumped, and ready.

Prepped? Check.

Aroused? Check.

Raring to go? Check.

The actual sex is practically the aperitif. Or at least we can say we've had drinks and delicious mouth-watering appetizers and are super-duper ready for the main course.

Unfortunately, once we've been with someone a while, we fall into ordinariness and expectation. We "know" how it's going to feel and be, so we don't bother bringing anything new. As with everything, we get into habits.

Fix it, fix it, fix it!!

HERE'S WHERE A RETURN TO YESTERYEAR IS CALLED FOR. Good sex keys:

- ✓ Go back to just-met-you-basics
- ✓ Think about the potential engagement far in advance.
- ✓ Spend time in your head getting worked up about it Do this instead of texting your friend or colleague on the way home—or instead of dictating one more memo
- ✓ Introduce something new into the sexual partnership. Call ahead and use your sexy voice to suggest a certain outfit. Or send that outfit from a store. Or make reservations at a hotel and have them meet you there. Leave an enticing note they're sure to find somewhere in the morning before you or they leave. Or suggest role-playing. Sure your partner might be reluctant or

shy about this, but even the suggestion alone might inspire

I'm thinking now about Daniel, who managed to simultaneously laugh and scoff when role-playing was suggested for him and his wife, Suzanna. He'd always been completely on board for *her* dressing up in lingerie as a stimulant, but this full-fledged fantasy business seemed to him a bridge too far.

I suggested they meet at a bar, acting as if they didn't know each other. The trick was to turn everything upside down—with her being the aggressor and him acting shy. Reluctantly, he agreed, more out of desperation than anything else as the sexual aspect of their long relationship had become dull as dirt.

In the case of Daniel and Suzanna, the results were spectacular, putting them on an entirely new relationship track.

Of course, this isn't everyone's cup of tea, but you'll never know unless you pose the possibility to your partner or give it a try yourself. Now, it doesn't usually happen that one such adventure turns the tide, but no matter what, it's a great reinvigoration start.

Look, obviously there are hundreds of possibilities. The idea is to be inventive, just like you would if it were someone you were just starting to date.

This reinvention and reinvigoration of relationship really wants to happen in multiple areas over and again. This is true everywhere in our lives. We need to reinvent ourselves at work. We need to reinvigorate our friendships.

Stunner: To stay refreshed, we must be refreshing.

Q: But how do I learn to stay faithful in relationship when I never have?

THIS IS A TOUGH, COMPLICATED SUBJECT. Why we're unable or don't desire to stay faithful inevitably has long personal history behind it and deserves extensive exploration. To be brief, and to simply tickle the fancy of this far-reaching and oft-met conversation, we can begin by saying that most often the lack of fidelity (where fidelity is desired or agreed upon) reflects a compulsivity and the fear feeding that compulsivity.

We might even begin by calling it a **complex**, which translates in Latin to *connection.* But what are we connecting to?

What a complex most often references is a deep unconscious set of emotions and beliefs revealed through behavior. Now, just as everyone has defenses, everyone has complexes. And not all complexes are negative, nor do they negatively impact our lives. The question is not are they good or bad, but rather how do they affect the ways in which we move through the world.

With infidelity the effect can be difficult and, in some cases, devastating to an on-going, solid relationship. So what happens? First, some arousal occurs—a desire surges up in us. Where does this urge come from? That's where the personal investigation must begin. Is this over-and-again encountered "need" based in insecurity—such as an idea that if I can't get someone new to be interested in me, I'm no longer a viable, vital person in the world? Must I have such attention to validate me and show me I'm worthwhile? Am I somehow trying to prove my prowess and power? Am I afraid if I connect to one person only, and profoundly on every level, I'll lose my independence? These few questions barely scratch the surface of possibility.

Indeed, there are inevitably far bigger issues for which the chronically unfaithful individual is compensating. To reveal what these larger issues are, this query can and should go in many directions. Those truly interested in discovering the psychological stimulus for such an on-going "complex" would best engage such delving. This is where sitting with yourself and foraging your way through the forest of your own psyche can deliver extraordinary results. Once finding the *why*, we can deal with the how-do-we-shift.

Still, for now, let's go at the question from the easiest possible angle. Best case scenario, we begin by understanding our true relationship to sex itself. Partnership sex, for instance, is never really about orgasm. In fact, we can do that better and more efficiently all by ourselves.

Uh huh.

So what's it about? That's the question we want to approach when discovering more about our sexual proclivities in any and all ways, including habitual infidelity.

It's helpful to begin with a non-sexual gratification list. This is to include all those things, minus an orgasm, that you get out of partner sex—things like feelings of desirability, appeal, power, control, surrender, etc.

Take a moment to make your list now.

After figuring out what we're getting out of partnership sex, and noticing how particular needs are not happening in our primary relationship, we can potentially start discovering non-sexual ways to experience those needs, wants, and desires.

Now, maybe one of the things you get out of infidelity involves the newness factor; that is, the thrill of realizing "I've still got it!" If that's your deal, you're going to have to dig deep to find other avenues to allow for the same excitement; for instance, discovering fresh adventures to pursue like sky-diving or scuba, or innovative and creative projects to engage. Or, of course, you can decide infidelity is the way to go for you.

If so, there will be certain ramifications.

Notice, as always, I'm not trying to determine right and wrong here. I simply want to open awareness. Only you can decide what can be lived with and what can't.

PART III: FIXING MY LOVE LIFE

ALL RIGHT, SO READINESS FOR REAL CHANGE HAS KICKED IN. By now, you've come to some overall realizations about why you've been proceeding the way you have—time to get really specific, especially with regards to love matters.

As with everything, when it comes to heartbreak, we tend to quickly establish rituals. Discovering your current ways and means is fundamental for true shift.

When examining ourselves we always want to investigate the things we think and say, the way we feel, and the behaviors we engage.

One of the best ways to discover ourselves is through writing. The simplest version will involve *making lists*. Rather than saving the following explorations for the *Love Works* chapter, I've included them in the body of this section because they provide an important foundation for all that is to follow. Again, though, as with other sprinkled-in exercises, feel free to merely read through them at this juncture with an intention of going back later (I'm hoping) to ruminate fully. In the meantime, having entertained the questions even briefly, your psyche will begin working on your behalf.

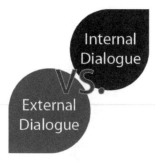

Sayings

THE FIRST THING TO DO IS NOTICE WHAT YOU SAY both to yourself and to others with regards to love and to heartbreak. We're very consistent really, so you'll find repetitive phrases peppering both inner and outer dialogue.

Here are a few examples:

It'll never be different;
Heartbreak is all I deserve;
There's something wrong with me;
If I can change them, it will mean I'm special.

Certain actual sayings or ways of thinking will be clear to you right away, while others will need nudging. Clarity ensues through attentive practice.

Try writing: Heartbreak is _____; Heartbreak is _____ Heartbreak happens because _____; Heartbreak happens because _____; When it comes to Heartbreak it's best to _____; When it comes to Heartbreak it's best to _____; Heartbreak never _____; Heartbreak never _____.

In other words, write the same lines many, many times and fill in the blanks.

By the way, if you *must* write on the computer, do so; however, writing by hand does stimulate a different part of the psyche, so you might attempt that as well.

Do your best to not think too much while attempting this exercise. Let the words flow without editing. We want to "catch" our true ways and means, while avoiding "right," smart, or sophisticated answers.

We're looking for organic here.

Let's go raw!

We need to know what we know to change what's next. So, besides the specifics of heartbreak, try listing the assumptions, myths, and overall ideas you have about love. Here are some samples:

Love happens by chance and is a crap shoot;
When it comes to love, obviously something's wrong with me;
When it comes to love, obviously something's wrong with the world.

To the best of your ability, write freely without considering what's coming out. Let the ideas you hold about love spill out upon the page, like faded letters from a fallen memory box. Maybe you'll discover your mother's old words written there, or your father's. Perhaps you'll hear refrains you didn't even realize you sang. Try not judging what's written. Become the fascinated witness of your own closely kept secret philosophies.

Ideas

Many operate primarily through thinking functions. If you fit into this category, you're likely to have lots of ideas about the effects of heartbreak and about how love works.

You'll be able to tell if you're mostly a thinker as your words reflect that. We're always describing ourselves through sentence structure and chosen phrases. Folks worrying about being misunderstood, for instance, can be heard to say:

✓ "Do you know what I mean?"
✓ "Does that make sense?"
✓ "I don't know how to explain this."

Others, wildly self-conscious about their potential and gifts, might apologize constantly. Thinkers, then, tend to often begin sentences with "I think," while feelers begin with "I feel." This isn't a rule or standard though—especially since in our current climate many have been told they need to talk about feelings more, so they start sentences with "I feel" but then progress to give their opinion about other people's behaviors. We'll soon discuss the *how-to* of good communication, which doesn't involve finger-pointing. Meanwhile, just pay attention to how you phrase things, the words you use, and also the pervading conclusions roaming through you. Perhaps you think things like:

*Because of all the potential hurt, I've decided relationship is too difficult
I just avoid it;
Love is for suckers. It just breaks you;
There are no good relationships;
Heartache is inevitable;
No one's really happy, but some folks are pretending.*

Remember that thoughts often guide actions.

Also, both thoughts and feelings get reflected back to us by the people and circumstances of our lives. If you believe love is for suckers you're sure to invite people who take advantage, are unavailable, or ignore your importance. If you believe a relationship is too difficult, you're sure to reject potential, delightful partners by putting up defensive walls. So, noticing your negative thoughts with regards to love is very important.

Feelings

CERTAIN INDIVIDUALS ARE FEELERS. There's no right or wrong here. However, if you're primarily propelled by emotion, you know it, so most of your list will sound like:

Love always seems to leave me sad;
I get heartbroken, then paralyzed;
I get furious and vow to never love again;
When relationships don't work out, I feel like I want to die.

All right then, you get the point.
The more we know what relationship beliefs we currently hold, the better chance we have of figuring out the basis for our love conflict. Sometimes, the other person is just not the right fit. Sometimes, no one will feel like the right fit. If we don't know what we're thinking and feeling it will be very difficult to shift into a fresh, vibrant, helpful perspective.

Invitations to love…

OVER THE YEARS, I'VE HAD SITTING ON MY COUCH countless individuals supposedly seeking true love. Many call themselves selective or picky.

It's inevitably code for "*I always find something wrong with the people I meet and date.*" Two things: first, there *is* always going to be something wrong with everyone. The idea is to figure out what's impossible for you to live with and what's not. **If you're looking for perfect, you don't really want a relationship.** Second, you're implying the rest of us aren't "picky" and that most people are settling. You're fooling yourself. What's keeping you from love is fear. Figuring out what supports that fear can change everything.

There are three *vital* invitation-to-love cornerstones. These three must be understood, accepted, and investigated before any real change can occur.

- ✓ **Cornerstone #1:** The majority of our complaints are actually problems of perception.
- ✓ **Cornerstone #2:** *Apparent* issues are really announcements and symptoms of *underlying "themes"* to be articulated, and more deeply understood.
- ✓ **Cornerstone #3:** Choices, reactivity, and actions are 100% our responsibility.

We talked earlier about the Nine Heartbreak Guarantees.

Now, I'm going to offer you nine solutions. For each solution listed here, the *how-to* has been well covered throughout *Our Love Matters*. This list is meant merely as a reference, then, and a yardstick list when you get tempted to lapse into old behavior.

And you will.

Don't limit yourself to primary love relationships when looking at these remedies. Maybe you've experienced heartbreak with friends, in your career, or with work colleagues? See how these alternatives might apply in all areas.

Heartbreak Solutions

✓ **Solution #1: Explore, examine, and appreciate personal responsibility.** Getting past the pain doesn't happen by ignoring or denying it. Look it in the eye. See its benefits. Acknowledge its burdens. Recognize what the past has taught. Don't erase—embrace.

✓ **Solution #2: Take contrary action.** A series of red flags mean walk away. Speak up instead of shutting down. Ask for what you need instead of expecting them to mind read.

✓ **Solution # 3: Consider reality.** Believe what people tell you. If a relationship is better in your head than in your bed, that's a problem.

✓ **Solution #4: Expect the best.** Fear prevents love. We get what we expect. When we walk through the world with boxing gloves on, we tend to meet many boxers.

✓ **Solution #5: Give acceptance.** Accept others in your life and you'll be more confident in expecting it for yourself. When you expect rejection, what you're really doing is rejecting yourself.

✓ **Solution #6: Practice presence** and go toward real, depthful understanding. The life in front of you calls. Strive to understand that life. Use magical thinking for inspiration not aspiration. The life in front of you calls.

✓ **Solution #7: Something's not better than nothing.** The best solution is to fall in love with the Self. Some terrible or lackluster or this-will-do match is never going to scratch that true love itch.

✓ **Solution #8: Understand your limits and the limits of others.** No one's perfect. You're not either. That's okay. Imagined control is the enemy of presence in all things including in love. Take care of today and tomorrow will take care of its self.

✓ **Solution #9: Stop reading from that old rulebook.** It's time to develop your own "rules"—things that work for you. There's no absolute right way to find and keep love.

Heartbreak Learning Points:

✓ Heartbreak has a purpose

✓ Most often heartbreak begins at home as a child

✓ Relationship tries to heal old wounds

✓ Love matters change when we take responsibility for our contribution to the problems

✓ Bad relationship is more than bad luck

Change Ways Chart

9 __Heartbreak Guarantees:__	9 __Heartbreak Solutions:__
#1. Refusing to recognize your contribution to the disrepair.	#1. Explore, examine and appreciate *your* responsibility.
# 2. Repeating old patterns of undermining behavior.	#2. Take contrary action.
#3. Refusing to hear.	#3. Consider reality.
#4. Expecting the worst.	#4. Expect the best.
#5. Living in expectation of rejection.	#5. Give acceptance and you'll be more confident in expecting it for yourself.
#6. Magical thinking as a substitute for inspired understanding.	#6. Be present to the life that is in front of you.
#7. Maintaining the illusion that something's better than nothing	#7. Something's not better than nothing.
#8. Trying to control outcome.	#8. Understand your limits and the limits of others
#9. Reading from an old rule book.	#9: Close the old rule book. Make your own new rules.

PART IV: WHAT'S LOVE GOT TO DO WITH IT?

The best things in life make you sweaty.
Edgar Allan Poe[xlvi]

EVERYONE POINTS TO LOVE AS THE BE-ALL, END-ALL OF RELATIONSHIPS. Buckle up because I've got a new truth to tell.

Stunner: In relationship love is never enough. **Love is the easy part.**

You know I'm right.

In relationship love is the first thing to come and last thing to go. My very first counseling internship was in a shelter for Abused Women & Children. The women would call in talking about how their partners drank all the money away, beat them, and disappeared for insane amounts of time.

Over and again, I'd ask: "Why do you stay?"

The answer was always the same: "Because I love him!"

Egads.

All right, these may be extreme circumstances but face it; we've all done similar things.

And worse.

Many believe love will carry the day.

It won't.

Now, I'm not saying love's irrelevant or unimportant—of course not. It's the tasty, sweet chocolate coating on the S 'more. But what's the graham cracker and where's the gooey, marshmallow holding it altogether? And where's the heat coming from to make it all work?

Throughout *Our Love Matters* I've been insisting that love is a verb. Like a wonderful fire, love continually wants stoking, attention, and new kindle. That means we need to stop grumbling about what isn't working and start changing our own behavior.

Maybe you've been thinking a relationship should just "naturally" flow. Or that once you have love, game over, and problem solved. Not so. Usually, finding the person to love or the job to love or the friends to love is only the beginning. Then the real "work" starts. Being a great musician takes work. Anything done well requires genuine diligence.

A relationship does also.

Happily, we don't need to be "all fixed" or even love ourselves entirely to find a terrific other. As described in the preface, my own story tells the tale.

Q: But how can I commit to someone when I feel conflicted myself?

Again, most of us simply can't wait until absolute readiness appears. And more importantly, perhaps, there's a certain kind of healing that can only occur *in* and through a relationship. We can't think our way into this kind of healing. It must happen experientially. It's like good sex. Talking about it just isn't the same as doing it.

The same equation is true in parenting as well. Certain remedial elements with regards to our own childhoods can only be done through the experience of parenting another. But not all of us will be parents. So what does that mean? Well, here's the thing: *Not everyone will or should heal every part of the Self.*

Radical therapist speak, huh!? And true.

Indeed, there are abundant ways and works that can produce and allow a fabulously manifested, enriched, productive, and contented life—with or without relationship, with or without children, with or without a stunning career, with or without an overflowing bank account, with or without hot sex, with or without family recovery and even with or without an acknowledged, conscious relationship to a Spiritual context. We don't need to massage every nook and corner of our bruised parts. In fact, I'd say, we simply can't cover it all. Most of it, anyway, will stay swimming in the unconscious. Some will work itself out through dreams and other sweet ways when our backs are turned.

That's a bonus.

But I don't believe that a genuinely wonderful life can happen without manifested love altogether—some way, somehow. Love of work or love with friends or love of humanity or love of Spirit, all of which, I maintain, starts with self-love and radiates out.

What I'm suggesting is that we work with the parts of healing we're most deeply called to. If it is relationship love, then go ahead and throw yourself into the fray—whether you feel ready or not. You'll quickly find out what you do and don't know. That's when it all gets truly exciting.

I mean it.

If it's love of work, attend that with equal vigor and use all the tools offered here to enhance your career experience. If it's love of community, become the most fervent, active, loving community member ever.

The long and short of it is: We can't fix our primary relationship issues outside of relationships; however, we can work with other connection quandaries and discover quite a wonderful level of health, healing, and love. And, too, getting into *any* relationship that comes along just because we're lonely or are working on healing, or hope everything will be fixed that way, is both dismal and unproductive.

So commit to *love* itself.

Commit.　To love.

PART V: HOW GREAT RELATIONSHIP WORKS

Even
After
All this time
The Sun never says to the Earth,
"You owe me."
Look
What happens
With a love like that,
It lights the whole sky. - Hafiz [xlvii]

The 4 C's of Great Relationship

I am certain of nothing but the holiness of the heart's affections. -Keats

Four C's of a Great Relationship

LONG HAVE WE STOOD IN THE SHADOW OF OUR WANTING, hoping for solutions to the undying yearning that our troubled thoughts might either find sweet peace as they are, or change direction altogether. We've grunted, prayed, read, and planned in all our love matters to feel anew the promise and dream we remember once enjoying. Here it is, what we've been working toward: Real solutions to genuine doubts, stranded dreams, and disturbing conclusions.

These solutions, called the Four C's, are:

- ✓ **Communication**
- ✓ **Collaboration**
- ✓ **Contribution**
- ✓ **Compromise**

Before diving in, though, let's start with remembering that people love differently—and also that whether in love or otherwise, they grow in various rhythms. Not only don't we express love the same way or in the same rhythm and timing, but also seldom do we experience love identically. For some, it's a pounding kettle drum announcing itself boldly. For others, it's quiet fingers gently tickling harp strings. Simple as this we-love-and-grow-differently statement might sound at first glance, it's actually an extremely layered declaration.

For instance, over time I've worked with many clients who simply don't "feel" the love they have for their partners. I'll call this way "thinking" the love. They know deep connected caring, but seldom experience it as emotionally overwhelming, blissful, or heart throbbing.

Meanwhile, others are primarily feelers. For them, most everything strikes an emotional cord. They're touched by many experiences including pain, need, and joy—and naturally by love as well. They cry easily and often.

Then there's the "doers"—those who show love through action. That can include, for example, fixing things around the house, making dinner, planning the vacation, or gift buying.

And that's just the beginning. There are slow-movers and fast-movers, talkers and non-talkers, social types and non-social types, extraverts and introverts, and on it goes.

When feelers and thinkers are partnered—or feeler/doers or thinker/doers, or any other configuration—there can easily be confused consternation unless they both come to accept and appreciate the love modality, as well as interactive style, of the other.

Why we choose partners so different from us has already been well covered throughout this book, but, of course, despite "good" explanations, we still manage to be mystified...and miffed.

Q: Isn't a relationship supposed to make life easier?

WELL, YES, TO SOME DEGREE. It should be the stable platform on which we stand; the anchor that keeps us from drifting out to sea, the place where all our hurts and hopes get expressed.

In fact, I've rarely talked to a couple, even amidst divorce, that didn't speak of their partner as best friend. In certain circumstances, what that means is somewhat bewildering. Do we withhold our true wants, needs, and hopes from our best friend? When we're unhappy with how our best-friend relationship is going, do we lash out or shut down?

Well, maybe your answer is yes because in truth, we do tend to treat our partners similarly to the way we treat everything and everyone in our lives—at least to some modest degree. Thus, even though the bright spotlight shining on the center-stage star called relationship makes our behaviors more obvious, we're always responding and behaving, to some degree, in pattern. That means, if we really try, we can spot our patterns revealing themselves everywhere to whatever extent.

The themes that poke at us and the well-established defenses that arise out of those themes don't simply dissolve when we leave the house. So yes, if you look carefully you'll see your relationship patterns showing up also at work, with friends, and even while driving. But, of course, when it comes to primary partnership, the picture shows in vivid, 3-D, Blu-ray, surround sound.

In other words, if shutting down instead of speaking up is your way of communicating to your mate, it's probable you do the same when problems arise with friends, family, and work as well. You may disagree with this at first, seeing the focused stress occurring in your relationship as unique, but remember some of that's cumulative and also constant—whereas in other places and situations we can keep leaving to regroup.

All right…how's it work?

IN ALL RELATIONSHIPS, THERE ARE THREE ENTITIES: ME, THEM AND US. This three-pronged standard includes mate connections, friendship bonds, work affiliations, and family associations. We might say there's even three with regards to the communal grouping called the Collective. We could talk about it this way: "THEM" is the world; "ME" is how I as an individual fit into the world (known as society); and "US" is how you and I together create what's called the world community.

Facebook is a wonderful example of how all three come together. When we go on Facebook, it feels very individual. Someone "likes" what we've written or posts a response. When that happens we, as individuals feel connected to that single other. When several respond, we are immediately reminded we've joined a community. If I post something from both my husband and me, we have joined.

All three parts of any affiliation deserve particular regard and respect. It's always valuable to check out what we are and aren't genuinely offering. Sometimes, for example, we're our own problem in the workplace; other times it's a particular work community dynamic that's the source of consternation, and in still other instances it's simply a bad fit.

It's the same, but more emphatically so, in primary relationships where it's always important for both participants to appreciate and take ownership of their individual contributions—especially when it comes to trauma and drama. Everybody's got a part. I like the idea of applying everywhere the couple's therapy work-concept that it's not 50/50, but rather 100/100; each party being responsible for 100% of their own behavior and psychological impact/input.

What this means to partnership…

ME: BY NOW, YOU'VE DETERMINED WHAT YOU WANT, NEED, AND DESERVE. Hopefully, you've also come to appreciate how personal history has thrown stumbling blocks into the middle of your relationship road. This understanding is crucial for full embrace of your 100%.

Here it's essential to remember the Fundamental: the bigger the response the older the material supporting the response.

I used to know a therapist named Rob who was very meticulous. By the time his second marriage rolled around, he'd discovered a great deal about himself and headed into it with his eyes open. Their life moved along nicely. One day fairly early on, he came home to find his new bride, Kate, had draped her freshly-removed coat on a living room chair. He immediately ruffled. "Please don't do that! Hang up your coat when you come in!!"

To her, he sounded like her father. Ouch.

Next day when Kate came in, she flung her coat on the chair and left her shoes on the living room floor. Upon arriving home, Rob exploded. Third day, Kate left her coat on the chair, her shoes on the floor, and a blouse there as well. The tension mounted.

Later that evening, Rob came to Kate: "You know, I've been thinking about this and I realize I've been really over the top with this neatness business. I know I'm kind of OCD about it all, but really it drives me nuts to see anything out of place. I'd so appreciate it if you'd appease me in this. It would mean the world to me!"

And with that, problem solved. Once Rob took responsibility and stopped treating Kate like an errant child, she was happy to accommodate his simple request.

Naturally, what we'd best evolve to is a mostly reactive-free life. That means being able to fairly easily pick and choose how much weight we want to give our feeling pinches. Would it have been terrific for Rob to get over the anxiety he felt when disorder happened? Sure. And would the best scenario include Kate no longer having to rebel against lingering father issues? You bet. Maybe, eventually, they both got over their individual glitches. One can hope. But meanwhile, quick self-assessment is the key.

In relationships, as everywhere else, we're unlikely to be "perfect," but we can stay alert.

THEM: It's important to stay aware of what's special about your partner.

During the first session with a couple, I often ask each person to tell the other things they find terrific about them—to describe what initially encouraged, invited, and excited them in their relationship. In answering this question, I'm constantly surprised by how many people talk about their "other" solely as a personal reflection. For instance, if you say your mate's great-looking, compassionate, spontaneous, playful, sexy, and smart, that's great. However, if all you know to reference is a series of statements like: I love how she takes care of me, shows me love, makes me feel good about myself, takes care of our kids, and always looks put-together when I get home, that's quite a different matter. In that case, you need to reach deeper. We always want to appreciate who our partners are as unique individuals having nothing whatsoever to do with us. If we're the happy recipients of their wondrous ability to nurture, so much the better, but it's that already-present ability we want to admire in the first place.

Get it?

Of course, it's vital that we go beyond the superficial. I ever-so-briefly had this one extremely young couple that when asked the what-do-you-love-about-the-other question both answered only: The way he (she) looks playing volleyball on the beach! Well, maybe in this case, it's patently obvious there's not much readiness for serious commitment. Still, I must say hundreds of times I've heard about their smell, shape, or attractiveness being the main draw. These things fade, shift or change. Then what?!

Of course, we must be attracted to our partners, no doubt about it, but when physical perfection is purely what we seek—or when the physical trumps every other aspect—it's a recipe for disaster. Additionally, the need to have a physically "perfect" other actually reflects deeper psychological stumbling blocks to real love.

The couple coming to mind here are Jan and Toby. Jan, a charming, attractive, physically fit, and financially successful person, came from a family of hugely overweight individuals. Jan worried that any partner he had would "turn into" his family. So the idea of slender, attractive, smart Toby suddenly becoming obese plagued him. It didn't matter that there were no signs of such a thing. Nor did it matter that Toby was interested in staying slim.

Jan's concern about weight began to spill onto other appearance areas. Was the hair exactly right? The clothing? The style?

It didn't take long for focus on physical appearance to become such a dramatic conversation between them that it threatened to derail the relationship entirely.

Naturally, Jan's real fear had nothing to do with Toby at all and related completely to family-of-origin matters. The complication, as it turns out, was that Jan's father had early on fled the family scene. Somewhere deep inside, Jan had equated that leave-taking with mother's appearance. Since he already entered a relationship with a fear of commitment that included concerns about somehow becoming a philanderer like his dad, some part of him thought if only he's manage to side-step all apparent physical issues, he could avoid repeating history.

Of course, Toby also entered a relationship with history-laden self-doubts and self-consciousness about being good enough to be loved in a sustained way. Thus, their mutual concerns nicely fed their relationship issues.

In any event, being attentive to the "them" of the equation means putting aside self-centered, often relationship-infecting preoccupations, to remember how much love matters.

US: Being in service to "us" means considering the needs of the partnership over our own self-centered wants. A simple example of this might be purchasing a house approximately halfway between your two job locations, so no one has to drive excessively.

I remember years ago when my husband's father was dying. One day I was thinking: "What if he dies when I've got a workshop? What will I do? Should I let all those folks down by being with my man at the funeral, or should I continue on with my work?" Now, I came from a family that never put family first, so it's not surprising that such a thought would cross my mind. Thankfully, it was brief. "Get a hold of yourself," I said. "Of course you shall be at your husband's side no matter what! Don't even think about it!"

Indeed, it's important to get your priorities straight.

Not long ago, singer Fiona Apple announced the cancellation of her South American tour dates because of the need to be beside her dying 13-year old pit-bull dog. Here's what she posted on a social media site:

It's 6pm on Friday, and I'm writing to a few thousand friends I have not met yet. I am writing to ask them to change our plans and meet a little while later. Here's the thing. I have a dog Janet, and she's been ill for almost two years now, as a tumor has been idling in her chest, growing ever so slowly. She's almost 14-years-old now. I got her when she was 4 months old. I was 21 then, an adult officially—and she was my child. She is a pit-bull, and was found in Echo Park, with a rope around her neck, and bites all over her ears and face. She was the one the dogfighters use to puff up the confidence of the contenders. She's almost 14 and I've never seen her start a fight, bite, or even growl, so I can understand why they chose her for that awful role. She's a pacifist. Janet has been the most consistent relationship of my adult life, and that is just a fact. We've lived in numerous houses, and jumped a few makeshift families, but it's always really been the two of us. She slept in bed with me, her head on the pillow, and she accepted my hysterical, tearful face into her chest, with her paws around me, every time I was heartbroken, or spirit-broken, or just lost. And as years went by, she let me take the role of her child, as I fell asleep, with her chin resting above my head. She sat next to me when I wrote songs, and barked any time I tried to record something, and she was with me in the studio, all the time we recorded the last album.

The last time I came back from tour, she was spry as ever, and she's used to me being gone for a few weeks every 6 or 7 years. She has Addison's disease, which makes it dangerous for her to go on the road with me...Despite all of this, she's effortlessly joyful and playful, and only stopped acting like a puppy about 3 years ago. She's my best friend and my mother and my daughter, and my benefactor, and she's the one who taught me what love is. I can't come to South America. Not now. When I got back from the last leg of the US tour, there was a big, big difference. She doesn't even want to go for walks anymore. I know that she's not sad about aging or dying. Animals may well have a survival instinct, but a sense of mortality and vanity they do not. That's why they are so much more present than most people. But I know that she is coming close to point where she will stop being a dog, and instead, be part of everything. She'll be in the wind, and in the soil, and the snow, and in me, wherever I go. I can't leave her now, please understand. If I go away again, I'm afraid she'll die and I won't have the honor of singing her to sleep, of escorting her out.

Maybe she'll fool me and live for a couple more years––maybe I'll lose my potential friends, in places I feel a longing to know. Sometimes it takes me 20 minutes to pick which socks to wear to bed. But this decision is instant. These are the choices we make, which define us. I am not the woman who puts her career ahead of love and friendship. I'm the woman who stays home, and bakes Tilapia for my dearest, oldest friend; and helps her be comfortable, and comforted, and safe, and important. Many of us these days, we dread the 'death' of a loved one. It is the ugly truth of life that leaves us feeling terrified and alone. I wish we could also appreciate the time that lies right beside the end of time. I know that I will feel the most overwhelming knowledge of her, and of her life, and of my love for her, in the last moments. I need to do my damnedest to be there for that. Because it will be the most beautiful, the most intense, the most enriching experience of life I've ever known. When she dies. So I am staying home, and I am listening to her snore and wheeze, and reveling in the swampiest, most awful breath that ever emanated from an angel. And I am asking for your blessing. I'll be seeing you.

Love, Fiona

Now, that's what I call having your priorities straight—and what a beautiful message. Love trumping all. As it should be and seldom is.

Yes, when it comes to priorities strict attention must be paid.

Good thing you're onto yourself in terms of themes, so you can first figure out if you're following old patterns or, rather, being present to genuine relationship need. This goes back to the self-care through boundaries versus the immature self-centeredness which encourages us to reject authentic service to a partner.

Now, there are many present-day circumstances putting pressure on the "us" and challenging sustained commitment. Good examples are current issues arising now, quite often, out of our challenging and changing economy. Say, for instance, he's lost his job and is staying home to be Mr. Mom, while she's the primary breadwinner.

First, there's the potential effect of their mutual abandonment of traditional roles. Perhaps she feels (deeply and unconsciously) unprotected; after all, he's no longer out slaying the fatted calf. While at the same time, he feels she's abandoned her "real" duties as, after all, she's no longer attending to hearth and home (again, this is likely to be unconscious). And second, he might believe he's abandoned his own manhood. Yes, indeed more advanced thinking might balk at this notion; however, that doesn't mean the more primitive parts inside us aren't up in arms. After all, what "real man" does laundry and changes diapers? Meanwhile, she could also hold an idea somewhere inside that she's abandoned her true purpose. After all, what "real woman" lets another soothe her crying baby?

Well, it can go on and on.

Because feelings of abandonment are so far-reaching, global and primary, we'd all do well to explore how and when they may affect a daily influence.

Our individual work in these instances, though, is as always to take ownership of the volume of our individual responses and to note how those reactions affect "us."

All of this is to say that practicing the Four C's of Great Relationships is vital. These amazing tools will hold you steady anywhere you are and no matter who you're with. So get going. Start today.

PART VI: COMMUNICATION

Practice Listening, Sharing, and Supporting

When you know how to listen, everyone is the guru.
- Ram Dass

TALK IS NOT A FOUR-LETTER WORD. In all my years as a therapist, and with the many thousands of couples I've met, 99% of the time, couples answer the opening "why are you here?" question with some version of: "We have terrible communication."

Pretty much everyone knows this is the crux of the matter—well, at least they know it's a problem their partner's got! Ah yes, we dearly love pointing the finger. "Fix them!" they say to me, having little idea they too have talk-right glitches.

Many things play into hog-tying communication, not the least of which is power struggling. Without doubt, it's feelings of powerlessness that most often inspire bad communication.

Everywhere.

On top of that, we generally have zero idea how to make it different. There's good reason for this. No one's teaching us.

Schools don't emphasize communication skills—home life often sadly doesn't as well. We're left dazed and confused.

There's a cure though—specific ways to make things better. Hooray.

As with everything, of course, the magic's in the doing. And no matter how simple the exercise sounds, consistent application will be more challenging than imagined. The trick is to keep your side of the street clean. In other words, don't tell your partner or friend or co-worker what they're doing wrong, but instead concentrate on *self*-improvement.

So how does it work? The key to good communication is to listen, to share, and to support. Now, it's easy to imagine we know what these three things mean—maybe not. Let's see.

PART VII: LISTEN

There is only one rule for being a good talker— learn to listen.
                                        - Christopher Morely[xlviii]

L ISTENING IS AN ART MOST ARE ACTUALLY QUITE ILL-EQUIPPED TO ENJOY. First of all, to listen well we need to stop talking, not just with our outside voice, but in our heads as well. This can be a sincere problem. We're so used to constant jabbering noise these days that worldly silence is seldom found, and interior silence is at just as much of a premium.

Certainly, brain chatter is one of the fastest ways to undermine good communication. We're constantly preparing answers while the other person is still formulating phrases. We evidence little patience and all too often jump the response gun. This is particularly problematic during arguments, where, it seems, we simply can't wait to make our point.

Is it that we're afraid we'll forget what we're about to say? Or do we imagine we know what's coming because we've heard it all before? Does our general anxiety push the jabber train?

Newsflash: You can't listen and talk at the same time.

Now, there are basically three fundamental pay-attention methods. We covered these while discussing Public Presence, so hopefully you've got a heart start on the how-to. Still, I repeat them at this juncture to insist on their specific relevant importance and value when it comes to partnership.

- ✓ **Method #1: Echoing**—which involves sound and sounding. That means responding with the kind of oh and ah we tend naturally to offer a baby. Echoing is simple and organic. No heavy lifting required
- ✓ **Method #2: Reflecting**—which involves responding with visual cues. We know instinctually how to do this also. Someone smiles and we find ourselves smiling back. A grim face gets a grim face. Again, this isn't a "doing" as much as a mirroring
- ✓ **Method #3: Active Listening**—which involves asking questions that encourage the story we're hearing to go further. For instance, your friend's telling you about her awful date last night and you interject: "Wow that sounds terrible. Did he get that you weren't saying a word? Did he not ask you anything?"

Notice that echoing, reflecting, and active listening don't involve advice, intervention, or opinion. Eventually, depending to who you're talking to and the circumstance, it might be appropriate to throw in your two cents. But when practicing, it's good to keep it simple.

On the other hand, there are some for whom *Taking Contrary Action* could be an immediate good plan. This means if you're used to interjecting a great deal, it might well be time to say less. But if you've been like one of those plastic empty nodding-head dogs propped in a car's back window—where it appears you're listening because you learned to sit mute in apparent agreement, but really you're far away or even silently rejecting or judging—then it's good to practice speaking your mind.

Whichever way you go—whether it's saying more or saying less—start practicing right away with co-workers, bank tellers, and baristas. Then move on to friends. You see—these are all "relationships" too. Don't save your relationship work for partners. Practice everywhere.

The idea, in other words, is to **use these listening techniques right now—today!** Practice and see what happens. A whole new experience awaits.

I can never think of what to say...

ALL RIGHT, MAYBE YOU SIMPLY CAN'T FIGURE OUT WHAT TO SAY when it comes to getting active in the listening procedure. Start by simply saying exactly that: "Gee, I hardly know what to say! What a story." It's called *State the Obvious*. Speechmakers do it all the time, beginning their lecture with: "I'm nervous to be here…"

Believe it or not, people can see our nervousness or confusion anyway. And even if they don't notice, they'll think nothing of our "confession", except that it acts as connection.

Or, if you really want to adventure into terrific communication territory, ask about feelings. I know, I know—that's SO personal. It is. Be a person. Person to person: Ask. *How did it feel to be ignored all night?*

What's the worst that can happen?

Repetition...paying attention...

NOW, TALKING ABOUT REPETITION—THIS IS THE DANDIEST OF ALL COMMUNICATION TOOLS. It is also really difficult at first, and harder than it sounds.

Repetition is meant to be done without creative interpretation. No "probably you meant…" or "I think what you intended…" or "you should…"

No.

Instead what's called for is clean, direct repeating.

The person telling you the story says: "*I simply didn't know what to do. I was terrified of what he'd think of me if I told him the truth.*" Now, tempted as you may be to "help" instead of "*that would be the worst thing to do,*" you respond with: "*Yeah, I bet you were terrified. What did you do then?*" Or, "*For sure, telling the truth is terrifying. What happened?*" Something like that. Notice that I incorporated the storyteller's exact words into my response.

The process works two ways:

- ✓ **Repeat/Respond:** As exemplified above, this means using the words of the speaker as part of our response, followed by a question furthering the story, as in: "*What attitude did he seem to have while you were talking?*" Once arriving at a place of comfortable ease with this process, you can practice a self-inclusive share, as in: "*I once had to tell a guy I...I thought I'd faint!*" Or with something like: "*I just think you're really brave to be so authentic!*" Get it?
- ✓ **Context/Response:** There are times when we want to initiate conversation—when feelings, thoughts, wants, and needs ought to be revealed. In this case, we still need to practice great communication skills by focusing on how the situation's affecting us, rather than putting the "problem" on the other person. So how do we do that?

It starts with context, which means the situation in which the hurt, concern, disappointment, or whatever occurred or occurs. Example: "*When you start texting while I'm talking to you...*"

That is then followed by feelings: "*...I feel abandoned.*"

Now, perhaps you even realize that your feeling of abandonment is over-the-top and based in family-of-origin history, but it's still your feeling and you're entitled to it. And certainly our current constant involvement with texting offers great fodder for this point. How many times are we talking to someone who glances down to read an incoming text? Or how many times do we take ourselves out of conversation to do the same? It's easy these days to feel overlooked, dismissed, devalued, and unimportant—and even abandoned. Whether or not the feeling experience seems highly charged to someone else, you have the right to address it—and should. Otherwise, resentment will grow. Resentment is the stealth bomber of a relationship and before you know it, we've turned away from love.

PART VIII: DEEPER STILL...

Only someone who is ready for everything, who doesn't exclude any experience, even the most incomprehensible, will live the relationship with another person as something alive and will himself sound the depths of his own being.

- Rainier Maria Rilke [xlix]

CERTAINLY, THE ABOVE OFFERED PROCEDURES TAKE TIME AND ENERGY FIRST TO LEARN, and then to integrate into daily communication. After that happens I have a real treat for you, which is another level of listening that allows a far more profound kind of relating.

I call it **Simultaneous Translation.**

Simultaneous Translation is a heartfelt procedure and, therefore, no easy matter until assiduously practiced—at which point it becomes second nature, like shaking someone's hand when you meet.

What's required is a real ability to allow the sometimes-faint strains of *what's really being said* to slip through the din and turmoil of what often passes for conversation, but really isn't.

Simultaneous Translation is a process of learning to hear the music underneath the words.

To accomplish this we need to:

✓ Shut down the inner clatter and clamor
✓ Refuse to get snagged on the words hurling toward us
✓ Access the heart part of ourselves that values love of the partner above "winning" the moment
✓ Remember the *who and how* of our beloved—the one underneath the defensive fighter
✓ Call upon the kinder, more curious, less-reactive person we can be

Sounds like quite the feat, huh? It can happen, though.

And when we're successful, the feeling and result is quite stunning. If you think about it, you'll realize how often ST is needed because of how commonly it occurs that we're saying one thing but meaning another—happens all the time, with things both big and small. But unless we eagerly train ourselves to listen, we simply won't hear. And we definitely won't hear if we stick with our usual ways of being wedded to pre-conceived notions about what the other person means or intends.

Here's another personal story—a sweet version of this magnificent ST listening process: One evening I arrived home after an extremely long, arduous workday riddled with client tears, fury, and pain. As I enter, my husband, from the cozy comfort of his library chair, says: "Hey honey, do me a favor and make me a cup of tea!"

I'm bone-tired. It's late, so I immediately speculate and assume that he's been sitting for quite a while. Inside, I explode. *Are you kidding me?* I think, as mentally a few well-chosen swear-word bombs detonate in my brain. But I shut down my fury. And instead of hurling my inner dialogue, I sigh heavily just to let him know how burdened I feel by his request and say: "Sure."

Of course, he registers my sigh. He knows me well.

"If it's a problem," he bluster-scowls, "don't bother!"

"No problem," I retort unconvincingly, but then trot off to do my diligence.

The next night and the end of another long day. Again as I entered the door: "Hi! Hey would you mind making me a cup of tea?" Inside thoughts race. *Are you nuts! What a selfish idiot. Don't you know how hard I work? How spent I am? Crap.* Out loud, I say: "Sure."

Again, he catches my tone and slightly snarls: "Well, if it's too much trouble…"

"No," I reply. And off I go.

The third day, I'm driving home when simultaneous translation kicks in. What is this silly request really about? My husband knows very well how hard I work and ordinarily does everything he can to make life easier so all I have to concentrate on the art of healing. So what's with the tea request at such inopportune moments? Uh, and by the way, he doesn't even drink tea. Where's the fellow who supports my strong efforts toward service in the world.

Oh. Oh. I get it: Service to others–to *others*. Ah ha, the dawn dawns. My dear partner wants, needs (deserves) to know there's still room for him in my consciousness and in my life. That he remains an important priority for me. That I'm not being all used up by my clients and, therefore, have nothing left to give him at home. That serving others will not mean refusing to serve our relationship also.

Oh.

That night I walk in the door and immediately say: "Hi baby. How 'bout if I make you a cup of tea?"

He grins from ear to ear: "Great!"

Next night I do the same—offering before he asks.

That evening, he answers: "No thanks. I'm good."

And that was that. He never asked again and I never offered. He'd gotten what he needed—such a small thing, that offering, but such a big deal. I'd "heard" him; heard the music underneath the words. Heard the want.

In a perfect world, and after practice, we hope simultaneous translation doesn't take three days to realize. We want it to occur in the moment. She says in a prickly way, "Are you going to be home in time for dinner tonight or what?" Actually, the underlying question might be: is she as important to you as your work? So, instead of huffing and puffing, you respond, "I'm not sure, honey, but I'll let you know as soon as I do." Then you lean over, give her a kiss, and say: "By the way, I love you so much!" Or maybe even: "Hey, why don't we do something special this weekend, just the two of us?"

Naturally, this is easier when we're not stressed or overwhelmed or stretched within an inch of our lives. But maybe that's simply not going to happen anytime soon. Plus, you know what, if you have to start over with a new relationship, you will magically find time to pony up. The stress, overwhelming circumstances, and stretch will be irrelevant because somehow you'll discover the energy to back your intention and exhibit kindness while carving out space for true engagement.

Besides, as I tell everyone, at the end of your life, as you're lying on your death bed, it's highly doubtful you'll regret not spending one more hour at the office or be upset over not completing one more deal or wishing you'd made more money. What's more likely is that you'll look around the room and notice how much love is—or isn't—coming your way. You'll think, then, about what you've given and what you've been able to receive in all your love matters.

That's all very fine and good, but...

WE MAY WANT TO BE THAT STELLAR RELATIONSHIP PERSON— —the kind that puts love first and overlooks petty moments—but there are simply times when partnership communication feels unbelievably arduous, like s/he's speaking a whole different language. The answers we get make no sense. We simply can't get ourselves understood and have no idea what's going on, at least at the surface level. Maybe we've said something simple like: "Don't forget, the Brittles will be here tomorrow night at 6:30!" And the return comment is: "Get off my back!" Or we say: "We really need to spend some time together," to which we get as a response: "You're never satisfied."

Huh?

The temptation is to stay mystified. Or to do what some foreigners do when new language comes toward them: instead of trying to understand, translate, or find alternative transmission styles, they repeat the same words while simply speaking louder. Obviously, a no-go when it comes to good communication.

So, what are the mechanics of this Simultaneous Translation? It's a bit like being one of those United Nations translators with the headphones where in comes Urdu and out comes English.

By the way, I know there are plenty of you reading this book imagining it's your job to convince your partner to follow you down the communication promise road. I suggest you reconsider that aim.

If your partner is eager to do so, then that's dandy.

But mostly that's not what happens.

Usually one member of a couple will be on board for radical change and the other not so much. What I alternately recommend, therefore, is that you focus on *you*. Make the changes you need to make and see what happens. I think you'll be astonished. As I am fond of saying: *I work on myself and work on myself and work on myself and am amazed how much my husband changes.*

Over and again I encounter stories like this. Linda, for instance, came to therapy husband in tow, at the end of her marriage rope. He showed up to session a few times but basically maintained that *she* had the "problem" and stopped coming. Of course, the problem wasn't hers. And it was. Because remember, it's 100% us and 100% them.

Well, Linda kept working on change even after hubby "officially" stopped. She worked on steadily opening herself and opening toward her husband. Loving him in new ways, without assuming or expecting reciprocity. Then something unpredictable happened. *He* began to shift. Notably and vividly shift. She was stunned.

Of course, it doesn't always turn out this way but far more than you might imagine. Besides there's no downside to self-focus!

Sharing

THERE'S ALREADY BEEN AN EARLIER CONVERSATION ABOUT CONTAINMENT, better known as *Shut It!* For some, good communication begins with saying less because "sharing" certainly does not simply mean being wordy. Many talk continuously but say little.

For those tending to blanket the relationship neighborhood with words (a defensive process called Spilling), try saying only what will fit on a 3x5 card, even if you must start with what will fit on the card front and back.

A good way to think about quality sharing comes through Indian Guru Sai Baba's injunction: Is it kind? Is it necessary? Does it improve upon the silence?

Quakers sometimes say the same thing this way:

The three sieves

ONCE DAY, A LITTLE BOY RAN INDOORS FROM SCHOOL and called out eagerly: "Oh, mother, what do you think of Tom Jones? I have just heard that—"

"Wait a minute, my boy. Have you put what you have heard through the three sieves before you tell it to me?"

"Sieves, mother! What do you mean?"

"Well, the first sieve is called Truth. Is it true?"

"Well, I don't really know, but Bob Brown said that Charlie told him that Tom—"

"That's very roundabout. What about the second sieve—Kindness. Is it kind?"

"Kind! No, I can't say it is kind."

"Now the third sieve—Necessity. Will it go through that? Must you tell this tale?"

"No, mother, I need not repeat it."

"Well, then, my boy, if it is not necessary, not kind, and perhaps not true, let the story die."

Getting good at *Speak It*Step Up*...

ON THE OTHER SIDE OF THE STREET, THOUGH, LIVES DIRECT COMMUNICATION, which I call *Speak It*Step Up*. This is particularly great for those tending to conduct most of the relationship in their head with little actually being revealed. This is called mental masturbation. It sounds like: *I'll say this and she'll* *say that; when I do such and such she always does so and so. I'm just not going to bother; besides s/he knows how I feel.*

But maybe your partner or boss or friend doesn't know how you feel. And even if they do know, or suspect, it's valuable for you to speak it. Of course it means risking vulnerability. Let's look at the ABCs of *Speak It*Step Up.*

✓ **A:** STORING COMPLAINTS LIKE NUTS IN WINTER ONLY MAKES US SQUIRRELY

Don't do it. Once we know what we want, we get to speak up about it. Not doing so only leads to complaint and even relationship collapse.

For many years, I worked with a fellow we'll call Bill, who'd long eschewed relationship. He was quite pleased to be alone and seldom considered the idea that being in a partnership was his cup of java. But then along came Harry, the apparent man of the dream he didn't even know he was having. Happily, they moved in together and even married.

Now, the main thing that worked for Bill was Harry's easy-going manner. Nothing much seemed to faze him and he accepted all Bill's long-standing, live-alone ways without fuss. Sure, certain collaborative changes were asked and mostly Bill was happy to accommodate, or when not happy found a way to do it anyhow.

Problems kicked in only when, after many apparently contented years, it turned out Harry had been harboring numerous unspoken wishes and disgruntlements.

As usually happens sooner or later, dissatisfaction surfaced, splashing rudely all over their tranquil life. Bill was shocked. He never considered the possibility that Harry had been hiding discontent. And once one thing came forward, so did other frustrations tumble out. As you can imagine, their connection became shadowed by stress and strain.

In the case of Bill and Harry, they were able to work through it all. It certainly could have turned out far differently than it did. Still, Harry's tendency to store concerns pokes at them from time to time. And each time, it chips away at the integrity and infrastructure of the bonding.

The long and short of it is: Don't keep emotional secrets.
It's not good for you.
It's not good for the relationship.

✓ **B: Invite don't instruct, or in trouble you'll get stuck**

All too often we imagine communication means exercising a commanding directive, as if we're in charge of educating the listener. This is dangerous territory indeed, especially in a primary relationship.

Instead, it's best to do one of two things depending on how you are as a communicator. For introverts, and most contained people, invitation is more a natural way to go. For extroverts, and more assertive people, the repetition and question procedure is a best bet.

✓ **C: Don't bully, browbeat, or compete, for you'll end in sure defeat**

Don't try to insist, cajole, or control another person's actions. Even when it comes to your needs, *ask* for what you want and see what happens. Or set clear, concise boundaries you're willing to back up with all you've got.

Let's discuss for a minute the differences and similarities between boundaries and ultimatums: Boundaries, meaning to establish mutually respected limits, often have as their main intention simple clarity. They put the furniture in place so no one trips over it.

An ultimatum, actually, is merely a power-punch-packed boundary. Folks get all bent out of shape about them. "Are you giving me an ultimatum?" he says ferociously.

"Oh no," you sputter, "I'm only saying what I need."

Well guess what—quite often an ultimatum is exactly what's called for. You've been wimping out long enough and waiting for things to change—waiting for the commitment to be made or the drinking to stop or the meanness to settle down. Stop it. Give an ultimatum. But first, of course, try figuring out why you've waited this long.

How has your lack of insistence been all about you?

I remember Stephan and Bonnie. For many years, Stephan was quite successfully employed in films, but that required him to be away from the family for months at a time. Initially, the family found a way to make it work. Bonnie would take the kids to join dad on set. It was fun visiting different countries. At first. But over time, this changed.

The change slowly but surely ate away at the relationship. Stephan got more and more unavailable. When things first started to go south, Bonnie tried hard to "fix" the situation. Nearly immediately though, it felt like knocking on a bolted shut door.

Eventually, when Stephan was away working, he'd rarely communicate much at all. Frustrated and feeling to some degree "out of a job" as partnership got further and further from view, Bonnie decided to re-initiate a career she'd had when she and Stephan first met. The startup meant an additional financial burden on the family budget. Stephan appeared to support her efforts, but began using apparent money worries as a further excuse to stop the expensive family film-set visits.

After a while, the kids got used to their dad being MIA, which was challenging enough but not even the worst part. Over the years, the business had gotten harder and harder on Stephan who sank into an awful depression—a tendency he'd long exhibited but had seemingly held somewhat at bay. He spoke constantly about feeling victimized by his circumstances and got rail thin, saying he couldn't even take time to eat while working.

Soon, even when home, Stephan had difficulty maintaining any version of presence. While with the family he barely interacted with anyone. Everyone soon got used to tiptoeing around his mood. Ultimately, they began looking forward to his absence.

This went on for a number of years. Finally, and way down the relationship deterioration line, Stephan and Bonnie showed up on my doorstep.

By the time I met them, she was completely pulled away and he was clinically depressed to a frightening degree. Bonnie's withdrawal exaggerated Stephan's belief in being a victim; Stephan's humongous depression exacerbated Bonnie's feelings of powerlessness.

A big steel door had been erected between them.

We worked together for a time; however, breaking Stephan's depressed, everyone-and-everything-except-me-is-the-problem stance proved impossible. Meanwhile, Bonnie was completely shut down, retreating back into a certain kind of remote behavior often exhibited in her family of origin. She didn't want to break up the family, but realized an ultimatum needed to be set. Either Stephan must seek and participate in the healing help that could work for him—including getting medicated for his depression, and break free of his staunch blaming position—or she'd need to leave.

Divorce followed. Is this a sad story? Perhaps in some ways.

However, what's obvious is that as the "family unit" stood, no one prospered. The children were learning no relational skills in terms of how a healthy partnership works. Bonnie was shutting herself further and further down, while the creative light she carried dimmed beyond seeing. And Stephan was only sinking into a deeper depression hole with every passing month. If any of them had a chance of thriving, clearly the entire family form needed breaking up.

Bonnie's ultimatum, then, way the only way to go.

I see this all the time with verging-on-divorce couples where one or both have apparently stayed "for the sake of the kids." Of course, breaking up when there's family involved adds bitter to the taste; however, when and if deep digging is done, most eventually realize they really stayed together way after the party was over primarily for themselves rather than the children.

This is hard to confront.

Really though, if your kids are seeing terrible fighting, watch you sleep in separate bedrooms, or witness constant coldness, what are you teaching them about relationships? Is that truly better than showing them the courage it can sometimes take to face your Self heart-on and do what needs to be done to move to the next hopeful moment?

But there's more...

ALONG WITH *SPEAK IT*STEP UP*, I'D LIKE TO INTRODUCE FOUR other important "sharing" procedures. When employing *any* new-to-you communication techniques it's important to realize what goes on with you as a result of the procedure. Do you get scared of rejection? Do you feel mean? Do you feel even more emboldened?

Start looking at what's been previously holding you back. As often writing is a terrific way to explore.

The first, I call:

✓ **Express the Hurt**, which is exactly as it sounds. I've given this its own category to emphasize importance. Few are good at this and most avoid such demonstrations altogether. Of course, certain feelings seem in most quarters more acceptable than others. We easily say: *I'm fuming; I've got angst/am nervous/anxious; I'm terrified.* But when it comes to hurt, all systems shut down. Why? Because expressing hurt—especially with regards to a partner—feels intimate and vulnerable like nearly nothing else. As a society, we relegate such intimacy to the shadows.

What is important here to remember is that expressing doesn't mean blaming or shaming. It simply involves letting the other person know our tender feelings. Whereas *Speak It*Step Up* covers the gamut from anger to anxiety to fear, *Express the Hurt* is exclusively about feeling wounded.

As always, the best communication style includes Context/Response as in: *When you say you're going to have dinner with me and then bail, no matter what good reason you have, I get really hurt and, silly as it may sound, feel abandoned!*

The second *Speak It*Step Up* subset is:

✓ **Express the Love**. You'd think this doesn't require pointing out but it does, especially in not-so-new relationships. We get complacent. We forget. Or maybe we weren't that great at it to begin with. Of course, showing it is important, but speaking it has value also. Try it.

The third subset of *Speak It*Step Up* is:

✓ **Fire with Fire.** Bet you can imagine how this works. This communication process is more direct and assertive. Indeed, there are certain times with particular kinds of persistent personality types when this is the only way to go if getting our point across has any chance of happening. It's not about being rude or doing character assassination. Rather, it means meeting the energy coming toward you in equal measure. Someone, for instance, aggressively insists you're in over your head and you respond, feeling the heat under your words: *Yeah, I get that you think I'm in over my head, but you're dead wrong! I have great confidence in my capacity here. I really think you'd better take another look at where this doubt in my abilities might be coming from.*

The idea is to paint your words with vivid, powerful emotion. No dulcet sounds. Be bold, but be sure to still include the repetition process.

The final subset of *Speak It*Step Up* might feel like the very opposite of communication; yes, it must be employed sparingly and never by people who already use disconnection as their primary "communication" style. It's called:

✓ **Walk Away*Step Out.** This is to be exercised under extreme conditions when all other communication tools and procedures have been tried. The idea is to give space, allowing for an emotional re-grouping. It's a kind of grown-up version of time out. When such experiences come forward, we really need to put the boundary brakes on because one thing's for sure: it's hard to sweep up during a tornado, so don't try it. Wait until the storm passes to take out the broom.

The bottom line when it comes to good communication is that for some less is more, while for others more is better.

Getting down to cases...

NOW, AUTHENTIC, DEPTHFUL SHARING IS A WHOLE OTHER BARREL OF MONKEYS. It means true revealing. There are some prerequisites for a full realization of such:

- ✓ **Know Thyself**: In order to reveal what's going on inside, we need to know ourselves well enough to have something genuine to say. That means: *Figure out your needs*. First and foremost, we must understand our own hearts and minds. If we don't know what works for us, how are we going to let others in on the secret?
- ✓ **Express Empathy**: Empathy is the ability to put ourselves in the other people's shoes. Without developing this compassionate aptitude, we'll be hard put to truly connect in a lasting way.
- ✓ **Acknowledge & Accept Opposite Points of View**: It's tempting to try convincing everyone to join our opinion team. I call it the I-Know-Better syndrome. After all, we certainly have no intention of holding a viewpoint we think is wrong. Well, unless of course we've simply adopted our parent's opinion, or someone else's, and have given the matter little real consideration. Funny how we can adamantly defend a position we've barely investigated in any real way. Odd. And common. Remember my rebellious atheist?

In any event, the true trick and treat is learning: *Agree to disagree*. Let me give an example. Off and on, I've long worked with a terrific couple who occasionally show up these days for a "tune up" inevitably spurred on by their differences of opinion about how to handle his family (from a long-ago first marriage). Sonya comes from a tiny family, while Jonathan comes from a brood, where he quickly became a caretaker. Also, Jonathan has grown kids who struggle, whereas Sonya's only child is thriving.

Quite often, Sonya becomes irritated as Jonathan insists on one more time rescuing a family member, which often involves what Sonya considers a home invasion. Throwing fuel on the fire is Sonya's comparing of what's done for her kid.

The conflict is easily resolved each time as Jonathan gets better and better at reigning in his controlling, co-dependence and Sonya improves in her efforts to stop ringing the fairness bell. Each knows by now they're carrying old conversations into current circumstances. But the truth is, they'll probably never completely agree on what's right and appropriate when it comes to each other's children.

PART IX: SUPPORT

They slipped briskly into an intimacy from which they never recovered. -F. Scott Fitzgerald, *This Side of Paradise*

EMOTIONAL INTIMACY: IT'S NOT JUST A "GIRL" THING ANYMORE. We're really lucky. For all my grousing about what we don't know intimacy-wise, and how challenging living in this technological age can be, I'd be hard put to refuse noticing how much more information is out there when it comes to the value of intimate communication. Everyone's on board—at least hypothetically.

But what the heck is intimacy, anyway?

Remember my prisoner story? Most use the word intimacy as code for sex. When I'm talking about sex, I use the word sex. When I'm talking about intimacy, I'm speaking of the emotional connection that comes from honest, vulnerable sharing.

Now, sincere, dedicated support invariably includes such intimacy. Easier said than done, huh? Certainly, such an adventure requires a few things of us:

✓ We must be free of the need to imagine control over other people's opinions of us. In other words, we need to expose ourselves while ignoring or overriding self-conscious fear

✓ We must know what we mean to say and then say what we mean, while understanding the difference between feelings and thoughts

✓ We must be *willing* to explore connection

Plus, when it comes to intimacy with our mates, perhaps above all we must remember to continue noticing the great parts of our partner and of our partnership. Tell you what though: It's amazing how fast we forget. Taking them and it for granted is as easy as slipping on a banana peel. Take your eye off what's right in front of you and before you know it, down you go.

Remembering to love our mates generously is hugely helped by remembering to love ourselves. Indeed, the more we love us, the more we can love them. So how do we build the self-esteem that reflects self-love? Well, self-esteem grows when we perform estimable acts.

Yep.

Doing good works builds character.

Try it. Be kind.

Go out of your way to help.

Be a valuable community member.

Summary: The pillars of good communication are listen, share, care, and support. Each element requires self-assessment. Each element gets to apply to us, too. Listen to yourself. Share from a place of self-knowing. Care for and about yourself. Support yourself by doing estimable acts. Also, recognize your needs and ask that those needs be met.

GOOD COMMUNICATION TOOL CHART

☛	REMEMBER what you love
☛	KNOW Thyself
☛	Express EMPATHY
☛	INVITE don't Instruct
☛	DON'T Bully
☛	Use REPETITION
☛	Speak It*STEP UP or Shut It
☛	Acknowledge & ACCEPT Opposite Points of view
☛	Practice SIMULTANEOUS Translation

PART X: COLLABORATION

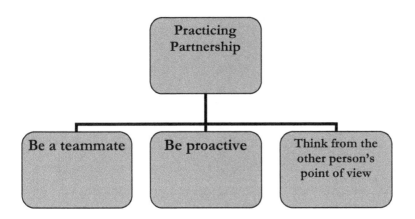

Where there is love there is life.
-Mahatma Gandhi

Be a teammate

I T'S EASY TO LOSE OUR WAY WHEN IT COMES TO GREAT PARTNERING. Once in a relationship—whether it's a lover, friend or even a job—we can slide into a cavalier forgetting to make the "other" a priority, operating from assumption and taking things for granted. We never do this at the beginning.

Nope. At first, we give it our all.

Try to make a good impression.

Put our nose to the partnership, job, or friendship grindstone.

Show our best selves.

Well, a new car is always fun to drive. We're very careful to avoid dings and scratches. We wash it frequently, keep it shiny, and treat it like a prize we worked hard for. We brag about it and show it off.

But after a while, we just assume it'll be available when we're ready to go somewhere. We stop looking at it as special. More often than not, we treat it as a convenience. If we're a certain kind of person, we quickly tire of it and wish we could have another new one. If we're another kind of person, we might drive it until its wheels are practically falling off because the familiarity makes us feel safe, if not excited. No matter what, though, if we don't get the vehicle regularly serviced, change the oil, and put gas in it, it will die on us.

As you can see having and keeping a relationship is much like having and keeping an automobile. To maintain a good one, we need to continue original efforts. Not every single second, of course. We all have bad days or weeks or, oh lord, months! But attention must be paid. Otherwise, things will most certainly fall into disrepair.

Over the years many couples struggling to find their way back to each other, try convincing me their problem is the exigencies of their lives—busy schedules, exhaustion, money stress.

I remember one couple who appeared in my office saying their relationship was absolutely fabulous. Why were they there, I curiously wondered? Well, they informed me, they had this one tiny problem. They couldn't find time to have sex together. Everything else, they continued, was perfect.

Were they still attracted to each other? Yes, they said.

Were there old, perceived relationship infractions they'd not discussed? No, they insisted. I asked many questions, but their answers stayed consistent.

Gently, I argued the point.

After all, as indicated, sex is like money—the concrete repository for our wishes, hopes, and dreams. It is the placeholder, to some degree, describing how we feel about ourselves in the world of relationship and in the world-at-large. So, if your relationship is fabulous, but you're having no sex—though you supposedly want it—something else is being advertised you've not yet realized.

What is it? Are you actually talking about sex or are you missing intimacy, as in emotional connection—or respect, attention, approval, or validation?

Well, the conversation with this couple went on for a few sessions while they continued to insist on their original point. It was just a matter of finding the time. Finally, I said the following:

We know it takes you approximately half an hour to get here and half an hour to get home. And you're here for an hour. Here's what I want you to do: Next week, instead of coming here, make an appointment with yourselves. Pay yourselves what you pay me, have a lovely two-hour date with the money, and end this terrific rendezvous with wonderful sex. I'll see you in two weeks and we'll chat about how it all went.

Two weeks later, the report was, guess what? No sex.

They couldn't find the time. Really?

I never seemed able to convince them that sex is not just sex or that the missing element in their relationship was something far more, shall we say, essential. But believe me that's so. Let me state this again: Sex reflects our inside feelings, hopes, needs, and preoccupations the way a beach reflector reflects the sun upon our face. The reflector isn't the source of light; it is the reporter of light.

The moral of the story is that one of the first cornerstones of being a good teammate is self-honesty. Then you can learn to be open and candid with your mate. Indeed, it's important to know the truth about what you're bringing to the relationship or withholding along with what might be truly inspiring your feelings, thoughts, and behaviors. Once you do know this, you can show up and be the best teammate possible.

Remember though, that **honesty is always about *our* feelings, not about the other person's behavior**. In fact, "I'm just being honest," is one of the most common phrases used in service of demolishing another. Like the individual who states, for instance, when their 20-year relationship is breaking up: "I don't know if I ever loved you! I'm just being honest." I've heard this "offered" numerous times. You know what: At that point, keep it to yourself. You're just being cruel.

Okay, besides honesty, being a good teammate means communicating both your needs and your appreciations. Your teammate is valuable.

Let them know that.

Good, honest communication breeds trust, which is the key for a well-functioning team of any kind. If we don't trust those we're surrounded by, we tend to pull our punch and hesitate to fully give our all.

If things aren't going as well with the team as we want, we always first want to check out our own behavior. What ways are we influencing and contributing to the problems? Are we not listening as well as we could be? Not communicating? Being controlling? Petulant? Demanding? Check yourself out and tell the truth about it all. Oh sure, this is no easy matter and I certainly don't mean to imply it is; however, understanding your own behavior—taking ownership of it—leads to success in every area, including places you've never even considered.

Independence, dependence, inter-dependence...

THESE ARE MORE THAN THROW-AROUND TERMS. They're vital to creating and establishing an extraordinary relationship.

In all relationships, no matter where and regardless of form, the idea is to know how to independently take care of ourselves in a way that leaves us feeling safe enough to allow our hearts to open to healthy Dependence, which then sets the stage for that delicious state known as Inter-dependence. But what does all this mean?

Independence...

MANY ARE AFRAID THAT INDEPENDENCE SIGNALS AN INEVITABLE LIFE OF ISOLATED LONELINESS. That perspective on independence gives rise to high-anxiety, which is code for fear.

So what are we afraid of?

That we can't do it; that we don't have the resources; that we'll die trying; that it means we're unlovable; that it means growing up? Whatever our particular hesitation indicates, those who hesitate are very often...well, lost.

There are two basic motivating forces: fear and love.

When we are afraid, we pull back from life. John Lennon said it as:

When we are in love, we open to all that life has to offer with passion, excitement, and acceptance. We need to learn to love ourselves first, in all our glory and our imperfections. If we cannot love ourselves, we cannot fully open to our ability to love others or our potential to create. Evolution and all hopes for a better world rest in the fearlessness and open-hearted vision of people who embrace life. – John Lennon[1]

In a healthy way, independence means living an I-know-how-to-take-care-of-myself manner. It includes a certain self-contained attitude. A knowing of our own voice, opinions, wants, needs, and even aspirations. Luckily, everything doesn't have to be neatly in place before considering ourselves independent. But I'll say that independence is far more than a money conversation, which is where most go when judging whether they are or aren't. Actually, like so many things, independence is a matter, to some degree, of a well-considered perspective.

Q: I value my freedom—a kind of independence, I'd call it, and relationships often feel so limiting. How can I be in partnership and still feel free?

VERY OFTEN, WHAT WE'RE *APPARENTLY* ASKING FOR IS REALLY NOT WHAT'S WHAT. What does *freedom* mean? The freedom to have sex with whomever we wish? If so, best to find a partner on board for that form of relationship. Or is it freedom to do what we want, when we want it, without consideration of our mate? If that's what we're wanting, best to stay alone.

Every relationship has requirements and requests.

Your boss is probably going to be miffed if you just "freely" take whatever time away from the job that suits you. Your friends likely will get peeved if you keep saying you're going to show up, but then stand on the "freedom" platform as a reason to bail.

I once had a young client whose parents had sent him to therapy, hoping he'd deal with his addiction to marijuana. Zack had already been thrown out of two colleges, lost jobs, and lost his parents' trust by age 21 because of constantly choosing drugs over showing up to his life. Zack and I made a bargain: No getting stoned before sessions.

We went along pretty well for a while, exploring his relationship to drugs and, more importantly, to growing up—until one day he appeared, reporting: "*I just want to tell you, I decided to get stoned before coming today!*"

"*I see*," I replied. "*Why is that?*"

"*Well*," Zack answered, with an I've-thought-this-through tone: "*I figured I wasn't going to let therapy decide what I was free to do and what I wasn't!*"

"*Uh, huh*," I answered, amused: "*So instead, you let the drugs decide?*"

The question needs to be not how can I be in a relationship that feels free, but rather how can I experience freedom within myself while also supporting relationship? As usual it's best to start with a definition.

Write about independence and freedom. What do they mean to you? When and how do you experience them? What blocks your sense of independence? What stops you from feeling free? What or who makes you feel tied down? What do you imagine would be different if you had the freedom and independence you crave?

My point is, *everything begins* with figuring out what we really, truly need in our lives. Once we're clear, we then take what we've come to understand about ourselves and apply it to our life choices.

Dependence…

THOUGH A RELATIONSHIP IS THE MUCH-TOUTED AIM FOR MANY, at the same time the urgency to maintain independence is completely understandable. We've long lived in a world that suggests the overriding value of pulling ourselves up by our bootstraps, getting over and on with it, and a variety of other don't-need-anyone, prize-your-independence ways. So, while certainly many get afraid of independence, especially during times where the Collective insists on keeping everyone eternally young, there are plenty of folks so committed to their independence they find real partnership nearly impossible.

Oh, they may be in relationships time and again, but really they're pretty terrible at the mating part, so everything keeps falling apart. What's often missing is an actual ability to allow *dependence*.

One of my very first clients was a terribly fragile young woman we'll call Delia, who'd never in her life been able to depend on anyone. Her alcoholic parents abandoned her many times, in numerous ways. Whatever relationships she'd had were distant at best with frightful men she'd maneuver and then leave. She was quite pretty and looked even younger than she was, so men were standing in line to be next.

When we first began working together, Delia refused to call our meetings "therapy." The whole concept made her feel squeamishly dependent. What if she came to "need" me, she'd wonder. In fact, initially we spent many session hours walking outside, as if we were merely two friends taking a stroll. The walking made her feel less claustrophobic.

As time went on, we became closer and closer. Delia let herself begin to trust me. She started looking forward to our time together. She began calling our work *therapy*.

Delia and I were together for many years. I knew her before my marriage and during. That piece was hard for her. She was certain my husband would take me away from her, just like alcohol had robbed her of quality parenting—but of course, it didn't.

Over time, I watched Delia blossom.

She stopped having dreadful liaisons and began to date actual potential partners. She went back to school and got a social work license so she could begin working with others to share what she'd learned about how to move through such an agonizing beginning. Eventually, she moved back to her home state, joined a social work agency, got married, and had kids.

Over the years, Delia would write me about her life and even once or twice came to California and stopped by to see me. On one of those visits, she informed me that while we'd been working together she'd done several secret things to maintain a constant connection with me, including: driving by my house to see that my car was still there and that I hadn't disappeared; calling my answering machine over and over to hear my voice; and finding a music video with an artist she thought I resembled so she could watch it repeatedly. (This was before websites and Facebook.)

As it turns out, Delia's strident punch against "need" was all the time based in her enormous pull *toward* it. Her refusal to allow real caring or to trust was compensation, guarding against the deep, aching she felt. In other words, her so-called independence showing up as a refusal to trust and a rejection of caring, was really a powerful defense against her throbbing want to depend completely.

This is true for us all, as most often we fervently protest our strongest desire. It's called the equal-opposite theory, wherein what we're most adamantly presenting is inevitably balanced by its opposite, deeply held element. Like how the schoolyard bully is actually the most scared kid there or the obsessively neat person is plagued with a hellish inside chaos. Much like any quality relationship, what's needed is some kind of compromise, communication, and collaboration among the warring inside parts.

Those familiar with the defense called counter-dependence, which basically takes an "I don't need anyone" or "I can do it better myself" posture, would do well to consider this Delia story. Are you running from your secret fear of dependence, afraid of the needy "weakness" you're sure will land you in an unbearable puddle of pain? Imagine what can happen if instead you take a deep breath and let in love.

How does such compromise happen?

WHAT DOES IT MEAN TO AFFECT A COMPROMISE THAT ALLOWS HEALTHY DEPENDENCE? *Being able* to lean on others in times of emotional, physical, or financial challenge is what that looks like. This doesn't mean constantly. It means collaboratively. It means vulnerably. Not instead of attempts to free ourselves from our gnarly dilemmas. Not because we've given up on our powerful capacities. Rather, because an emotional or physical helping hand is something we can allow.

It's walking a razor's edge though—for if we continue to be unable to permit moments of reliance, we remain alone. And if we're too constantly dependent on anything or anyone outside ourselves to furnish self-esteem and well-being, we're living a stunningly precarious existence. In fact, the definition of co-dependence is a complete reliance on anything outside of the self to furnish esteem. That means depending on money, property, prestige, looks, sexual appeal, status, fame, approval, importance, and on it goes—is a fragile and unhealthy proposition.

In the end, the idea is to establish *your* version of both independence and dependence so that you can enjoy the fabulous experience called…

Interdependence…

OF COURSE, I'D SUGGEST being able to embrace this inter-dependent state is the sweet crème brûlée desert. What it means is sometimes I do it myself, sometimes I rely on you; sometimes you do it yourself, sometimes you rely on me, and in the final analysis we collaborate. This experience can be practiced at home, work, and play.

And then compassion…

Love does not dominate; it cultivates.
- Johann Wolfgang von Goethe

THERE ARE TWO OTHER IMPORTANT IDEAS TO PAY ATTENTION TO when it comes to establishing *quality* team experience. The first is making sure we're offering compassion to our teammates. That requires first slowing down long enough to notice what's really happening with them; and second, figuring out how to address what we observe. This can test our patience if their primary concerns don't match ours. But that's one of the dandy things about partnership of any kind—it asks us to be more than we tend to be without it.

Experiencing and expressing compassion lets our mate know we value them. It's not about "fixing" anything, but really more about acknowledgment. We all need this. You can't imagine how far offering a heart-full hug or soft ear can go to enhance your relationship.

A fan of the team…

> If we have no peace, it is because we have
> forgotten that we belong to each other.
> **-Mother Teresa**

THE SECOND IMPORTANT BALL TO KEEP YOUR EYE ON IS a version of what I mentioned in The Grand Connection Trifecta: Be a fan of your team. In other words, though important, it's not simply about being their fan as individuals, but more about being a fan of the team itself and of the idea of the collaborative process.

Now, for many this being-a-fan-of-the-team is quite a mountain to climb. Coming from collapsed families, for instance, or living in a society emphasizing an every man for himself mentality, don't necessarily lead us to prize union. Still, I'd postulate, some part of us does long for this team experience. Look at all the excitement about sports and check out the television shows with team competitions. These pop culture expressions report our deeper collective desires. Organizations are also climbing on board to appreciate the importance of teams. So, when it comes to home life, we need to rouse ourselves and be the CEOs who celebrate the family team.

Why be on a team in the first place?

MAYBE IT'S THAT PRIMITIVE URGE TO RECOVER ORGANIC BEGINNINGS and to get back to the way it was in the womb, or perhaps it's that existential loneliness nipping at our heels, but whatever tickles our need-to-connect funny bone and even if it's merely the way we let our pets become our precious personal posse, one thing's for sure: Come hell or high water, we'll find a way.

Sometimes that's good news and sometimes not.

Joining a team at any cost can have dire consequences (gang life; bar-fly life; gangster life; dreadful partnering), so attention must be paid to the where and when of it. Luckily, there's plenty of wonderful "clubs" with which to associate.

Now, if you only want to be a member of a club, or partnered with folks who don't want you, as Groucho Marx famously said:

"I refuse to join any club that would have me as a member," be suspicious. It is time to go back to the self-esteem drawing board.

How does collaboration work?

LET'S LOOK AT THE BOTTOM LINE WHEN IT COMES TO TERRIFIC COLLABORATION.

Fundamental: Focus on what you can give, rather than what you expect to get.

Be proactive

Proactivity is anticipatory, change-oriented, and self-initiated behavior in situations. Proactive behavior involves acting in advance of a future situation, rather than just reacting. It means taking control and making things happen rather than just adjusting to a situation or waiting for something to happen. [ii]

WHEN TALKING IN TERMS OF COLLABORATION, BEING PROACTIVE IS A BIT TRICKIER than it might seem at first glance. Why? Because it's easy to slide from mutual well-opinioned collaboration to a take-control "do it my way."

To avoid that means appreciating that we (not I) are in charge. For instance, we've split up the household duties in a particular agreed upon fashion. As long as what we're doing works, we keep doing it. When it stops working, we renegotiate. Sounds perfectly simple until "I" start thinking about why you're not doing things my way: loading the dishwasher with the cups all in the back; taking out the garbage in the morning versus the evening; or waiting until the last Sunday afternoon of the month to pay bills instead of paying them as they arrive. The damaging perspective is: Why aren't you doing it the way I would?!

Collaborative partnership negotiation, then, includes figuring out who does what and letting them do it without interference. Now, people hate when I use the negotiation word in terms of partnering. Why not? A relationship is a negotiation. In all entwining there are must-give-ups that smooth the fabric for desirable new design outcomes.

Of course, if I'm more a pattern-maker than an actual seamstress kind of person and especially if I'm partnered with someone who prefers following someone else's pattern design, it's tempting to unilaterally make all the decisions and delegate. Those preferring this style of interaction must proceed carefully because everyone involved in any project, be it home life, work life, or friendship life, needs to feel the value of their contribution. Without that discontent or at least apathy are sure to set in.

Not so great for creating a sense of team.

The solution, or at the least the beginning of a solution, is conversation. Start with each person on the team creating a list of what they think needs changing. Remember, optimally, we realize why we want or need particular changes. When I work with corporations on team building, even the most minor of players has an opinion on what can be improved.

Additionally, it's handy to realize what part of us is requesting the change. Remember Rob and his new bride's flinging of her coat on the living room chair? Did he need the clothes removed because: it simply aggravated him to see them there (a visual issue); it felt like he'd eventually be overtaken (a psychological issue); or maybe he felt disrespected (a defensive emotional issue)?

Once we know what's driving our want, sharing can ensue.

Together, we can pick what seems to be a priority.

Q: But what if I'm already pretty good at certain things I feel to be important, but my partner isn't? For instance, what happens if my partner is quite unromantic and I crave romance?

IN A RELATIONSHIP WE'RE ALWAYS TEACHING EACH OTHER WHAT'S WANTED AND NEEDED. That means when we're not getting our needs met, it's time to open discussion. Unfortunately, this commonly does not occur. Too many keep their desires to themselves expecting their partner to mind read––if you really love me, you'll know what I need without me telling you.

This is deadly for relationship.

Happily, it turns out when we ask for what we need or want, and then get it we're still as content as if we'd received it spontaneously. Now, if we have to ask for the same thing over and over and over, that's another colored horse.

Think from the other person's point-of-view

ONCE SOMETHING'S BEEN REQUESTED, putting ourselves in the other person's shoes lays the foundation for better, more effective dialogue. For instance, my client Tommy gets very nervous when his beautiful girlfriend, Lola, is less affectionate in public than when at home, believing her to be focused on getting public attention from others, especially men.

Tommy has been quite verbal about his concerns and the angst this gives him. Lola, meanwhile, tends to reject his concerns as overblown and silly, emphasizing that when they're out, she just gets a bit preoccupied with making sure everyone's having a good time.

Tommy's worry about Lola's need for male attention is mostly based on his own insecurities, since he's imagining she'll soon find someone better and more worthy than him. Meanwhile, for Lola, public displays of affection are slightly uncomfortable because mostly she's under the influence of prickly, public parental memories where being out "as a family" seldom went smoothly. Also, she's wrestling with some profound please-daddy-notice-and-love-me issues pushing her to excessively crave male attention from every quarter.

The solution is for Tommy to realize that neither Lola's hesitations nor her need for male attention have anything to do with her level of caring for him, and nor do they mean she's looking for someone better. Meanwhile, Lola needs to push herself beyond what's comfortable and exhibit more public affection than usual to allay Tommy's fears.

In the final analysis, Tommy will need; of course, to solve his own esteem issues while Lola will need to change her relationship to parental history. Meanwhile, though, they shall both be well served by tenderly addressing the needs of the other.

So, the next time you're looking at your partner like s/he's got two heads because you've been told something you'd prefer to reject outright, pause, take a couple big breaths, and imagine seeing yourself as your partner sees you.

What do you discover?

Maybe they've got a point.

Perhaps you should take a closer look. Hopefully, such shifting of perspectives will invite the new behavior that leads to a partnership able to embrace you like a toasty cloak on a stormy night.

Collaboration Tool Chest

- ✓ **Be a teammate**
- ✓ **Be proactive**
- ✓ **Think from the other person's point of view**
- ✓ **Develop inter-dependent skills**
- ✓ **Feel and exhibit compassion**
- ✓ **Be a fan of the team**
- ✓ **Be willing to negotiate**

PART XI:
CONTRIBUTION:
PRACTICE SERVICE

Life is not accumulation, it is about contribution.
- Stephen Covey

IT MUST BE SAID THAT WHEN IT COMES TO CONTRIBUTION, most get stuck in outdated or shallow explanations of what that means. It used to be: he brought home the bacon and she fried it up. Then we switched to everybody's doing both. No matter how much has changed, it's easy to see we're still lugging around old myths and outdated "rules."

Yes, deep-rooted notions poke through all the time in so-called "modern" couples struggling to define contribution. Or more exactly, not actually tussling to define it, but instead being unconsciously dragged around by concepts they're hardly aware of having.

As always we need to start where we are if we can expect to move to where we want to go. That means telling ourselves the truth. So ask yourself: How does contribution work for and in me? How do I learn to value my own contributions, as well as the gifts of my partnership? Of my boss, my friends, or my family?

It's great to begin with the idea that contribution has nothing to do with money. Well, except when it does. I mean, if what we primarily bring to the party is what we have earned, that's fine too. But that's not the only version. The money conversation is similar to our previous sex chat. What *else* besides the obvious commonly accepted financial "value/orgasm" definitions are present when it comes to our contribution? Good to know.

So much has changed in our world, and so little.

If we don't know how we feel and what we believe underneath it all, we're likely to continue down the mystification road when it comes to how to put a relationship on a healthy, healing track. This is both for those already involved with committed love and those still looking. When it comes to our viewpoints about what contribution is, and how it can best work, it's enormously important to be on the same page with our partner. There really are only a few areas where commonality is essential to quality conjoining, and this is one of them. Another would be what can be called the No-Turning-Back Issues: I know you can't have children and I thought I really wanted my own; I don't want children under any circumstances (some might argue many frequently do go back on this, but I strongly suggest sorting this out at the beginning); which state or country do we start our referral business in; or I know you have a potentially communicable disease, but I chose to be with you anyway.

The no-turning-back matters are unfixable.

These kinds of issues are obviously few and far between.

You can refuse to bring your child up in the religion of your partner, but go back on that decision later. You can say you never want to see your family of origin again, but change your mind. Still, it's best right at the starting gate to check out how your own No-Turning-Back prerequisites square with the person you're dating.

Q: What if I don't have that much to give?

PROBABLY THE MOST IMPORTANT PART OF LEARNING HOW CONTRIBUTION WORKS is to push the boundaries of assumption with regards to our own limitations. Believe that you have capacity beyond up-to-now experience. I guess "give 'til it hurts" is not entirely out of line here, though perhaps a better way of saying it would be *give with feeling*. Urge yourself to discover what you can offer that you've never before considered offering. And as always, when it comes to contribution, *do the inconvenient thing*.

Summary: It's helpful, maybe even critical, to write about what you believe contribution to include. Uncover your hidden ideas about relationship roles. Again, thinking about it isn't the same as writing about it, making a collage about it, or painting about it. Certain fragments of history or feeling-driven precepts are unlikely to come to light through thought alone.

Thus, to be a quality contributor, you will need to recognize what you bring, appreciate what you receive, and extend beyond yourself.

PART XII: COMPROMISE: PRACTICE CATCH & RELEASE

Catch and release is a practice within recreational fishing intended as a technique of conservation. After capture, the fish are unhooked and returned to the water before experiencing serious exhaustion or injury. Using barbless hooks, it is often possible to release the fish without removing it from the water (a slack line is frequently sufficient). [lii]

W E MIGHT HAVE AN IDEA OF HOW TO TAKE CARE OF OUR INDEPENDENT SELVES AT THIS POINT, maybe even have figured out some ways to make partner-needs a priority. But when it comes to the "US," it's easy to get snagged.

In this regard, compromise is basic and the key.

Just as with fishing, compromise is about conservation. When done in a timely, gentle manner, it protects the relationship from harm and does so without wearing down the connection. Compromise is not about trying to convince or lure the other person into doing it our way, but about finding a true middle ground. There's no fooling them into thinking we're in mutuality.

It needs to be real.

In other words, we need to truly, actually, release.

We can't pretend or "submit" or keep a secret tally of wins and losses. This is a practice of letting go and finding something inside ourselves that can *appreciate* the middle-ground solution. If, instead, we hold on to our grumpy "it shoulda been my way," we're sure to undermine our relationship—whether in the moment or in the long run.

In relating of all kinds, compromise is needed constantly. Be aware. Start noticing how it works at home, at work, and everywhere in the world, in fact. Even in a chat with a friend, we might be chomping at the bit to get our point across, but have to compromise our jump-in want. Or maybe at work we're pretty darn certain a project would work better our way; however, there are other team members on the assignment voicing their input as well. Or at our corner restaurant they're out of our favorite fish.

Sometimes there are rules, like when two cars get to the stop sign around the same time the one on the right turns first, but even then often it's a judgment call. Mostly, we're attempting (or variously forgetting to attempt) civility when it comes to in-the-world activities.

Sure, go ahead of me.

Oh, let me get that door.

Each move we make asks us to compromise something—our time, energy, or desires. Funny though, at home we often fall short or simply don't want to. It's odd really, when you think about it. Home is where we should really, by all rights, exhibit the best of us, not the worst. It seldom happens that way. Do we take our partners for granted, imagining we can be whomever we wish and they'll just take it? Are we testing? Do we imagine no-need-to-be-on-my-best-behavior there because home-is-where-I-go-to-relax. Do we suppose the unthinking, unkind version of ourselves to be the "real" us? Actually, home is where we ought to bring our *best* selves. After all, who's more important than our mate?

Think about this. Figure out why you're less thoughtful, kind, solicitous, impressed, funny, or whatever at home than you are wherever else you go.

In any event, when compromising with our partners, as noted, barbless hooks are recommended.

That means putting away our snide, aggressive (passive or otherwise) ways of interacting to allow truly helpful decision-making methods. These decisions can be little or big, including anything from what kinds of curtains to buy, where the kids should attend school, where to eat on Saturday night, or where we should move.

And in compromise, as in fishing, slack lines are frequently sufficient; in other words, when entering discourse it's best to participate gently, rather than trying to tug and grunt the topic into submission.

Trouble starts when we feel reactive to circumstances or requests. Such reactivity tends to inform what we're saying and how we're saying it, weaving through our words and ways like tangled line.

Where does that reactive "energy" come from anyway?

History, of course.

In the case of a relationship, it usually includes family of origin or upbringing history, but can be precisely stimulated by what we can call *local history*—issues arriving over time in the partnership. This local history ordinarily begins with particular requests going unfulfilled, again and again. Probably the urgency of those requests was based on earlier childhood remnants hanging around the partnership like dangling participles at the end of a sentence. Still, it never helps to have our jeopardy doubled through current frustrations. By the by, here's a dandy "never ever" set of relationship rules:

- ✓ Never ever accuse your partner of being in any way like their father or mother, or your father or mother
- ✓ Never ever threaten to break up unless you really, truly, absolutely mean it. All too often *we're finished!* is used as a way to throw the **hear-me** bomb in the middle of the room. This is especially prevalent among passionate fighters. One hint is that intentional, well-considered break-ups seldom happen during a screaming fight
- ✓ Never ever move to abuse of any kind

By the way, I personally find it constantly annoying how often the statement "where's your sense of humor" comes up in the wake of vile behavior, whether in word or deed. It's a common go-to for abusers. When we're stabbing people, there's nothing funny about it. And further, if you find yourself to be a person who turns everything into a joke (called the Defense of Humor), you'd do well to investigate what's really going on with you. No doubt, you're involved in a process called deflection, which means distracting the eye from the real deal, the way a magician distracts to affect his trick.

Are you avoiding real connection?

Are you afraid to look some fear in the eye?

It's fine to use humor in life, of course, and how could we even survive or thrive without it? However, when humor is a defense, it becomes our go-to for *all* circumstances, even those easily recognized by most as inappropriate.

Please note all three of the above-mentioned never-ever-do statements are most often efforts to connect—even abuse. Terrible choices, huh? And though they're the true never-ever rules, pretty much *everyone* breaks one or more of them. To save yourself the heartache of this rule-breaking process try figuring out *before* your next fight what needs to be said or confronted that's flying under the radar. Also, as always, try noting where your enormous angst, fury or hurt might really originate.

The compromise tackle box...

WHY IN THE WORLD AM I TALKING ABOUT FISHING?

Well, finding the part of ourselves that can put aside the my-way-is-always-better, I've-been-doing-it-like-this-all-my-life, or but-I-don't-wanna voices, means fishing around inside ourselves in often pristine, undeveloped territories. The question becomes: how can we get past all the accumulated resentments so we can fully invest in the wonderful world of compromise?

Whether we're adventuring through new love terrain, or trying to fix what feels broken, understanding how to use the compromise tackle box holds us in good stead.

Looking for love...

THERE'S PLENTY OF FISH OUT THERE AND QUITE A VARIETY AT THAT. That's partially why our gigantic challenge when it comes to trying to find love often strikes us as a mystery.

Nevertheless try we do, again and again.

Are we diving right in—letting ourselves hang out in the deeper waters, or are we sitting on the dock where maybe we feel safer, merely throwing out the thinnest of lines? Are we in some kind of transition with regards to our approach, which looks like fishing off a bridge with legs dangling over the side? And what kind of gear are we using—what's our tackle method?

What's our bait?

Our lure?

Have fun with this. Ask yourself these questions and see what answers pop up. Delighting ourselves in the way we explore inner regions can inspire us to dig deeper.

By the by, I'd like to emphasize this point: Self-discovery work doesn't need to be a constant sludge march through the murky swamp in the dead of night. I know I was talking just a few pages ago about humor as a defense, but sincere healing can, and in fact should, include laughter and play. We want to find a rhythm that allows moments of light-hearted release. Indeed, it's well documented that laughter also heals. American political journalist, author, professor, and world peace advocate Norman Cousins said: "Laughter is a form of internal jogging. It moves your internal organs around. It enhances respiration. It is an igniter of great expectations."

At times, in truth, when it comes to healing, laughter can be more important than anything else.

Making love work...

YOU'VE ALREADY GOT A COMMITTED RELATIONSHIP AND YOU THINK MAYBE YOU'D LIKE TO FIND A WAY to re-inspire, sustain, and even elaborate it. How does that happen? The first question to ask is: Do you still see your relationship as an adventure?

Well, in certain situations, it's easier than in other circumstances. Fishing waters can be tumultuous, meaning your history separately and together can be complicated; or the fish might be big or nasty, meaning you might have hooked a difficult partner.

Still, if you're in it to win it, re-upping your level of investment is necessary. Truth is: If you were content to leave things as they are, it's unlikely you'd be reading this book. So get in there. Roll up your sleeves and go to work. An inspired life awaits.

If the relationship's tough going...

OFTEN THE MOST CHALLENGING RELATIONSHIPS HAPPEN BECAUSE the psyche wants to grow us in super-extraordinary ways and the bigger the obstacle, the higher the jump. Of course, it might be because that's what you knew and got comfortable with growing up; or because you're somehow convinced struggle is your lot in life; or numerous other hard-boiled perspectives.

Whatever the reason all along, we want to ask ourselves: *Why has my psyche chosen such a thorny relationship? What might I be trying to heal? How does this relationship reflect me now and how does it reflect my history?*

One thing is guaranteed: Primary relationship potentially offers extraordinary possibilities found nearly nowhere else. And yes, discovery can be as complicated or as simple as you choose. As with all things, sometimes less is more, while other times more is better.

Start with the basics and use extra-sophisticated gear as you move along. Always honor your own pace and the speed with which your particular psyche wants to accommodate change. A relationship is no place to practice our overachieving tendencies. Try to resist powering-through as a solution to your relationship complexities. Tackle recovery piece by piece.

Summary:
When attempting compromise:
- ✓ Find a true relationship middle ground
- ✓ Follow the three never-ever rules
- ✓ Keep figuring yourself out.

PART XIII: BETTER LOVE EVERYWHERE ALL THE TIME: NINE WAYS & MEANS

Ready to fish for a better relationship…

ERE ARE NINE DANDY, USEFUL WAYS TO FISH THE COMPROMISE WATERS. This gear is actually appropriate for all situations, whether with new potential partners, long-standing mates, with friends, at work, or anywhere we travel in the world.

Remember: wherever we go, there we are. Which is why changing partners, jobs, housing, cities, and even body shape doesn't fix our lives. Our best shot at changing is to offer our most intentional, integral Self in all places. And don't wait for "feeling it" to kick in. Sometimes, we have to act as we'd like to be before we can be who we want.

Here's what you need to pay attention to remembering that all these better-relationship expressions ask of us a certain level of consciousness. It might first feel awkward and like over-analyzing. Do it anyway. Nothing's going to shift if you refuse new procedures. I will talk about each here; however, when ready for the "How-To" of true shift, turn to the *Love Works* chapter for full exercise explanations.

#1: The upward-turned palm

OPERATING FROM TRUE, COMMITTED RELATIONSHIP *INVITATION* IS CRUCIAL TO HEALTHY OUTCOME. All too often we fool ourselves into imagining we're actually open to a relationship when it's far from true. How do we know if our invitation is real?

Recall the **Stunner:** the evidence of our intention is visible in the way our life unfolds. No matter what we say, think, or believe, if we don't have love it's likely we're not inviting love. If we really want to change tedious circumstances, we need to root out resistance.

Well, discovering underlying issues can take a while. Meanwhile, happily, there are do-it-now paths to walk. Twelve-step programs will often say: *Take the action and the mind will follow.*

Of course, I must rush to remind you—changing behaviors without profound appreciation of the underlying dynamics will be only brief stopgap measures sure to lose long-term power. So gear up, get your equipment cleaned and ready, decide where you want to start, and get going. But always keep your eye on catching the big fish called True Self.

#2: Take Ownership

THIS IS THE CENTERPIECE OF *ALL* CHANGE. It means recognizing who, where, when, and how we are being besieged by the defenses that report our history, as well as the beliefs we hold about that history. I've been drumming this loudly and constantly, so by now I'll bet you've accumulated some excellent understandings.

The idea now is to reveal them.

#3: Move from Complaint to Compromise

IT'S SO EASY TO LIVE IN THE COMPLAINT, ISN'T IT? Whether with friends, on the job, or at home, we can always point to something that's not working. Why do we so often focus on what's missing? We know it keeps us unhappy. We know it robs us of joyful experience.

Some imagine complaining creates change.

It doesn't.

Others jump on the complaint bandwagon as a kind of solidarity move. You know, *all* women do such-and-such and *all* men do so-and-so.

Ugh. No solutions there.

In other cases, complaining is synonymous with blaming, which is about getting the spotlight off us. What is it for you? Answer this important question for yourself.

Now, it's great to be discerning—to know the difference between what works and what doesn't; however, being trapped in the world of constant critical grievance is not the same thing.

Notice that I've juxtaposed complaint and compromise.

By that I mean to indicate complaint as a kind of power play. Well, it's far from the only version and maybe not even the most egregious because, in fact, *everything that's not about love is about power.*

Everything.

When we're angry, that's about power.

When we're pleading, that's about power.

When we're playing the victim, that's about power. Terrible choice for getting so-called power, huh? Thus, complaint is power also. Mostly, we don't seem to notice that these choices aren't working. Well, we notice something's not working, but hardly ever realize it's *us.*

All right, so power-playing is the enemy of compromise.

Actually, *power-playing is the enemy of love.*

That means compromise is actually the surrender of power. You can tell there's surrender in it because you're not exactly getting your way. And believe it or not, that's a good thing.

Q: Okay, so how do I do that? Surrender sounds so…demeaning. I'm already afraid of being smothered!

FIRST, THE FEAR OF RELATIONSHIP SUFFOCATION IS ONE OF THOSE IT'S-ALL-ABOUT-HISTORY DEALS. If your current partner is a smothering type, there's a reason you've chosen that. Maybe you get to practice boundary setting. Or perhaps you're healing a mom problem.

Another version of this is called fear of entrapment. It involves worry about getting caught without an escape route. An individual plagued with this chafes at boundaries and limits on so-called freedom and finds restriction intolerable. For this kind of person, real relationship commitment can be nearly impossible. They often move from person to person and even job to job—or find a career that involves constant change, like, say, advertising or acting, where every project is like starting over.

Obviously, the intensity of such apprehension pushes away commitment. If we imagine being swallowed by a whale as inevitable, we are certainly going to avoid swimming in the ocean.

It's not that being this kind of person is a problem exactly; it's only recognizing the crux of your ideas of self and figuring out how you want to handle it. Do you want to change your relationship to it, or accommodate it?

Again, I'm only on the side of clarity.

Most importantly for our purposes, it's vital to realize there's absolutely nothing demeaning about the kind of surrender being recommended here. It's not raising the white flag in defeat, but rather yielding—the way one might gently let go of physical rigidity during a luscious dance in order to feel the rhythm. It's actually more of a joining with the energy of the other, or with the experience, rather than struggling against that energy.

There's a delightful Japanese martial art called aikido developed by a man named Morihei Ueshiba that beautifully describes the intention of surrender:

> Aikido, a synthesis of martial studies, philosophy, and religious beliefs, is often translated as "the Way of unifying (with) life energy" or as "the Way of harmonious spirit." Ueshiba's goal was to create an art that practitioners could use to defend themselves, while also protecting their attacker from injury. Aikido is performed by blending with the motion of the attacker and redirecting the force of the attack rather than opposing it head-on. This requires very little physical strength. [liii]

Actually, blending and redirecting is a delicious definition of collaborative intimacy. Everyone's well served through this. As always, we want to practice *deeply* becoming the person with which we'd like to partner. Or be in business with. Or be friends with.

Newsflash: The face you show shows back to you.

What does this mean?

What we're talking about is the *inside face*—the one we imagine no one really sees and the one even we sometimes don't "see." This face carries our feelings, more deeply held thoughts, and our most earnest desires. Now, here's the squirrely part: *It's that inner face the world reflects back to us.* That's right. Not the mask we so carefully don each day; you know, the appearance assiduously chosen to accommodate circumstance.

Thus, if somewhere inside you hold contempt for or about relationships, no matter what you 'say' or pretend, the people gravitating toward you will know it. And if you're terrified of heartbreak, they'll know that, too.

Therefore, when your partner isn't doing what you want and need—or isn't being as good to you as you wish—check out your own behavior or be brave enough to venture into the secret nooks and crannies of your thinking. Look carefully beneath the discarded fabric scraps.

Sometimes, it's easier to begin by examining how we treat ourselves. Are we as kind to our Self as we'd like our partner to be? Are we regarding the Self with the respect we crave?

In the final analysis, the main problem with constant complaining is that it erects a barrier between us and others. This is obviously counterproductive when it comes to creating a healthy intimate relationship. Don't judge yourself for this please, just start by noticing.

#4: Don't travelogue

OH, HOW VERY MUCH WE LOVE GOING OVER AND OVER JUST-WALKED TERRITORY. Going round and round about who was standing where and who said what: "No, I was in the dining room when you started yelling…" Or "Oh please, I never said that…in fact what happened was we were in the bedroom and you took out your phone and…"

On and on it goes; each person trying to 'prove' their point through endless re-examination—traipsing muddy footprints all over the relationship floor. By the time we're finished, we can't even remember what we're fighting about. The contest has long ago shifted from how we fix this, to who's right.

What a mess.

At work, as well as with friends and family, we tend to engage what I've dubbed "traveloguing"—by which I mean the play-by-play review. It's a familiar dance most of us know well that takes us nowhere and is exhausting and fruitless.

At times, "traveloguing" includes bringing out the old laundry list of long-ago incidences and perceived infractions. When we do this, we're most likely getting some kind of *oomph* out of reliving the original anger and resentment we felt. Of course, this merely pushes us away from the present moment, and away from the true underlying issues stimulating conflict. We do this, mostly, to back our play, thinking history can validate our current position. It's the same thing we're doing when we say things like: "All your friends say this about you…" Or, "Everyone knows how you are."

These trips to nowhere merely salt the wounds.

Fundamental: We can never fix a problem at the level of the problem.

The thing is our problem is not really about taking out the trash or even getting home on time, or any other superficial complaint. It's about the basics of respect, value, abandonment, attention, and the like—which means, once more we need to dive beneath the surface. Maybe we're just fishing in wrong waters or using incorrect equipment. Whatever's going on, our procedure needs adjustment.

#5: Pick your battles

CERTAINLY, YOU'VE HEARD THIS OFTEN-SUGGESTED ADVICE NUMEROUS TIMES, but what does it mean and how does it happen? Firstly, we need to know what's sincerely important to us. Once we learn to keep our eye on the three or four thematically important matters, we can stop sweating the small stuff. To find out more, check out the *Love Works* chapter.

#6: Do the inconvenient thing

IN RELATIONSHIPS, WE'RE OFTEN CALLED UPON TO PERFORM TASKS WE'D PREFER SKIPPING. To stoke the great relationship fires, we simply need to put our preferences aside and do the called-for deeds. We must see their relatives when we'd rather watch a game, do the laundry when we'd prefer getting a massage, go to dinner when lying around the house is far more appealing, have a conversation when we'd rather collapse in bed, help with their computer problems when we'd rather cuddle.

Actually at work, roaming around in the world, or with friends, we do it all the time. Go to lunch with a co-worker we're not that crazy about, agree to a work plan we'd prefer to avoid, or go to the bank at lunch when we'd rather dine leisurely in a decent restaurant.

But, as mentioned a few pages ago, at home we want a pass.

Remember that becoming the person you'd most like to have as a partner is the aim. It's a good deal, whether you're on a first date or a fifth decade with someone.

By the way, this idea of wanting later in relationship what we at first had confuses me. Well, of course, we all want the initial spark. However, in the best of all worlds, over time we get better as individuals and thereby get better in our relationships as well. Wouldn't we rather have, then, the more dimensional, rich-layered, been-through-so-much-and-survived relationship we've developed—especially if we can also keep that beginning excitement spark glowing?

It *can* happen. Imagine it.

#7: Continued Individual Development

AS I'VE CLEARLY EMPHASIZED, JUST BECAUSE WE FIND OUR BELOVED doesn't mean everything stops. In fact, I'd say a relationship can be both the instigator and platform for furthering unique, individual development.

I'll assume if you're reading this you're the kind of individual who wants continued growth. As you may then already have figured out, the more we discover, uncover, and reveal about ourselves, the more we have to contribute—both to personal relationships and to the world.

The good news is that a healthy relationship supports personal evolution. Still, it can be tempting to sit back and drift, counting on what we've already exposed and known as "enough." Thing is: at each stage of development, as mentioned, we're able to learn and unearth things not previously available to us at earlier stages.

Yes, we continue to have only a few themes, and most certainly we can grouse about returning constantly to them, as in: "Oh for Pete's sake, I just read my diary from when I was 12 and I'm still talking about the same stuff! Crap!" Or we could celebrate the insistent nature of our journey.

I choose door number two.

When I was about 11 or so, I wrote a story called "Destiny." It was about a town called Destiny where everyone went to find—you guessed it—their destiny. Okay, a little narrow.

Still, look at what this book's about…really, truly being able to fulfill your love destiny. So, as it turns out, when it comes to our thematic narrow focus, we've been slapping away at it from the beginning and it is what it is. And what it is: is good.

#8: Practice Trust

I'VE USED THE WORD TRUST MANY TIMES—trusting in terms of Faith that something outside us operates in our best interest; trusting the value of our own instincts, intuitions and capacities; trusting the concept and construct of a relationship itself. Believe that love can be a healing proposition. But how the heck are faith and trust connected? To quote Alan Watts:

To have faith is to trust yourself to the water. When you swim you don't grab hold of the water, because if you do you will sink and drown. Instead you relax, and float.[liv]

Trust involves confidence. It's a faithful knowing that we can withstand whatever comes our way because we trust that heartbreak won't kill us—trusting that a panicked grabbing at the relationship will only sink us. Instead, we need to relax. But of course, that often takes a belief that life is on our side--a trust that we're resourced. And, underneath it all, we need to trust that whether you like or love me or don't, I'm okay and that even if the rug is pulled out, I'll survive and eventually thrive...again and again.

This is how the question often gets posed:

Q: But how do I know I can really trust my relationship? I mean, what if I surrender and get squashed?

ACTUALLY, SURRENDER ISN'T EXACTLY ABOUT TRUSTING THE RELATIONSHIP or even the person with whom we're in a relationship. It's about trusting the Self, knowing that floating in the water is as sure as walking on solid ground. Certainly, we want to choose wisely. Partnering with a thief or pathological liar or someone violent is not a particularly good plan and could easily pull us under, of course. But for the most part, no matter how badly we want to imagine our trust problems to be about the world or specific others, they aren't.

I can't emphasize this enough.

What must be trusted is our own ability to be reactivity-free when it comes to other people's responses to us, to what we offer or ask for, and to whom and how we present. When we fundamentally believe in the Self, we can speak our emotional truth clearly. When we trust ourselves, we can risk surrender for we have no fear of "losing ourselves."

Newsflash: If you're afraid of losing your Self it means you haven't found that Self the first place.

Is genuine self-trust possible? Absolutely. However, patience and practice are required. A lifetime of thinking differently is not summarily discarded.

Back in the day, we used to do trust exercises. While surrounded by a group, an individual would close their eyes and fall back into the supposedly waiting embrace of those assembled. As we fell, we'd count on being caught. It was scary, but let's face it—what facilitator was going to actually let the participant fall. Tucked away in our minds, then, we had a kind of failsafe.

Trust is much like this.

We need to assume there's a failsafe, even if we can't see it. Actually, the failsafe is to be found in our own capacity to endure disappointment, loss, embarrassment, or whatever other feeling theme is the crux of our matter. By the time we're entering relationships, we've most often already built this capacity—through family challenges and peer difficulties.

On top of that, we did it when we were smaller with many far fewer resources. Think back. You've already survived the worst parts, and in a far more fragile circumstance than you're experiencing now, because the big people were in charge. That means, you absolutely have the ability to face the life and apparent challenges currently before you because early on you developed resources you're simply yet to realize. See and know the truth of what I'm saying.

I'm asking you to look at the evidence reported by your experiences. When disappointed, even betrayed either as a child or adult, did you die? Obviously not. Did it hurt? Sure. And? Oh, I know you didn't like it; no one does. But not liking what happened is not a reason to shut down and shut off. Love is worth the excursion, even through the densest of territories.

Love is a choice. Choose love.

Trust is a choice. Choose trust.

Q: But what about the fact that every time we go into a new relationship, we inherit the issues the other person brings in from their previous relationships! Even if I trust myself, it doesn't mean my new partner will automatically trust me. How do I overcome that?

Such a big question calls for an in-depth answer. Indeed, in all new relationships everyone arrives with fully packed bags and it's inevitable that we'll have to deal with what was earlier referred to as the crowded bed, which I remind you means all parents (and previous partners as it turns out) climb in with us.

The question is not whether our partner brings luggage, but how much luggage they bring. Is it a small carry-on or a steamer trunk?

While exploring this question, there are two primary things to keep in mind:

- ✓ Our job is to *work on us* rather than fixing, deciphering, or instructing anyone else. Lead by example.
- ✓ No matter what, relationships of betrayal, unkindness, hesitation, or vile treatment are announcements of original wounds unmet—something in us needing exploration and healing. Let me hearken back to the magnet to refrigerator concept, where right material sticks to right material. Therefore, each primary engagement is an opportunity to look ever more deeply at what unmet inner material is being reflected. That's going to be your deciding factor when asking: Do I pursue this bonding or not? You're completely entitled to choose the most or least wounded birds out there. Just do it consciously.

Fundamental: Hear what your date, lover, or potential mate (your new friend, coworker or boss) says about past partners (past friends, past coworkers, past employees) as indicative of something you're eventually in some fashion guaranteed to bump up against yourself.

This means: "She was crazy" is likely to become you are crazy; "He never made enough time for me" turns into you never make enough time or you're too unavailable. "I just lost sexual desire!" That, too, will ultimately be about you, no matter what you believe at the beginning.

Thus, next time you enter a new relationship and the person starts talking about how so-and-so cheated on them, you might want to wonder how come. If your date starts talking about their cheating ex, try to remember such behavior rarely comes out of nothing—unless that ex was a philanderer to begin with, and how come they didn't recognize that anyway? But if the ex-partner wasn't a natural player, how did the partnership contribute to such behavior?

No matter what the nature of the description about a previous relationship breakdown, the question coming to mind wants to be: *what was your participation in the challenges and collapse of that relationship?* Now, maybe that's not a first-date question, but before getting too far in it's a goody. And if they don't know, that's also info for you—though unfortunately it's admittedly a question few consider.

Stunner: Whatever happened in the other person's last relationship is likely to happen in yours, somehow, some way.

This includes such issues as "sexual betrayal". The following question dialogue does not mean to "blame" the person being cheated on, but is rather an example of a way to simply explore. Thus, is the person you're beginning to date or in a relationship with hyper-vigilant and suffocating or, alternatively, do they withdraw affection? Either could encourage the mystery of betrayal to occur. Or are they in a long-standing family pattern they play out? Have any of these things led them to appear less immediately trusting of you than you'd prefer or imagine you deserve?

This is all good information for you. So when it comes to feeling trusted, rather than trying to convince the new person of our reliability we must:

- ✓ Look at why we've drawn such an untrusting person to us at this point in time.
- ✓ Do the work to expand understanding of the ways in which we too exhibit mistrust.
- ✓ Decide if we can live with the possibility that this fabulous new individual might never "trust us" the way we prefer.

It's not our job to prove ourselves in order to overcome *their* history. You get to decide if you want to continue or not considering the heavily packed designer bags they've brought with them. If *you're* ready to stay, begin unpacking your own cases; because at this point, if you truly want to practice having a trusting, loving relationship, you're going to need to jump in with both feet.

The Dance of Love and Betrayal...

Q: What moves people to do relationship work?

COUPLES ARE ENCOURAGED TO ENTER THERAPY because certain common stimulants come into play. Basically, it's one or more of the following four things listed here in no particular order:

- ✓ We have terrible communication
- ✓ Our relationship has lost its pizzazz (which can mean no romance; no time with each other; no emotional intimacy; no sexual intimacy)
- ✓ There's been sexual betrayal
- ✓ There's been emotional betrayal

Throughout this book thus far, I've offered many examples of these challenges. I want, however, to reinforce how betrayal in some form or other is most often at the crux of our matter—whether the betrayal is literal or it involves a betrayal of expectations as in: "I thought our relationship would turn out to be such and such and it hasn't at all gone that way."

Of course, feelings of betrayal are most often at the center of our early history, whether based-on-home-life betrayal, peer-member betrayal, or a perceived betrayal of our own potential and dreams. At a profoundly deep psycho-spiritual level, we might even feel betrayed by the very process of birth itself. [10]

Now, obviously the form adult-to-adult betrayal takes is often called "cheating," which is surely not to diminish financial betrayal, promise betrayal, business-partnership betrayal, friendship betrayal, spilled-secrets betrayal, and more.

I'm fascinated by what a huge issue sexual betrayal is, actually, even in the face of so many other forms of disloyalty. Like the one woman I worked with who discovered her husband had

---

[10] This conversation references birth trauma about which there's been much investigation from various angles. It can even include a discussion of the "being cast out of Eden" conversation. Though these are fascinating areas of exploration they do not exactly serve our purposes here. Still, I encourage you to someday adventure into these ranges.

secretly taken a huge chunk of their money and invested it, unbeknownst to her, in a losing gold mine. Zero discussion had ensued about this major investment that had simply been done behind her back. They also did not discuss his unilateral and cavalier attitude toward their future security. These she overlooked, while at the same time being quick to caution: "If he ever cheats with another woman, that's it!"

In any event, just to put a fine point on the "cheater" piece, here are three different story versions:

Betrayal Story # 1:

This is the story of Bruce and Lance. When arriving in my office, this couple right away evidenced great love for each other. They'd enjoyed a 20-year relationship by that time, and had the kind of entangled life so many years usually engenders.

Initially, they were full of hearty compliments for each other, but included how they were both sexually pulled away. In fact, they'd not had sex in several years.

Slowly, over the first couple months of work, it came forward that Bruce had, in fact, gone outside the relationship for sex. Lance was furious and devastated. Bruce insisted it was merely for the physical experience and took nothing away from the love they shared.

Together, we explored how they'd both set the relationship up for this inevitable experience. Bruce recommitted his fidelity and they began a sexual exploration together again, while we continued to investigate why each of them individually had shut down in the first place.

Betrayal Story #2

Sandra and Phillip had been in a loving relationship for years. Both were reasonably successful actors, which means neither were household names but managed to support themselves through their careers.

They married and began a family.

To all appearances, everything was going well.

Sandra was an emotionally complicated artist type, with a strong sexual appetite. Phillip was a steady-as-a-rock, dependable partner. Their sex life was fine, if unremarkable.

For Sandra, however, romance and newness poked at her desires like the Sirens on the rocks. In the old mythological tale of the Sirens, the three tempting creatures would sit on their rocks singing a song so painfully beautiful that passing sailors would be irresistibly drawn to them—even knowing they'd be crashing against those rocks and thereby going to their deaths. So sweet was the song that defiance was impossible. We all have our Siren song and best we figure out what it is so we can, like Odysseus eventually did, lash ourselves to the mast of our ships and thereby avoid going to our metaphorical deaths.

Now, some of the time, Sandra could resist the call of her appetite for new male attention and other times she could not. Sandra and I worked hard to discover what lay beneath this temptation. She became more and more successful at battling it. Phillip never discovered her secret.

Betrayal Story #3

Bryce and Lulu had been married over 20 years when I met them. At first he'd been the breadwinner and CEO of the relationship. As time went on, Lulu became well known in her field and began making so much money she could easily support them both in high style. They moved to Los Angeles, which was a town Bryce never liked, to accommodate Lulu's upward trajectory. Bryce started trying ways to discover a new version of Self—one that could both offer him the same thrill Lulu's job gave her, while allowing him to feel important, powerful, and manly in the relationship, which he no longer did.

In the process of this journey of discovery, Bryce started getting ever more disgruntled with Lulu's style of interaction, which was quite self-centered. She wanted everything to revolve around her. She seemed always to get her way, which is often something being the money-maker affords and seems to entitle if such an adventure is not accompanied by clarity and consciousness.[11] Meanwhile, Bryce, at that point, knew only how to exhibit power through complaint and negativity.

Lulu loved the attention of men. She drank quite a bit, which didn't much interest Bryce, and would party with her work friends. She especially liked the very handsome, flirty younger men as being around them made her feel more desirable. She never "crossed the line" with any of the fellows, but it was clear she was frequently involved in what we might call emotional affairs—allowing an intimate ebullience with them she never exhibited with her husband.

Eventually, Bryce also began seeking the attention of another. He too never "actualized" the affair in physical terms; however, it was obvious that he and the woman he closely befriended shared an intimacy not at all present in the marriage. Lulu found out and was horrified. Unable to see her part in the scenario, she couldn't get over the circumstances and the marriage ended in an ashen heap of shared vitriol.

Q: So how the hell am I to practice trust, compromise, and surrender with all the sad, bad, mad stories out there?

WHEN WE'RE TALKING ABOUT COMPROMISE AND SURRENDER, we're speaking of a new approach to life itself. Holding fast to our long-standing story perceptions while regarding them as precious causes us to squeeze the very life out of love. That's why I've been emphasizing the value of fresh perspective. We need this for a balanced life. And we need this for all our love matters.

I once worked with a couple we'll call Mira and Jason; they'd found each other through the Internet from halfway across the world.

Now, as I've clearly stated before: when trolling the Internet waters, great care must be paid. Indeed, it's super important to be cautious when surfing the 'net for love. Please diligently check out who's on the other side of your communication.

---

[11] On this note: It's essential that the family money-maker, no matter the gender, stay awake to their responsibility to honor the contributions of the non-money making partner, and that they conscientiously avoid waving a power flag.

There are scam artists aplenty!

For example, there's a brand new Internet issue called Cat fishing:

> The phenomenon of Internet predators who fabricate online identities and entire social circles to trick people into emotional/romantic relationships over a long period of time. [lv]

Now, besides such techno terrors there are, of course, also the standard operating procedure confronts with Internet dating, like the distance issue as well as the extra pesky layer of challenge when we consider how uber-romantic fantasy can so easily explode onto the scene. When we've only got words on a page or a voice. Indeed, we concoct, imagine, and envision who we decide and hope them to be with only the thinnest evidence to rest on. A rich canvas for romantic projection. Add that to what inevitably happens in any scenario when we meet someone new and it seems like a recipe for disaster.

And yet, I've worked with numerous couples discovering successful love this way. Mira and Jason are just such a couple and though the usual delicate elements immediately presented, they managed to overcome them all to meet, marry, and after a few years of getting to know each other, begin a family.

In any event, Mira, who was quite a bit younger than Jason, came into the relationship with a disastrous early family story—a tale leaving her wildly mistrusting not only of relationships, but of the world-at-large. Meanwhile, Jason also had a challenging history, plus a previously collapsed marriage under his belt. Still, as indicated, they were together several years and thought they had a decent sense of each other before beginning to have children, and yet that's when the trouble started.

Wanting her children to experience a far different life than she had, Mira became hyper-vigilant with regard to safety. Additionally, both her local family-of-origin experience and her cultural roots supported a rather aggressive manner of communication that landed on Jason as critical and assaulting.

But Jason wanted her and everyone else in his life to be happy. In fact, his main psychological development involved being the good guy who takes care of everyone. He'd always been that way in his all-female, no-dad family. To accomplish his care-taking ends (and naturally, because it was his aim-for-success style anyway) he worked harder and harder in his thriving business.

Early on, Jason had become the man of the house and as part of his early life; he'd trained himself to overlook infractions, which means he'd sometimes have the habit of inviting less-than-trustworthy people into their home. Of course, this only exaggerated Mira's fears.

The long and short of it was: Jason was the glass half-full guy and Mira was the glass half-empty person. In this way, they were opposites, or what we early hinted about as Shadows of each other.[12] As we know, this kind of "opposite" can make or break couples.

In any event, feeling pushed far away by Mira's guardedness, the couple began to fight in that bitter way that so often leads to the end of a marriage. Then they stopped sleeping in the same room. They had lots of excuses about the why of this, but it really was mostly symptomatic of their relationship deterioration.

When I met Mira and Jason, they were on the verge.

But one truly important thing in such cases, as previously stated, is the willingness to turn things around. To figure out if this is possible, we have to look at how much goodwill is left. Now, once bitterness and resentment set in, goodwill flees the scene.

It can be reclaimed with diligent effort.

Happily, both Jason and Mira were willing to check out their individual histories and make the relationship changes needed. It didn't mean she became instantly trusting of one and all, nor did it mean he necessarily stopped his co-dependent make-everyone-happy stance; however, both were able to shift their most obvious characteristic ways of proceeding to allow the deeper discoveries that promised real change.

---

[12] The Jungian term *Shadow* refers to discarded, unknown, unmet elements of self thrown away or repressed as an accommodation to our family system, or perceived peer member requirements or assumed societal mandates etc. Couples often (in fact, usually) carry shadow elements of each other—lost parts wanting reclamation. . Facing our Shadow parts is one of the gifts offered by relationship!

In the long run, Mira and Jason were able to move forward in their relationship; however, there will no doubt be a revisiting of their fundamental issues over and again throughout their marriage.

Q: How do I find balance?

PERHAPS THE WAY OF UNDERSTANDING HOW THIS BALANCE BUSINESS WORKS IS to envision a seesaw. I used to imagine balance to mean each person on the seesaw strongly holding position. In life, that would translate to a trying to achieve a stable, trusting experience by strongly holding firm. Looked at carefully though, that starts to resemble zero movement. Picture it: two kids are on opposite ends of the seesaw, feet planted decisively on the ground. No one budges. No seeing or sawing—just staying still.

Not so much fun, huh?

Then notice the difference if you envision one child going up while the other goes down. Spirited movement: That's more like it! Now that looks like a good time.

A healthy working relationship is similar.

It has motion and flow.

It may seem, at any given moment, as if one individual's "dominating" the action, but really it takes both to make the experience happen. In the case of Mira and Jason, for instance, she needed in the long run to learn to surrender her vigilance guns, while he needed to let go of the idea that he could please all the people, all the time. Thus, it turns out balance is not static and stasis is not flow. Both personally and relationally, we need flow to grow.

I promised you nine…

THERE'S ONE MORE BETTER LOVE WAYS & MEANS, and after this long but important dialogue about trust, here it is. It's a killer, so brace yourself.

#9: Drop it

THAT MEANS, LET THE TOPIC REALLY, TRULY, ABSOLUTELY GO. No putting it on your drag-it-out-later list. No beating the topic into submission. No more repeating.

Boy, if you're anything like me this is a hard one. After all, we've not made our point, haven't felt heard, need to be understood, require response, and want correspondence. That's what we think anyway.

Yes, I know.

Sometimes, though, we've got to come to realize the fight simply isn't worth it. After all, more likely than not you've landed on some more or less superficial issue you're now beating the crap out of. Think about it. Is this *really* the point you want to be making? Besides, believe it or not, you did make your point—20 times. If your partner didn't "get it," and if you've really tried all angles of good communication, then no amount of cajoling, convincing, or demanding will change things.

Thus, instead of repeating yourself for the billionth time and maybe landing on "well I guess we're done then," try figuring out why, and if, your insistent point is truly that vital. More importantly, attempt to discover the actual underlying issues.

Yes, once more into the breach.

When you understand what's driving the conversation on your side of the equation, you can actually let the little point go. After all, you've got bigger fish to catch and fry. Thus, the *Drop-It* tool reminds us that we can't solve a problem at the level of the problem. It's the release portion of the catch-and-release program.

Then you get to decide if the unmet, barely approached, or badly discussed fundamental concern is a deal-breaker or merely a problem-maker.

Nine Better Love Ways & Means

1. Make sure you're operating from true, committed invitation

And continue with:

2. Take ownership
3. Moving from complaint to compromise
4. Don't travelogue
5. Pick your battles

Maintain by evidencing the willingness:

6. To do the inconvenient thing
7. Participate in continuing individual development

Perpetuate by:

8. Practice trust
9. Practice the art of *Drop It*

PART XIV: THE ROAD TO RELATIONSHIP HEALTH

> I am not sure exactly what heaven will be like, but I know that when we die and it comes time for God to judge us, he will not ask: "How many good things have you done in your life?" Rather he will ask: "How much love did you put into what you did?"
>
> - Mother Teresa[lvi]

IMAGINE HAVING A RELATIONSHIP THAT FEELS, LOOKS, AND SOUNDS FABULOUS. Naturally, the yawning hope is that when we find our true long-awaited love match, *all* our dreams will be satisfied.

Sorry, they won't.

Seriously.

Come on. I know you've been listening and realize by now that even the greatest relationship isn't the "fix" for all that ails us, right? *We* are the fix. Relationship of any kind, like happy employment of any sort, is merely the cherry, and maybe the sprinkles too, topping our delicious self-esteem ice cream parfait.

Still, having a love that matters and reflects our personal sense of well-being—supporting and elaborating the best parts of us, while confronting and offering to shift the worst parts—is pretty darn great.

It can also be central to a life of wholeness and health.

The following essentials are meant to support an extraordinary life, whatever that means to you specifically. For some, that's about creating great works, while for others that's about creating great families.

One's not better than the other.

The idea is: Are you, as American mythologist, writer and lecturer, Joseph Campbell would put it, following your life's bliss?

> If you follow your bliss, you put yourself on a kind of track that has been there all the while, waiting for you; and the life that you ought to be living is the one you are living. When you can see that, you begin to meet people who are in your field of bliss, and they open doors to you. I say, follow your bliss and don't be afraid, and doors will open where you didn't know they were going to be.[lvii]

The 10 love matters essentials

Power without love is reckless and abusive,
and love without power is sentimental and anemic.
- Martin Luther King

NOW, WHEN WE TALK ABOUT RELATIONSHIP most think personal love and certainly this book has variously emphasized that as well. I do want to continue making the important point that a primary relationship isn't for everyone. That doesn't mean those who don't have a satisfying mate-type partnering can't achieve a spectacular life. If, in fact, you allow and embrace the following *ten healthy love matters essentials* in friendship, in work, and really everywhere you go, your life can still be vivid, splendid, and extraordinary.

The following must-haves are the foundation stones for any solid sustained relationship structure. At best, we'd use this basis for *all* our relationships both at work and at play, and in every context including family and career. Obviously, some will be more essential in private settings, while others should be included in public scenarios.

You'll find here certain definitions of health. Take what you like and leave the rest. As always, you'll want to discover and develop meanings plus methods that suit *your style* of being in the world.

The most necessary elemental idea, though, is that we form a fundamental perspective that promises to guide us through both the obvious challenges life inevitably offers, and through our demanding blind spots. Think of the essentials, then, as the side-mirrors of your vehicle. Even when our eyes are on the road ahead, we know they're still available at any moment to protect us from being sideswiped; therefore, glance at them occasionally when in traffic.

You'll recognize much of what's listed here as being things previously touched on. I organize them now for you, however, as a convenient summary and in some cases, elaboration.

✓ **Essential #1: SAFETY**
✓ **Motto:** *I've got your back!*
✓ **What that means:** Creating a context and/or arena of safety is an imperative emotional procedure. It can include things we "do"; however, those doings mostly reflect who and how we are. Safety in a relationship happens when we feel our most authentic selves supported. It says: Be who you are. Show me your good, bad, and ugly, and I will be behind you 100%.

This never means we can behave in any 'ole way. Absolutely not. Nor does it recommend saying thoughtlessly anything that comes into our brains. Kindness and authenticity are not enemies. Remember the previously mentioned injunction: *Is it kind? Is it necessary? Does it improve upon the silence?*

✓ **Essential #2: TRUST**
✓ **Motto:** *We say what we mean. We mean what we say. We walk the talk.*
✓ **What that means:** As stated, trust starts with us. We often look to circumstances or others to create an

emotionally hazard-free atmosphere. And sure, that's desirable as well, for the situation we're in should be reliable, consistent, and honest. For many, this will be a new experience, having had no such thing in childhood. Those of us who come from alcoholic homes, for instance, are constantly looking for landmines. For us, vigilance becomes a way of life. Numerous other circumstances likely prepared us similarly. Practicing trust of our surroundings, and the folks therein, eventually frees us from such vigilance. If we just continue to act as if everything's as awful as ever it was, things will remain the same.

Obviously, we can't always have an absolute, solid sense of security in every physical or emotional condition, but what we can have is a sense of *security within*. Show up authentically by being trustworthy in word and deed. Watch what happens. Exhibit the qualities you most long for in and from the world, and discover the wonderment of reflection.

- ✓ **Essential #3: INTIMATE FRIENDSHIP**
- ✓ **Motto:** *I get who you are and I'm there for you*
- ✓ **What that means:** We've spent many pages describing intimacy; however, in the long run, you're the one who gets to decide how your relationship feels. And this includes our relationship to occupation. Does it satisfy the heart of us? Are we in our bliss?

Q: How can I reinvigorate my relationship/s? I'm just not feeling cherished or appreciated or, as you say, intimate.

It's important to ask the question: *Was there was an initial spark in the first place?* Did your relationship stimulate and thrill you? Or, did your job inspire you? (Remember when we're talking about relationships that means all the circumstances of our lives, which is to say most answers will be useful and applicable across the board.)

Anyway, if there was no initial spark—if the sex, for instance, between you and your partner never was very exciting, it's unlikely it will magically become exciting now. Or if your job never felt thrilling and everything remains equal, that's probably not going to change. Basically, in those cases, we're working with wet kindling and nothing's going to spark a flame.

Just answer honestly. If that's something you can live with, so be it. On the other hand, if there was excitement in the beginning, then reinvigoration is possible and up to you. Certainly, don't wait for your partner or boss or friend to make things better and different.

Do it yourself.

Yes, to reinvigorate relationships we need to find the generator of our original interest. That sparkle is *inside*, so stop waiting for someone else to make it happen.

Begin by cherishing and appreciating others and circumstances as the way you'd like yourself to be cherished and appreciated. You can do this by treating your partner or friend or job like you've just met. It's called Beginner's Eyes—the eyes of a child. Stop assuming you know how that partner or boss or friend is going to respond.

Offer something new.

- ✓ **Essential #4: MUTUAL RESPECT**
- ✓ **Motto:** *I don't need to agree with you to support you.*
- ✓ **What that means:** Happily, we don't require exact correspondence with every viewpoint, attitude, and even action to feel respected. Different strokes, as they say. The idea is to stay in contact with our sense of vigorous regard for the people and situations with which we find ourselves involved. When that respect is gone we best ask ourselves questions like: *Have I changed so much that this circumstance or these individuals no longer reflect me in a beneficial way?* An example of this might be when someone gets sober and discovers most previous so-called friends were actually drinking buddies. Reassessment is in order. Or, in the case of job circumstance: *Have I outgrown this job?* Or, *does the current atmosphere at work support my emotional well-being?* These questions can also easily be applied to love matters everywhere.

The bottom line is that when it comes to maintaining mutual esteem, we must be able to acknowledge, accept, and respect the situations and people with which we're associated. Of course, as always, it's best before making any radical moves to figure out what negative contribution we bring to the party.

✓ **Essential #5: COLLABORATION**
✓ **Motto:** *Let's be a team.*
✓ **What that means:** We've spoken extensively of this. Remember to be a teammate, be proactive, and think from the other person's point-of-view. If you ignore what your companions have to offer, you'll be shortchanging yourself.

✓ **Essential #6: BELONGING**
✓ **Motto:** *We're in it together!*
✓ **What that means:** Even the most reclusive among us want a sense of fitting in. Outcasts belong to a tribe called outcast. Cults sometimes sweep such individuals into their container. Strong religions do the same. The want to belong is innate.

Truth is: we do "belong," whether we mean to or know it or not. To begin with, we belong to the time era in which we're born. We even keep finding generation names for it. Here are a few:

2000/2001-Present: New Silent Generation or Generation Z
1980-2000: Millennials or Generation Y
1965-1979: Generation X
1946-1964: Baby Boomers
1925-1945: Silent Generation
1900-1924: G.I. Generation

Additionally, it's common for us as we grow up to find clicks or a *posse* or groups to hang with—fraternities and sororities of sorts. This is all in the service of having a sense of connection.

For most, family roots become the center of this belonging or not-belonging story. Relationships, be it with co-workers, friends, or mates, want to allow us to feel met and known—to give us a sense of "family". The nature of the original family usually determines our reaction in those circumstances, especially if greeted with little consciousness. Naturally, positive actualizing of these possibilities will depend on what we're ready for and able to express.

✓ **Essential #7: AFFECTION**
✓ **Motto:** *I want to show you how I feel about you.*
✓ **What that means:**

> Ardent emotional attachment or involvement between people; a strong, sometimes short-lived attachment, fascination, or enthusiasm for something; a childhood romance with the sea; a mysterious or fascinating quality or appeal, as of something adventurous, heroic, or strangely beautiful. [lviii]

Now imagine applying the idea of being ardent to a friend you love, to a project you feel adamant about, or to an adventure you're entertaining. This conversation begins to nibble yet again around the edges of the question: *How do we express love in all our matters?*

There are all versions of affection including physical, emotional, and verbal. Many come from families where affection simply wasn't shown in any way, while others grew up experiencing very specific forms of loving warmth and care. Some histories make learning to express more challenging, whether that's because fondness was rarely conveyed or because it came forward in inappropriate ways.

But when it comes to the personal "shoulds," we need to figure it out for ourselves. You know by now there are no rules. That means: While some like to save their "displays" for primary partners, others tend to follow full-time express-affection programs. There's not a right and wrong to this. What's important is not how, but that you **find** *some* *way* **to express your love.**

Love's a muscle.

It gets stronger, better, and bigger the more you use it.

Yes, it's true that expressed affection grows itself. Like working out at the gym builds stamina until, before we know it, we can do more than ever anticipated. When we articulate or reveal affection, we're encouraged to more of the same.

Thousands of times in my career I've been told: "I've never said 'I love you' to my father, but he knows!" Or, "My friends know how much I love them!"

Maybe. Maybe not.

But in any case, that's only part of the story.

Articulating affection is not only for the other person—which is motivating enough—but it's also vital *for us*. Why? Because thinking, feeling, being, living, and conveying authentic love affects our perspectives and attitudes *toward everything* in the same way putting glasses on blurry eyes clarifies vision. Seeing through a love lens actually enables us to perceive more beauty in the world. This, in turn, increases our sense of personal well-being. Like water reflects sunlight, we reflect back the beauty we see around us. This isn't about ignoring what doesn't work or isn't so lovely. Not at all. It's about recognizing both the dark and the light as integral to living and then, even in the face of that recognition, choosing to appreciate all with affectionate love.

The cherry on top is that people tend to give what they get. When we offer ourselves, the offer is often returned. But don't by any means do it for payback. Do it because you can. Do it because you refuse to let hesitation or fear stop you. Do it because growing into love is your intention.

Q: I get that general idea, but truthfully my partner seems at this point unavailable for specific displays of affection of any kind. What can I do to encourage romance?

The idea, as always, is to be proactive. We don't need to wait for permission to change our way of relating love, so lead by example and don't expect your partner to be a mind reader.

Of course, beginning with a frank discussion is likely a good idea. Inevitably, there's going to be some underlying material afoot—something not being attended, either inside the individual or within the relationship. Find out what it is. Keep in mind most behaviors are symptoms of something left unsaid and unmet.

- ✓ **Essential #8: SELF-ESTEEM**
- ✓ **Motto:** *The more I love and like myself, the more I have to offer you.*
- ✓ **What that means:** Well, this self-appreciation and self-love piece has been central to *Our Love Matters*, so I'll assume by now you've got plenty of tools in your arsenal. Use them.

Always what we can do to get ready for love with another is attend to self-love. Self-love and self-esteem are inextricably linked.

- ✓ **Essential #9: SELF-ACTUALIZATION**
- ✓ **Motto:** *I'm becoming and revealing the unique individual I am!*
- ✓ **What that means:** Realizing our highest and best selves is a lifelong journey. The important idea is to realize that self-realization is a process with no finish line to cross. This means evolution is constant.

I find it variously annoying and amusing when folks believe there's a self-improvement endgame. Actually, *the process is the point.* Planning the journey is one thing, but heartily enjoying the road trip is quite another.

And besides, ever notice how reaching a goal simply gives rise to a new objective? Yep, as it should be. When we stop reaching toward a different tomorrow, a dull fog rolls in. I've often told people that I hope as I take my final breath, I'll have one more realization and the strength to share it! Here's a plus: By continuing self-discovery, we gain further capacity to contribute both to a primary relationship and to the world around us.

- ✓ **Essential #10: APPRECIATION OF THE WHOLE OTHER**
- ✓ **Motto:** *I know and embrace all of you, even the parts I don't like.*
- ✓ **What that means:** This can be tough for many, but really it's what we all want. That is: even when we

show our ugliest, darkest parts, we hope to be accepted and loved anyway.

Naturally, this best starts with us being okay with the Self. Then being discovered, as it were, gives us no pause or consternation. It helps us to realize that everything lives inside us all in some measure—sometimes small and sometimes great.

Refusal to believe and acknowledge this can keep us away from love—both of the Self and of other. Shame, judgment, perfectionism, disavowing, denial, and resistance are only a few of the devices refusing healthy wholeness.

Exclusively acknowledging and allowing only what we prefer limits us in ways we can barely imagine. The more we appreciate how we're part of the unified, well-woven fabric called humanity, the happier, more satisfied, and less self-loathing we become. In the words of Kevyn Aucoin:

Today I choose life. Every morning when I wake up I can choose joy, happiness, negativity, pain... To feel the freedom that comes from being able to continue to make mistakes and choices - today I choose to feel life, not to deny my humanity but embrace it.[lix]

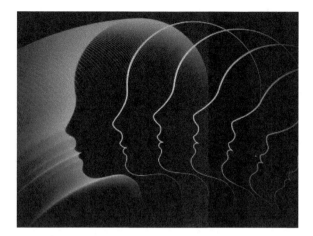

CHAPTER FOUR
WHEN ALL IS SAID AND DONE

> He allowed himself to be swayed by his conviction that
> human beings are not born once and for all on the day
> their mothers give birth to them, but that life obliges
> them over and over again to give birth to themselves.[lx]
>
> - Gabriel Garcia Marquez

IT'S COMPLICATED—THIS FINDING LOVE BUSINESS, AND REALLY NOT COMPLICATED AT ALL. Mostly, the difficulty comes from our refusal to look history in the eye, to embrace authentic, vulnerable behavior, and to remember faith.

When I was a little girl, I thought love meant getting attention.

When I grew into shape, I thought love meant being desired.

When I grew into a relationship, I thought love meant being needed.

When I became a teacher, I thought love meant being helpful.

When I become silent, I think love is Divine inspiration.

I don't *know*. Not really.

For a thoughtful person, lack of definition promises both freedom and fear. We want containers for our liquid offerings. We require parameters to frame our dialogues and delineate our territories.

But more important than any definition is to recognize the ways we have lost track of ourselves: how we've turned away from the Heart of the matter; how we've fallen prey to our baser fears, foibles, and follies.

In this, then, we've lost touch with our Divinity.

But change *is* possible.

And not only that, but when we truly attend our inner work, we find such change to be upon us like a sweet surprising rainbow appearing in the after-rain sunlight. That means there's hope. And armed with hope, courage, awareness, intentionality, and a true willingness to take action, the future turns bright. That's what *Our Love Matters* has offered you—a brightly-lit future.

I'm told we're in a new Renaissance—a promised rebirthing.

I am certain, if this is so, we will learn to fall in love with True Love again. We will remember ourselves. And in doing so, we shall, perhaps, find our way back to each other. In every way we can imagine. It matters in the boardroom and in the bedroom. It matters in the bright day's sun and during the darkest night. It matters when we're with others and when we're alone.

When we can put aside defensive, self-annihilating behaviors and perspectives, love's just hanging around every corner— humming a tune, waiting for us to stroll by and take an outstretched hand. It may not match our fantasies. It may not answer our long, insistent fathomless need. It may not deliver us from frustration, self-doubt, or thirst.

But what it will do is offer a platform on which to stand and arms in which to rest. And most of us are so very tired, aren't we. So weary of fighting the good fight; tired of answering the inner hunger driving us like pounding rain on a bleak night.

Leading the way...

WHAT YOU'VE BEEN READING IS A RELATIONSHIP GUIDEBOOK—a map to a better relationship future in every area of your life: be it at work, with friends, with family, and, of course, in a primary partnership. If you've followed the offered exercises and tips, you've already begun to experience real change.

Most of all you've opened a window into the Self.

Along the way I've shared stories, both about clients and about my own journey. In my personal tales, I've shown how I too have gone from dismal to delightful with regards to love matters; but even more importantly, I've revealed how change is an inside job. I know this path to be truly helpful because I walk the talk. I know also that the journey is never-ending.

We're always works in progress. And that's a good thing.

Look, we all have questions, concerns, and worries when it comes to relationships. Those in relationships worry about how to make it better. Sometimes they worry about whether they should stay or go. Those who don't have a partner worry about how to get one; and more particularly, how to get the right one.

That's what we've been talking about: how to have the relationships you want and want the relationships you have; and most importantly, how to love yourself amidst all the ups and downs of daily life.

I don't expect you to love yourself every minute.

I don't expect to love myself every minute.

Mistakes will be made.

Stitches dropped.

The question is not can we live perfect lives, but can we greet the unanswered questions, rise up to meet the incoming tide and stand proudly upright to face the beauty of life's sometimes harsh truths. And when we can do these things—when we open both our mind and heart to life—we find ourselves entering truly sacred territory, the land where love lives.

I've said it before and often: When all is said and done, there's only one thing to be talking about and that thing is love—because love is all that really, truly matters. Everything else is a reflection of this oft-times intangible, sometimes elusive, inevitably desirable state of being and doing. Curing cancer is about love. Planting a garden is about love. Finding your bliss is about love. Any artistic endeavor well met is about love. Sitting in considered silence is about love.

What do you know now?

WHEN IT COMES TO WHAT IS STANDING BETWEEN YOU AND A FABULOUS RELATIONSHIP, obviously *Our Love Matters* has covered many topics. I hope you feel enlightened.

We've been looking at how and when we tend to focus more on what we're not getting than on what's great about our relationships, jobs, friends, homes, etc. We explored how to know when a relationship is mostly working, so we can stop complaining and make it even better. We talked about when it's not working, how to either fix it or get out.

We investigated patterns—those appearing through relationships and those showing up for us everywhere we go: with partners, friends, colleagues, bosses, and employees. Bravely, you looked at how you behave in relationships, ever attempting to stop blaming and begin claiming responsibility. Of course, we recognize that there are problematic larger influences magnifying our love challenges. For instance, the current, rampant self-absorption where most seem never to move out of their it's-all-about-me stance. This means a world full of people believing everyone's talking, thinking, and behaving in a personal way.

You know how this works.

You do it too, hearing yourself say such things as:

"Oh I can't do that—she'll think I'm nuts!"

"My boss looked at me funny today. He's up to something."

"I just don't get along with people. Everyone thinks I'm stupid."

Why are we so preoccupied with what others do or how we perceive them to regard us? Oh sure, it's a lack of self-trust. But more, I suspect this other-directed focus means to "save" us from the self-investigation we're certain will leave us even more lonely and longing. Terrified of what we'll find inside, we flee by any means possible. If I let you tell me who I am, I don't have to figure it out for myself.

By now, you have a sense of that all-important relationship element called communication. You've been alerted to your communication skill, ability, and lack thereof. You've been given detailed, practical tools for improvement.

Yes, at this point you know what's great and not so great about the way you share yourself with others; plus, you've come to recognize the family roots supporting your relationship dilemmas and endeavors. In that regard, we checked out problem sources including local context, heritage pieces, global conditions, and more. Indeed, if you've followed the bouncing ball of this book, you've done enough work to grasp the idea that you've been running like hell from old childhood monsters.

Remember that dangerous kid's closet of mine?

Guess what? No one's hanging around in there waiting to harm you. Quite the contrary! What awaits is a better you—far better. You're struggling to get out now—fighting to be seen.

Let your Self free. Let us know you.

You have nothing to lose but your loneliness.

You know now that love does not happen by chance, but by choice. You've come to realize that to shift our relationship we must discover true intention, recognize the thinking and feeling blocks to love, and then change the way we do things.

Whether you've been reading *Our Love Matters* to better understand your spouse, partner, boyfriend, girlfriend, parents, kids, or friends; to take charge of the way your relationship life is unfolding; to find that special someone in your life; to discover how to love your career, body, mind, heart, God; or even to figure out how to have a more profound relationship with life itself, I sincerely trust you have taken much away from what you have read.

At last…

WHAT WE KNOW BY NOW is that we've been telling a story about ourselves in all our associations—our relationships with circumstances and with specific others called friends, co-workers, parents, and lovers. Stories about our potential, our career, our money, our self-image, about life itself and, of course, we've been telling ourselves stories about who, how, and what we are.

Finally, we've been designing our lives based on limited and limiting notions.

Newsflash: You are far, far more than you have imagined yourself to be.

The stories we've been claiming to define us were formulated long, long ago in the dark, quiet recesses of psyche and mind; in the sad corners of our secret lives, where no solace could be found.

It is time to give up those old fictions. You can do it. Stop frantically clinging to outdated ideas of the self. Realize you can become the person for whom you've been searching.

Each day, remember this: *How life feels is primarily up to you.*

It's a matter of perspective.

The beat goes on...

Owning our story can be hard, but not nearly as difficult as spending our lives running from it. Embracing our vulnerabilities is risky, but not nearly as dangerous as giving up on love and belonging and joy—the experiences that make us the most vulnerable. Only when we are brave enough to explore the darkness will we discover the infinite power of our light.

- Brene Brown[lxi]

HERE'S A FINAL PERSONAL STORY. This tale is hardly ego-enhancing for sure, but I offer it because, as you most certainly know by now, walking the talk is essential to all my teachings. Any teacher who doesn't continue to move toward self-discovery has very little to teach others. I ask you to plunge, plummet, and even sometimes free-fall, vulnerably exposing yourself.

I must do the same, so, here it is.

Not so very long ago, my husband and I faced the greatest battle of our long marriage. Besides all the glorious years of travel, making and losing friends, house-buying, growing my business, surprise parties, the zillions of events attended, witnessing deaths together, and the usual list of hopes lifted up and lost, we'd already together driven through financial storms; challenged and slaughtered his cancer dragon; insistently tackled the trials of my paranoid, dementia-burdened mother, while at the same time meeting and daring to face certain historical family sorrows of his. We'd individually, and together, tried to repair our damaged pasts. All in all, the years have been filled with both grace and contest. And through everything, our love has continued to grow.

Then something unthinkable happened. I caused a wound so profound there seemed no recovery from it. My husband was rightly furious and hurt.

And too, the wound I'd leveled came out of unspoken sorrow of my own; it was a feeling of being unmet in certain ways—of being unconsidered. I had tried hitting what I decided to be the problem head-on, but was unsuccessful. My response at that point to his perceived infraction was in pattern, of course, which means I did some version of what I've always done when deeply pierced. That's what we all do—go back to what we know, whether it's silence or rage or something else.

Let me repeat: When we're hurt or hugely disappointed, we go back to what we know, behaving the way we always have. Awareness helps, but does not heal. We must take new action to sustain and perpetuate long-term change. However, in the process of practicing fresh attitudes and new actions, we can, from time to time, get side-swiped by old, deeply held wounds. These events and experiences, I believe, are meant to encourage further awakening, to remind us of our amazing humanity, and to keep us in contact with life-affirming vulnerability.

To tell you the details will help nothing, because, as usual, details are only symptoms. They announce but don't define. Remember how right from the start I've insisted how we are not to be described by our stories? When it's all about the he-said, she-said, they-did, or when we get tangled in the minutia, real change becomes impossible. Because fixing the scratches on the table top will never repair the broken, wobbly legs holding the table up. Instead, we must set our sights on working with the deep breaks and cracks—for as long as they're ignored, we risk deadly peril. We must not get caught up in the symptoms. Like the alcoholic who thinks if he stops drinking, he's solved the problem. He hasn't. Then we wonder why nothing significant changes in our lives, or why we're still in such daily pain.

In any event, the important part about my tale is that even as I'm writing this book about love matters, I found my own partnership in trouble. For days and weeks, I wasn't sure we'd make it.

I tell you all this by way of exemplifying a potential process for you and also to let you know that as great as my marriage is, it's far from perfect and still very much a work in progress. That being said, it grows me constantly and wonderfully. That fits into my version of a healthy relationship.

With my husband I tried everything. I used all the tools: communicated my hurt, while also recognizing his; fought fire with fire; walked away; expressed empathy; acknowledged his point-of-view; set boundaries; apologized.

You name it, I did it. Nothing helped. We started imagining who would take which animals and where we'd each live. Then something happened. I realized there was one thing I'd not done. Not really. Not entirely.

I'd not surrendered. No. I'd not surrendered.

I was still trying to get *my* point across. Trying to get him to see his part, instead of profoundly dealing with the aspect *inside me* I'd also wounded—the sad, humiliated, little unloved creature I'd forgotten. The one I'd gotten too busy to include in my growing up.

So, I began to work with myself. I meditated and prayed.

I used all my resources. I embraced the young inside hurt crying out constantly in the dark—the innocent one waiting for so long to be remembered. The one only *I* can hold and heal and help. Into my arms the distressed creature flew, clinging on for dear life.

And in the end, when I'd truly seen the depth of my own desperation, and had been confronted by the real ancient source of my agonizing, I began to interact with my husband from a new place.

That place, I'd call: Surrendered to love.

Maybe from the outside, everything looked the same.

But inside, at least for a glimpse, all felt altered.

I didn't try to get absolution. I didn't try to fix anything. I stopped pointing out the error of his ways. I stopped focusing on the table-top scratches. Instead, I simply kept working inside myself with the lonely, grief-stricken, abandoned one.

Then something unpredictable occurred.

My husband softened. He began to talk of finding our way back to each other. As we looked at all the grand and even tumultuous years, our vision cleared.

As of today, and as of this moment, we've decided to hold on—to hold onto love. We simply have too much of a solid, long-term, amazing soul connection to let go. And truth be told, from my perspective our relationship today is the strongest it's ever been. We walked through the fire and emerged triumphant. Astonishing.

I can't tell you this is easy, nor can I assure you that the work is over for us. In fact, I'd say we're entering a new stage in our relationship journey together. How will it all turn out? I can't say because we never know, and that's not the point.

But no matter what, I sincerely believe we're worth it. I'm worth it. Love is worth it. This lifelong journey of learning to surrender to love is what I'm here to study and to teach.

I continue to entreat you to follow suit. Know love as more than a train stop or fantasy or sloppy gotta-have-it effort. Understand and appreciate its profundity. The bliss it offers. The grace it invites. The sincerity it demands.

When all the creatures of the earth have fled and all the flowers are wilted to dust and all the memories burnt on the pyre, love is what remains. Before anything and after everything, there is love.

May you find it now.

Our Love Matters

Ancient hills, recent gullies and stark plains
Tender streams and blustery tides,
All sound our names
Calling us
Toward a dense gathering
Where many wait
In honest celebration.

Only we have become afraid,
Our backs nudged up against the corner,
Seeking nothing
Even from the frozen trees
Directly outside the garret window,
Where we hide.

Again our name is called.
And again.

Still in our corner, resisting,
We imagine something better.
There must be an easier way
To ease this heart
Of ache and pitch and storm.

But the brave warrior
Knows well the arduous path of true surrender.

DR. NICKI J. MONTI

The brave warrior
Knows well
Surrender.

Determination arrives
Carried on the bent backs
Of those who've gone before.
Bow down
We must.

Still, we hope for kind mercy.
At times it comes.
At times it does not.

We stand beside ourselves.
We consider returning to our garret.

Finally, placing our fate in Love's hands
We become willing to suffer Love's indignities.
We become willing to suffer.
We become willing.
We become.

How is it so?

Because…
At last,
Astonishingly,
Passionately,
We know it to be
Love most able to paint our lives
In stunning colors of glad and gold.
We know love, more than anything,
Can release us
From the shackles of our own history.
We know love offers us the truest glimpse
Of Sacred Eternal light.

And for these promises

Our Love Matters

We will suffer anything.

And for these promises
We will balance with the angels
On the head of a pin.

We know now
Without doubt,
Above all, below all, beside all
Love matters most.

Today, then,
We willingly lay our open Hearts
Upon the altar table
And with palms turned upward
We join the celebration.

Newsflash: If you want a different life, you need to do things differently.

When we began, I said: **Relationship is an Art that requires Action.** Yes, love is a verb—an action you must take. I said it and I mean it.

You need spend no more time pining for love, because love is at your fingertips. Look in the mirror. See? Quality love is just a glance away. Sound pat? It is. And it isn't. Real, true, lasting love begins in and with you. Start inside and work your way out.

I wish for you a life of willing discovery—where the stark sun, the glimmering moon, the pounding rain, and the struggling children all live in your heart with equal measure. I wish for you the gifts, both great and small, of love. I wish for you an awakened heart that you may see yourself and the world around you as a precious gift to be celebrated.

It's time for you to face the fact that change starts with you. You can read a book and take some things away from it; however, it has been my intention to change not your mind but rather your living process—change the way you live your life. To do that you need to participate in the activities offered in the *Love*

Works section, which follows this chapter. It has handy touchstone lists of all the go-to material offered throughout.[13]

You're trying to make a change. You now have the tools and the desire.

Now, go out there and do it.

---

[13] On my website at http://www.stucknomore.com/love_matters_book/, you will find print outs of the e-book pages of the activities. All you need to do is enter the website you purchased your e-book from to be able to download the materials to work with.

LOVE WORKS:

Exercises and Activities to expand, explore, and apply what you've learned

ALL ALONG, I'VE BEEN INSISTING that to truly, fundamentally, lastingly change your relationship to love matters, you're going to need a sincere effort. The good news is there are definite steps to take. Those steps and procedures can be found described below.

Though I've listed them in a particular order it's not important that you do them that way but rather that you begin with the ones that attracts you most.

Treat each like a new potential lover. Dance closely. Let yourself lean in. Feel their arms swaying you across the floor of your life.

Spend a good amount of quality time and effort with each one before moving on to dance with another. Speeding through won't be useful. Savor each. Let each surprise you

It's *very important* that you allow yourself to discover ways of approaching the specific assignments outside of what's written on these pages. Treat the exercises as a gift rather than an obligation drudgingly accepted. And believe in the potential efficacy of all you pursue. As with everything, attitude will make a difference as to outcome success.

In each exercise I will describe the *why* and the *how*. Your job, then, will be implementation. Enjoy.

EXERCISE #1: LOVING SELF-TALK

Throughout this book, we've been talking about self-love as the cornerstone and essential foundation of every aspect of our love matters. The positive internal conversation that can reflect this self-love, then, is vital and means to carry you through the challenging times, amplify the grand moments, and expand your capacity in all areas. In other words, it will serve you well in every encountered circumstance for, indeed, the way we feel about ourselves not only impacts how others respond to us, it also affects how we treat those we meet and greet.

That means, naturally, we best start there.

Understand that taping over all long-established self-denigrating, self-defeating, self-sabotaging, love-undermining ways of thinking, feeling, and behaving will take concerted effort and fervent intention. Still, like anything else, self-love is a muscle that can be built up over time, so starting *now* is clearly better than not starting at all.

The *initial purpose* of this exercise is to begin establishing a positive, self-esteem enhancing, self-supportive internal go-to dialogue. The *eventual purpose* is to be able to **know your true worth by valuing the essential you.**

Don't worry about veering into arrogance or self-centeredness as your lifelong practice of doubt will always drag you back to center.

What we're working with here is your *attitude* toward self, while at the same time you can and do at this point realize some of your behavior to be unacceptable. Yes, you can acknowledge what's great about you and simultaneously notice how some of your behavior doesn't report that greatness. Working specifically with that unfortunate behavior is something we'll do as we move along.

The point is, we need to begin with self-appreciation for if we don't know how terrifically worthwhile we are, it becomes super-duper difficult to acknowledge and accept the not-so-ego-enhancing parts. Being mean to yourself is part of that unacceptable behavior—usually, being mean to others trails not far behind.

At first, you may have difficulty knowing what to say or may feel so awkward you defend against the positive self-talk process with humor—or some other form of change rejection. Plow through. Do the exercise. The more you practice, the easier it will get.

Appreciate that this process may at first feel kind of silly. Of course, it never feels silly to talk to yourself in mean ways!

Funny, huh? Let's turn the tables.

All right, so even when you feel odd—or worry if anyone finds out what you're doing they'll make fun or think you're nuts—do it anyway. Let's begin.

How To:

Get comfortable. Find a spot at home that's both quiet and safe. Make sure you can remain undisturbed.

One of the easiest entry points into loving self-talk is to imagine a younger version of you. Often, it's helpful to use a childhood picture to start with. One taken of you around seven years old or younger is often preferable as ordinarily, know it or not, by then we've started diligently working on our powerful negative self-view.

You might choose to actually gaze at the photo, or instead vividly establish the picture in your mind's eye.

Now begin talking to that younger you with what's called *unconditional love* and acceptance. That means speaking to yourself in soothing, supportive language, the way as you might talk to a frightened or sad or simply sweet child. Perhaps you'll be saying things like: *I want you to know I believe in you. You are entirely lovable just as you are. There's nothing you can do to make me abandon you. You are beautiful. All your feelings are okay with me. You can always trust me. You don't need to look or act a particular way for me to love you.*

The point is to talk to yourself the way you wish you'd been spoken to growing up. What we're aiming for here is a *real* sense of safety, security, and love.

Even when you feel odd or idiotic or uncomfortable, stay the course. Even when grief or fury or any other feelings begin to surface keep at it.

At best, you'll be attempting this self-talk process no less than 60 seconds a day. Eventually, two minutes is even more effective. Set a kitchen timer or set the timer on your watch.

Once you feel in the flow of this process, commit to every day for 30 days. Notice what happens.

Imagine how differently you might feel about yourself and about love today if you'd been told such unconditionally loving things for two minutes a day from ages 1-18!

Perhaps you'll be moved to write about the surging feelings coming out of this procedure.

Each day and evening, especially when you feel particularly challenged to appreciate who and how you are, refer back to the inner supportive dialogue. Keep practicing.

Eventually, you'll notice your own loving words jump into view spontaneously. You'll hear them in the middle of your board meeting; or when someone's berating you; or while sitting quietly in the garden. That's when you'll know *real* self-love has begun to grow roots. A fabulous new career, amazing friendship or stunning partnership cannot be far behind.

Exercise #2: The Autobiography Exercise

When it comes to writing, I'm a big, big fan. Writing sorts things out and brings forward certain awareness just thinking in our endless-loop kind of way does not. An autobiography in particular means to reveal points and patterns seldom appearing when we're just spinning our brain circles. Best of all, putting things on paper allows nearly immediate realizations.

Do I hear a heavy sigh with regards to this assignment?

Well, I rarely suggest autobiographical writing where it's not greeted with wrinkled-nose doubt and even loathing. Thing is it's really, truly helpful. And the good news is you don't need to write every single detail to unearth potent discoveries. Anything you scribe will yield terrific information. Now, if you're the kind of person who does better starting with bullet points, so be it—but then go back and write unfettered prose for every point mentioned.

Prose, please.

The idea is to begin surveying the landscape of your history. To truly understand the historical picture, you need to *see* it. Most often, when we write the story down new understandings and realizations instantly pop through. It's a bit like those old figure/ground perception photos where different impressions show up depending how you look at it.

Is this two people or a vase?

How To:

When writing an autobiography, start anywhere you want, but start! It doesn't matter how often you've told the pivotal stories out loud—writing them down will shed new light. Let yourself freely roam the landscape of your history with as little thinking as possible.

Just allow the words to flow.

Take your time. You'll most likely want to do this writing in numerous increments. You might, each time you write, choose to cover certain periods of your life. That's fine. Or, alternatively, you might want to simply allow whatever arrives upon the page to surprise you. Either way, I suggest you carve out a minimal time for exploration with each writing adventure—a half hour, for instance—and then if you're on a roll just keep going until you feel entirely played out at that juncture.

Additionally, it doesn't matter if you go in linear order of life events and experiences or jump around. Let yourself be guided through the process by instinct. Trust yourself to know what's best in your particular case.

You'll want to explore, in detail, how your primary caretakers interacted both with you and with each other. Being specific as to their style, manner, and method will go far in helping you realize when and how *their* voices and messages first started ringing in your head. Over time those voices have morphed to seem like your voice. But mostly they're not yours and in the end, the idea will be to take what you like and leave the rest instead of continuing to operate on automatic by simply *assuming* all pre-established notions, attitudes, and apparent solutions still need adherence. Perhaps you notice certain thinking, and feeling responses to early environmental experiences arise as you're writing. Once the scribing is completed, you'll want to check out these feeling states more thoroughly. Be rigorous in your attempt to discover early experiential inspirations for current feelings, behaviors, and attitudes. Pulling your punches won't lead you to the crux of your matter.

Very often, this process allows our three or four lifelong themes to dance clearly forward. Pull out those themes so you can later track the way they continue to be revealed in your life.

EXERCISE #3: MIRROR, MIRROR ON THE WALL

The purpose of this exercise, first touched upon in Chapter One, is to explore the phenomenon called Projection. Our two-pronged aims throughout *Our Love Matters* has been: a) to lead us to our True Selves; and b) to learn to alter the undermining behavior preventing that discovery. Why? Because it's those two appreciations that allow the extraordinary life we want to be revealed.

As a reminder: We tend to loathe or love characteristics perceived in others as if those traits have nothing whatsoever to do with us—while in fact they have *everything* to do with us, for what we see in other people is a direct reflection of a corresponding attribute living inside us.

Of course, many times the last thing we want to imagine is our association with some irritating or loathsome characteristic noted in a friend, co-worker, boss, dry-cleaner, or partner.

Well, the truth is *everything* lives inside each of us, more or less. This understanding, if you recall, is great news. It allows us to profoundly understand and appreciate how the world works. Also, it walks us toward compassion which beautifully reinforces our own humanity.

It's important during this investigation to include things you admire about others that seem, at this point, unobtainable to you. That's projection also. I'm not talking about acquiring "stuff," but rather about, say, their charisma, likability, ease of communication, and such.

Now, the loathed or admired characteristics don't always take the same form for us and in us, as they do with people who irk or shine in our estimation. For instance, maybe your mother is aggressively controlling and always telling everyone around her what to do. That's annoying and you have carefully avoided being that way, right? But now you need to go deeper. What *are* the ways you exhibit control in your life? Do you maneuver to get things to go your way? Do you control your own desires, squeezing the very life out of them? Do you control your friends with your constant lateness?

Get it?

Or in another way, do you know someone who seems to attract everyone with their indefinable "glow," while meantime you think of yourself as shy and lacking in charisma? What if I told you that so-called charisma lives richly inside you as well!

Nuts, right?

Well, for now just record what specifically attracts you about that other individual and see if you can find some glimmer of their qualities inside yourself.

What I'm saying here is that discovering your personal relationship to the dreaded or desirable characteristics often requires creativity and thinking outside the box. So, perhaps our partner's anger is obvious and volatile making it at first easy to refuse identifying with it, but look deeper. Like maybe you have just as much anger, but express it more covertly—as in making snide remarks, being late all the time, through snarling gossip, or some other subtle method. Or perhaps you just *think* awful, vicious things about people and situations—roaming the mental land like a saber-toothed tiger looking for mental prey.

And that's another important point. The disdained characteristics may show up in actual doing or might live primarily in your thinking. Everything counts when it comes to understanding ourselves.

How To:

Make a list of the people who've most impacted your life: family members, lovers, intimate friends, bosses, etc. Beside each, list their qualities—everything that describes their attitudes, behaviors, and ways of interacting.

Now, go back over the list and in some way mark the qualities that most annoy you as well as the ones that most impress.

When somewhere down the line you're feeling particularly brave, take the qualities one by one and start investigating how that characteristic exists inside you. Be thorough. Check out your thinking, feeling and behavior. Remember: the way your boss criticizes is not going to be exactly the way you do it. In this case, for instance, it's easiest to start with how you treat *yourself* critically and then move onto how you treat others in a critical fashion—whether out loud or secretly in your own judgmental brain.

Clearly covering all the characteristics is going to take a while. No rush. Also, though, you're likely to quickly notice similar annoying or desirable traits weaving amongst the various people listed. Really, in the long run, there will probably be a short list in each category to be working with.

Obviously, telling the truth about these things takes some digging. And it takes courage. The more thorough you are here, however, the faster you'll gain an entirely new perspective on your life. Realizing our problems, irritations, and promises are clearly within reach is incredibly powerful––allowing us a very real sense of authority. The idea is to operate through clarity. Once you truly realize what you've been so far doing, plus how your thinking and feeling is generating that doing, you can figure out how to change course, steering, then, toward a more bountiful life.

EXERCISE #4: THE PRACTICING PRESENCE EXERCISE

This exercise from Chapter Two is, in many ways, *essential* for the truly stellar loving life you crave. After all, if we remain disconnected from the moment, from Self, from others, from life, how are we really to terrifically impact our love matters?

Hopefully you began these practices when first encountering them in this book. If so this will be a reminder of why and how. If not, enjoy now this wonderful new adventure called presence.

The exercises presented here address public as well as private presence. Both serve as an important foundation for every successful experience we have. We'll start with the first one, which involves developing tremendous listening-to-others abilities.

Public Presence
How to:

The Practice: **Responsive Listening**.

Responsive listening involves four primary areas: 1) how we think; 2) how we witness; 3) how we respond; 4) and how we further the speaker's story. This wants to be applied with friends, co-workers, acquaintances, partners, store personnel, etc. In other words, perform this exercise everywhere you go.

1) **Thinking:** When with others *repeat* exactly what speakers are saying. Start this process by doing it inside your own head. Articulate the words precisely. Don't interpret, edit, or get creative. Right away, you'll notice that to truly do this you need pay careful attention. That's why others immediately recognize, whether they say so or not, that they're being heard.

2) **Witnessing:** During responsive listening you'll be communicating through *reflection*, meaning your face will naturally exhibit receptivity. This doesn't ask you to "make faces" or be inauthentic to show how you feel or

that you're hearing well. It's organic and as such, like pesticide-free fruit, such listening nourishes.

3) **Responding:** Responsive listening invariably includes *echoing*. Like reflection, echoing does not rush to "show" the speaker anything, but simply offers a natural auditory response as in an "ah," "I see," or "uh huh." No heavy lifting required.

   Summary: Responsive listening includes *repetition, reflection,* and *echoing.*

Now let's move on to Active Listening, which involves moving the speaker's story forward through inquiry. Asking questions reveals our involvement with the speaker. It furthers connection and turns a monologue into a collaborative venture.

4) **Active Listening:** Active listening includes curiosity. In Active Listening, the key again is repeating and echoing out loud what's heard, and then incorporating the speaker's precise words into a responsive inquiry. For example they say: "I was on the phone with my mother and as usual she was criticizing everything…" And you say: "Ugh. I know your mother's criticizing makes you crazy! What did you do?" Thus, active listening involves repetition, curiosity, and story advancing.

   Summary: Quality listening includes *repetition, reflection, echoing,* and *active investigation.*

Private Presence
How to:

The Practice:
You're in your car. Try thinking *specifically* about what's going on at that very moment: "I feel my hands griping the steering wheel. I see the yellow car in front of me. I hear the radio music." This routine is called **Grounding,** which means remembering that we have bodies and, at best, are aware of being inside those bodies. Through grounding we learn to keep our feet on the earth by

attending to what precisely we're seeing or experiencing from second to second. This is a terrific anecdote for dissociation, obsession, ADHD and anxiety, among other things.

You're at home. Again the idea is to be specific in your attention to what's happening in the immediate. Practicing presence can be as simple as allowing yourself to focus completely on the movement of broom against floor as you sweep; or on the petting of the beloved animal lying upon your lap. Again, you can say to yourself: "*Ah, I see the broom gliding along the floor. I feel the floor under the broom. I feel the soft fur of Puddles under my fingers. I hear her purr.*" Or you can simply, to the best of your ability, "watch" what you're doing with a relatively empty mind. Perhaps concentrate on *listening to/hearing* the broom's swoosh.

You're in a business meeting or a lecture. This might seem like we're veering into public presence practice but I want to emphasize how often we use brain 'isolation' , even with others, to take us out of presence. So the next time you're with others and find yourself drifting off try taking notes or, again, repeating in your head all that's being said. When private thoughts tempt to take you away from the situation at hand, notice and, as quickly as possible, bring yourself back.

Learning to sit quietly: All right then, it is time to learn the joy of stillness, both physical and mental. Sure, stillness positions us for extraordinary discovery and that's what I'd love you to aim for; however, that's not even the first fabulous result. What happens immediately through stillness is a nearly indefinable peacefulness that has the potential of removing the angst, frantic concerns, sense of impending disaster, need to control, or any of the other preoccupations that ordinarily plague you.

I realize that the whole idea of true stillness, especially as it regards mental cessation, might seem right now like a remote possibility. I promise it's closer than you think. But as with everything, effort is required. And in the case of stillness, this effort will need to happen more than once or twice. Eventually, though, you'll be hugely surprised by what you can do.

We begin by turning everything off: no phones, no computer, no radio, and no television. Oh, and by the way, if total silence feels like a completely awful idea, you can start this process with a background of patient, easy, wordless music. There are countless "meditation" albums from which to choose.

Now, settle into a private, quiet spot—either in-home or somewhere that delights. Get completely comfortable. Lean back. Close your eyes.

Try imagining yourself approaching a beautiful, deep, calm body of water—perhaps an ocean into which you are choosing to dive or even a small pool into which you can dangle your feet.

Begin breathing in your nose and out your mouth.

Let all concern or anxiety or fear leave you.

Breathe.

Nothing terrible can happen in this experience.

Breathe.

Know that you are entirely safe in this moment.

Breathe.

Begin slowly concentrating on bringing your breath down into the center of your body. There's a point on the sternum between the breasts called the Heart Center. You'll notice this isn't exactly where the actual heart is. For those who know something about energy points, this is called the fourth chakra.

Place your right hand on that energy point, and your left on top of the right with thumbs touching. Be comfortable. Don't hold your elbows up in the air like wings, but rather let them sit comfortably. Be sure you're resting at the Heart Center rather than the solar plexus right below.

Imagine a slippery waterslide inside, extending from the tiny point between your eyebrows where you've probably noticed Hindus sometimes place a red dot (the sixth chakra sometimes called the Third Eye and often considered part of Intuition), down the throat area (the fifth chakra usually representing communication), and then down into that fourth chakra heart area. Choose a simple word to let gently roll down the slide: a word perhaps like "serenity," or, as earlier suggested, how about "Love."

Just breathe this way for a long time.

No hurry.

No plan.

Simple.

If words or thoughts come in, let them move on through like clouds—so you're not attaching to the word thoughts or developing them. If you think, for instance, "I'm hungry" that's fine, but don't develop a lunch menu in your mind. Just notice the idea and go back to focusing on your breath.

You're now mediating. The more you repeat this process, the easier it gets and the deeper you're likely to dive.

EXERCISE # 5: THE TRUE INTENTIONS EXERCISE

In this exercise, you'll be able to apply what you learned in part three of Chapter One, when looking at Wheel #3, where the intention was to figure out why you've *chosen* relationship sabotage. At that point we talked about the fact that our true intentions are absolutely revealed in the lives before us. It's vital to appreciate this notion, even if it makes you squirm or there's still some skepticism about it. Do, then, what's called "acting as if" by just for now endeavoring to fully embrace what at this point might still seem like an odd idea. There's an incredible amount to learn by doing this, and you can always reclaim your old ways of thinking and proceeding at any point.

How to:

Choose a challenging question and sit with it. You know now about stillness, so start there. In this case though, you're letting the question be what moves down that water slide.

Here are a few examples:

- *Why do I always date mean people? Even when they don't start out that way, they seem to turn into that! Why does that happen?*

—   *How come everyone else seems to find love, but I don't?
Everyone I meet seems unavailable or turns out to be.*
—   *Why isn't my career on track?*
—   *Why can't I manage to have the body I want?*

As you can see, you can go in any direction. Sometimes it's easier to start with something not quite so confronting. Still, do whatever you can to be rigorous—both in your efforts and in your willingness to face whatever truths come forward.

Take one question at a time in any given "session" of attending this exercise. Again, there's no rush.

Write down the ideas, images and feelings that arise. If you hear yourself veering into blaming or victimizing, recognize it, take a second to comfort yourself, and start again.

Now, dive beneath the first few answers you come up with. Such first-glance responses are superficial no matter how plausible they sound.

You'll know you've hit pay dirt when you get a chill or the hair stands up on the back of your neck or you feel an "ah-ha" surging through you.

Once you hit "the" answer, you've entered a new stage. Now, the idea is to sit with that response. Feel into it. See where in your body the answer might live. Is it in your stomach or genitals or throat? Wonder why.

If you feel particularly adventuresome, you might decide to throw paint on canvas or collage to describe the feelings underneath the answer. Or maybe you'll dance them. The more we can take understanding out of the brain and appreciate them as living "creatures", the more we come to understand how they've been impelling and compelling our lives.

So, with all this investigation have you arrived back at the start? Has your family of origin popped onto the scene as part of the equation? That's usually the case. Indeed, those three or four lifelong themes resurface again and again. That's okay. There are terrific solutions for the behaviors, thinking, and feelings that come out of those themes.

Exercise # 6: The Template Exercise

The template exercise mainly formats an easy-to-read list of what you've thus far discovered, uncovered, and revealed. I've included here one already recognized "story" as a reminder, and added one additional example. I'll take the first and break it down step-by-step, but finding the most germane ideas to explore will be up to you. Please note, however, that this process is far from easy, so do the best you can to hold your frustration at bay. Diligence here will serve you well.

How to:

The Idea: This is the belief we've been generally holding and quite often sharing with anyone who'll listen. Well, of course, some stay silent about their viewpoint because they're so embarrassed to be seeing things that way in the first place—or more exactly, embarrassed because they absolutely believe it's a truth about them they're hoping others aren't onto. For instance: *I don't have a relationship because I'm fat;* or, *I'm too stupid to succeed;* or *Everyone knows I'm damaged goods.*

Payoff: This is where it's imperative to tell yourself the truth. Hopefully, you've discovered this truth in the previous True Intentions exercise. If not, go back and try again. The easiest way to figure out the payoff is to simply write down the facts of your life. If you hate your body and think that your body is keeping you out of relationship, and you're aware of how to get a better body but simply don't do it, then its best to accept some part of you isn't ready to have a better body. Remember: we're not talking about *all* parts of you being on board for the sabotaging procedure. Some inside aspects do want change. But the aspects running the show up until now don't. We know that because the facts support the hypothesis. So the payoff of being out of shape is: *I don't have to seek relationship.*

Truth: The question quickly becomes: Why? Underneath all the symptoms of our disrepair—beneath ideas of what we should have versus what we do have—lives a series of feeling-drivers. In this case, for instance, the answer might be: *I don't have a relationship because I'm terrified.*

Origin: That's very fine and good, but why might that be the case? Inevitably, at this point, we're going to be looking at beginnings and where all our lessons, ideas, and concerns got started. That means, of course, the family. Maybe what you right away get to is something you easily discovered in the autobiographical writing: *Mom & dad had a terrible relationship.*

Underlying Dynamic: Okay, so you know where the lousy thinking and feeling started, but what's that have to do with anything? Well, now it's time to truly take the plunge and figure out what profoundly held idea supports the self-defeating behavior you've been exhibiting. This means looking yourself in the eye and realizing the sometimes secret, always humiliating image, you carry. *Being fat confirms and maintains my long-held belief that no one will ever want me.*

Current Behavior: Now that you've dug into the nitty-gritty, it's easy to see how you're manifesting and confirming these awful impressions of self-value. Looking at your behavior in this regard is very important, because changing that behavior is pivotal to acquiring and maintaining the new life you want and deserve. Let me press this point: We need both behavioral shift *and* a fundamental attitude and belief system adjustment for real, sustained, sustainable change to occur. Here's one tiny thing in this example that might behaviorally be happening: *I assume no one is or can be interested.* When it comes to the behavior part of the disrepair program, stay aware that we're most likely to go at self-sabotage from several angles simultaneously.

All right, let me use love language as a further sample:

- ✓ **The Idea:** *There's no one out there for me.*
- ✓ **Payoff:** *I don't really have to risk my heart.*
- ✓ **Truth:** *I'm afraid it's inevitable that I'll get my heart broken.*
- ✓ **Origin:** *My dad left when I was four and I never saw him again.*
- ✓ **Underlying Dynamic:** *I believe if I were more lovable he'd never have left.*
- ✓ **Current Behavior:** *I push anyone away who is really interested in me and only go after the unavailable ones.*

Now, make a list of the most apparently daunting ideas you carry. These will be obvious because you hear them in your head, or coming out of your mouth, every day. Pick several categories or start with the one that seems most pressing. Then apply the above-described process. Again, only handle one topic each time you engage the process. Too much too soon will threaten to shut you down permanently.

EXERCISE #7: THE FOUR A'S: CONNECT-THE-DOTS EXERCISE

Continuing the work begun earlier in part three of Chapter One, we arrive at Connect-The-Dots. This process has resonance back to that old drawing exercise, where by connecting the dots we create a picture. That's exactly what we'll do here.

The specific purpose of this exercise is to track how the need for accolade, appreciation, attention, and approval weave through our lives—how they affect our decisions, reactivity, and behavior; and most of all, where it all started. However, the Connect-the-Dots process is a dandy way to chart other questions coming forward for you as well. Basically, you're again being asked to do the brave, quite interesting work of tracing the roots of who and how you are today.

Your discovery of how this has all worked for you began when you wrote your autobiography. Now, a quick graph is recommended. Working here with the Four A's will give you a solid outline of how it works.

How to:

Pick one of the Four A's:

- ✓ **Accolade**
- ✓ **Appreciation**
- ✓ **Attention**
- ✓ **Approval**

Chart where and how it all started. Start with current behavior. Just notate the facts and behaviors in service to those facts, plus the feelings, if possible, that arise out of those behaviors. Here's an example of what that might sound like:

Now: *Fact:* I need to be constantly helping everyone. *Behavior:* I'm always on the go. *Feeling:* I always feel better when I'm being useful.

Then: *Fact:* My dad was always drunk and my mother depressed. *Behavior:* I helped him when she wouldn't, but also made sure she was all right. *Feeling:* Sometimes it made me feel important, sometimes I got mad, and sometimes everything just felt unfair.

Conclusions: Right from the gate, I knew I was the only one who could keep the family together. Today, I believe it's up to me to keep everything afloat. I don't believe I can depend on others. I expect to be disappointed. I place my value in what I can do. If I stop being helpful, no one will want to be around me.

Follow this procedure recognizing as many areas as possible of your thinking, feeling and behaving. Investigate all the four A's to see which shoes fit best.

Every new realization intends to be in service to your overall understanding of self. Clarity begins to allow you to make new choices, so your future need not imitate your past.

EXERCISE #8: THE 100% EXERCISE

The purpose of this exercise, first discussed in Chapter One, is to encourage an exploration of your true willingness and readiness to commit. Often, we imagine eagerness because we *say* we're ready for love, success, a great body, sobriety, a healed relationship, or whatever, but our lives tell a different story. The 100% exercise is designed to let you stop talking about what you're doing and feel what it's really like to stand unreservedly on both sides of the commitment fence.

In this procedure you're asked to take chunks of time to *completely commit* inside yourself to living a life that's all in or living a life that's all out.

Naturally, no matter what, as we move along in our lives we're likely to have periods or moments of vacillation. Particularly challenging times can do this. Frustration can do this. Exhaustion can do this. But if you're an individual tending to fence sit over and again, you know what I'm talking about. That sabotaging position needs to be confronted if you're ever to have the life you say you want.

The idea here is: whatever the focus of your consternation, spend periods when you're completely uncommitted and periods where you're completely committed. This looks and sounds like: *I absolutely adore this job*, then: *this job will never satisfy me*. Or: *The things that don't work in my relationship are far less significant than what works, so no matter what, <u>I'm in</u>!* Or: *this relationship is entirely draining and gives me less than it takes from me, so <u>I'm out</u>.*

This in/out position is done interiorly. You don't announce or proclaim it. You simply entertain it inside yourself. But the most important part involves checking out your feelings either way. To do that accurately you've got to really sit still in one position or another *for periods of time*. Guaranteed you'll never figure out which way to go by constantly jumping back and forth.

How to:

Try briefly, truly exploring the two possibilities, both at work and at play. First, spend a day or two, or even better a week, holding both all-in and the all-out positions alternately: 100% out for two hours; 100% in for two hours. Be specific with your intention and time yourself. No matter how you'd like to change gears, don't. Stick to your commitment or non-commitment guns through thinking and through behavior.

Notice what happens. Write about it. How long were you able to tolerate and sustain each position? What did you feel and think?

Delve even further into those thoughts and feelings. Where did all this waffling start? What do you imagine would happen if you made an absolute commitment?

Now, how about upping the ante? For the next week, increase the time on both sides of the equation to half a day each. If you can, go even further by being all in for an entire day, then all out for an entire day. After each experience write about what you feel, think, and know.

You can attempt this exercise with whatever troubles you most. The way you feel and behave about your relationship, your job, your food intake, or anything else. Once you've looked at both sides, proceed to do what you think best. Should you stay or should you go? Is this the job for you or is it not? Is this the partnership for you or not? The friendship for you or not? The way to eat or not? Is drinking a good plan or not?

The 100% exercise is also an excellent tool to discover how committed you are in an overall way to the life you're living and to the living of your life. Of course this is enormously challenging as you'll constantly want to veer to the other side, but do everything you can to remain firm one way or other.

What do you realize?

Exercise #9: The Four Gateways Exercise

The purpose of this exercise is to further open your eyes. We've already well discussed in former exercises the last three gateways mentioned in the body of *Our Love Matters*. Now we'll delve more deeply into the first gateway: Awareness.

Just to remind you, gateways 2-4 are:

✓ **Historical triggers:** This gateway involves understanding clearly how, when, and with whom the past leaps forward to manage our lives. Through your autobiographical writings you've begun to acknowledge this.
✓ **Confronting Stuckness:** This gateway involves our old stories told and retold, plus the long-standing defenses reporting those old stories and ideas. Again, the

autobiography starts us on the road to understanding while working the Template clarifies.

✓ **Practicing the Art of Self Love:** Walking through this gateway began our exercise program, as we adventured into positive self-talk. In addition, attempting estimable acts as we move through the world is also an elegant way to boost self-esteem.

Awareness

How to:

Awareness: Write about your self-denigrating thoughts. A simple list will suffice as a vivid report. Buy a small notebook and *write down these thoughts every day* as they arise. Or record them in your phone. Transfer them to your computer. Be sure to date everything. Eventually, you'll be able to recognize themes.

Once we know our themes we can easily see how they appear everywhere in our lives—at work, play and in love. If, for instance, one of our themes is: *No one ever listens to me,* we'll easily be able to notice how that concern and complaint weaves into all our activities. Then, as by now you might expect, the work is to trace the origins of that theme.

The great news is we absolutely can change our relationship to such ideas and eventually have a life not run by damage.

EXERCISE #10: BODY MIND CONNECTION EXERCISE

The purpose of this simple exercise is to get you in touch with that all-important vehicle called the body. The body is often talked about as a miracle but frequently ignored or taken for granted. Being in touch with our body allows us to fully engage life in heretofore unmet ways. You might be surprised to find out what happens. Try it.

Here you'll be able to apply what you've so far learned about presence.

How to:

Begin by engaging the Private Presence exercise. Once comfortable, proceed to bring your focus to your body. Try to feel the blood flowing through you into all parts. Take your time with this. Ease down your neck and arms and chest. Move into your solar plexus and then downward.

- ✓ Leave no part out.
- ✓ As you do this, feel your body parts come alive.
- ✓ Is there a kind of buzz, a heat, or increased calm?
- ✓ Also notice where the energy flow feels "stuck". Take a moment to breathe into that stuck part.
- ✓ Trust whatever happens.
- ✓ Try this exercise every day for two weeks.

After completing this portion of the exercise, try staying aware of your body as you move through the world. Notice your posture and your feelings as they get reported in your body and your sensations. Even sitting at your desk again, imagine the blood flowing through you. Write about what comes up for you.

Now here's one more part to attempt: Spend a portion of your day—an hour even—listening to your body mind. Let it guide your food intake, for instance, or even your choice of companions. Let it touch another's hand or take a nap or go for a walk. Listen carefully. What's it telling you? Write about it.

When we're fully in touch with what matters to/in our body and to our body matters, we are greeting Life Force. We can see the results of that in how we walk, carry ourselves, touch others, express, allow embrace, enjoy our meals, have sex and a multitude of other ways. The body is our gift. Love it.

EXERCISE # 11: THE CHANGE-IT-UP EXERCISE

This four-part pay-attention procedure maps out the "how-to" of the manifestation of your best, most evolved Self. I'll repeat and review the four Change-It-Up plan ways, but elaborate the "how-to" in each case. The idea is to consciously and conscientiously practice real change by opening your mind and heart, followed by taking new action.

Contain: This exercise is about exhibiting new boundaries around habitual, distracting, self-sabotaging thoughts and actions. *Everyone* can profit from such a practice. Do it.

How to:

When it comes to self-defeating procedures practice saying "no." Of course, you'll need to start with a list of what those current gnarly ways are. Make the list comprehensive. Cover all areas of your life. Adventure into areas of thinking, feeling and doing. Be thorough in intent and attention.

Now the idea is to stop. If you eat sugar every day, stop. If you complain all the time, stop. If you constantly pick up all the checks at restaurants, stop.

Do it for a day, a week, a month. See what happens.

In each case, write about the feelings coming up for you. For more information Connect-the-Dots as in where, when, and how did this behavior begin.

Take Contrary Action. This means do the reverse of what you've been doing.

How to:

Again, start with a list of what you're currently doing, then beside each note what the opposite behavior would be. Now, attack them one at a time, engaging the new behaviors for no less than two days each.

If you've been saying yes to everyone, practice saying "no." If you've been saying no, say yes. If you've been shutting down, speak up. If you've been blabbing constantly, contain. You get the drift.

At the end of each experience, write about what comes forth. New behavior invariably invites new response. Your friends or coworkers or lover might notice. Certainly you will.

Invite Discovery. Turning things upside down in terms of routine behaviors and ways of thinking opens new doors. We get into so many habits. Some are not bad, but all of them can leave us stale. Having new conversations with ourselves, and with the world, is essential to eventually allowing fresh perspectives on everything. I'm not suggesting this shift in behavior be permanent—only that it can be an invigorating dip in a backyard pool during a summer heat wave.

The idea, as always, is to stay awake. Life is immeasurably improved when we do so.

How to:

Write down your wishes and dreams—the ones you had as a kid, and now. Notice what's changed or hasn't. Are you going toward those dreams?

Read a book about something you've never explored before. Draw or dance or collage or photograph or write poetry or throw clay. Express your love, appreciation and/or gratitude to various others no less than twice a day for 30 days. No simple "I love you" or "thank you" please. Those can be catch-all easy ways out! Be specific, as in: "*I love the way you dress,*" "*I love you more each day,*" or "*thanks so much for your constant generosity.*"

Allow recovery. It's not that all this work means to turn you into an entirely new person—not at all. What's wanted, rather, is to uncover and reveal a deeply buried version of "you"—the one you've been hiding from the world thinking it unacceptable, or even hiding from yourself for the very same reason. It's actually easier to like and appreciate this version of the self than you probably believe. Let's start simply.

How to:

Every night, make a gratitude list for all you appreciate about your own day's accomplishments. This list should include:

a. embraced feelings

b. expressed feelings
c. effective containment
d. contrary actions taken
e. presence encountered
f. freedom from reactivity
g. actualized moments

In other words, it should include what you do (*I organized my desk*) and what you don't do (*I didn't surf the net while at work*), along with things you express (*I told my friend how much she means to me*) or don't (*I was tempted to gossip about my boss and what a pain she is but didn't*).

Every new morning read the list from the night before out loud. Listen to your own written words. Notice what comes up for you. Express what you're learning about yourself to valued people in your life. Acknowledge what's great about you.

I want to remind you that this isn't bragging. When we're telling simple truths, we don't feel all puffed up about it but rather as if we're merely authentically acknowledging something. In that way, *I've got hazel eyes* becomes equal to *I'm great at organization* or *I love cooking for people and I'm good at it.*

The intent of such expression is not to garner a particular response but only to practice the kind of sharing that can engender real intimacy. As a side benefit, it teaches others how to share in similar ways.

Alter actions. All the new information plus acquired tools have given you new ways of being, and fresh eyes with which to perceive your life. Now, of course, maintenance is the key. It's important to keep rotating those tires, get that car washed, and change the oil, even when the luster of new wears off.

How to:

Increase your contrary actions list and follow that list.

Review your latest acquired tools, noticing which ones serve best under which circumstances. Try some of the tools you haven't picked up yet.

Celebrate your mind, body, heart, and spirit as often and as thoroughly as possible. Continue to devise new ways of doing this. Dance as though you've never danced before. Read a book you would never have previously considered. Go to a temple you've never before entered. Embrace something you've always rejected.

The idea of such engagements is, again, to wake up, wake up, wake up. Slogging your way through life serves no one, least of all you.

EXERCISE # 12: NINE BETTER LOVE EXERCISES

The purpose of the following nine approaches to relationship touched upon in Chapter Three is to *guarantee you* an extraordinary love life. These exercises can and should go with you everywhere. There is, in fact, no corner of your life that can't be improved by following these suggested attitudes and actions. Let love blossom with you and for you. Change your way of walking through the world and your life is guaranteed to become what you've been hoping it will be.

Before jumping in, however, I'd like to attend the three most constantly posed and seminal relationship questions. With each question you'll notice invitation to change your thinking and feeling and behavioral procedures. Take the hint seriously.

Q #1: How do we know if we've found the right partner?

The answer is—oh yes, I bet by now you know where I'm going—first BE the partner you're seeking.
But of course there's more. Here it is.

Fundamental: When partnership is right, we find ourselves growing and expanding. That means that "right" partners support and applaud our continued evolution. Now, what evolution means is wildly diverse. But *you know* when you're stagnant. Stop thinking nothing can change at work, at play, or at home. That's an idea you've landed on, not a truth. Convenient if you want to give up, but certainly not healthy. Your right partner should believe in and applaud your potential changes also.

Q #2: How can I find satisfaction with the relationship I've already got?

To start with, look at the cheese and not the holes. In relationships, we often get so used to focusing on what's missing, we neglect recalling, realizing, and relishing what's present and the things that work well. Try remembering love and see what happens.

Q #3: Should I stay or should I go?

This is a toughie. Ordinarily, I suggest making a list of burdens and benefits. If the burdens outweigh the benefits, off you go. If the benefits outweigh the burdens, hang in there.

However, there are always complicating factors.

Like how deeply have you looked at your contribution to the burdens list? And why might your psyche have chosen this particular person in the first place? If you leave now without meeting and greeting the interior dynamics originally bringing you into the relationship, you're guaranteed to simply repeat the pattern in the next. Faces change, but essential relationship patterns remain the same.

Now, this doesn't mean you stay in lieu of sincere actualization. Point is: it's best to first discover what you're doing to incite, contribute, inspire, or elicit the behavior you're complaining about *before* jumping ship. Naturally, if you've hit an iceberg and the ship is going down, jump!

Remember that no relationship is going to be perfect; also, no relationship on earth is going to dissolve the angst inside. Nothing can fill the cracks and fissures formed by your past— except diligent self-work.

So, make that burdens and benefits list, but be sure your side of the street is clean before packing your bags. Because guaranteed, your next relationship will turn out the same way unless you shift the drama and trauma living inside.

Besides, clearly something's keeping you there.

Otherwise, you'd already be gone. Try hearing what your inner voices are trying to say. What's the underlying, real nitty-gritty reason you're staying? Toss out the first three or four rationales, as those are likely to be superficial. No, it's not because of the money. Not because of the kids. Not because it's easier. Keep digging.

Find the truth.

That's where the work begins. Focus on *that* piece as it relates to your family-of-origin history, to your defenses, to your fears, and to the stories you've been telling yourself about love. At the end of that work, your decision is likely to be clear.

Oh Wait!!

One more thing. Before moving forward into the Nine Better Love exercises, let's prepare you for love! Answer the following twelve questions. As always, take your time and be thorough, working diligently one-by-one.

Preparing For Love

- ✓ Define love.
- ✓ Describe why you think the relationship you have isn't working the way you want or why you haven't yet found the relationship you desire.
- ✓ At this point you think of the ideal partnership as…?
- ✓ What story have you thus far been telling yourself when it comes to you and love?
- ✓ Describe your relationship to Faith.
- ✓ When and how have you felt wounded by love?
- ✓ Describe your relationship to the idea of abandonment.
- ✓ How, when and where have you felt betrayed? What was your response?
- ✓ Define Heartbreak.
- ✓ Where, when, and with whom are you most courageous?
- ✓ Where, when, and with whom are you least courageous?
- ✓ List all the love relationships in your life that have had impact. Include mother and father. Once the list is complete go back and list under each one the

characteristics of the individuals (the traits that define who they be, not what they do). Also, with love relationships, list the characteristics of the relationships themselves (he was in charge; I took care of everything, etc.) plus how long they lasted and what ended them.

And now, the Nine Better Love Exercises!

#1: The Upward-Turned Palm
How To:

Find a comfortable place to sit. Nearby should be a piece of paper and pen, or some other recording device. Writing or recording as you go along can be effective; however, if preferred, it can be done afterward.

Begin with gentle breathing to get yourself settled and present. Now that you're truly "here", gently turn your palms upward, resting them on your thighs. Look at them. What are your first thoughts? Keep breathing. Let your mind wander. There are no rules of right or wrong. Organization of those thoughts is not essential at this juncture.

Now, what do you feel? If any concern or fear arises, what's the nature of such? Are you comfortable with palms turned upward or not? At this point, it's helpful to wonder what's great about the upward-turned palm. What's worrisome? Write down your discoveries.

Once having identified thoughts, feelings, hesitations, and possibilities, it's time to move into action. One way to go is that as you walk through your day, you let yourself *imagine* those palms turned upward in the manner previously practiced. What happens? Does your opinion of others change? Do your interactions shift?

Notice your feeling responses. Once in a while, you might even (publically) try actually turning your hands upward in this manner, just for the experience. Are there inner or outer reactions when you do this?

Try this practice for 30 days, again, recording as you go—perhaps at the end of your day. See what happens. The feelings, thoughts, and experiences that occur will garner great information, while at the same time taking you into ever clearer, more refreshing waters.

#2: Take Ownership:
How To:

When something happens in your relationship to anyone or under any circumstance, it's important as quickly as can be managed to tell the truth about your contribution to the consternation. The trick is to do it without excuses. Don't say, "I did get mean to get so angry or be rude, but you pushed me so hard!" Their push does not justify your reaction.

Of course, being able to do this starts with understanding where your reactivity's come from. Hopefully, through both the autobiography and Connect-the-Dots, you've accumulated some understanding of these origins.

Still, understanding is always only a beginning and it's important not only to appreciate that you invariably have other response options, but also essential that you choose to take action employing those alternatives.

So the "how-to" is pretty simple, at least in concept: recognize your contribution to whatever has happened and make amends. Immediate is better than later, but any timing version of taking ownership counts.

Do it.

Remember: Taking ownership in no way lets the other person off the hook or validates the squirrely work circumstance or permits your friend to continue bad behavior. But what *they're* doing is their responsibility. You're welcome to set boundaries, of course, but please don't do it at the same time as owning up to your part, as that procedure right away invalidates the amends you've just offered.

#3: Move from Complaint to Compromise
How to:

First, as always, you need to be able to recognize the ways in which, and how often you're currently engaging in complaint. Track yourself. Get a small notebook or use your phone. Keep a record of all complaints. Note the nature of them, the circumstances/context, the style, and even what's going on with you physically. For instance, are you particularly tired or hungry when complaints arise? In other words, you'll want to record:

- ✓ Personal physical context
- ✓ Personal emotional context
- ✓ Circumstantial context, including type of people involved
- ✓ Timing
- ✓ Nature of complaint/content
- ✓ Style of conveying complaint

Pretty quickly, you'll notice themes. This is good. Once themes are identified, it's easy to uncover the source and subsequently to determine the best applicable solution to apply.

#4: Don't Travelogue

Traveloguing is commonly found everywhere but is especially noticeable in primary relationships. It's a trip to nowhere. Nothing ever gets "fixed" by going over and over tired old territory. It's that trying-to-fix-the-problem-at-the-level-of-the-problem business. Reversing traveloguing tendencies requires great driving skills, terrific control of the wheel, and a true willingness to get the job done.

How to:

Here's the hard turn: You're driving down disaster road, going over worn territory. **Stop.** Image an actual stop sign. Now step on the breaks, which means breathe.

Again, breathe.

Once more.

At this point, begin wondering: What's the underlying issue we're arguing over? In a perfect world, all parties involved would be attending this question, but still, we can start on our own.

Drop below-the-surface nattering and recognize what really wants to be conveyed. If you can't do this in the moment, shut the conversation down altogether until it can be figured out (*Walk Away*Step Out*).

Remember: This Walk Away*Step Out doesn't mean simply going silent, which is a favorite defensive move for many. It means making a clear, cogent statement of intent, something on the order of: *"We're not getting anywhere and have lost the thread of our real conflict. Let's figure out what we each need and talk about this later."* But then do what you've suggested by proactively bringing the topic back up. This isn't meant as a device to merely shut down conversation and then sweep it under some already lumpy rug.

If your partner, for instance, can't let it go, take stronger measures, as in: "I can't continue until we cool down. I love you and want to resolve this, but don't know how at this exact moment." If that doesn't work: "Okay, I'm walking out right now. Not walking out on you, but on this useless fight!"

If you, in your busy, noisy mind, can't let go, try wondering (in writing) what you're getting out of clinging onto the conversation. To whom must you really prove your point? (Look back…way back.) What will be accomplished if you overcome doubt? What theme does this process plug into, as in: I never feel heard; if I'm wrong, I'll be thrown away; giving up means giving in.

#5: Pick Your Battles

As we've been discussing the entire book, figuring out what's important to us means first recognizing and understanding our themes, so that we can rightly notice how those themes are reflected through all the various parts and relationships in daily life.

Take the common topic of abandonment, for example. Now, it can be confusing trying to determine if there's actual, present-time abandonment happening or if you're in tender reactivity based on family-of-origin history.

It's best to start by checking in with *you*.

Is there an underlying resentment you've neglected to address? That pick-a-little, pick, pick, pick process some get into known as bickering is inevitably a sign of deeper unaddressed matters.

So before going into fight the fight, wherever that might be, make sure you're not simply dunking your donut in an old story. A good clue here is to notice if what you're talking or fighting about includes sentences you often hear in your head or notice coming out of your mouth. Plus, it's always helpful to remember the bigger the reaction, the older the material supporting the reaction.

As is often said in healing circles: if it's hysterical, it's historical.

How to:

The easiest way to proceed is to make a list of now-known themes. Use Connect-the-Dots to see where they started. Work within yourself first to ease the tension around perceived infractions.

When clarity ensues, share your discoveries with your partner, friend, coworker, or family. Try doing this without accusation. Even in the face of, say, meanness, this can happen as in: "When you're aggressive with me I feel like I'm 12. I remember standing in the kitchen, trying so hard to be helpful, while my mother just screamed at me. No matter what I did, it wasn't good enough."

Are you afraid your partner or friend won't understand, or have patience for your meandering? Try it anyway. If you get rejected, *that's* worth a battle.

#6: Do the Inconvenient Thing

In all relationships, whether at work or home, in order to thrive we must learn to play well with others. This means putting ourselves in positions and situations we'd generally prefer skipping. We need to go to a boring luncheon, a family event, a friend's child's play, a party we're way too exhausted to attend, a business meeting for which we're pretty certain we're irrelevant, and more.

Every single relationship lasting more than a nanosecond will at some point call upon us in cumbersome, tiring, or even stressful ways. Just as we call upon others in the same fashion. There's no way around it, so we might as well pony-up.

How to:

With regards to doing the inconvenient thing the "how-to" is easy. Say YES. Go to the hospital to be with your sick friend. Pick up dinner for everyone on the way home even though you're beat. Attend the birthday party you don't want to go to. Make dinner for the partner's boss. Take care of your neighbor's cat. Accept help. Offer help. You get the point. Do it.

#7: Continued Individual Development
How to:

For us to maintain growth and change rather than simply resting on our laurels, the idea is to do the work laid out in this book not once, but many, many times. Naturally, also include whatever other sources for change that you choose to consult. Maintain your investigation of the how, where, when, and what of the circumstances, events, and people that irk, trigger, dismantle, and undermine—along with insistently working to discover what supports, expands, invigorates, and excites you. Keep checking out the root causes of your choices. Notice when and how particular themes persist. Do the work. Celebrate the journey.

#8: Practice Trust

In the body of this book, we extensively explored the importance of understanding that trust has nearly nothing to do with anyone or anything else. The idea, rather, is to get to the point where you trust your own ability to withstand other people's reactions to your authentic and especially vulnerable truth. Knowing you will land upright no matter what happens— being aware of both your own resilience and of clarity of purpose—changes completely the way we walk through the world.

How To:

Here's the trust practice drill: Every day for whatever extended period of time you commit to (the 30-day plan is always a dandy start), tell two people something you don't usually reveal. They can be little points like how you're feeling in the moment or thoughts and feelings concerning big issues, which might include some piece of personal information you'd usually keep to yourself. A good practice here is telling one stranger/distant acquaintance *and* someone you consider close to you.

At the end of each day, or even right after each sharing depending on time and circumstance, write about what you discover.

If you attend this exercise consistently, over time you'll hopefully notice that other people's reactions don't matter so much and that even when they seem surprised by what you offer, you're fine. *Your* feelings are really the point. And guess what: you're exploring intimacy also.

#9: Drop It

This is exactly as it sounds. You're building your case, repeating your point, expounding on your grievances and suddenly magic happens when that knowing, still inner voice— the one that's smarter than your ego mind—insists you shut up.

And you do.

Oh yes, nearly everything in you wants to keep going. But you don't. You let yourself recognize the wisdom of simply letting the argument die on the vine. Both you and whomever you're talking to have said, or are on the verge of saying, things difficult to take back.

This is going nowhere fast.

At this point, a stop sign may not do the trick.

You'll just roll right through. Still, hopefully by now you've discovered which battles are worth it. And even then, the question becomes: *How is this important battle best fought?* If you're at war about something, negotiation often feels fruitless. It's hard to come to a détente amidst flying bullets and exploding grenades.

How To:

Settle down.

Breathe.

Go write about what you're trying to convey. Be sure to double check whether this is, in fact, present-day relationship material—or if your own history is rearing its insistent head.

When you figure it out, ask for a "conference" to deal with the core issue as it exists from your perspective. At this point, the idea is to drop the fight at hand. Get off the "traveloguing" train and attend to the real-deal issues triggering and empowering the superficial conflict. I promise there's no downside.

Exercise # 13: Rituals

Briefly in the body of *Our Love Matters*, I mentioned rituals. A more elaborate investigation of this elegant and important procedure will be far beyond the scope of this book; however I wanted to touch slightly upon this delightful topic, for in truth all of us are involved with ritual on a daily basis.

The question we first asked in Chapter One with regards to ritual was: how can we come to understand the *unconscious* rituals with which we're already involved?

The easiest way to start involves, as always, observation.

Keep it simple.

Notice, for instance, what your morning procedure is. Do you begin with brushing your teeth or do you make coffee or jump in the shower or what? Yes, that's ritual, which simply means you're following a series of "prescribed" actions.

The idea will be to see what you're doing now and then determine what habitual procedures can stay in place and what needs to be changed or added.

A fun way to tickle your fancy is to switch things up—do what you do in a new order and see what feelings arise.

Okay, these are the easy-breezy things. But of course there's more. You want to start asking questions like: *How do I tend to approach the day in terms of attitude?*

What if you switched that up too? Imagine instituting the ritual of saying immediately upon arising: *This is going to be a great day!!*

What all this means is that you're changing unconsciously pursued rituals to consciously expressed rituals.

Now, why am I calling this ritual rather than simply habit? Because I want to underscore the sacred nature of such engagements. In fact, from my perspective pretty much everything we do can be viewed in a sacred light, meaning deserving of veneration.

In any event, obviously not every little thing in your life needs changing. It's fine to start your day with teeth-brushing. However, we have dozens of daily ways of undermining our joy and happiness with ritualistic attitudes and actions—negative procedures and habits that send us off on the wrong direction. Let's ferret those out and shift them.

As always, be thorough when investigating your ritualistic behaving, thinking and feelings. Once you determine what you've been doing you can decide what you'd prefer to do.

You can choose to make supportive choices through healthy rituals. Weave them into your life as you move forward into change.

EXERCISE # 14: A NEW STORY TO TELL

When we first began feasting on our tasty *Love Works* chapter exercises, I suggested you write out your autobiography, paying special attention to family ways and messages. I'm hoping you did that and also subsequently have come to recognize the three or four themes running and ruling every aspect of your love life––including how you love your work, your friends, your co-workers, your partners, and how you love the very life you engage with every day.

Now you have an opportunity to create a new script—to write the story of either how you see yourself at this moment, or perhaps how you look forward to seeing yourself in the near future.

I've been anxious to impress upon you that the way you perceive your life very much influences and directs how your life will unfold. Perception, then, determines experience.

Shall this be a glad day or a sad day?

You decide.

Does love carry for you the meaning you intend or not?

You decide.

Can you leave your self-sabotaging ways mostly behind?

You decide.

How To:

Get comfortable.

Start writing: Let the words flow.

Don't judge yourself.

The fourteen exercises here offered are the beginning. In the course of doing them you hopefully came up with a few new investigatory procedures of your own. But most importantly please realize these processes can and should be done over and again at different stages of your development. It's fun, handy, and helpful. Then, keep the recorded work you do in order to look back over time to recognize and appreciate the flow and go of your life.

Be bold. A bright, glorious new view awaits.

EPILOGUE

O UT OF ALL THAT'S BEEN WRITTEN AND SAID HERE, one thing's certain: Changing our relationship to love, whether about self-love, partner love, career love, body love, or love of life, is anything but simple. Like great crime drama, love has many twists and turns. But in the end, as I've insisted from the start, it's all worth it.

Because our love matters! Indeed, it does.

By now you know what you need to do to make everything different. If you want a great job that brings you bliss, supportive, stunning friends you're glad to know, a body image that satisfies, a bank account that doesn't strike terror, self-esteem you're proud to express, a life that reflects your inner beauty, and of course, a love-life that provides a sturdy, thrilling platform on which to stand, then you'll embrace what's offered here.

I'm so excited for you.

In this epilogue, you'll find reminders of what's to be found throughout the pages of *Our Love Matters*. Here, seminal points not covered by the exercises are mentioned. The idea is simply to tickle your remembrance fancy. If you've forgotten what particularly stimulated you about a specific topic, it's best to re-read that book section. But as I've made clear, this is the kind of book that will serve you well with several readings. Each time you re-enter, you're likely to make new discoveries about something in your life or a development wanting attention.

The Stunners, Newsflashes, Fundamentals, and Universals lists also follow—offered as wonderful touchstones of the important perspective changes needed for on-going love success.

Enjoy them.

Delve further into them.

Meditate on each line, one at a time, to arrive at your own conclusions. Make notes, or other kinds of visual prompts, reminding you about certain phrases or ideas that feel particularly important, or helpful in your particular instance, and place them strategically around your home. Occasionally, review all of them again, trying to read them as if for the first time.

What I'm not intending in this epilogue is any kind of intense re-visiting of a particular topic. Again, I mean this as a handy go-to review.

Real Change...

No matter how deadly your relationship history is, it's really, actually possible to change your relationship to love matters! To review, it works like this:

- ✓ We begin by accepting that we have the life we've unconsciously designed
- ✓ We become willing to figure out the root cause of that unconscious sculpting
- ✓ We recognize that it's our *unconscious* intentions that require changing
- ✓ We accept that it's up to us to shift the behaviors that report those intentions

Change happens through a combination of *preparation* (which means getting ready), *procedure* (which means understanding what to do next), and *perspiration* (which means taking action). All three are necessary for long-lasting effects.

There are no short cuts.

Now, part of our preparation includes recognizing that we live in a pattern. *Our Love Matters* discusses these patterns in terms of:

- ✓ **Soul Patterning** which includes heritage material plus genetic coding
- ✓ **Environmental Patterning** which notices the influences of family, community, and the global historical times in which we live
- ✓ **Developed Behavioral Patterning** which includes defensive developments

These three pattern developments have sub-categories like: **Organic Patterning**—innate tendencies and temperament, consisting of instinct, intuition, and genetic coding; **Nurturing Patterning**, which addresses all our environmental influences; **Local Nurturing**, talking about how well we're physically fed, housed, and taught as a child—what peer member influences we had, the physical location in which we're raised, and the historical times in which we were reared.

Here, we spoke of how important it is to stop blaming and start claiming responsibility. This is one important key to shift.

In other words, it's not about pointing our fingers toward our ineffectual, negative, or even cruel parenting—or toward, say, the school bullies who made us miserable, toward our childhood poverty, our most horribly challenging times, or anything else. Rather, it's about understanding the impact of all these experiences and events on us and on our lives. What happened, what was our perception of what happened, and what did we take away from the experience?

Most importantly, naturally, what can we do about it all now?

One essential thing discussed over and again in various ways throughout this book is the idea that nothing is actually personal (though, of course, pretty much everything feels that way).

The more we can understand this, the better we fare.

All right, as we delved into pattern material we started exploring the importance of context, which is not only about whether we were born in the city or the country—which is called *community context*—but more particularly about what's going on in the world, which refers to *historical context*. We looked at the effects of attitudes toward ethnicity, religion, gender, and sexuality to suggest a few.

Another pattern sub-category to appreciate is *Soul Pattern*, which is best described as the blueprint describing us. We saw the ways in which this inner design is often referred to as the essence, core, or psyche.

One more important pattern we dove into involves the *actions, deeds, activities, and manners of conduct we exhibit in everyday life*. These expressions, more commonly known as defenses, are here called:

Developed Behavioral Patterns

THE IMPORTANT PIECE TO RECALL IS THAT DEFENSES ARE EVERYWHERE, most of the time. Everyone has them and exhibits them. Absolutely no one is distinct from this truth.

The bottom line with all pattern discussions is to encourage the realization that everything influences how we turn out. It's not as simple as what our parents did, how we got bullied at school, some terrible divorce or even a terrible parental death. Sure, big events often have big effects, but I maintain that *more importantly than precisely what happens to us is our response to what happens to us*—which is going to rely on numerous things, including the nature with which we are born. All this affects how we relate to the idea of love, along with how we pursue, express, and reveal ourselves everywhere and all the time. This means that the how, when, where, and who we love is a long, multi-layered process.

Along with understanding patterns, it's vital to appreciate the idea that the road to real relationship success *always* starts with US. Focusing on who did what to us will not heal us. The idea instead is to assess the impact of the life events and people we've come across.

The how of it all...

NO MATTER WHAT, WE NEED TO REALIZE THAT ALL GREAT LOVE BEGINS WITH THE SELF. Until, and unless, we love ourselves deeply, loving any part of our lives becomes amazingly difficult and unsustainable. Indeed, love is an art that demands our active participation—and our courage as well. Why courage? Love reminds us how very human we are and in the face of that humanity, how very vulnerable.

We're so continuously afraid of abandonment in some form or other. Poet and teacher David Whyte puts it beautifully when he says: "To feel abandoned is to deny the intimacy of your surroundings." You see we cannot really be abandoned— not in the way we generally talk about it. Not if we realize our ever-present link to all that has ever existed and does exist right this minute.

Well, the long and the short of it is that to love anyone, including ourselves, we must discover the beauty of True Intimacy—which I define here as heart-to-heart vulnerable, authentic connection. For this intimacy to develop, we must:

- ✓ Stop imagining we have any control over other people's opinions of us
- ✓ We must know what we mean to say and then say what we mean
- ✓ We must understand the difference between feelings and thoughts
- ✓ We must be *willing* to explore connection

Most of us have misunderstood what vulnerability really means. In this book we began with what it isn't:

- ✓ Vulnerability in no way allows us to say *everything* that occurs to us
- ✓ Vulnerability doesn't let us tell everyone else what's going on with *them* or what they should do to improve their lives
- ✓ Vulnerability doesn't mean a disastrous collapse into a sickening emotional puddle or that we're waiting to get run over
- ✓ Vulnerability doesn't mean we are weak

From my perspective, what vulnerability *does* mean is the clear, non-accusatory, and non-reactive communication of feelings and experiences. We need to understand our needs, motives, drives, and intentions. Once this understanding kicks in, having the courage to vulnerably express our deeply held feelings and thoughts changes everything in our lives.

Everything.

Mother, Father, Child…

REMEMBERING THAT WE HAVE ONLY THREE RELATIONSHIPS OUR WHOLE LIFE to deal with is pivotal to all my teachings. I keep hammering home the point that this is a good thing, not a problem. Because it means all relationships are combinations of, or even a direct replica to a degree, of your mother, your father, or yourself as a child. Once we understand how those three relationships are determining our behaviors, and impacting our lives, we can quickly move to actualizing change.

Most get caught up in the story they're telling themselves about who they are and what's going to happen. It's easy to assume that all the things that happened while we were growing up were personal.

Really, they weren't.

But taking them personally and thinking that abandoning, confronting, hurtful, bullying, or any other kind of experiences need to describe and define us, starts to strangle the very love out of us. We behave in ways, then, that confirm our worst notions about ourselves. This basically means that the crux of our lifelong love difficulty is threefold:

- ✓ *Our attitude* toward the blueprint established within the above-mentioned various patterning
- ✓ The *story we tell ourselves* about how and who we are
- ✓ *The behaviors we establish* to defend those distorted, negative ideas of self

What can we change?

OVER AND OVER, WE WORRY ABOUT WHAT CAN WE REALLY CHANGE? Turns out we don't need a new job, a new house, or a new area of the country in which to live. What we need is a new relationship to the Self.

Actually, realizing that things don't "go away," but rather we just change our attitude toward them, is terrifically liberating. It means everything that's ever happened to us contributes to a better version of us—once we know how to sift through the ashes.

In this regard, the salient questions will be to figure out what our attachment is to the story we've been telling, and how we've wrapped our identities around outdated stories. After answering those questions, we can figure out who we *really are*. Then we can apply what we've figured out to our love matters.

Why are we attracted to who we're attracted to?

TO SOME DEGREE, LOVE INEVITABLY FEELS LIKE A MYSTERY. But really there are some good reasons why we're constantly attracted to certain kinds of people. The trick is to discover what inner dynamics support these attractions.

Insistently in the course of *Our Love Matters*, I emphasized the importance of getting to the root of what ails and drives us. This begins when we:

- ✓ Notice when and how behaviors initially showed up
- ✓ Recognize the original childhood triggers for those behaviors

I encourage you to remember that behaviors of every kind are symptoms, not problems. Triggers to those behaviors get established quite early on. Every time those triggers are pulled, they threaten to undermine love everywhere.

Luckily, we only each have three or four underlying themes. It's essential for a true curing of our love matters that we figure out these themes. Certainly, they travel with us at all times. Once we understand the themes and know the triggers stimulating those themes, we can choose from a handy list of solutions. Yes, our themes will always be our themes, but our responses to those themes can radically shift.

The first rule is to become the person you want to be in a relationship with. You'll know when this happens.

The long search for wholeness...

RIGHT FROM THE START, WE BASICALLY FEEL CUT OFF FROM THE SOURCE OF WHATEVER FEELS GOOD AND RIGHT. That is to say, once we're pushed out of the womb, we feel to some degree lost. It's interesting to notice that the doctor's words at the time of our birth are: *Push! Push!*

And out into this strange Universe we come.

At that point, I believe, we nearly immediately begin searching for wholeness, for a connection to our true nature. Most feel cut off from what we'd call the Self, as we quickly have that connection interrupted by life's traumas, trials, and dramas. Mostly, the problems stem not from the events themselves, but rather from the story we tell ourselves about these events.

This sense of disconnection from who we intuitively know we're supposed to be gets included in, and reflected by, the way we search for love. Most of this is unconscious. *Our Love Matters* emphasizes the understanding that the aforementioned *unconscious* is actually an *ally* collaborating with us to re-unite us with our selves.

What stands in the way, as I've said, is the battle fatigue showing up very often as post-traumatic stress disorder. Warriors frequently experience this, as well as car accident victims. Many, if not most of us, are also suffering the signs and symptoms of this disorder.

Indicators include anything from self-consciousness and compulsivity to self-contempt. They'll show up in three prime ways: thinking, feeling, and behaving.

Naturally, what we're going for here is healthy self-esteem.

Healthy self-esteem means healthy self-regard.

For most of us, that requires commitment to change, and a willingness to appreciate the difference between where we are and where we can be along with the true intention to overturn our PTSD symptoms.

The idea is to stay awake and aware. All perspectives can change and we can give up the symptoms reporting our profound self-contempt, early-established doubt, mistrust, and self-sabotage.

But for all this to happen, we have to tell ourselves the truth. Basically, we've not been doing that. Most imagine they have little power over how their lives are going. A central theme here is that whether we believe it or not, we have what we intend to have. If we want a change, we'll need to appreciate that we-are-living-our-intentions. It's time to change those intentions.

It's not really that hard to decide...

MOST OF US KNOW, DEEP DOWN, WHETHER OUR RELATIONSHIPS ARE GOOD OR NOT SO GOOD. Of course, paying attention to what we know is another thing altogether. What we want to go for, really, in all our relationships including our relationship to career can be described as: **THE GRAND TRIFECTA**—the win-place-show triple play that describes a terrific relationship.

- ✓ Win: Your partner should ALWAYS be your biggest fan
- ✓ Place: Your partner should cherish you
- ✓ Show: Your partner should have your back

If these things are present for you, that's terrific.
If not, better re-access the idea of staying in the situation.

Heartbreak Hotel is a lonely place...

THE TOPIC OF HEARTBREAK IS EXTENSIVELY COVERED THROUGHOUT OUR LOVE MATTERS. No matter how "strong" we think ourselves to be, heartbreak usually lands on our self-esteem like a heavy mallet.

Here I emphasize two points: first, heartbreak is unavoidable; and second, heartbreak gives more to us than it takes from us. It enhances our humanity, increases our capacity for compassion, and expands our ability to love better the next time—if we learn from it.

Besides, mostly we're nursing a childhood heartbreak from which we've never recovered. So we've got a bruise just waiting to be bumped by a passing poke.

Anyway, when it comes to heartbreak or any other part of love, there are three vital aspects that must be understood, accepted, and investigated before any real change can occur. These, I consider to be the cornerstones of healing.

Here they are again:

- ✓ **CORNERSTONE #1:** The majority of our complaints are actually problems of perception
- ✓ **CORNERSTONE #2:** Current issues appearing to be important are actually announcements of underlying "themes" needing articulation and understanding
- ✓ **CORNERSTONE #3:** Choices, reactivity, and actions are 100% our responsibility

What's been going wrong at home?

WHEN IT COMES TO IDEAS OF RIGHT AND WRONG, it's handy to keep in mind three primary things:

- ✓ What we attract reflects something in us needing exploration and healing. Remember the magnet to refrigerator concept. Each annoying person and circumstance gives us an opportunity to look deeply at ourselves. The question to ask is: What inside story or remembrance or assumption is stimulating our big reaction?
- ✓ Our job is to *work on us* rather than fixing, deciphering, or instructing anyone else. We get to and must lead by example.
- ✓ Relationships of betrayal, unkindness, hesitation, and vile treatment are announcements of original wounds unmet.

Finding True Love...

I SUPPOSE AFTER ALL THIS, IF I HAVE ONE ENORMOUS PIECE OF ADVICE it is: **Stop settling for easy answers!**

You deserve better. You deserve more. You deserve to discover how to do what comes naturally, which is to love. You deserve to figure out how to reconnect with the things that truly excite you, and how to do those things with full intention. You deserve a love that invites moments of real bliss. This can honestly be yours, if you do the work. If you commit first, and foremost, to *self*-love.

Be Love.

Now.

TOUCHSTONE LISTS TO GUARD AND GUIDE

The Stunners: Ideas meant to alert you!

- ✓ **Stunner:** You don't have what you say you want because you haven't been ready!
- ✓ **Stunner:** Our lives consistently reveal the truth of our intentions.
- ✓ **Stunner:** We love who and what we love because we're trying to re-member ourselves—put ourselves back together again. We're actually born to love, but have merely forgotten how because fear has taken the place of faith.
- ✓ **Stunner:** The only real authority we have in life involves the choices *we* make.
- ✓ **Stunner:** Living in your head instead of in your life is undermining your happiness.

✓ **Stunner:** Current insistent ways of thinking, behaving, and feeling actually have little or nothing to do with NOW!

✓ **Stunner:** Where we come from is not the problem. It's the promise.

✓ **Stunner:** What you're doing now—the defensive struggle you're in to maintain old stories about the Self and the world, the clinging to being uncomfortable in your own skin—is actually harder than change!

✓ **Stunner:** There's no "I'm done" point when it comes to change.

✓ **Stunner:** The most effective solutions for how to live a quality life live inside you.

✓ **Stunner:** To stay refreshed we must be refreshing.

✓ **Stunner:** In a relationship love is never enough. Love's the easy part.

✓ **Stunner:** Whatever happened in the other person's last relationship is likely to happen in yours, somehow, some way.

The Fundamentals: Elementary, essential thoughts supporting everything you are and do.

✓ **Fundamental:** If you do what you've done, you'll get what you've got.

✓ **Fundamental:** Extreme behavior and/or defensive behavior are symptoms, not problems.

✓ **Fundamental:** We live in a house of mirrors.

✓ **Fundamental:** What we intend to have, we have. We live the life we intend.

- ✓ **Fundamental:** When we tell the truth about our profound complicity in the disrepair of our relationships, we find new freedom.
- ✓ **Fundamental:** Everything we do—*every behavior we engage in*—has a purpose.
- ✓ **Fundamental:** We can never fix a problem at the level of the problem.
- ✓ **Fundamental:** You are the centerpiece of your own story.
- ✓ **Fundamental:** Everything *appearing* outside us is actually inside us.
- ✓ **Fundamental:** Accept and appreciate that you'll always be flawed, without interpreting that to mean you're "defective and insufficient."
- ✓ **Fundamental:** Vulnerability is critical for true transformation.
- ✓ **Fundamental:** Focus on what you can give, rather than what you expect to get.
- ✓ **Fundamental:** Hear what your date, lover, or potential mate says about past partners as indicative of something you're eventually in some fashion guaranteed to bump up against yourself.
- ✓ **Fundamental:** When partnership is right, we find ourselves growing and expanding.
- ✓ **Fundamental:** Live in your life instead of your head.

Newsflash: Wake-Ups!

- ✓ **Newsflash:** Perception rules and determines 90% of our life experience. That's why conscientious awareness prepares us for great real-world impact.
- ✓ **Newsflash:** *You are exceptional,* but it's not because of the excruciating, stunning, or even potent details of your daily experiences.
- ✓ **Newsflash:** The problem isn't how we're put together—the problem is our attitude toward how we're put together.
- ✓ **Newsflash:** Our experiences are not mistakes.
- ✓ **Newsflash:** The only way through it is into it!
- ✓ **Newsflash:** We can only face our lives—we can't force our lives.
- ✓ **Newsflash:** "Other people" are not the point.
- ✓ **Newsflash:** Joy-fullness is an inside job.
- ✓ **Newsflash:** *Nothing* is personal. Nothing is *personal.* Nothing is personal.
- ✓ **Newsflash:** All sabotaging preoccupation is about lack of self-love.
- ✓ **Newsflash:** If you're not having a relationship, it's not because you're overweight, unfit, too short, not rich enough, or anything else—it's because you're making yourself unavailable.
- ✓ **Newsflash:** What keeps us in our sad, bad, troubled relationship to the Self, to others, and to life is primarily our refusal to give up the habitual behaviors that report old beliefs.
- ✓ **Newsflash:** Society only reflects the trends and tendencies rising up from within us.
- ✓ **Newsflash:** If you want a different life, you need to do things differently.
- ✓ **Newsflash:** You can't listen and talk at the same time.
- ✓ **Newsflash:** The face you show shows back to you.
- ✓ **Newsflash:** If you're afraid of losing the Self, it means you haven't found the Self in the first place.

Universals: Never-changing fundamental rules fitting everyone.

- ✓ **Universal:** That which wounds us offers to heal us.
- ✓ **Universal:** Our true intentions are revealed by the reality that stands before us.
- ✓ **Universal:** If you do what you've done, you'll get what you've got.
- ✓ **Universal:** The only way through it is into it.
- ✓ **Universal:** The search for Wholeness is the rule, not the exception.
- ✓ **Universal:** The bigger the reaction, the older the significant stories supporting the reaction.
- ✓ **Universal:** Be the person you want to date!

These two lists are your Healthy Relationship Mandates. Remember them.

The details of both lists are well covered in the body of this book. I only offer them here as a check-in for you.

The Relationship To-Do's:

- ✓ Shut It!
- ✓ Speak It*Step Up
- ✓ Express the Hurt
- ✓ Express the Love
- ✓ Fire with Fire
- ✓ Walk Away*Step Out
- ✓ Know Thyself
- ✓ Express Empathy
- ✓ Acknowledge & Accept Opposite Points-of-View
- ✓ Simultaneous Translation

The Relationship Tenets

✓ **Relationship Tenet #1:** Don't expect your partner's pace to be identical to yours.

✓ **Relationship Tenet #2:** Realize that just because your partner isn't changing at your pace, doesn't mean they're not changing at all.

✓ **Relationship Tenet #3:** Understand that your way is not the only way.

✓ **Relationship Tenet #4:** During the "dry" times, try focusing on the cheese and not the holes. Remember what you like and love about your partner. Stop looking at what's missing and see what's present.

✓ **Relationship Tenet #5:** Focus on your own changes. Changing your part of the equation will change the entire equation. It may still not turn out as you prefer, but you'll have learned something that will most likely announce what's next.

✓ **Relationship Tenet #6:** Stop discussing the relationship all the time with your partner. There's an old saying: "If you're talking about the relationship all the time, you're not actually engaging in the relationship." Remember: the work to be done is primarily *inside you*. Do that work first.

✓ **Relationship Tenet #7:** Check out your relationship patterns to see what's being repeated: do you always find something wrong; do your disgruntlements tend to surface in a particular timing; do your relationships tend to last the same length of time?

✓ **Relationship Tenet #8:** Don't assume sameness. Check with the folks in your life to see what *they* want and need.

Resources

[i] Rumi, *The Essential Rumi*

[ii] Rainer Maria Rilke, *Letters to a Young Poet*

[iii] Marianne Williamson

[iv] Online dictionary

[v] Wikipedia

[vi] Maya Angelou

[vii] James Hillman, *A Bue fire*

[viii] Dictionary.com

[ix] Thomas Merton, *No Man Is an Island*

[x] British Library

[xi] Carl Jung

[xii] Cynthia Ocellio, Speaker Reference

[xiii] Hesse, Hermann *Bäume. Betrachtungen und Gedichte*

[xiv] *Carlos Castañeda*

[xv] Oscar Wilde

[xvi] David Byrne

[xvii] Elie Wiesel

[xviii] Martin Luther King Jr., *A Testament of Hope: The Essential Writings and Speeches*

[xix] Craig Freudenrich, Ph.D. and Jonathan Strickland

[xx] Eleanor Roosevelt

[xxi] Truth About Deception

[xxii] Austin Tree Experts

[xxiii] Orkin

[xxiv] C.S. Lewis, *The Four Loves*

[xxv] *Psychology Today*; Mathew Hutson; March 2008

[xxvi] Wikipedia

[xxvii] *Psychology Today*; Mathew Hutson; March 2008

[xxviii] Wikipedia

[xxix] Anaïs Nin, *The Diary of Anaïs Nin, Vol. 1: 1931-1934*

[xxx] *Thich Nhat Hanh*

[xxxi] E.E. Cummings

[xxxii] Yahoo Answers

[xxxiii] Jim Hyland and Matthew Clemons

[xxxiv] Austin Tree Experts

[xxxv] Rainer Maria Rilke, *Letters to a Young Poet*

[xxxvi] Pablo Espada

[xxxvii] Rainer Maria Rilke, *The Selected Poetry*

[xxxviii] Free online dictionary

[xxxix] Wikipedia

[xl] Wikipedia

[xli] Anthon St. Maarten

[xlii] Institute of Heart Math

[xliii] Wikipedia

[xliv] Rainer Maria Rilke, *Letters to a Young Poet*

[xlv] Louise Erdrich, *The Painted Drum LP*

[xlvi] Edgar Allan Poe

[xlvii] Hafiz

[xlviii] Christopher Morley

[xlix] Rainer Maria Rilke, *Letters to a Young Poet*

[l] John Lennon

[li] Wikipedia

[lii] Wikipedia

[liii] Wikipedia

[liv] Alan Wilson Watts, *Love in the Time of Cholera*

[lv] Urban Dictionary

[lvi] Mother Teresa

[lvii] Joseph Campbell, *Reflections in the Art of Living: A Joseph Campbell Companion*

[lviii] Wikipedia

[lix] Kevyn Aucoin

[lx] Gabriel García Márquez

[lxi] Dr. Brené Brown, *Power of Vulnerability* from Ted Talks